The River Nile fascinated the Romans and appeared
descriptions, texts, poems and paintings of the dev
Tantalised by the unique status of the river, explor
find the sources of the Nile, while natural philosop
on its deeper metaphysical significance. Andy Merrill
*Geographies of the Nile*, examines the very different
river that emerged from these descriptions – from an
figures, brought repeatedly into Rome in military triu
the frequently whimsical landscape vignettes from the
peii, to the limitless river that spilled through the pa
*Civil War*, and symbolised a conflict – and an emp
end. Considering cultural and political contexts along
Niles that flowed through the Roman world in this per
provides a wholly original interpretation of the deeper
geographical knowledge during the later Roman Repu
Principate.

ANDY MERRILLS is a Senior Lecturer in Ancient Histor
versity of Leicester. He is the author of two books: *Hist*
*raphy in Late Antiquity* (Cambridge University Press, 20
*Vandals* (with Richard Miles, 2010). He has held researc
at Cambridge University, the University of Wisconsin–M
University of Cincinnati and the University of Sydney.

# ROMAN GEOGRAPHIES OF THE NILE

## From the Late Republic to the Early Empire

ANDY MERRILLS

*University of Leicester*

CAMBRIDGE
UNIVERSITY PRESS

# CAMBRIDGE
## UNIVERSITY PRESS

University Printing House, Cambridge CB2 8BS, United Kingdom

One Liberty Plaza, 20th Floor, New York, NY 10006, USA

477 Williamstown Road, Port Melbourne, VIC 3207, Australia

4843/24, 2nd Floor, Ansari Road, Daryaganj, Delhi - 110002, India

79 Anson Road, #06-04/06, Singapore 079906

Cambridge University Press is part of the University of Cambridge.

It furthers the University's mission by disseminating knowledge in the pursuit of education, learning and research at the highest international levels of excellence.

www.cambridge.org
Information on this title: www.cambridge.org/9781107177284

First published 2017

Printed in the United Kingdom by TJ International Ltd. Padstow Cornwall

*A catalogue record for this publication is available from the British Library*

ISBN 978-1-107-17728-4 Hardback

Additional resources for this publication at www.cambridge.org/9781107177284

*For Mum and Dad*

# Contents

# Figures

# Acknowledgements

Like the Nile, this book had several distinct points of origin and had to travel some considerable distance before it assumed a recognizable form. Like the Nile, in the final reckoning, it proved to be rather longer than anyone was expecting. On the simplest level, the project was an attempt to expand and develop some of the ideas laid down in my first book – an examination of the importance of 'historical' texts to the dissemination of 'geographical' ideas in the middle centuries of the first millennium CE. Where that study sought to show how important historical narratives were in shaping ancient assumptions about the wider world, I hoped that my next study would cast the net rather wider and approach similar questions by considering a whole range of different media. Flush with post-doctoral pride (and buoyed by the support of more than one funding body), I felt confident that the project would be a manageable one. But research projects are rarely so simple. Having chosen the River Nile as an appropriate object of study, two things rapidly became apparent to me: first that the later Republic and early empire would provide the most fruitful area for exploration, thanks to the sheer proliferation of different Niles that flowed through those troubled decades; and second that I was poorly equipped to stray into such a well-populated field of scholarship. As the project developed, these feelings intensified, even as the implications of the research became more intriguing. I slowly became aware of source materials that I hadn't considered, and vast scholarly traditions that I hadn't fully appreciated, while new publications presented a wealth of thought-provoking perspectives on all of this material. It was only through extensive conversation and collaboration with many colleagues and friends that these challenges were overcome and my unseemly post-doctoral hubris was transformed into something like a finished book.

I have benefitted greatly from the generous support of a number of institutions, during the slow gestation of this work. The earliest stages of research were undertaken as a Post-Doctoral Research Fellow on the

'History and Theory of Description' Project at King's College, Cambridge and as a Friedrich Solmsen Fellow at the Institute for Research in the Humanities at the University of Wisconsin-Madison. Discussions with other students and fellows at each of those institutions shaped this work profoundly in its formative stages. In the period that followed, I also benefitted from extended periods of work at the Blegen Classics Library at the University of Cincinnati, first as a Margo Tytus Fellow, and then as a visiting researcher. It was during the long and pleasurable summers in that library that much of the present book was written, and I am very grateful to Getzel Cohen, Jacquie Riley and the staff and graduate students at Cincinnati for making me so welcome. My greatest institutional debt, however, is to the School of Archaeology and Ancient History at the University of Leicester. My time spent in the School, first as an RCUK Fellow, and then as a lecturer, has shaped this book immeasurably. Without the unstinting support of colleagues and students at Leicester, this work would be much the weaker. Different sections of this book (at different stages of development) have been presented to audiences in Madison, Durham, Leicester, London, Cambridge and Sydney. I am grateful to audiences in all of these places for their comments and suggestions.

The images in this book have come from a variety of places, and I am grateful to the copyright holders for permission to reproduce them. I would particularly like to thank Jackie and Bob Dunn, the curators of the extraordinary website 'Pompeii in Pictures'; Pim Allison; Jan Haywood and Debbie Miles-Williams. I am also grateful to Michael Slade, Erica Graber, Anne Turkos and Fabienne Read for their help in securing specific images.

I am lucky to have been able to draw upon the expertise and patience of many friends and colleagues, and the book that follows has depended greatly upon their help. Alfred Hiatt, Jen Baird, Dan Stewart, Naoise Mac-Sweeney, Dave Edwards, Cori Fenwick, Graham Shipley, Andrew Morrison, Mairead Macauley, Molly Swetnam-Burland, Neil Christie and Julia Farley all read chapters of the book and provided helpful suggestions. Michael Sharp and the three anonymous readers from Cambridge University Press also saved me from embarrassing errors, encouraged me in sharpening my focus and aided in the direction of my thoughts. I am grateful to them all.

Many other friends and colleagues listened with great forbearance to my intemperate ramblings, gently suggested where I might be going wrong and shared valuable observations of their own. These individuals are too many to list, but I am particularly grateful to Christina Pössel (who heard much of what follows over the course of innumerable long walks in Derbyshire and the Welsh borders), Richard Talbert, Anne Rogerson, Elly Cowan, Bob Cowan, Simon Loseby, Mark Gillings, Francois Furstenberg, Dan Vyleta, Jason Morris, Jan Haywood, Mary Harlow, Laurel Fulkerson, John Marincola, Claire Taylor, Lesley McFadyen, Ollie Harris, Bill Grundy, John Ryan, Charlie Campbell, Andrew Connor, Adam Squires, Susan Reslewic, Paul Stephenson and Eric Blaum.

This book is dedicated to my parents, John and Dariel. For everything.

# Abbreviations

Ancient sources are cited using the abbreviations in the fourth edition of the *Oxford Classical Dictionary*.

In addition the following abbreviations have been used:

| | |
|---|---|
| Achilles Tatius | Achilles Tatius, *Leucippe and Clitophon*. S. Gaselee (ed. and tr.). *Achilles Tatius, Leucippe and Clitophon*. Loeb. (Cambridge, MA, 1969). |
| *Ad Herr.* | *Rhetorica ad Herennium*. Harry Caplan (ed. and tr.) *Cicero. Rhetorica ad Herennium*. Loeb. (Cambridge, MA, 1954). |
| *Alla ricerca di Iside* (1992) | *Alla ricerca di Iside. Analisi, studi e restauri dell'Iseo pompeiano nel Museo di Napoli* (Naples, 1992). |
| Ambrose *Ex in Ps* | Ambrose, *Expositio de Psalmo*. Michael Petschenig (ed.) *Sancti Ambrosii Opera. Expositio de Psalmo CXVIII*, Corpus Scriptorum Ecclesiasticorum Latinorum (Vienna, 1913). |
| Athanasius, *Contr. Gen.* | *Athanasius, Contra Gentes*. E. P. Meijering (tr.), *Athanasius, Contra Gentes* (Leiden, 1984). |
| *Carm. Bell Act* | H. W. Benario (ed. and tr.) 'The "Carmen de bello Actiaco" and Early Imperial Epic', *Aufstieg und Niedergang der römischen Welt* (1983), II.30.3: 1656–62. |
| Chaeremon, *Fr, Test* | Pieter Willem van der Horst (ed. and tr.) *Chaeremon. Egyptian Priest and Stoic Philosopher. The Fragments collected and* |

| | |
|---|---|
| | *translated with explanatory notes* (Leiden, 1984). |
| Epiphanius *Adv. Haer* | Epiphanius, *Adversus Haereses* Frank Williams (tr.), *The Panarion of Epiphanius of Salamis.* 2 vols (Leiden, 1987–1993). |
| Eus., *Prep Evang.* | Eusebius, *Praeparatio evangelica.* Karl Mras (ed.), *Die Praeparatio Evangelica.* Die griechische christlichen Schriftsteller der ersten Jahrhunderte. 2 vols (Berlin, 1982–1983). |
| *It Ant* | Otto Cuntz (ed.) *Itineraria Romana.* vol. 1: Itineraria Antonini Augusti et Burdigalense (Leipzig, 1929). |
| Lydus, *De Mens* | John Lydus, *Liber de Mensibus.* Richard Wuensch (ed.), *Ioannis Lydi Liber de Mensibus.* Teubner (Stuttgart, 1967); Anastasius C. Bandy (ed. and tr.), *On the Months. (De Mensibus), by John Lydus* (Lewiston, NY, 2013). |
| Origen, *Contra Cels* | Origen, *Contra Celsum.* M. Marcovich (ed.), *Origenes Contra Celsum. Libri VIII* (Leiden, 2001). |
| *Pan Lat* | *Panegyrici Latini.* R. A. B. Mynors (ed.) *XII Panegyrici Latini* (Oxford, 1964); C. E. V. Nixon and Barbara Saylor Rodgers. (tr.) *In Praise of Later Roman Emperors: The Panegyrici Latini* (Berkeley, CA, 1994). |
| Philae | André Bernand (ed.), *Les Inscriptions grecques de Philae* 2 vols (Paris, 1969). |
| Philo *VM* | Philo, *Life of Moses.* in F. H. Colson (ed. and tr.) *Philo. On Abraham. On Joseph. On Moses.* (Cambridge, MA, 1935). |
| Pomponius Mela | Pomponius Mela, *Chorography.* A. Silberman (ed. and French tr.) *Pomponius Mela. Chorographie* Budé (Paris, 1988); F. E. Romer, *Pomponius Mela's Description of the World.* (Ann Arbor, MI). |
| Porphyry *De abst* | Porphyry, *De abstinentia ab esu animalium.* Jean Bouffartigue, M. Patillon and Alain-Philippe Segonds (ed. and French tr.), *Porphyre. De l'abstinence* 3 vols., Budé |

|  | (Paris, 1979–1995); Gillian Clarke (tr.) *Porphyry. On Abstinence from Killing Animals* (London, 2000). |
|---|---|
| *Pseudo-Scylax* | Pseudo-Scylax, *Periplous*. Graham Shipley (ed. and tr.), *Pseudo-Skylax's Periplous: The Circumnavigation of the Inhabited World* (Liverpool, 2011). |
| Ptol. *Geog.* | Ptolemy, *Geography*. C. F. A. Nobbe (ed.) *Claudii Ptolemaei Geographia* (Hildesheim, 1966); J. Lennart Berggren and Alexander Jones (partially tr.), *Ptolemy's Geography: An Annotated Translation of the Theoretical Chapters* (Princeton, NJ, 2001). |
| *Res Gestae* | *Res Gestae Divi Augusti*. P. A. Brunt and J. M. Moore (ed. and tr.), *Res Gestae Divi Augusti: The Achievements of the Divine Augustus* (London, 1969). |
| Solin. *Collect.* | Solinus, *Collectanea rerum mirabilium*. Kai Brodersen (ed. and German tr.), *Wunder der Welt: Collectanea rerum mirabilium* (Darmstadt, 2015). |
| Strabo | Strabo, *Geography*. S. Radt, *Strabons Geographika*. 10 vols (Göttingen, 2002–2011); Duane W. Roller (tr.) 2014. *The Geography of Strabo* (Cambridge, 2014). |
| Varro Atac. Fr | Varro Atacinus, Fragments, in Adrian S. Hollis. *Fragments of Roman Poetry c.60 BC–AD 20.* (Oxford, 2007), 165–241. |
| Xenophon of Ephesus | Xenophon of Ephesus, *Ephesian Tale*. Jeffrey Henderson (ed. and tr.). *Longus, Xenophon of Ephesus. Daphnis and Chloe. Anthia and Habrocomes.* Loeb. (Cambridge, MA, 2009). |

Standard editions of all texts have been used throughout. Where appropriate I have used published translations of Latin and Greek texts. Where no publication is listed, translations are my own. Where I have deviated from published translations, this is marked in the footnotes.

# Introduction
## What We Talk about When We Talk about Roman Geography

> Your desire to know Nile, Roman, was shared
> by tyrants Pharian and Persian and of Macedon,
> and no age is there which has not wished to grant the knowledge
> to the future – but up to now its natural power of hiding is victorious.[1]

Midway through the tenth book of Lucan's gruesome epic *The Civil War* is a long digression on the River Nile.[2] Taking the form of a learned discussion between the Egyptian priest Acoreus and the insatiable Julius Caesar, the passage sits somewhat uneasily in the narrative of the poet's final book. Caesar, having just contemplated the disembodied head of his great rival Pompey and replete from his revelry with Cleopatra, sees the long-standing mystery of the Nile as the perfect opportunity for some post-prandial intellectualizing and a stage for asserting his own imperial aspirations. As conflict with the young Ptolemy XIII looms, the dawn will return both Caesar and Lucan to the brutal realities of war, but the prospect of the Nile offers the poet and his anti-hero a brief respite. Through his contemplation of the Egyptian river, Caesar could imagine a claim to dominion even over the 'unknowable' south, a dream that was to sustain imperial exploration in the interior down to the expeditions of the Royal Geographical Society in the nineteenth century. For Lucan, the Nile offered an image through which he could demonstrate his own erudition and reiterate the principal themes of his magnum opus as it staggered towards its untimely end.

The description of the Nile in *The Civil War* must have had considerable contemporary resonance for the immediate audience of the poem. It was composed in the mid-60s CE, at a time when the rule of the emperor Nero was fluctuating between inspired cultural ambition and deranged excess. Some months before Lucan composed this passage, probably in around

---

[1]  Luc. 10.268–271. tr. Braund (1992), 214.
[2]  Luc. 10.172–331. This passage – and the epic in which it appears – are discussed in detail in Chapter 6, below.

62 or 63 CE, Nero had sponsored an expedition up the Nile, which had recently reported back with its discoveries from the heart of the Meroitic Kingdom in what is now Sudan.[3] At around the same time, Lucan's uncle, the Younger Seneca, had written his own lengthy discussion of the Nile as part of his *Natural Questions*, a book of natural philosophy ostensibly intended to instruct another courtier in the principles and practices of Stoicism.[4] These emperors, authors and their audiences would also have been familiar with a variety of other impressions of Egypt and its famous river from the city around them: statues of the personified Nile had been frequent features of the triumphal processions which marked Roman military victories in the late Republic and were to become still more familiar as static monuments within Rome over the decades that followed. Egyptian landscapes, featuring idealized and sometimes grotesque scenes of life on the banks of the river, had also recently come back into fashion as the subject of wall-painting and other domestic decoration.[5] Such motifs had been familiar in mosaics and frescoes from the later second century BCE and reached a peak at around the time when Egypt was formally annexed by Augustus in 30 BCE, but had briefly fallen out of use for a generation or two. In the reign of Nero, however, this Egyptomania seems to have recovered its popularity: by the time of the eruption of Vesuvius in 79 CE, Egyptian scenes were a very common sight on the walls of the houses of Pompeii.

Lucan's description of the Nile is remarkable for its detail and precision, not least because the sudden didactic tone of this section represents something of a break from the madcap helter-skelter of the narrative up to that point. Having been dizzied by a rapid account of the collapse of the Republic and the visceral brutalities of civil war, the audience is stopped short by a measured natural philosophical reflection on the Egyptian river. The passage discusses several different aspects of the watercourse. First, Acoreus provides a detailed description of the Nile from its murky origins in the distant interior of Africa to the Mediterranean. He then briefly recounts the attempts made by earlier tyrants to find its origins, and closes his digression with a summary of the major theories put forward to explain the summer floods of the river. Throughout this digression, the priest (or rather the poet) provides a fair approximation of contemporary thinking about the mysterious river. As we might expect, Lucan seems to have drawn quite heavily on the philosophical writing of his uncle Seneca in this part of his epic, but we may also detect echoes of earlier poets including Virgil,

[3] The expedition is discussed at 206–15 and 270–3 below.　[4] See Chapter 5.　[5] See Chapter 3.

Ovid and Propertius, as well as the influences of other Roman representations of Egypt, including wall paintings, triumphal displays, itinerary
descriptions of tourist voyages and perhaps the reports of the Neronian
explorers. Lucan's is undeniably a poetic river – an epic Nile – but is also
unmistakably one which ran through Neronian Rome.

Yet there is something missing in this discussion. Lucan includes no
reference within his account to the great maps of the world, often supposed
to have ornamented the walls of early imperial Rome, or to the formal prose
treatises which we know to have been composed at around the same time.
Lucan's is among the most detailed descriptions of the Nile to have survived
from the early imperial period, and yet it makes little reference to the sorts
of geographical expression that have dominated modern discussions of the
subject. His is a vivid reminder that Roman responses to the world could
be expressed in a variety of different media and could be conceptualized
in a number of ways. When inhabitants of the early empire wished to find
out about the wider world, they did not have to turn to maps or dry prose
geographies in order to do so; there was a variety of different lenses through
which they could view the infinite variety of the now-conquered world.

Studies of ancient 'geography' – of the ways in which Greeks or Romans
conceptualized the physical world around them and communicated this
understanding – have tended to emphasize prose writing over poetry,
itinerary records of physical journeys over imagined voyages and maps
over landscape paintings and mosaics.[6] Over the last generation or so,
much of this scholarship has been brilliant and ground-breaking. Various
attempts have been made to chart the generic limits of different types of
ancient writing on the wider world – to understand how modern concepts
of 'geography', 'cartography' and 'ethnography' might map onto the textual
productions of the classical Mediterranean.[7] The simple fact that no recognizable maps have survived from the classical world has stimulated extensive
debates about the function of cartography within Greek and Roman society
and prompted reflections on the different ways in which space might have
been conceptualized in these worlds.[8] Equally importantly, those texts that
have survived – works like Strabo's *Geography*, Pliny's *Natural History* or
the geographical tables of Ptolemy – have been read with a sensitivity to

---

[6] Typical of this is the recent survey by Dueck with Brodersen (2012), which includes a short chapter on
poetry and historiography, but emphasizes the technical material. Cf. Talbert (2010b) and Brodersen
(2010).

[7] See esp. Janni (1984) (on cognitive assumptions); the collected papers in Prontera (2011) and the
important articles of Pascal Arnaud, esp. Arnaud (1989). On changing attitudes to ethnography (and
definitions of the form), see esp. Hartog (1988), Gruen (2010) and Skinner (2012).

[8] See esp. Brodersen (1995). The topic is discussed in greater detail in Chapter 1.

their literary and political contexts.[9] The technical literature of antiquity
has been radically reassessed, even over the last decade, and 'geographical'
texts have certainly benefitted from these changed perspectives.[10]

Other forms of geographical and spatial expression have also inspired
recent work. The painted landscapes known from the ancient world have
been subject to considerable scrutiny; study of Roman wall paintings in
particular have benefited from the parallel investigation of poetic topography, with significant results.[11] Detailed consideration of ancient concepts
of visuality has had important implications for the study of attitudes to
the wider world, and the modes of its representation – a theme that has
again been explored through text as well as image.[12] More broadly, the
corpus of Classical, Hellenistic and Latin literature has been assessed as a
repository of geographical and ethnographic information, and as a medium
for negotiating the relationship of societies to the world around them.[13]
Historiography, too, has been examined as a medium for geographical
information, from Herodotus down to Ammianus Marcellinus and the
historians of late Antiquity.[14]

Yet for all of this diversity, there have been surprisingly few attempts
to address how this material fitted together, and the study of 'ancient
geography' remains a field dominated by technical and prosaic texts.[15] This
demands a number of questions: How was popular understanding of the
developing Roman empire shaped by wall maps, landscape paintings or the
peculiar symbolism of military triumphs? And how did the spectators of
such events reconcile these different media into a coherent mental image
of the world as a whole? To what extent did descriptions of the world in

---

[9]   Most obviously Dueck (2000); Naas (2002); Carey (2003); Murphy (2004). Jones (2012) provides
      a superb introduction to Ptolemy. On Strabo, see n.9 below.
[10]  Cuomo (2007) is central within this. See also the collected papers in Taub and Doody (2009).
[11]  Leach (1988) and Fitter (1995), 25–52.
[12]  See for example Bartsch (2006); Elsner (2007); and the collected essays in Richlin (1992); Bergmann
      and Kondoleon (1999) and Fredrick (2002a).
[13]  Spencer (2005) provides an excellent recent discussion. See most obviously Thomas (1982); Horsfall
      (1985).
[14]  See esp. Clarke (1999) on the late Hellenistic period; the late Antique material is discussed in Feraco
      (2011) and Merrills (2005).
[15]  The point is perhaps illustrated best by a counter-example. The edited collection of Geus and
      Thiering (2014) purports to examine 'common-sense' geography in the classical world, as distinct
      from the mathematical approaches of scholars like Eratosthenes. The use of recent psychological
      literature on spatial cognition and acquisition, particularly in Thiering (2014) recalls the method-
      ology of Janni (1984), and is very welcome, but the project as a whole rather reifies a distinction
      between 'scientific' and 'experienced' responses to space. This leaves little room for examining the
      interaction of contrasting modes of spatial comprehension in different physical, social and generic
      contexts and among different members of society. Dan (2014) hints at the value of this in a study
      of Xenophon's Anabasis.

verse or prose draw upon a wider frame of reference that would have been familiar to their audiences? What role did visual commonplaces or poetic *topoi* play in shaping assumptions about the wider world? And how did all of these different media help to situate their expected audiences within the political hierarchies of the city and the empire? Lucan's description of the Nile is significant not only as a fragment of epic poetry, and as a reflection of Latin natural history, but as both of these things at once. His poem is a reminder of the complexities of ancient geographical understanding and a prompt to further investigation.

The present book is an attempt to investigate the political, social and cultural resonances of geographical knowledge during the later Roman Republic and early Principate. It interrogates different modes of geographical representation that were known within Roman Italy, and crucially how they related to one another. To do this it will look in particular detail at representations of the River Nile that circulated from the later-second century BCE to the end of the first century CE. It will examine the ways in which the river appeared in a range of different media from large display 'maps' to domestic landscape paintings, triumphal monuments and works of natural philosophy. It will also consider the different political resonances of each of these representative modes, not just in framing the balance of power between the imperial authority and its subordinate provinces, but also in defining hierarchical relationships at home. The study seeks to provide an original reading of some of the most important visual, textual and archaeological creations of the later Republican and early imperial periods, and to use these studies to cast new light upon the evolving geographical understanding of the societies that created them.[16]

My attention here will focus primarily on the representations of the River Nile which emerged in Roman Italy between the mid-first century BCE and the mid-first century CE. Appropriately enough, the study sometimes overspills these chronological banks. It is difficult to understand the Roman response to Egypt without some appreciation of the important Greek precedent. Some of the multiple Niles explored here are anticipated in earlier writing, and Herodotus, in particular, casts an important shadow

---

[16] Talbert (2010b), 269 notes the desirability of a wide-ranging study of this kind. 'I am convinced that the immense range and variety of surviving texts, images and material objects will repay fresh appraisal in a continued quest to achieve fuller, more nuanced understanding. Recovery of Roman worldview in its intriguing variety – not all of it even detected to date perhaps – remains a work in progress.' The essays in Mutschler and Mittag (2008) display the potential for looking at Roman conceptions of space through a variety of different lenses and – still better – through systematic comparison with modes of representation in Han China, but there is little focused attempt to draw these strands together.

over much of what follows.[17] Elsewhere, reference to earlier periods is more explicit: extensive attention is paid, for example, to the famous Nile mosaic from the Temple of Fortuna in Praeneste, which is generally thought to have been created and installed towards the end of the second century BCE. This mosaic is important both as the first of many Egyptian 'landscapes' known from countless domestic contexts over the next two centuries, and is also commonly invoked in discussions of Roman 'mapping': for these reasons it could scarcely be omitted. Similarly, a small number of later imperial and late antique texts are also discussed in order to illuminate points made in the main discussion. But the last century of the Roman Republic and the first of the new Empire provide an exceptionally rich body of material in themselves. These include the major works of Roman prose geography, many of which describe the Nile at some length; the principal representations of the river in military triumphs; the overwhelming majority of visual 'Nilotica' from the walls of Pompeii and Rome; two crucial works of Latin natural philosophy by Lucretius and Seneca; and several relevant works of epic and elegy (including Lucan's *Civil War*). These decades also encompass the period in which Roman power spread throughout the Mediterranean world and was consolidated in the political domination of the Principate, a period which certainly witnessed dramatic changes in Roman attitudes to the wider world and the ways in which these were expressed. This period provides us with an unrivalled range of sources for explaining the multi-faceted nature of geographical understanding in the classical world, and its sometimes fractious relationship to political power.

## Roman Geography Triumphant

Modern understanding of Roman geographical thought, and particularly its political function, has been shaped to a remarkable degree by the scholarship of Claude Nicolet. Crucial here was his inspirational monograph of 1988, *L'inventaire du monde: Geographie et politique aux origines de l'empire romain*.[18] Nicolet's nuanced survey stressed the importance of geographical imagery to Roman political power from the first half of the first century BCE, but argued that it changed dramatically during the Augustan Principate. In his view, both the politics and the practices of geographical

---

[17] On Herodotus, see esp. Vasunia (2001). Herodotus' contemporary context is explored further at 177–8 below.

[18] Nicolet (1988). This material was subsequently delivered in English as the Jerome Lectures and published as Nicolet (1991).

description were transformed under Augustus.[19] From 27 BCE, the triumvir Octavian remodelled himself as Augustus, assumed something close to autocratic power in Rome and remade the constitutional (and physical) fabric of the state in his own image.[20] The same period witnessed an intensification of quantitative data gathering in census and cadastral surveys and the systematic reordering of the new empire: it saw the establishment of large-scale representations of world in the imperial city, and very probably marked the period in which the first descriptive prose geographies in Greek (and perhaps Latin) were composed. Given the widespread modern fascination with Augustus' ideological programme of renewal – his 'propaganda' in the common modern terminology – and the frequency with which assertions of universal imperial power appear in the poetry, monuments and even coinage of the period, the correspondence between 'Imperial' geography and 'Empire' seems clear enough.[21]

Three specific documents are granted a particular prominence in Nicolet's discussion. Augustus' *Res Gestae* was a posthumous inscription of the emperor's accomplishments that was erected outside his mausoleum in the Campus Martius and subsequently circulated around the empire.[22] The *Breviarium totius imperii* is known only from its title, but seems to have been a summary of the dispositions of the imperial army and the state of the fisc and was said to have been passed to Augustus' successor Tiberius upon his assumption of power.[23] The third text within Nicolet's study, and certainly the most important for our purposes, is the so-called 'Map of Agrippa' said to have been produced by Augustus' son-in-law and lieutenant Marcus Agrippa and erected in the Porticus Vipsania after his death.[24] Like the *Breviarium*, the Agrippa map has since been lost, and its precise form and function have been much debated (as we shall see). At the very least it seems to have included a visual component that is often assumed to have been a map of the world, as well as a written commentary of some kind. For Nicolet, this 'map' represented the heart of Augustus'

[19] The 'revolutionary' features of the period are famously delineated in Syme (1939) for politics and Wallace-Hadrill (1997) and (2008) in intellectual and cultural terms.

[20] Eck (2007) and the papers in Galinsky (2005) and Bowman, Champlin and Lintott (1996) provide good introductions to Augustus and his age.

[21] Zanker (1988) is the (now classic) discussion of Augustan 'propaganda'. And cf. also Galinsky (1996) which sets the literature of the period in a similar frame.

[22] *Res Gestae*. Suet. *Aug.* 101.4; Dio Cass. 56.33.1. Nicolet (1991), 15–27.

[23] The title is from Suet. *Aug.* 101.4; Dio Cass 56.33.2 plausibly refers to the same document. Nicolet (1991), 171–87.

[24] Nicolet (1991), 95–122. The key textual references to the 'map', and the modern scholarship surrounding it, are discussed in detail in Chapter 1.

ideological project and was a necessary cartographic gloss to the textual information presented in the other documents. It was through this work, he argues, that the princeps displayed the scale of the imperial state to an admiring city. Equally importantly, it was this map that acted as the public face of the great geographical archive of the new Empire. This was a demonstration of the authoritative knowledge of a new kind of state in the ancient Mediterranean.[25]

Recognition of the intimate relationship between political power and the production and control of knowledge had transformed the study of historical geography between the 1970s and the 1990s.[26] Scholars increasingly appreciated the importance of maps and other practices of spatial representation to the articulation of state power, and Nicolet brilliantly adapted these observations to the fissiparous world of late Republican and early imperial Rome.[27] Certain aspects of his argument seem incontrovertible: whatever form the Agrippa 'map' took, for example, there can be little doubt that it was primarily intended to celebrate the magnitude of imperial rule and thus represented something like an 'official' view of the empire. Similarly, the broad thematic correspondence of a range of different texts on episodes like the Roman conquest of Egypt, or the extension of military authority to the edges of the world, can be meaningfully viewed alongside one another to present a more or less coherent 'imperial' discourse of domination and control.[28] Roman surveyors can likewise be viewed as agents of empire, manifesting the imperial presence in occupied territory, even as they compiled knowledge about these regions.[29] If we can credit Augustus with some power in the creation of his own ideology (and surely we must), it is not too much of a stretch to see the function that geographical imagery might have played in this.

Nicolet's argument provides a bravura demonstration of the importance of power at the root of all geographical production, but somewhat

---

[25] Arnaud (2007–2008) 46–7 traces the intellectual antecedents of Nicolet's argument. Dion (1977) presents an earlier survey of political influences on classical geography, but focuses on the texts, rather than the context.

[26] J. B. Harley was central to this process, especially in his adaptation of the ideas of Michel Foucault and Anthony Giddens to historical geography. See esp. Harley (1988) and (1989), and the collaborative *History of Cartography* project of Harley and Woodward (1987–). Andrews (2001) crisply introduces Harley's work.

[27] Nicolet is not particularly forthcoming in discussing his debts to this developing tradition of historical geography, but the broad parallels are clear enough. For roughly contemporary discussions of more modern imperial mappings, compare the important survey of Livingstone (1992) and the essays in Godlewska and Smith (1994).

[28] See for example Bellen (1991).

[29] Morris (2016) provides an important reappraisal of these processes, and the social role of the surveyors themselves.

oversimplifies the political and intellectual context from which the discourse that he identifies emerged and obscures the divergent geographies that circulated in the decades after Augustus' rule.[30] In spite of its strengths, the epistemological issues at the heart of Nicolet's reconstruction remain unstable. Two aspects are particularly problematic. The first relates to Augustus' ability to translate his political power into intellectual authority – the extent to which he was able to sanction a preferred representation of the world and exclude contrasting or dissonant readings. The second concerns the media through which he expressed this privileged geography. Nicolet understandably emphasizes the importance of the *Res Gestae*, the *Breviarium* and the Agrippa 'map' within his text, as the closest ancient analogues to the atlases, reports and tables of modern imperial bureaucracy.[31] In doing so, however, he not only frames lost works in ways that may be anachronistic, he also occludes the huge array of other texts that have survived from the period, or appropriates them into his own model.[32] Nicolet implies that Augustus created an archive from which points of data could easily be retrieved, and which other writers were compelled to use if they sought trustworthy geographical information. In fact, as we shall see, geographical authority remained contested throughout the early imperial period and existed in perpetually ambivalent relationship to the apparatus of state power. As shall be discussed, moreover, information about the wider world could be gathered, displayed and even archived in this period without any expectation of eventual retrieval or practical use.[33] These observations have important implications.

Nicolet's view of the Agrippa 'map' – and of Augustan geographical discourse more broadly – is founded on a seemingly straightforward piece of reasoning. Speaking of the importance of the 'map' to the *Res Gestae*, particularly in illuminating its long lists of obscure toponyms, he notes:

---

[30] Virlouvet (1988) and Purcell (1990b) provide perceptive immediate responses.

[31] Cf. Nicolet (1991), 10: 'Once listed, classified, and stored, these documents will constitute, at the center of power, an administrative memory and picture of the world that will correspond more or less to those geographic images that we have studied.'

[32] This is perhaps clearest in his identification of Ovid as 'a poet in Augustus's entourage' at Nicolet (1991), 114. Which substantially simplifies the peculiar political position of that writer. Cf. Barchiesi (1997). Ovid's ambivalent appropriation of imperial geographical motifs is further discussed at 86–91 and 244–6 below.

[33] A point hinted at in the review of Nicolet by Talbert (1989), 1351: '. . . there is a questionable acceptance that, because Roman administrators gathered a mass of information, they shared the passion of a modern bureaucracy for retrieving and analyzing it.' Virlouvet (1988) and Purcell (1990b) also highlight the anachronism behind Nicolet's assumptions. Wallace-Hadrill (2008), esp. 259–314, offers a nuanced view of how different aspects of this 'knowledge revolution' might have operated on the ground. Moatti (1997) and (1993) discuss archival practice in the Roman world.

> All these names, and especially the latter, were known to the Hellenistic
> geographers . . . but they were certainly less familiar to the Romans. They
> could not have been appreciated without some illustration.[34]

And goes on to question:

> Is it to be believed that that the emperor was resigned to speak in a void,
> and not to be understood by the public when he employed a rare toponym,
> or when he described, in a subtly rhetorical manner, the Roman Empire
> extending over almost the entire region bounded by the northern Ocean
> ("from Gades to the mouth of the Elbe") or stretching towards the southern
> portions of the *oikoumene*, to the "Ethiopian" border? Surely not.[35]

Nicolet argues from this 'commonsensical' reasoning that the Augustan city
must have had maps of the world, because such documents would have been
necessary to make sense of the extraordinary proliferation of information
in circulation at the time. He enables this logical step by elsewhere asserting
that spatial cognition among the Romans was essentially the same as our
own.[36] Because modern scholars are so comfortable referring to maps as
repositories of authoritative information, in other words, because we turn
so easily to the atlas or to Google Maps to clarify a toponym or geographical
concept that is unfamiliar to us, it is easy to assume that the same must
have been true in the classical world. Indeed, it is sometimes difficult to
conceptualize how else these materials might have been understood, but
we should still try.

Nicolet's conclusions have proved enormously influential, and his work
has been much cited, among classicists and historians of geography alike.
This is not to suggest that his arguments have gone unchallenged. In particular, the likely form and function of the Agrippa map have been much
discussed, as we shall see in the next chapter.[37] Nicolet's contention that the
Augustan period witnessed a particular transformation in Roman attitudes
to the world has also been further nuanced, not least in the important
work of Pascal Arnaud.[38] Similarly, Strabo, who appears as something of an
Augustan echo chamber in Nicolet's work, is now appreciated much more
fully as an author in his own right.[39] Yet Nicolet's interpretation of the

---

[34] Nicolet (1991), 23.     [35] Nicolet (1991), 23.

[36] Nicolet (1991), 70–4, at 70: 'We should not put forward a "natural" difference between the ancient
     way of thinking and ours.' In response to the arguments of Janni (1984).

[37] See below, 27–38.

[38] See esp. Arnaud (2007) for a survey and García Moreno (1994) on African material. On Nicolet
     specifically see Purcell (1990b), 180–1.

[39] Cf. for example, Nicolet (1991), 74. Radt (2002–11) is the newest edition of the text, Roller
     (2014) an up-to-date English translation. Clarke (1997), (1999), 193–7, Dueck (2000), 1–30

somewhat monolithic political function of many of these representations, and his implicit trust in the authority of conventional geographical and cartographic media, remains widely shared. Many recent writers have happily concurred that a bedrock of established knowledge must have lain beneath the more unusual modes of geographical expression in this period – that maps or detailed prose descriptions were necessary to 'make sense of' triumphs, landscape paintings or poetry, and that such works did not enjoy a cognitive authority of their own.[40] Others have accepted that these media operated together as a seamless *inventaire du monde*, without closely assessing how this might have worked in practice.[41] It has been suggested, for example, that triumphal parades must have included maps among their trophies, both as a display of Roman military technology, and as a means of making the display legible to viewers; from this it has been concluded that these military plans helped transform the depiction of space in other media, like landscape painting.[42]

Yet Nicolet's paradigm runs the risk of obscuring the complexity of Roman responses to the world. Strikingly diverse modes of representation, including public 'chorography', triumphs, landscape painting, itinerary lists and descriptive prose, have too often been lumped together as manifestations of a dominant 'imperial' conception of space that is suspiciously similar to our own, with little attention to the diverse ways in which

---

and 145–86, and Dueck, Lindsay and Pothecary (2005) are helpful introductions to the author and his text. Koelsch (2004) is a thoughtful assessment from the perspective of a modern geographer. Dueck (1999) makes a persuasive case for dating the composition of the work to 18–23 CE and summarizes the earlier scholarship. See also Pothecary (2002) and Prontera (2016).

[40] Nicolet (1991), 113. Cf. for example Clarke (2008), 213–4 (on the ways in which audiences could understand triumphs): 'For that, they needed the geographer, the mapmakers, the constant rearticulations in different media of what it meant to rule the world . . . the theatrical show, the dinner party, the triumph were all parades of the special and significant features, *which would become crystallized on the map and in verbal descriptions*, giving the vast scope of the Roman Empire meaning in both text and image.' (my italics). Compare Rodriguez (1992), 84; Evans (2003), esp. 255–6; Manolaraki (2013), 24.

[41] Cf. Murphy (2004), 23: '. . . map, triumph and encyclopedia were all educational media, and as such functioned as intermediaries between the authority of Rome and the world it ruled.' Cosgrove (2001), 52: 'The absence of actual globes and maps from antiquity makes it difficult to verify claims about the actual production, circulation, and consumption of such artefacts. Certainly, in both textual and architectural representation global concepts and narratives articulated a language of empire.' Both statements are justifiable, but the means by which these discourses were effected demands closer investigation.

[42] See for example Holliday (2002), 22–121 and the observation at 105: '[paintings carried in triumphs] appear to have made use of chorography and topography, types of cartographic illustration that were undoubtedly crucial to the military successes encoded by later paintings.' The difficulties with these assumptions (not least the absence of evidence for the use of maps or landscape paintings in triumphs), are discussed below at 77.

they actually worked.[43] Practical issues – of mass-producing any sort of 'maps' for triumphal display, of determining their legibility for audiences unfamiliar with their conventions, or of explaining their precise function in clarifying other triumphal trophies – remain unexplored. That Roman views of the world were heavily implicated in contemporary issues of power is not to be doubted, but seeking a homogeneous mode of understanding does justice to neither the evidence nor to the complexity of the society that produced it. As our understanding of social, political and economic relations of this period develops, so too should our appreciation of the roles that geographical expression played within this.[44]

The present study has been motivated by three principal objections to the view of imperial geographical knowledge initially proposed by Nicolet, and since widely accepted. First, the media traditionally associated with the dissemination of official knowledge – chiefly the so-called Agrippa 'map', but also textual administrative materials, triumphal geography and monumental inscriptions – cannot have provided a definitive archive of material in the way that is frequently assumed. We know little about the practicalities of triumphal displays, and still less about the public 'maps' assumed to have ornamented the imperial city, but the material available to us does not suggest that either medium could have functioned particularly well as an effective geographical archive for the presentation, recording or retrieval of specific information. Textual references to display maps from the later first century (termed 'chorographies' in the discussion that follows) strongly imply that these took a variety of forms, variously depicting cities, provinces and perhaps the empire as a whole, and presumably adopting different visual conventions in order to do so. This variety, and the practical difficulties in reproducing maps before the invention of printing, argue against the view that such works provided a convenient repository of factual information about the world. Nor can they have included a great

---

[43] Cf. Moffitt (1997), 240: 'In sum, both the literary and particularly the surviving artistic evidence shows that Roman compositional conventions for historiated mural paintings were hybrid, combining flattened scenography seen from on high with people and significant monuments viewed laterally. This mode of narrative, topographical representation, perhaps often captioned, could well have provided a precedent for the historiated mappaemundi of the Middle Ages.' This tendency to identify overarching 'Roman' attitudes towards geographical space, rather than explore dissonances and idiosyncrasies remains widespread. Skempis and Ziogas (2013) take Pietro Janni as their inspiration, rather than Claude Nicolet, when they stress that the Roman tendency to view the world in 'hodological' terms 'has been influential in shaping the epic discourse along with its narrative elaborations.' While there is much to be said for this as a conceptual starting point, the simplification remains striking. On 'hodological' representations, see Chapter 5, and on narrative geographies, Chapter 6.

[44] Arnaud (2007), 26–40 provides an important starting point.

deal of detail: if citizens really did wish to set the boasts of the *Res Gestae* in context, in other words, they would have had to turn to other media than maps in order to do this. Triumphs pose similar problems. Although these ceremonies might well have brought a vast body of information before the *populus* – one source records almost two thousand distinct toponyms in a single parade – their mode of presentation was almost anti-cartographic.[45] Important places were represented prominently within the triumphs, but smaller trophies appeared as little more than abstracted symbols, or names on placards, and were paraded with no reference to their original spatial context. No spectator would have been able to reconcile the jumbled parade of obscure triumphal trophies with the schematic 'map' of Agrippa, and to assume that they would have attempted this obscures the cognitive relationship between these contrasting modes of display.

   This connects to the second objection – that the most prominent modes of geographical representation known from this period did not fit together into a seamless discourse, as has frequently been assumed. Public display maps, inscribed lists, triumphs, landscape paintings, itineraries for travel and descriptions in poetry and prose all placed spectators in different positions with respect to the world that they described, and to the wider institutions of empire. An individual who stood within a crowd of fellow citizens, and who caught glimpses of a statue of the personified Nile as it was jostled along in a military triumph, for example, would experience a different appreciation of the river from one who gazed upon a perspectival landscape, painted on the dining couches of his own garden. In one case, the position of the viewer as a subject of empire would be emphasized, one citizen among many and part of the collective validation of military conquest of abstracted foreign territories; the other manifested a more personal response to domination of distant regions, which might be experienced on a more subjective level. Similarly, disinterested itinerary accounts of the course of the river, marked by a succession of stopping places, make very different cognitive demands of their audiences from consciously evocative descriptions of the river in flood, which allude to the primordial waters. All of these accounts reflected Roman geographical knowledge, in some sense, and all contributed to the wider appreciation of a distant province of empire, but they did so in contrasting ways, and with different expectations. The simple assumption that all of these forms were motivated by essentially similar political impulses remains

---

[45] Plut. *Vit. Pomp* 45.1–2 (including a thousand forts and almost nine-hundred towns, as well as fifteen 'headline' trophies). On this account, see below 79–80.

implicit in much writing about early imperial geography and deserves to be challenged.

The third objection comes from the recognition that discordant or subversive geographies also circulated within this period and challenge the view that the imperial administration monopolized knowledge of this kind. One well-known example illustrates the point. According to Suetonius, the emperor Domitian executed the aristocrat Metius Pompusianus for the apparent crime of carrying a parchment representation of the world on his person.[46] But we are left wondering precisely how Pompusianus had access to this information, how these images were circulated and displayed and just how widespread such affectations may have been among his contemporaries. Significantly, other forms of contestation were also possible, even among those who did not aspire to imperial power themselves.[47] Lucan's description of the Nile, for example, appropriates many of the familiar motifs from contemporary natural philosophy and poetic geography, and is conventional in much of its content and form, but did so in order to evoke a river that actively eluded the enquiring gaze of an avaricious ruler and ultimately resisted straightforward textual description. In so doing, Lucan both lent his epic a somewhat nihilistic (and Nile-istic) conclusion to the story of Julius Caesar and made a subversive comment on Nero's aspirations to discover the source of the river for himself. It is from this perspective, too, that we need to consider many of the domestic Nilotic landscapes that became popular among the regional aristocracies in around this period. While these should certainly not be read as marking active claims to the imperial throne in the manner of Metius Pompusianus, they did, perhaps, represent a series of collective aspirations to agency within the empire. Through perspectival paintings like these, provincial householders could approximate the seignurial gaze that they felt was their due as citizens of the colonizing power. As several commentators have noted, then, these paintings played a fundamental role within Roman 'imperial' views of the wider world, but they functioned very differently from the administrative documents or chorographies ratified by Augustus. Paintings like these related only tangentially to the forms of geographical knowledge displayed by the state in the streets of the capital. They were not a part of an official imperial discourse, of the type that Nicolet explores, but they did contribute substantially to the geography of empire. Understanding

---

[46] Suet. *Dom.* 10 describes a *depictum orbem in membrana*, Dio Cass 67.12 implies that the representation was on his wall. See esp. Arnaud (1983), and briefly Brodersen (1995), 105.

[47] Tan (2014) provides a reading of subversive geography in Tacitus' *Germania*.

such gestures, their political implications and their relationship to other media, is crucial to this study.

The need for a reappraisal of Roman representations of the world is intensified by developments in other fields of historical geography. That geographies of empire are typically polyvalent has become a commonplace in scholarship on later periods.[48] Modern studies of British imperialism, for example, have readily explored the role that schoolroom geography, imperial rituals, changing fashions in fiction and pulp literature, scientific enquiry and military activity all had in the creation of congruent imperialisms.[49] The representations that they produced have also been fruitfully examined as the means of perpetuating or challenging conventions of gender and social hierarchy and relations between the colonizers and colonized and as testing grounds for new epistemologies. The surveyor and the schoolboy, the home decorator and the cartographer, were all shaped by the grand economic and political currents of empire – and all shaped it in turn – but to assume that they all contributed to this discourse in the same way, or that the journals of a missionary represented imperial space in a way that was interchangeable with the maps produced by the Admiralty, is clearly unsatisfactory. Recent studies have investigated the production, dissemination and reception of geographical information in their immediate contexts, and have particularly examined the different historical and cultural operations of particular media.[50] The conclusions drawn in these histories of imperial geography cannot be imported directly to the study of the ancient world, where social, political, technological and cognitive contexts are sufficiently different to demand wholly new assessments of comparable phenomena. But this scholarship still has a great deal to teach us, and the study that follows has been influenced profoundly by this work.

[48] Morrissey (2013a) and (2013b) survey recent geographical approaches to empire. On historical empires specifically, see esp. Edney (2009) and the other papers in Akerman (2009).

[49] The scholarship is rich (and richly rewarding). Important specific studies include: Edney (1990) and Cohn (2006) (on interdependent modes of representation of 'British' India); Blunt and Rose (1994) and McClintock (1995) (on gender and race in imperial geography); Hudson (1977) (on education); Said (1993) on literary geographies of empire, with specific studies of Bishop (1989), Phillips (1997), Piper (2002) and Goldsworthy (2013).

[50] The disparate processes involved in the creation of 'imperial' geography are further examined in Carter (1987), Burnett (2001) and esp. Driver (2001). See also Fitter (1995) (on specific modes of representation and their interdependence); Mitchell (1988) (on metropolitan exhibition); Richards (1993) (on forms of archive); Casey (2002) (on the relationship between panoramic and sublime landscape images and maps in the American West); Pratt (2008) (on dissonant travel accounts as part of the wider imperial discourse). Also see the papers in Akerman (2006a), on cartographies of travel, and Jacob (2006) – a translation and development of Jacob (1992), which explores audiences' responses to maps more broadly.

## Why the Nile?

The Nile has been chosen as the principal focus for the present study for a number of reasons. Chief among them is the startling range of representations of the river in the late Republic and early Empire. The Nile was a familiar feature of multiple triumphal processions, prompted speculation from a number of philosophers, surfaced regularly in epic and elegiac writing and was described with almost forensic scrutiny by a number of prose writers. It may also have appeared on maps of the world, although quite whether it did – and if it did, how these maps may have presented it – are further questions that can only really be answered by looking in detail at the different sources available to us. This remarkable generic variety also provides a practical advantage: by looking at one single geographical feature, even a tremendously important one like the Nile, it will be possible to provide close readings of specific sources or modes of representation and examine their interdependence, with a scrutiny that might not be possible were the frame of reference any wider.

I am largely interested in the Nile, then, because the Romans were. This fascination was prompted by a number of aspects. The first is simply that the Nile was unique within the known world, thanks to its unknown origins and summer floods, and Greek and Roman commentators struggled to find a convincing explanation for its eccentric behaviour.[51] As understood today, the Nile has two principal sources: the 'Blue Nile' (*an-Nīl al-Azraq*) has its origins in Lake Tana in Ethiopia, the 'White Nile' (*an-Nīl al-Abyad*) in the Great Lakes of Central Africa.[52] These tributaries meet at what the ancients called the Island of Meroe, now the city of Khartoum, to form the body of the river as it flows through northern Sudan (Nubia), passes the last ('First') Cataract to the south of the modern city of Aswan and then enters the Egyptian Nile Valley. The Nile's sources were unknown to the inhabitants of the ancient Mediterranean, but were the cause of perpetual speculation, as they were for later imperial powers down to the nineteenth century.[53] The narrative of Nilotic exploration during the modern Scramble for Africa is well known and has been admirably summarized in a number of popular history books (and television series), but speculation on the

---

[51] French (1996) 110–12 provides a succinct overview.
[52] The modern bibliography on the Nile is substantial. Ludwig (1937) provides a thorough introduction to the river, Collins (2002) a more recent survey of similar ground. Moorehead (1960) and (1962) are the classic travel narratives in English. Morrison (2010) is a worthy recent addition to the tradition.
[53] Stanley (1899), 7–9 connects his own enquiry to those of the ancients.

sources was similarly intense during the classical period.[54] During the Ptolemaic occupation of Egypt, trade contacts with the Kingdom of Kush and hunting expeditions to the interior provided some information on the middle stretches of the river which circulated in Hellenistic texts. Trade along the east African coast and sporadic contact with the interior may also have generated further knowledge about the upper Nile, although this was frequently vague. While some classical descriptions of the source of the Nile seem surprisingly accurate, most were not, and many writers contented themselves with assertions of ignorance. Indeed, the hidden origins of the river were a poetic commonplace in both Greek and Latin.[55]

A second feature which fascinated Greek and Roman commentators was the unusual summer flooding of the Nile.[56] During the late Spring each year, heavy rainfall in the Ethiopian highlands causes the Blue Nile to swell. Between June and September the lesser of the two tributaries contributes around two-thirds of the water in the river and the Nile floods as far as the Mediterranean. While the completion of two major dams at Aswan in 1902 and 1970 changed this picture substantially, the inundation was crucial to the prosperity of the region in earlier periods. The unique summer floods transformed rainless Egypt into one of the most fertile regions of the Mediterranean world. This prodigy was central to Egyptian cosmology and religion and posed an intellectual puzzle to outside observers from Greece and Rome, particularly following the successive occupations of the region. In the absence of a straightforward explanation, natural philosophers suspected that the Nile floods might offer a key to understanding the essential nature of the world and the cosmos. Their interpretations drew upon existing geographical knowledge and the methodologies of philosophical enquiry, but created from this a view of the Nile that delighted in uncertainty and instability. Simultaneously, the spread of 'Egyptian' cults throughout the Mediterranean took with them an appreciation of the Nile that was shaped by local cosmology and was less bound to the geographical assumptions of imperial power. Esoteric as these perspectives might at first seem, these attitudes proved surprisingly influential in poetry and even prose geographies.

Finally, the Nile was important because of its close association with Egypt and was significant to Roman commentators because of the history

---

[54] There are many studies of nineteenth-century exploration on the river. Jeal (2011) is an accessible recent overview.

[55] See Chapter 6, below.

[56] Pliny does note at *HN* 5.90 that the Euphrates also flooded in the summer (and at *HN* 6.65 that the Ganges also had unknown sources), but the Nile remains his point of reference for these eccentricities.

of that region's incorporation within the empire.[57] Ptolemaic Egypt had lingered on the fringes of the Roman sphere of influence since the second century BCE. For around a century and a half, powerful figures within the Republican Senate had been content to influence the politics of Alexandria from afar, while pursuing wider diplomatic strategies in the eastern Mediterranean. This changed substantially following the collapse of the First Triumvirate. After his defeat at the Battle of Pharsalus in 48 BCE, Pompey the Great sought refuge in Egypt, only to be killed on the instructions of the young Ptolemy XIII. This murder effectively handed political authority to Julius Caesar and secured the place of Egypt in the prolonged power politics of the next two decades.[58] The two alliances of Cleopatra VII, first with Julius Caesar and then with Mark Antony, are among the most familiar narratives of romance (and tragedy) from antiquity, but also catalyzed hyperbolic views of Egypt within Rome. In part captivating, feminine and exotic, in part corrupting and tyrannical, Egypt was frequently presented in terms strongly reminiscent of more modern orientalisms.[59] As in later periods, such caricatures were partly a conscious political creation, which helped justify Octavian's political and military action against Cleopatra and Antony in the 30s CE, and partly a genuine reflection of ambivalence towards one of the richest regions of the Mediterranean. In many ways, the post-Actian Nile encapsulated the delights and corruption of this territory in the eyes of the wider Roman populace, just as Herodotus' river had symbolized the same territory for earlier audiences. Impossibly fecund and rich, the river was also subject to unpredictable patterns of behaviour. After the formal incorporation of Egypt within the Empire in 30 BCE, these issues became still more relevant. The great grain fleets that travelled from Alexandria to Rome each year, and fed the imperial city, were a reminder of the dependence of the economy on the vicissitudes of a temperamental river. While a succession of governors struggled to chart the levels of flood, and were well aware of the implications of this for the well-being of the province (and the world), they could do little to affect them.

The ties that bound Rome to Egypt (and Egypt to Rome) have been well-treated by modern scholarship. Several studies have examined Greek and Roman views of the region, particularly in drama, historiography, ethnography and poetry.[60] A number of works have analyzed Greek and

---

[57] Sonnabend (1986), 19–68 introduces this clearly.
[58] This narrative is accessibly presented in Capponi (2005), 5–23.
[59] A great deal has been written on Roman representations of Cleopatra; some of this is engaged with in Chapter 6. Kleiner (2005) is a wide-ranging introduction.
[60] See, for example, Sonnabend (1986); Vasunia (2001); Maehler (2003); Manolaraki (2013).

Roman responses to the Nile floods specifically, in a variety of different literary modes.[61] Attention has also been placed on the peculiarly Roman tradition of visual representations of Egypt and the Nile, particularly in the domestic contexts of Rome and Pompeii.[62] A burgeoning sub-discipline has also explored the circulation of Egyptian religious practices within the Greek and Roman Mediterranean, traced through material culture, visual art and textual representation.[63] As a consequence, the intellectual, cultural, economic and political integration of Rome and Egypt are perhaps better known (or at least more thoroughly studied) than virtually any other region in the Empire.

This is a rich body of scholarship with which to work, and the present book has benefitted greatly from this material. Where this scholarship has cast a considerable light on Egypt, the Roman occupation of Egypt and the reception of the region within the Roman world, the present study is intended to examine the geographical discourse itself in all of its variety. Just as important as philosophical reflections on the flood of the river, the poetic treatment of Egypt, or perspectival representations of the Nile on the walls of Pompeian dining rooms (and all of these are certainly significant) are the relationships between them – the extent to which a wealthy Pompeian might have been prompted by a landscape image into reverie on sublime cosmology as she ate, or the philosopher was influenced in his reflection on the Nile floods by the commonplaces of contemporary poetry. It is only by looking at these representations alongside one another, and the contrasting implications of these media, that we can start to get a fuller picture, not only of the way in which Egypt was regarded within late Republican and imperial Rome, but of the way in which the developing empire as a whole was understood, and how the individuals who made up the metropolitan state comprehended their own positions within it. To my knowledge, this is an approach that has rarely been attempted. Miguel Versluys's study of Roman 'Aegyptiaca' hints at such a reading in its final chapter, but only approaches this (to very good effect, it should be stressed) through ethnographic comparanda.[64] More recent studies by Eleni Manoloraki, Jonathan Tracy and Molly Swetnam-Burland have provided wonderful illumination on specific textual responses to the Nile and the incorporation of 'Egyptian' motifs within imperial Roman aesthetics, but again without detailed consideration of the implications of this material for

---

[61] Most obviously Bonneau (1964) and Postl (1970).    [62] Roullet (1972); Versluys (2002).

[63] See esp. Malaise (1972a), (1972b); Tran Tam Tinh (1972); Takács (1995b); Lembke (1994). And the collected papers in Bricault (2000), Bricault (2004) and Bricault, Versluys and Meyboom (2007).

[64] Versluys (2002), 422–35.

the geographical knowledge of the period.[65] Perhaps the closest antecedent is Grant Parker's extraordinary survey of Roman views of India, which has certainly directed my thinking considerably.[66] But the Nile occupied a very different position in the Roman *Weltbild* to India, and casts different light upon modes of geographical thought.

It is worth reiterating, by way of apology if nothing else, that this is not a book about Roman Egypt. Many studies have examined the imperial occupation of this important province, and the unique social and cultural amalgam that resulted.[67] Detailed discussion of how Strabo or Seneca (or the painter Studius) viewed Egypt may tell us a great deal about the *mentalité* behind Roman imperialism, but can offer little to discussions of social and political interaction within the region itself. Similarly, while administration of the Nile floods was clearly a central feature of government within Egypt, and some appreciation of the river was important to this process, there is relatively little in this study that relates directly to the practical issues of water management as an aspect of imperial government.[68] What follows is broadly a discussion of Roman views of Egypt (and hence of the empire as a whole) from outside the province. What this book seeks to be, then, is a contribution to discussion of Roman 'geography' in its broadest possible form. It wishes to examine and interrogate how 'the Romans' saw the changing imperial world around them, and to consider how this discourse worked and (perhaps) what it meant to be 'Roman' during this period. In order to do this it adopts a close investigation of a specific case study which happens to be located in Egypt.

## The Structure of the Argument

The **first chapter** considers the grand public mapping projects, or 'chorographies', often assumed to lie at the heart of early imperial geography. Visual displays of the wider world were a relatively common sight in the late Republican and Augustan capital, and a number of texts allude clearly to several different works of this kind. These 'maps' have been intensively studied for more than a century, in spite of the limited evidence. The few

---

[65] Manolaraki (2013); Tracy (2014) and now Swetnam-Burland (2015). I am very grateful to Molly Swetnam-Burland her for allowing me to see sections of this book before publication.

[66] Parker (2008), and cf. Purcell (1990a) for a similarly nuanced approach to Cisalpine Gaul.

[67] Bowman (1996) provides a clear survey of Egyptian history in this period. See also Lewis (1983); Bowman (1986); Capponi (2005); Dörner (2014) and the collected essays in Riggs (2012). Blouin (2014) is a sensitive recent study of Roman Egypt from the ground up, focused on the Mendes Nome in the eastern Delta.

[68] On which see esp. Bonneau (1971a).

textual descriptions that we have do not allow us to reconstruct these works (they tell us nothing about size, shape, form, number or the integration of textual and visual elements), but they all say something about the ways that such displays affected their immediate audiences. It is argued here that these surveys were primarily important as objects of collective scrutiny, rather than as archives of specific points of information – as a means for meditating on one's position in the world, both through the omniscient gaze enabled by the work itself, and through the presence of other spectators. The 'maps' produced by Agrippa and others were certainly not important as definitive interpretations of the physical world. But they did allow the populace of the city a means to define and practice their collective sense of imperial community.

 This chapter considers the role of these public displays in shaping contemporary responses to the world by looking in detail at two well-known works, which featured the Nile prominently. The first is a visual source on the world's rivers which was apparently used in Vitruvius' treatise *On Architecture*. Vitruvius alludes to the 'painted and written works of chorographers' (*chorographiis picta itemque scripta*) as support for his contention that the Nile arose in the far northwest of Africa, and could be traced across the Sahara, before it turned to the north at Meroe and flowed through Egypt.[69] Vitruvius clearly appealed to the authority of a visual work of some kind in asserting this origin for the river, but it is proposed here that most of his geographical information was taken from textual sources. This is argued from internal evidence in his account, including the striking level of detail, and some surprising omissions. From this it is suggested that visual representations could be invoked as authorities, but were probably not helpful as archives of specific geographical information. The second case study in this chapter is the well-known Nile mosaic from Praeneste. Probably established towards the end of the second century BCE, the Nile mosaic provides an extraordinary – and indeed unique – representation of the whole of the Nile valley, from Alexandria to Nubia. Attempts to read the mosaic cartographically, however, have largely foundered. It is suggested here that the representation was intended for display, admiration and discussion, but again not as a cartographically ordered representation of the Nile valley, or as a definitive and detailed rendering of the territories of Egypt.

 **Chapter 2** is concerned with other more or less formal articulations of geographical knowledge by the state, and how these were received by

---

[69] Vitr. 8.2.6.

the *populus* more broadly. To this end it looks in detail at the role played by geographical trophies in triumphal processions, including personified figures, allegorical representations and inscribed *tituli*. Ceremonies of this kind were a crucial means by which the inhabitants of Rome found out about the conquered world, and an important source of information for poets and prose geographers alike. The didactic function of these military parades has long been recognized, but the precise mechanisms by which information was gathered, transmitted and understood have never been closely investigated. This chapter attempts such an interpretation, and argues that the essentially chaotic presentation of material was central to the impact of a new form of imperial geography – in which the component parts of the world were consciously fragmented in order to be reassembled within the city. This stripped individual regions, places or geographical features from their spatial and historical context and created wholly new associations within Rome itself. These new geographies were authoritative only because they became the objects of the collective gaze of the city.

The second part of the chapter considers the varied cognitive cartographies that were assembled from these disparate parts and which the inhabitants of Rome might create from the city around them. Some of these new 'maps' were straightforward enough – it is likely that personifications of individual provinces were assembled in the so-called 'Porticus of the Nations', for example, thereby creating a reordered image of the world. When Vespasian formally consecrated his Temple of Peace in the early 70s, it is likely that this structure did something similar. A substantial botanical garden would seem to have been included in the Temple, alongside a diverse assemblage of military plunder and symbolic statuary. This complex collected together the plants, art and constituent parts of the world in a sort of museological and natural historical *Wunderkammer* for the delight of the Roman *populus*. But less formal microcosms were also possible. The fragmentation of the wider world effected by the triumphal displays allowed *tituli*, architectural motifs, or plunder like the captured obelisks to be endlessly reordered by the citizens of Rome into an infinity of different world 'maps'. By this process, plants, paint pigments or even food taken from all over the expanding empire could be comprehended as representations of the world in miniature.

Rather different issues of spectatorship and belonging arise in the discussion of domestic wall paintings in **Chapter 3**. Visual representations of the landscape of Egypt were known in Italy as early as the late-second century BCE, when the famous Nile mosaic was installed in the Temple of Fortuna in Praeneste. Over the following two centuries, similar representations proliferated in the houses and gardens of the Italian elite. There were particular bursts of interest in Aegyptiaca in the Augustan period and in the 60s and 70s CE, shortly before the eruption of Vesuvius. Interpretation of these works has frequently centred on their symbolic or religious functions, and occasionally on issues of taste, not least through the obvious parallels with orientalizing art in modern Europe and America. This chapter does not dispute these interpretations but also suggests that the paintings were important in shaping contemporary views of Egypt, and had a political significance in their own right. It argues that idealized perspectival landscapes can only be appreciated as reflection of a wider discourse on visuality and seeing. The paintings themselves were placed in a variety of different contexts – from small fragments of complex decorative schemes to large vistas which could occupy a whole wall – but always required some reflection on the visual context in which they appeared. Although the responses that these images demanded of the viewer were different, all were intended to provoke and engage their audiences.

Crucial to understanding these images is the recognition that the specific framing of these perspectival landscapes emphatically placed viewers in a privileged position – they presented the distant regions of the empire beneath the 'managerial gaze' of the provincial aristocracies. It is suggested that the choice of Pompeian and Roman householders to adopt these motifs reflects, whether consciously or unconsciously, a significant personal engagement with the politics of empire at this time. If the triumphal geographies that dominated the public spaces of the city demanded that its inhabitants confront their shared position as members of an imperial community, the domestic geographies that we see here reasserted their power as individual Romans. This was a form of 'imperial geography' every bit as resonant as the monumental cartography thought to have been erected by Augustus, or triumphs, but one which is frequently neglected in discussion of the reception of these texts. From a close reading of three examples in particular, the chapter further argues that visual geographies of this kind were shaped as much by pictorial convention as by a deference to authoritative geographical texts or cartographies. It is suggested that the precise way in which these perspectival landscapes exhibited exotic territories before the privileged gaze of the individual spectator also performed an important role in connecting provincial aristocracies to the new empire. Nilotic paintings created their own geographical discourse – one which was connected to other forms of geographical understanding, certainly, but was by no means deferential to them. It is also significant that the implications of these decorative conventions – that 'Egypt' was imagined as a

series of more or less undifferentiated places along the Nile, for example –
provides a link between the metonymic geography discussed in Chapter 2
and the cognitive associations prompted by itinerary writing and 'hodological' views of space, which are assessed in Chapter 5.

**Chapter 4** moves from spatial to temporal understanding and considers
the metaphysical significance of the Nile in more detail. The river provided
an important case study for natural philosophical investigation in the work
of both Lucretius and the Younger Seneca, just as it had for earlier scholars.
Although these philosophers comprehended the cosmos in contrasting
ways, their attitude to the Egyptian river was remarkably similar: both
recognized that the systematic application of philosophical reasoning to the
puzzle of the Nile floods offered a fine model for rational contemplation
and a challenge to superstition or hubris. Both also hinted that the deeper
secrets of the river might link to the greater wonder of the universe as
a whole. In order to accomplish this, both writers approached the Nile
through doxographical discussion, as many natural philosophers had before
them. By enumerating the various theories put forward by earlier scholars
to explain the causes of the Nile floods, and systematically refuting them,
Lucretius and Seneca did not seek to establish a definitive solution to the
problem, but rather to instruct their audiences in approaching intractable
problems. As part of their discussions, both writers introduce sublime
aspects to their philosophical enquiry and recognize the point at which
active mental contemplation might surrender to awe at the colossal scale
of the universe. More widely, similar themes can also be detected in the
relatively frequent assertion of the similarities between the annual Nile
floods and the original creation of life in the universe, and in the links
between the Nile and the recognized antiquity of Egyptian civilization.

The second part of the chapter investigates the importance of the Nile
to the so-called 'Egyptian' cults as they spread throughout the Roman
world. The river was, of course, central to the cosmogonies of Pharaonic
and Ptolemaic Egypt, but these theologies were changed substantially as
syncretistic cults developed and expanded beyond the Nile valley. By looking at the multiple representations of the Nile in the Iseum of Pompeii –
as personification in a mythological scene, schematic setting for an Isiac
myth, Egyptianizing landscape and water cistern – some of its metaphysical resonances are explored. Again, it is striking that many of these images
appropriate conventions of representation familiar from elsewhere in the
Roman world, but adapt it to dramatically new ends.

**Chapter 5** considers the linear nature of the Nile, as a line of connection
to be travelled along and as a mode of conceptualizing the physical relations

between different places. By far the greatest body of 'geographical' literature to have survived from the classical world are itineraries and *peripli* (or *periploi*) – variously schematic lists of placenames, narratives of individual voyages or abstracted 'road atlases'. The sheer proliferation of these texts, and the peculiar way in which they refashion the world for the convenience of the traveller, has led to considerable recent discussion about ancient geographical cognition. It has been argued that these works reflect an essentially 'linear' or 'hodological' conceptualization of the world as a place to be travelled through, and that cartographic maps (or other forms of two dimensional representation) were exceptional in classical antiquity. This chapter engages with this debate by looking at the representations of the Nile as a routeway in the texts of the period. This is accomplished first through a close investigation of the expedition sent upriver by Nero in the early 60s CE. It is argued that the explorers travelled with obsolescent itineraries, marking their progress along them and ultimately producing an annotated itinerary text of their own, and not a 'map' as has commonly been assumed. The discussion then turns back to Strabo's geography of Egypt, which reveals how a travelled itinerary might be translated into descriptive prose. Strabo's account was based in part on his own journey up the Nile and adopts a structure derived from an itinerary. Recognition of this point allows several important aspects of his description to be drawn out, including his surprising simplification of the course of the Egyptian Nile. Significantly, this view of Egypt as a succession of places strung out along the Nile gave way to further caricature, not least among authors and audiences who only knew the region at second-hand. Several later texts, including Tacitus, Juvenal and the Ancient Greek Novels, present plausible sounding but nonsensical geographies, which may have been intended satirically. These passages have generated considerable debate and have been read either as deliberate distortions for literary ends, or as reflections of the incompetence of their authors. It is suggested here that confusion of this kind was an inevitable product of modes of 'hodological' representation and has considerable parallels in later descriptions of Nile travel.

**Chapter 6** turns to the representations of the river in the epic and elegiac poetry of the period and brings us back to Lucan. Poetry was an authoritative form of meditation on the physical form of the world – a point clearly demonstrated by Strabo's lasting deference to Homer throughout his *Geography*. Poets also help us to chart how ideas about the natural world shaped by triumphs, paintings and formal geographical writing disseminated through the literate population of Rome. The Nile appears relatively infrequently within the poetry of this period, but its most significant appearances are considered in some detail here. It is suggested that Virgil's *Aeneid* was formative in shaping Augustan responses to the river. His description of the Nile in the *ekphrasis* on Aeneas' shield in Book VIII drew heavily upon the triumphal imagery of the Actian ceremony of 29 BCE and helped popularize these symbols for a contemporary audience. This conceit blurred the distinction between the Egyptian river and the Augustan trophy and further associated the Nile with the other trappings of the ritual, including Cleopatra, her sistrum, the god Anubis and the snakes. This illustrates the resonance of triumphal imagery in the popular imagination, but also established a specifically poetic template against which later writers could work in fashioning their own responses to imperial power and the domination of the wider world. The chapter goes on to examine the manipulation of these themes in elegies of Propertius and (perhaps surprisingly) Ovid. The chapter closes with a detailed discussion of the multiple roles played by the Nile in Lucan's *Civil War*. Lucan was far more ambitious in his treatment of the Egyptian river than earlier poets – as we have already seen – but the precise manner in which he created his poetic geography represents a remarkable confluence of the different rivers which have appeared in the volume as a whole.

The **Afterword** looks back at many of these themes through the lens of Pliny's *Natural History*. Pliny's work is increasingly recognized as a profoundly political work, as a celebration of the Flavian carnival of empire, which gathered together a colossal body of knowledge in celebration of the new dynasty. While Pliny's political aspirations have been much discussed, the fragmented and frequently contradictory nature of his text also reveals a great deal about the nature of 'imperial geography' in this period. By looking at some of the representations of the Nile within the work, including geographies which trace its origins to three distinct sources, superfluous and contradictory descriptions of its course through Egypt and some surprising appearances of the river in Rome, this discussion highlights the essential polyvalence of early imperial attitudes to the wider world.

# CHAPTER I

# A World Full of Maps?
## Public 'Chorographies' in Late Republican and Early Imperial Rome

In the last decade of the first century BCE, a monumental representation of the world was erected inside the Porticus Vipsania, in the southern part of the Campus Martius in Rome. The work was based on reports compiled by Augustus' lieutenant and heir presumptive Marcus Vipsanius Agrippa, and it must have been an important monumental addition to the Augustan city. Conventionally labelled the 'map' of Agrippa in modern scholarship, the survey has since been lost and is known primarily through a handful of fragmentary allusions in the *Natural History* of the Elder Pliny. At first glance, Pliny's account would seem to indicate the importance of this great 'map', and the authority that resonated from the imperially-sponsored work:

> Agrippa was a diligent and careful man. Who could believe that he – and along with him the Divine Augustus – made a mistake when he displayed the *orbis terrarum* to the gaze of the world? For he [Augustus] finished the porticus begun by his sister, following the design (*destinatione*) and *commentarii* of Marcus Agrippa.[1]

The finished work in the porticus was evidently impressive – a spectacular visual connection to the wider world for the citizens of the imperial city. Yet Pliny also turned to the survey – or an associated text – for specific points of information.[2] Agrippa is named around thirty times in the geographical sections of the *Natural History*, and modern commentators have identified numerous other sections which may also have come from the same source.[3]

---

[1] Plin. *HN* 3.17.
[2] The relations between these texts and the 'Agrippa' survey were discussed by Joseph Partsch (1875) and (1907), who argued that they derived from a written commentary that accompanied a visual map, and Detlefsen (1906), who suggested an indirect dependence, via circulating annotated copies of the original map. Sallmann (1971) discusses the intellectual content within which Partsch and Detlefsen worked. Arnaud (2007–8), 45–51 provides the best general summary of this scholarship. Cf. also Tierney (1963), 152–4; Nicolet (1991), 95–7; Brodersen (1995), 284–5.
[3] Agrippa is cited by name at: Plin. *HN* 3.8, 16, 17, 37, 86, 96, 150; 4.45, 60, 77, 83, 91, 98, 103, 105, 118; 5.9, 40, 65, 102; 6.3, 36–7, 39, 57, 136, 163–4, 196, 207, 209. On other fragments associated with Agrippa, see Brodersen (1995), 273–4; Arnaud (2007–2008), 48, 52; Arnaud (2016), 207–10.

A small number of later Roman treatises are also sometimes associated with the Agrippa project, although none of them makes this connection explicit. These texts make for somewhat dry reading, but cover a substantial swathe of the earth's surface from India in the east to the Spanish provinces and Britain in the west. If they were derived from the survey in the Porticus, even at several removes, then it was evidently a very wide-ranging work.[4]

The uncertain relationship between verbal and visual modes of spatial representation – between textual descriptions and 'maps' – remains a fundamental point of anxiety in analyses of ancient geographical thought. There is plenty of evidence to suggest that visual representations of the wider world were well-known within later Republican and early imperial Rome. The Agrippa 'map' is the most famous example and has been the most discussed, but other representations of a similar kind seem to have been familiar enough. An earlier survey of the world may have been undertaken during the dictatorship of Julius Caesar, and it has been suggested that a handful of late antique texts and medieval maps were derived from this work, rather than Agrippa's more famous project.[5] In the mid-20s BCE, Vitruvius knew of visual and verbal (*picta itemque scripta*) accounts of 'chorographers' and referred to them in order to clarify his account of the rivers of the world.[6] Vitruvius is unlikely to have been referring Agrippa's work here for chronological reasons, and scholars have frequently taken this to be an allusion to an earlier world map. There is reason to doubt this interpretation, as discussed below, but Vitruvius' reference remains important evidence that visual sources of some kind were known and valued. According to Livy, Sempronius Gracchus placed a panel in the Temple of Magna Mater in 174 BCE which included a *forma* ('shape' or 'outline') of the island of Sardinia, supplemented with 'visual representations of battles'.[7] A generation later, Lucius Hostilius Mancinus is said to have put up a plan of Carthage in the Roman forum, which he used to explain his own heroic actions in the capture of the city.[8] Both of these images may well have been visible for some time after their initial erection, and

[4] Debts have long been identified in the preface to the *Divisio orbis terrarum* in Riese (1878), 15–20: *terrarum orbis... quem diuus Augustus primus omnium per chorographiam ostendit*. And cf. *Dimensuratio provinciarum* in Riese (1878), 9–14. Arnaud (2007–2008), 65–8 discusses the relationship between these texts and the Agrippa project and previous scholarship.

[5] Cf. Nicolet and Gautier-Dalché (1986); Wiseman (1992), 22–44; Brodersen (1995), 262–7 provides a sceptical overview of this argument.

[6] Vitr. 8.2.6. On this passage, see 40–50 below.

[7] Liv. 41.28.10: *Sardiniae insulae forma erat, atque in ea simulacra pugarum picta*. On this *forma* cf. Lehmann-Hartleben (1926), 123 with the comments of Brodersen (1995), 157–60; Holliday (1997), 135–6; ibid. (2002), 105–6; Pittenger (2008), 284–5 and Östenberg (2009), 192–5.

[8] Plin. *HN* 35.23.

it is certainly possible that many more public depictions of this kind were known in the imperial capital.

Roman scholars were certainly well aware of Hellenistic traditions of mathematical cartography by the mid-first century BCE, but how widespread this knowledge was, and how far these conventions of spatial representation permeated the public sphere may be doubted. In a famous letter to Atticus, Cicero lamented the tedium of his attempts to translate Eratosthenes' work into Latin, but in so doing hinted at some of the esoteric interests of his circle.[9] The Hellenistic tradition was certainly well known to Strabo of Amasia, who composed his long description of the world in Rome during the early years of Tiberius' reign.[10] In this opening section of his text Strabo refers to a *geographikos pinax* and a *chorographikos pinax*, which apparently included the coastline of the three continents, rivers, mountains and the location of cities.[11] Whether these allusions were to the same work, to separate works or to an idealized 'map' which never existed in reality is unclear.[12] Regardless, Strabo evidently expected his audience to be able to conceptualize visual representations of some kind when reading his text. Other displays may have been inspired by Hellenistic antecedents, but these are hardly more illuminating, and it is probably wisest to be cautious when speculating on their likely form. In one of his late elegies, Propertius describes a young woman, mourning her lover's absence and gazing wistfully at a *tabula pictos ediscere mundos* ('a panel to show painted worlds'), which would seem to have depicted the main climatic zones.[13] Again, this may not refer to a specific map, and says little about the precise form it may have taken, but the hint is clear enough. Varro refers in passing to a *picta Italia* ('painted Italy') on the wall of the Temple of Tellus, that has variously been interpreted as a geometrical design following the principles of Eratosthenes, an idealized landscape painting, or a personification of the province.[14]

While these references do suggest that visual representations were relatively common in late Republican Rome, it remains an awkward truth that no large-scale public maps have survived from the Roman period.

9  Cic. *Att.* 2.6.1; cf. 2.4.1; and see also 2.20.6 and 2.22.7 on other works that he had borrowed.
10 Recent scholarship on Strabo is outlined above at 10, n.39. On the Tiberian dating of the text, see Dueck (1999).
11 Strabo 2.5.13, 17. At 1.1.22 Strabo evidently expects his audience to be familiar with a basic geometrical outline, perhaps from works of this kind.
12 Prontera (1984), 244–6; Arnaud (2014), 37; Lightfoot (2014), 121–3.
13 Prop. 4.3.37–40. The possible content of the *tabula* is suggested by the following lines of the poem. Brodersen (1995), 101–2. On similar themes in the *Panegyric to Messalla* (which does not allude directly to a map), see Schrijvers (2009), 149–51.
14 Varr. *Rust.* 1.2.1–3. On which see esp. Brodersen (1995), 152–5 and Spencer (2005), 57–61, 69–85.

Those works which are known to have existed, moreover, may not have been quite as prominent as some commentators have made out: it remains noteworthy that none of the descriptions of the Porticus Vipsania from the imperial period make any reference to the Agrippa survey adorning the walls of the building.[15] Agrippa's survey, Strabo's *pinakes* and Vitruvius' chorographers' images have all been lost beyond recovery, and the absence of any comparable works from the period make speculation on their likely form a futile operation. To be sure, certain forms of visual representation have survived and counsel against complete despair on this issue. We know from Roman surveyors' manuals and epigraphic references that these were also produced in bronze for civic archiving, as well as (presumably) more portable materials for use in the field.[16] A number of marble *formae* are extant, which would seem to date to the early imperial period. These were apparently monumentalized records of cadastral surveys, at the scale of the individual estate.[17] The great Severan marble plan of Rome is the most vivid example of this tradition, and certainly represented spatial representation at its most dramatic and its most public – a clear reminder that the *populus* of the city appreciated different forms of cartography turned to spectacular ends.[18]

Rather different methods of depicting space are apparent in the bird's-eye landscapes which start to appear from the later second century BCE, on a variety of different scales.[19] The earliest, grandest and best-known of these is certainly the spectacular Nile mosaic of Praeneste – a unique work which combines a panoramic view of the river valley from Alexandria to Nubia with detailed vignettes of life in Egypt and Ethiopia. The work has been described by Eleanor Windsor Leach as 'the fullest example of a maplike painting', and by Mikhail Rostovtzeff as 'a zoological atlas'.[20] On a more local scale we might note the famous axonometric riot fresco from the House of Actius Anicetus in Pompeii (I.3.23), which depicts the amphitheatre and the surrounding neighbourhood.[21] Similar schematic representations of urban space can be found in the miniaturized images of

---

[15] Cf. Dio Cass. 55.8.3–4; Mart. 1.108.1–4; Tac. *Hist.* 1.31.2; Plut. *Vit Galb.* 25.9. And see Brodersen (1995), 276 and (2001), 20, n.9. Remarkably, Strabo makes no reference to the Porticus in his description of the Campus Martius, on which see Wiseman (1979) and Arnaud (2016), 209. On the Porticus itself, see Gallia (2002) and Coarelli (1999).

[16] On the production and use of these plans, see now Morris (2016).

[17] Rodríguez-Almeida (2002) provides a clear introduction.

[18] Trimble (2008), with further references.

[19] Leach (1988), 89 and Holliday (1997), 40–1 on the striking originality of the form. Brodersen (1995), 29–31 is rightly sceptical of the tendency to label this tradition as 'cartographic'.

[20] Rostovtzeff (1941), 318; Leach (1988), 91.

[21] Holliday (2002), 109–10. And cf. Tac. *Ann.* 14.17 on the riot itself.

Troy on the so-called *Tabulae Iliacae*, a number of inscribed tablets which combine imaginative visual detail with complex arrangement of textual summaries of the Homeric cycle.[22] It is possible that these appealing urban vignettes may hint at the form of Hostilius Mancinus' plan of Carthage, or of other schematic diagrams alluded to in texts.[23] In each of these cases, the spectator is provided with a privileged bird's-eye view as a crib to the unfolding narrative, and it is easy to see how representations of this kind would have provided the ideal prompt for a soldier's bravado.

The space between the textual allusions on the one hand, and the varied forms of visual display on the other, has posed something of a challenge within studies of ancient geographical thought. The sheer proliferation of different modes of representing space in the later Republic and early empire have prompted a diversity of scholarly questions about geographical understanding in this period. Studies have attempted to ascertain what was new about the visual and verbal descriptions of the first century BCE, and whether these were dependent upon earlier forms of representation. Since the important work of Claude Nicolet, particular attention has been paid to the role of 'maps' within the developing political, cultural and intellectual discourses of the period, as we saw in the introduction.[24] But important questions remain: To what extent can the form of lost Roman *picturae*, *tabulae* and *pinakes* be reconstructed from the texts that either describe them or were derived from them? How did the grand projects mentioned by Pliny or Strabo, which seemed to represent the inhabited world as a whole, relate to mappings of smaller regions or to developing landscape art? Can textual descriptions themselves be viewed as part of the same process, and hence conscripted to the business of reconstructing these lost works? And to what extent was all of this bound up in the political transformations, first of the later Roman Republic and then, ultimately, of the early Principate?

Into this vacuum, scholars have projected their own views of Roman cartography, imperial power and modes of monumental display, in an attempt to deduce what the lost 'maps' may have looked like. By placing this early imperial mapping in a variety of different teleologies – the 'translation' of Hellenistic cartography, the evolution of medieval *mappaemundi*, the origins of later imperial modes of display – modern commentators

---

[22] On the *tabulae* see Brilliant (1984), 53–8, Squire (2011) and Petrain (2014). Cf. also Purves (2010), 24–64 on how the 'eusynoptic' nature of the *Iliad* lent itself to spatial representation in this manner.

[23] Note for example the plan of Troy, traced in wine on a tavern table in Ov. *Her.* 1.33–6. And cf. Brodersen (1995), 243.

[24] Nicolet (1991), and see above 6–15.

have cast these works in an extraordinary diversity of forms, rarely entirely
comfortably. The speculative reconstructions of the Agrippa 'map', that
have proliferated over the last century or so, illustrate this point especially clearly. Attempts to reconstruct the work have leaned heavily upon
spurious comparanda, with predictably varied results.[25] Agrippa's project
has variously been compared to the Hellenistic maps of Eratosthenes and
his predecessors (which are no longer extant), the *picta Italia* on the wall
of the Temple of Tellus (which has also been lost) and Ptolemy's mathematical *Geography* (which may never have been rendered in graphic form
in the ancient world).[26] One interpretation has claimed that it took the
form of a great triptych, in which each continent was depicted on a separate wall of the Porticus;[27] another that it was probably composed of
interlocking geometrical shapes, in the manner of some contemporary
Hellenistic cartography.[28] Other points of comparison have included the
second-century Severan marble plan of Rome, medieval *mappaemundi* and
the so-called Peutinger Table – a late medieval manuscript supposed to
have derived from a late Roman original.[29] A further school of thought
has argued persuasively that Agrippa's 'map' had little or no cartographic
content, as it is conventionally understood, and is probably best viewed
as a series of inscribed lists.[30] Most recently, Pascal Arnaud has questioned

[25] Contra the extraordinary claim of Nicolet (1991), 101: 'it is quite legitimate to try to reconstruct
the [map] from preserved textual fragments. It has been successfully done and so it is not necessary
to go over it in detail here.' At 102 Nicolet cites Detlefsen, Klotz and the 'reasonably accurate'
tableaux of Kubitschek. For more recent reconstructions, compare Tierney (1963) and Moynihan
(1985). Hänger (2007) represents the most recent attempt.

[26] Tierney (1963), 160–1 and Aujac (2001), 107–8; Marcotte (2000), lviii (Hellenistic 'Maps'); Holliday
(2002), 106 (who argues that it was a 'chorographic painting' in the manner of the *picta Italia*); Klotz
(1931) and (with reservations) Schnabel (1935) (Ptolemy). The sheer variety of these interpretations
is catalogued with amusing irony by Brodersen (1995), 269–72.

[27] Trousset (1993).

[28] Hänger (2007); Arnaud (2007), 24; Arnaud (2007–2008), 83–4; Arnaud (2016), 210–14.

[29] Tierney (1963), 152 proposes a visual similarity to the Severan Plan; Miller (1895–97), VI. 145–7
reconstructs the Agrippa map according to the obvious model of medieval *mappaemundi*. On the
intellectual context of this reconstruction, see esp. Gautier Dalché (2008), 32–3. Moffitt (1997) con-
fusingly ties Agrippa, the Praeneste mosaic and medieval *mappaemundi* together as 'chorographies'.
Trousset (1993) is one of several scholars to draw links with the Peutinger Map, and cf. Rathmann
(2016), 347 who suggests that Agrippa and the Peutinger Map may share a common (Hellenistic)
ancestor. The latter text is examined exhaustively in Talbert (2010a).

[30] Cf. Syme (1988), 233: 'Sooner or later the question of maps will impinge. At Rome the typical
product had nothing to do with cartography. It was the itinerary, registering stages and distances
along known roads and comparable to a mariner's periplus.' A comparable reading of Agrippa's work
is proposed by Brodersen (1995) 268–85 and hinted at in Purcell (1990b). Brodersen's interpretation
is disputed in Salway (2001), but see also Brodersen (2001), 20, n.9 for a reiteration of the position.
Talbert (2012), 169 proposes a sensible 'middle way': that Agrippa produced a 'map' of some kind,
but the precise form is uncertain and it was probably original in form.

whether the work was genuinely innovative in scholarly or technical terms and has suggested that it adopted established Hellenistic practice.[31]

Clearly, there is little consensus about the precise form of the Agrippa 'map', and attempts to reconstruct our other lost works have been similarly inconclusive. There is an essential futility to this methodology which it is hard to escape: by adducing different possible principles for the reconstruction of Agrippa's map, these studies tell us rather more about the concerns of modern scholars than they do about ancient views of the world. But the problems of this approach run still deeper and relate to the implicit collapsing of the distinction between text and image as distinct modes of geographical representation. At one extreme, the common assumption that cartography represented the most important medium for the 'scientific' representation of the world risks subordinating texts like Pliny, Vitruvius or the late antique geographical treatises to the lost 'maps' upon which they purportedly depended. The particular value of verbal description as a means of making sense of the world thus becomes obscured.[32] At the other extreme, some scholars have concluded prematurely that public cartography cannot have existed in any meaningful form in the late Republic or early empire.[33] Simply because Roman writers rarely describe maps in detail, or derive from them information that could just as easily have been taken from texts, it has been argued that visual sources did not influence textual geographers at all, and therefore may not have existed. This rather nihilistic position runs the opposite risk of neglecting the importance of the visual within the later Republic and early empire in favour of the written word. Both approaches effectively ignore the extent to which texts and images responded to the wider world in different ways, and audiences responded differently to them.

In many ways, the simple assumption that the Agrippa map was a work of particular intellectual and political significance has done most to confuse its interpretation.[34] The enormous importance of archival knowledge in the development of modern empires, and the fundamental authority of cartography within contemporary conceptualizations of state power, have

---

[31] Arnaud (2016), 216: 'The image we can have of his work is that it was at the same time very conventional and largely second-hand, as far removed from the secret weapon some have seen in Agrippa's work as it is from the huge innovative survey of the world ordered by Augustus.'

[32] See, for example, Shcheglov (2014) which reduces Pomponius Mela's idiosyncratic text to a lost Hellenistic 'map' which anticipated Ptolemy's work. Broderson (2011) and idem. (2016) argues persuasively that Pliny's *Natural History* was purely textual in form, and gained a visual dimension only with the recension of Solinus in the third century.

[33] Most conspicuously Brodersen (1995).

[34] Arnaud (2007–2008), 47–8 discusses the origins of this interpretation in the later nineteenth century.

shaped the scholarship surrounding the Agrippa project profoundly, at the risk of some anachronism.[35] Thanks largely to the important scholarship of Claude Nicolet, the 'map' in the Porticus is most frequently regarded as the public face of the Augustan archive – a spectacular demonstration of imperial power, founded upon the privileged accumulation of knowledge about the newly conquered world.[36] According to this reading, political authority and geographical authority are interdependent and unified within the 'map' itself: the project makes a claim to a definitive representation of the world on the strength of its association with imperial power, and the empire itself is supported – even reified – by this impressive depiction in visual terms.[37]

On the face of it, this would seem to be a defensible interpretation, given Pliny's description of Agrippa's project. After all, in the passage quoted at the start of this chapter – his fullest reference to the work – Pliny states explicitly that the trustworthiness of the survey as a geographical source is guaranteed by Agrippa's political stature and particularly by his association with Augustus.[38] In this way, the association between political and geographical authority could scarcely be clearer. Yet the picture is not quite so simple. In the very next section of his text, Pliny goes on to challenge the data provided by Agrippa. He notes at some length the errors in the measurements that the survey gives for the dimensions of the province of Baetica, and adduces several other sources in the hope of providing more accurate figures.[39] This is a pattern followed throughout the *Natural History*: when Pliny refers to Agrippa's survey it is frequently as one source among many, and the information from the Porticus rarely stands on its own as absolutely authoritative.[40]

The point here is not that Pliny did not trust Agrippa. Quite the opposite, Pliny clearly regarded the Agrippa project as a valuable source of a

[35] See the discussion above 6–15.

[36] Nicolet (1991), with comments of Brodersen (1995), 23–5. On the archival impulse in this period, see also Moatti (1993) and (1997), with the comments of Naas (2002), 74–7.

[37] Carey (2003), 63: 'Even greater than the sense of conquest evident in being able to hold the world in your hand, here the whole world was unfurled, measured and deconstructed, its anatomy placed on view in the centre of Rome. In representing the world as it had not been seen before, in detailing it where it had simply been spherical, the map made a strong claim to autopsy, which in turn implies conquest, particularly when linked to a man who had been a military commander in almost every part of the empire.' Compare Brunt (1963), 175–6 (on the grounds that it served no practical function); Arnaud (2007), 19; Arnaud (2007–8), 50–3.

[38] Evocatively put by Arnaud (2016), 207: '[Agrippa] was also the tongue of truth, and the God Augustus was his warranty.'

[39] Plin. *HN* 3.18; Arnaud (2007–8), 76 notes that these other figures may themselves have come from Agrippa.

[40] See, for example, Plin. *HN* 3.86–7; 4.45, 77, 91, 98; 5.40; 6.3, 36–7, 57, 163–4, 196, 207, 209.

specific kind of information. This was why he cited the work by name so frequently, and indeed, why he firmly asserted the political foundations upon which the authority of the 'map' was based. Pliny does go out of his way to explain these discrepancies, and his apologia on Baetica in particular has justly been compared to the work of the Homeric scholiasts in explaining the idiosyncrasies of those great texts.[41] But it is evident from Pliny's engagement with the survey in the Porticus that Agrippa's work did not hold a monopoly over geographical knowledge within the early Principate and was viewed by the later writer as being absolutely authoritative in itself. Pliny clearly did not regard the work – or *any* single work – as being an absolute arbiter of geographical knowledge. Instead, different sources of information were regarded as trustworthy or relevant in different contexts, even within the (relatively) restricted confines of an individual text.[42] If Pliny and other geographical writers of early imperial Rome desired a definitive source of information on the geography of the known world, they did not find one fully formed in the Porticus Vipsania: they had to go about creating one for themselves.[43]

Equally significant is the type of information that Pliny drew from Agrippa. As several studies have pointed out, the vast majority of Pliny's references to the survey relate to precise measurements, sometimes involving dimensions of whole regions or provinces, at other times the relatively short distances between specific places.[44] These are data that are more easily transmitted in a text than an image, and speculation has increasingly focused on the verbal component of Agrippa's project, which must have been quite prominent. As we have seen, this has led some commentators to assume that the survey in the porticus was essentially a massive inscribed list. This form of display could certainly be impressive, as studies of other monumental inscriptions have shown.[45] Others have suggested that Pliny may have drawn upon written *commentarii*, produced by Agrippa in preparation for his survey, or perhaps inscribed alongside it.[46] These are all justifiable interpretations, but they sidestep the essential contradiction in Pliny's treatment of the work: Agrippa's survey was a trustworthy authority because it was so widely familiar within the city, and yet the specific data that was drawn from it would have lent itself poorly to spectacular display. There are two operations at play here – the visual and the verbal – and

---

[41] Arnaud (2007–8), 54 and cf. Burns (1964), 256.
[42] The issue of Authority in the *HN* is discussed more fully in the Afterword.
[43] On Pliny's approach to this problem, see below 288–90.
[44] Winkler (2000), 158–9; Carey (2003), 64–5; Arnaud (2007), 24–5; Arnaud (2016), 210–14.
[45] Cf. for example Thomas (1994).        [46] Discussed in Arnaud (2007–8), 87–8 and (2016), 218–21.

we should not assume that they can be perfectly reconciled. Even as Pliny emphasized the visual aspect of the Agrippa survey in other words – that its principal function was 'to set the *orbis terrarum* before the eyes of the world' – his own exploitation of it was primarily for discrete numerical data.

A number of important studies on ancient art have recently explored similar tensions between the status of text and image.[47] Where it was once common practice for modern commentators to view visual representations in essentially verbal terms – to 'decode' paintings or sculptures of mythological or religious subjects following cues from extant texts, and to assume that ancient viewers did much the same thing – such strategies no longer seem appropriate in the assessment of classical art. Instead, greater emphasis has been placed on ancient fascination with the interplay between different representative forms. Michael Squire's recent study of the cryptoporticus of the House of Propertius in Assisi, for example, which dates from the later first century CE, has shown that the curious juxtapositions of Greek epigrams and mythological wall-paintings were not intended as simple labels or illustrations, in which either the visual or verbal elements would be privileged. Instead, they appear as playful meditations on the strengths and limitations of each medium, and as a perpetual reminder of the active role of the spectator in imbuing the assemblage with meaning.[48] Similarly, recent work on the visual and textual components of the *Tabulae Iliacae* have revealed how pictorial and written elements can complement and complicate one another in important ways.[49] Comparable approaches have been particularly effective in recent studies of *ekphrasis* as a literary phenomenon. Classical authors' fascination with the cognitive, physiological and aesthetic experiences of sight, and their attempts to replicate these responses through text, have been recognized as part of an ongoing exploration of different aspects of visual culture.[50] Increasingly, text and image are not regarded as completely distinct, but as two parts of an interlocking discussion of visuality, which can accomplish very different things.

Adopting a similar approach to the puzzle of ancient public mapping allows us to think in rather different terms about what Pliny, Vitruvius or Strabo were doing when they alluded to *formae, picturae* and *pinakes*, and yet refrained from discussing the content of these images in detail. Theirs

---

[47] See, for example, the different approaches of Stückelberger (1994); Elsner (1995); Clarke (2003); Elsner (2007); Stewart (2008), Rutledge (2012), 79–121 and esp. Squire (2009). And compare Alpers (1983) for a seminal study of early Netherlandish art in similar terms.

[48] Squire (2009), 239–93.      [49] See esp. Squire (2012) and Petrain (2014).

[50] On *ekphrasis*, see below 239–46.

are not ecphrastic descriptions in the strict sense, and they were evidently not concerned with capturing the emotional or intellectual effects that such images might have on their viewers.[51] Instead, Pliny and his predecessors adopted a different approach to the depiction of the world in these images – one which was framed in narrative, rather than synchronic terms, and which was defined by discrete points of textual or numerical information rather than the promise of taking in the known world at a single glance. Visual and textual strategies could certainly overlap, whether through the incorporation of text on 'maps', or the use of evocative visual language within written descriptions. But these means of representing the world were essentially distinct, and were recognized as such by their creators.

Here we may turn again to Pliny's description of the Agrippa project, designed as it was to 'display the *orbis terrarum* to the gaze of the world'.[52] This can tell us next to nothing about the precise form that the 'map' may have taken, and little about the political value of the text beyond the recognition that the work had a monumental function. Indeed, Pliny describes the text of the *Natural History* itself in similar terms, as a declaration of its magnitude.[53] But the statement does emphasize the visual impact of the Agrippa survey, and the means by which its audience accessed it: Pliny's use of the verb *proponere* is almost always deployed within the *Natural History* to refer to objects rendered meaningful by public display.[54] At once, it becomes apparent that the Agrippa survey – and perhaps other works like it – were defined primarily by their position before the collective gaze of the *populus*. In demanding a visual and even physical engagement on the part of their viewers, they enjoyed a different status to other forms of geographical representation. This public visibility is also one of the few things we can say for certain about the representations of Sardinia and Carthage mentioned by Livy and Pliny. Varro's allusion to the *picta Italia* on the wall of the Temple of Tellus is immediately followed by a long account of an imagined conversation that it provoked among a crowd of passers-by.[55] This suggests we should think of these 'maps', not as lost 'texts' that might be pieced together through painstaking *Quellenforschung* among later 'recensions', and which were primarily valued for the discrete points of information that they contained, but rather as visual displays that provided one means

[51] Brodersen (1995), 277; *pace* Evans (2005), 55.
[52] Plin. *HN* 3.17: *cum urbem terrarum ubi spectandum propositurus esset.*
[53] Plin. *HN* 6.211. Cf. Brodersen (1995), 277–8; Arnaud (2007–8), 87–8.
[54] Plin. *HN* 1.35; 10.5; 35.22, 23, 84, 140. Cf. Arnaud (2007–8), 54 and (more cautiously) Arnaud (2016), 220. The one exception is *HN* 35.151 (which refers to the hardening of clay 'exposed' to fire).
[55] Varr. *Rust.* 1.2.3–8.

by which citizens could begin to comprehend the world around them and appreciate their place within it. These were works that helped to inspire and impress the spectator: like many public maps, indeed like many maps, they placed their viewers in a position of apparent panoptic authority, presenting the whole world beneath their gaze.[56] But these responses were framed by the static, architectural settings of the works themselves, and the collective nature of this audience engagement.[57] Appreciating these visual displays in this way need not contradict their interpretation as essentially political tools, but it does nuance it, and highlights the importance of the audience to the meaning of the political message.

Viewing the issue in these terms, we can appreciate how important visual language was to textual geographers without assuming that physical maps provided the essential bedrock of geographical understanding in this period. When Manilius identified his brief description of the world as a *figura*, or Strabo appeared to recommend the construction of impossibly complex *pinakes* as a prelude to his textual geography, we can see this as a form of *enargeia* – a metaphorical mode of conceptualization – rather than a simple deference to a superior medium of geographical exposition.[58] In her recent study of the *Periegesis* of Dionysius, J. L. Lightfoot demonstrates how that second-century poet does precisely this. Dionysius' verse shifts easily between different visual registers, evoking a series of pseudo-cartographical perspectives which would be impossible to reproduce on a single map, even if they can readily be brought to mind.[59] Maps may not have been especially important as sources of information, then, but visual frames of reference remained an important medium for the comprehension of the world.

The Nile provides a useful starting point for examining the cultural, cognitive and epistemological function of visual media of these kinds, not least because the Nile featured particularly prominently on two of our best-documented examples. Frustratingly, the Agrippa survey does not seem to have represented the Nile in any particular detail. It is possible that the Nile and other rivers appeared within the work, but there is no evidence to

---

[56] Jacob (2006) is fundamental. Cf. also Stewart (1993), 37–69 for comparable messages in different media.

[57] Jacob (2006), 94: 'The intended function of the building naturally influences how the map is perceived. A private house, a scientific institute, and a church or palace count as different stagings of the map that reserve its spectacle to the happy few or the masses, on ceremonial occasions or in the course of everyday life.' All of the references to these public displays in Rome would seem to be to works that were viewed collectively and by a wide audience.

[58] Manilius 4.586; Strabo 2.5.13, 2.5.18, 2.5.26. Lightfoot (2014), 18.

[59] Lightfoot (2014), esp. 18–19 and 121.

support this contention.[60] Certainly Pliny never defers to the source when discussing the river, and the later texts sometimes assumed to have derived from the survey are also silent.[61] Instead, we are limited to two contrasting case studies. The first of these is (or are) the 'chorographic' works to which Vitruvius refers in the eighth book of his *De Architectura*, shortly before a substantial digression on the course of the Nile. Whether these 'painted and written accounts' refer to ancestors of the Agrippa survey, landscape paintings of a type that were increasingly common in Augustan Italy, or diagrams within an illustrated scroll is uncertain. What is clear, however, is that Vitruvius felt it necessary to appeal to the authority of images as well as texts in framing his description of the Nile course, and was evidently confident that his audience would be familiar with the types of work he was talking about. The second example is the great Nile mosaic of Praeneste, which has survived from its original creation in the later second century BCE, albeit in fragmented form. This work is unambiguously a visual representation of a large region, which was clearly intended for public display, and was intended to evoke the broad form and specific features of Egypt in a stylized manner. By reflecting on the form and function of the Praeneste mosaic, and comparing it with extant textual responses to the same region, we can begin to unpick the means by which different media shaped popular responses to the wider world.

## The 'Chorographies' of Vitruvius

Vitruvius' *De Architectura* (*On Architecture*) is the best-known prose didactic treatise of the Augustan period.[62] The work was almost certainly composed in the 20s BCE, during the difficult first decade of the Principate, at a time when Augustus was consolidating his political authority and

---

[60] Contra Postl (1970), 25–6 (who assumes that Agrippa prominently represented the 'western' course of the Nile), presumably on a misreading of Vitruvius, and Arnaud (2016), 217 (who implies that Agrippa placed the source of the Nile in the far south thanks to his presumed deference to Polybius).

[61] Pliny cites Agrippa several times on rivers, but only as provincial borders, or in measuring distances between their mouths and other points of interest, never as an authority on their courses as a whole. See, for example, *HN* 4.81 (Ister and Vistula), 4.91 (Borysthenes); 4.105 (Rhine); 6.136 (Indus, Tigris, Euphrates) (as provincial borders), and *HN* 4.77 (Ister), 5.9 (Subudum, Salat, Quosenum, Masathat and Darat) (as river mouths). At *HN* 6.196 Agrippa is cited only as an authority on the size of Africa as a whole and is conspicuously absent in Pliny's account of the distances between settlements on the Nile; this passage is discussed in more detail in Chapter 5 (below). On late antique Nile geographies (and their absence in the *Divisio orbis terrarum* and the *Demensuratio Provinciarum*), compare Oros. 1.2.27–33 and the comments of Merrills (2005), 79–87.

[62] McEwen (2003) provides the best general introduction to the text. See also Wallace-Hadrill (2008), 144–212 on the cultural and intellectual context and Baldwin (1990) on dating. Janvier (1994) provides a full discussion of Vitruvius' geographical passages.

beginning his great programme of urban renewal. The text comprises ten books and was intended in part to accentuate the political and cultural status of architecture within the changing imperial state, and perhaps also to bolster the author's own position in society.[63] Quite how successful Vitruvius was in either of these ambitions is open to question. While Vitruvius does not seem to have enjoyed particular advancement as a result of the text, his work did chime well with the spirit of the age. The wide frame of reference within the text helped make sense of the world, and imbued the new imperial capital with the Hellenistic cachet that Augustus craved. Within it, Vitruvius discusses topics as diverse as the ideal location of towns and ports, the appropriate form of religious, public and private buildings, domestic decoration, water supply, sundials and clocks, and the role of the architect in war. His intention was to demonstrate both the essential order at the heart of the Augustan project, and the unique role of the architectural writer as arbiter of this.

Vitruvius refers to visual depictions of the world, and to the River Nile, towards the start of the eighth book of *De Architectura*.[64] Book VIII concerns the importance of water within the well-planned city, and in the world as a whole. This corresponds closely to broader themes of order throughout Vitruvius' text and exemplifies the role of the architect in identifying and accentuating this balance. The book opens in suitably grandiose style with an account of the creation of the universe, and goes on to assert how an understanding of the circulation of water throughout the world both reveals these generative forces at work, and allows the careful observer to divine hidden sources.[65] Vitruvius then turns to established geographical knowledge. His contention is that the great heat of the south means that moisture is absorbed from these regions, borne away from the region by winds, and deposited in the north:

> The sources of rivers can serve as proof that these things happen as we have described, for most of them, and the greatest, are to be found to emerge in the North, in the *orbis terrarum* as it is painted and written by chorographers.[66]

Vitruvius had to go to some lengths to justify this surprising contention, not least in his contorted description of the Nile, and we will come to the specifics of his geography shortly. Equally important are the authorities

---

[63] König (2009).
[64] Vitruvius also includes geographical descriptions at 2.10.1 and 6.1.1–12 (with no explicit reference to the sources that he used).
[65] Vitr. 8.Praef – 1.     [66] Vitr. 8.2.6 after Rowland and Howe (1999), 98.

to which he appeals in making this statement. His appeal to 'chorographers' and to their 'painted and written' accounts – *picta itemque scripta* – has important implications for our understanding of popular geographical knowledge in this period and the different ways in which this was transmitted to a wide audience.

It is important to establish explicitly that Vitruvius' reference to 'chorographers' cannot tell us very much about the nature of these *picturae* and *scripturae*. In a much-analyzed passage from the mid-second century CE, the Alexandrian mathematician Ptolemy distinguished *geographia* from *chorographia* at the opening of his great work on cartography.[67] Ptolemy states that *geographia* demanded the representation of the world as a single continuous whole, which could be taken it at a single glance by a viewer, and which would be produced according to mathematical principles. In itself, this would seem to correspond to contemporary uses of the term, which had appeared only relatively rarely in earlier Greek and Latin, and was typically associated with the work of Eratosthenes and the mathematical cartography of Alexandria.[68] *Chorographia* seems to have been a more ambiguous term, and Ptolemy's concern to distinguish *chorographia* from *geographia* may in fact indicate that such distinctions were unusual, rather than commonplace, at the time of his composition.[69] Ptolemy's account states first that *chorographia* was concerned with individual parts of the world, rather than the entire *oikoumene* – the 'ears' and the 'eyes' in his simile, and not the whole head.[70] He goes on to state that chorographers were responsible for capturing the character of particular regions or places and should concern themselves with qualities rather than quantities, likenesses rather than precise positions in their works.

In broad terms, Ptolemy evidently regarded *geographia* as mathematical 'mapping' on an ecumenical scale, *chorographia* as the description – whether textual or visual – of rather smaller regions. But these distinctions blur upon closer scrutiny, and it is impossible to infer from Ptolemy's definition precisely what form Vitruvius' 'painted and written accounts of the chorographers' may have taken. References in Strabo's great first-century survey of the world certainly underscore the association between *geographia*

---

[67] Ptol. *Geog.* 1.1. For various readings of this passage, compare Leach (1988), 91; Meyboom (1995), 186–90; Ferrari (1999), 379–80; Rouveret (2004), 333; Prontera (2006/2011); Cosgrove (2008), 7–8; Rathmann (2012), 208–12; Lightfoot (2014), 18–19; Rathmann (2016), 348–51.

[68] Cic. *Att.* 2.4.3, 2.6.1. The works of Eratosthenes were certainly known in later Republican Rome and were commonly identified in these terms; cf. Strabo 2.1.1–2 and *passim*.

[69] Cf. Prontera (2006/2011), 102–3. Contra Moffitt (1997), 246.

[70] Ptol. *Geog.* 8.1 notes that practical considerations might sometimes lead cartographers to produce regional maps, which were fragments of the whole, but were still geographies.

and the Alexandrian tradition, but he employs the term *chorographia* more loosely.[71] In his description of Greece, for example, Strabo cites a definition from Polybius and Ephorus that more or less directly contradicts Ptolemy's later account:

> We will show things as they now are, concerning both the position of places and the distances between them, for this is most suitable for chorography.[72]

At different points in his text, Strabo does use *chorographia* to refer to regional surveys, and he notes that the 'chorographers' of India might view the world differently from Greek savants.[73] Yet he also describes an imagined plan of the whole world as a 'chorographic' *pinax*, rather than a geographical text as Ptolemy's definition would seem to demand.[74] Vitruvius, too, was evidently referring to a work which was more or less universal in scope, and which certainly included the major rivers of the world, both characteristics which Ptolemy would associate with 'geographical' works.[75] At times 'chorography' seems to have been associated with very precise mathematical measurement – as in Strabo's deference to 'the chorographer' (*chorographos*) on distances between settlements in the western Mediterranean, or the common use of the term among surveyors in the imperial provinces.[76] At others it could refer to short literary descriptions of the world as a whole, most famously in Pomponius Mela's written account of the mid-40s CE, which circulated under that title in the medieval manuscript tradition, but also in the verse *chorographia* of Varro of Atax which was written in the mid-first century BCE, and which has survived

---

[71] On the identification of Eratosthenes' work as *geographia* specifically, see van Paassen (1957), 34 and 364, nn.44–5; Prontera (2006/2011), 97–8.

[72] Strabo 10.3.5 (= Polyb. 34.1.5); tr. Roller (2014), 453. And cf. also Strabo 2.4.1 (= Polyb. 34.5.1). Prontera (2006/2011), 97.

[73] Strabo 1.1.16. The same passage uses *geographia* and *chorographia* more or less interchangeably. Compare also Strabo 2.5.1.

[74] Strabo 2.5.17. A 'geographical' *pinax* is introduced in 2.5.13. On the blurring of these distinctions by Strabo see esp. Brodersen (1995), 281–2 and now Lightfoot (2014), 18. Rathmann (2012), 209–10 and (2013), 36–7 is much more confident in the precision of Strabo's language. Meyboom (1995), 187 suggests that any vignettes in this work are better regarded as topographical, rather than chorographical – a term that would seem to be equally ambiguous in this period.

[75] Ptol. *Geog.* 1.1.

[76] Strabo 5.2.7; 5.2.8; 6.1.11; 6.2.1; 6.2.11; 6.3.10. This *chorographos* was long identified with Agrippa. Cf. Tierney (1963), 152; Nicolet (1991), 107–8; Dueck (2000), 127–9. Gruen (1992), 184 regards this as 'a tempting but not particularly probable interpretation'. Brodersen (1995), 280–3 is similarly sceptical on chronological grounds. Arnaud (2007–8), 60–4 demolishes the argument that Strabo's source was Agrippa. On surveyors as *chorographii*, cf. Morris (2016). I am grateful to Jason Morris for bringing these texts to my attention and for extensive discussion about their implications.

only in fragments.[77] Various scholars have tried to explain away these contradictions by arguing that Strabo and Vitruvius drew upon works that combined 'chorographic' and 'geographic' elements – perhaps including painted vignettes within a broadly cartographic outline.[78] Others have argued that these writers were simply unaware of the type of works they were looking at, or were unable to read them.[79] Such explanations simply emphasize how little we know about these lost sources, and other allusions only intensify this confusion. Within this context, Vitruvius' *chorographi* may be writers or painters (or both), who depicted the whole (or part) of the world, with an emphasis on either geometrical or imaginative principles. In short, his use of language cannot tell us much.

Vitruvius' appeal to the written and visual works of chorographers (in the plural) does imply that he grouped a variety of different modes of representation together under the same broad label. At one end of the scale, this may refer to public 'mapping' projects somewhere in the imperial city. These cannot have included the Agrippa map: Vitruvius almost certainly composed his text during the 20s BCE, and the survey in the Porticus Vipsania cannot have been erected before 7 or 6 BCE, when the building was completed.[80] But it is certainly possible that Vitruvius was referring to an earlier map of a similar sort.[81] At the other extreme, Vitruvius' allusion to images may refer to little more than simple diagrams in otherwise wholly textual descriptions of the world: papyri and early medieval manuscripts offer some corroboration for this view, not least through the sketched illustrations and diagrams recently identified on the so-called Artemidorus papyrus dating to the first century CE.[82] Others have argued that these 'chorographical' images can only refer to evocative landscape paintings of the kind known from Rome and Pompeii and alluded to elsewhere in the *De Architectura*.[83] Again, this interpretation is perfectly plausible – and the

77  Lightfoot (2014), 14–6 succinctly summarizes this tradition and notes that the *hypotyposis* of Strabo 2.5.18–33 and Manilius 4.585–696 could plausibly be included in this tradition. On Pomponius Mela see esp. Silberman (1988), xiv–xx; Brodersen (1995), 2; on Varro Atacinus, see Hollis (2007), 166–70 and 181–92 (which discusses links to the Hellenistic tradition). A lost work of Cicero is also described as a *chorographia* at Prisc. *Inst.* 6.8.2. And see also *Divisio Orbis Terrarum* 1 in Riese (1878), 15.
78  Compare Nicolet (1991), 107; Prontera (2002), 243–4; Arnaud (2014), 39–40.
79  Rathmann (2012), 212. If it could indeed be demonstrated that Vitruvius (one of a tiny handful of possible references to visual cartography) was unable to 'read' a map, this would be tremendously important for our understanding of the function of such works in the imperial city. As it is, it seems more generous to assume that he understood what he was looking at, even if we cannot tell what it was. Cf. also Rathmann (2016), 350–4.
80  Dio Cass 55.8.3–4. Cf. Brodersen (1995), 275.    81  Janvier (1994), 59 suggests this.
82  On which see Gallazzi, Kramer and Settis (2008); Brodersen and Elsner (2009).
83  Vitr. 7.5.1–2.

author and his audience clearly knew works of this kind very well – but the case is far from straightforward. Vitruvius' reference does not in itself prove the existence of a specific mode of 'chorographic' landscape painting that was at once uniquely Roman and authoritative. It merely reveals that the writer expected his audience to think of geographical sources in visual as well as textual terms.

Yet we can still learn a great deal from this short passage. Viewed in context, Vitruvius' insistence upon the apparent interdependence of image and text is revealing. This formulation, and the description of the Nile which follows, provide a starting point for thinking about how different modes of representation may have been viewed and used by contemporaries within the city. Vitruvius clearly depended on textual sources in putting together his unusual description of the Nile – and indeed tells us as much later in his discussion. But this did not mean that visual representations were unimportant: They may in fact have been vital to his understanding of the world, and his didactic method. For Vitruvius, it would seem, images offered spectators a means to genuine geographical autopsy – a glimpse of the imperial world as it actually was. Yet this authority could only be rendered legible through the mediating influence of verbal authority.

Vitruvius supports his assertion that the major watercourses all flow from the mountainous regions of the north with a list of examples:

> First of all, in India, the Ganges and Indus arise in the Caucasus; in Syria the Tigris and Euphrates; in Asia, in Pontus: the Borysthenes, Hypanis, and Tanais, in Colchis: the Phasis; in Gaul, the Rhodanus; in the land of the Celts the Rhenus; in Cisalpine Gaul the Timavus and the Padus; in Italy, the Tiber . . . [84]

River catalogues of this kind were a relatively common *topos* in the poetry of the Augustan period, and allowed writers to advertise the breadth of their interest with little reference to geographical specifics.[85] Vitruvius deviates from this pattern with a much fuller description of an African river, which is eventually revealed to be the Nile:

> In Maurusia, which we call Mauretania, from Mount Atlas, the Dyris, which after arising in the northern region proceeds through the west to lake Eptagonus, where it changes its name and is called Agger. Then, from Lake Eptabolos, it flows underneath the desert mountains through southern regions, and flows into what is called the swamp, circles Meroe, which is the kingdom of the southern Ethiopians, and from these swamps it rises through

---

[84] Vitr. 8.2.6. tr. Rowland and Howe (1999), 98.
[85] See P. Jones (2005), 81 on this material. Lightfoot (2014), 88–99 on the geographical catalogue.

the rivers Astanasoba and Astoboa and many others, to pass through the mountains to the cataract, and hurling itself over this it continues toward the north between Elephantis and Syene, and the Theban countryside in Egypt – and there it is called the Nile.[86]

To the modern reader, the most striking feature of this passage is Vitruvius' insistence that the source of the Nile was in the Atlas Mountains of north-west Africa. This interpretation fitted well with the author's broader contention that great rivers tended to spring from large mountain ranges towards the north, but also corresponded to several contemporary theories about the westerly origins of the Nile. As early as the sixth century BCE, Greek natural philosophers had speculated on the confusing hydrography of interior Africa, variously speculating that the Nile had a second, oceanic mouth on the west coast, or simply that the Egyptian river ran east through the Sahara before turning north at Meroe.[87] Whether these theories arose from fragmentary knowledge of the Upper Niger, from a misunderstanding of the hydrographical connections between the Saharan oases, or from an assumption that the easterly course of the Danube in Europe was reflected in the great river of Africa, the deduction was a popular one.[88] Herodotus was the best-known exponent of this theory, and traces of these assumptions are apparent in Vitruvius' account.[89]

The view that the Nile originated in the Atlas mountains was relatively widespread in the Latin geographical writing of the late Republic and early empire. In the mid 40s CE, Pomponius Mela included a similar account of the headwaters of the river in his own prose geography.[90] Pliny, similarly, suggested that the Nile rose in Mauretania, and identified Juba II as his principal source:

> . . . the origin, so far as King Juba was able to establish, was in a mountain of Mauretania Inferior, not far from the Ocean, where it forms a stagnant lake called Nilides. The alabeta, coracinus and silurus fish are found there. A crocodile was also found there and was dedicated in the Iseum of Caesarea to prove this argument, and can still be seen there to this day. Moreover, it has been observed that the Nile increases as snow and rain saturate Mauretania.[91]

Juba II was an exact contemporary of Vitruvius; a *belle-lettriste*, gentleman naturalist and Roman client king, he was a crucial authority on natural

[86]  Vitr. 8.2.6. after Rowland and Howe (1999), 98–9.
[87]  Hes. *Theog* 338; Diod Sic 1.37; A western course (from a source in the Ocean), is attributed to Euthymenes of Marseille by Sen. *Q Nat* 4a.2.22 and cf. Hdt. 2.21.
[88]  On the different western Niles see esp. Bonneau (1964), 143–50. On Vitruvius' debts to these traditions see also Callebat (2003), 79–80.
[89]  Hdt. 2.31–3.    [90]  Pomponius Mela 1.50–2.    [91]  Plin. *HN* 5.51.

philosophy for many later writers.[92] He was installed as ruler of the newly-created realm of Mauretania in 25 BCE, which had a capital at Iol Caesarea in what is now northern Algeria. Here, he established something of a court of letters, aided by his own education in Latin, Greek and Punic, and the substantial intellectual support provided by the Ptolemaic entourage of his young wife, Cleopatra Selene – the daughter of Cleopatra VII and Mark Antony.[93] Juba's writings survive only in the fragments of later authors such as Mela and Pliny, but they certainly included dedicated regional studies of both North Africa and Arabia.[94] Juba's discussion on the Nile was presumably included in the *Libyka*, an account of the continent of Africa written in Greek. As ruler of Mauretania, with influence stretching into the pre-desert and beyond, Juba had good reason to express an interest in the river. His confident identification of the river's headwaters in the hinterland of his own kingdom could only magnify the importance of Mauretania in the eyes of the wider world. As the husband of the last member of the Egyptian Ptolemaic dynasty, moreover, Juba may also have exploited this 'discovery' as a statement that the Nile symbolized the union of the two African kingdoms under the aegis of Rome, a point emphasized by his supposed display of the crocodile in the Iseum at Caesarea.[95]

Vitruvius was certainly aware of the importance of Juba's Mauretanian kingdom, and may even have known the king personally, but the influence of the *Libyka* upon his writing is not completely clear. He seems to have drawn upon Juba in a short passage on the poisonous soils of North Africa, in which the building projects of King Juba (or his father) are noted with approval.[96] Yet chronology argues against Vitruvius' direct knowledge of the finished work. Juba is unlikely to have started writing the text before his formal installation in Mauretania in 25 BCE, and it may have been written as late as the last decade BCE.[97] If Vitruvius was himself writing in the later 20s BCE, as seems likely, we should probably conclude that both he and Juba were independently influenced by common contemporary

[92] Roller (2003) provides an excellent introduction to the king. On Juba's African geography, see Sirago (1994) and Roller (2003), 183–210. Cary and Warmington (1929), 183–4 propose that Juba's 'western' Nile derived in part from knowledge of the Niger.

[93] Plut. *Vit. Caes.* 55.2 praises Juba's intellectual breadth; Strabo 6.4.2 and 17.3.7 describes Juba's kingdom (the second having been written after the king's death). On the kingdom itself, see Roller (2003), 151–62.

[94] Sallmann (1971), 85–8 discusses Pliny's use of Juba and cf. below 285.

[95] Roller (2003), 187–93.

[96] Vitr. 8.3.24. Cf. Rowland and Howe (1999), 6, n.44 and Callebat (2003), 124–7. Baldwin (1990), 427 also detects an echo of Hor. *Carm.* 1.22.15–16 here, which may (or may not) have been inspired by Juba.

[97] Janvier (1994), 59–60 on relations between texts.

geographical debates about the western origins of the river. Both Strabo and Pliny state that speculation of this kind was widespread, but this was by no means the only theory in circulation.[98] Strabo acknowledged that some theories placed the Nile source in the west, but for his own part asserted emphatically that the river originated in the south, a conclusion which he linked explicitly both to the mathematical reasoning of Eratosthenes and his Hellenistic successors, and to the more allusive testimony of Homer.[99] A generation later, Pomponius Mela also acknowledged the argument for a western Nile, but placed this alongside several other theories, including a possible origin in the inaccessible regions to the south of the equator.[100] Pliny too noted the possibility that the Nile arose in Mauretania, but also expressed his uncertainty about its precise course in the regions beyond Meroe.[101] Remarkably, at different points of his *Natural History*, Pliny identifies possible sources for the river in the far west, the deep south, and at different points in between.[102]

Read closely, however, Vitruvius' description of the westerly course of the Nile is remarkably disjointed. This fragmentation is emphasized by its confused nomenclature. Vitruvius names the Dyris, Eptagonos, Agger and Eptabolus, Astanasoba and Astoboa before he finally identifies all of these as parts of the Nile. Some of these features were commonplaces in contemporary writing on the river. The Astanasoba and Astoboa clearly recall the similar names which were given by Hellenistic geographers to the two branches of the Nile as it passed the 'island' of Meroe.[103] Juba, similarly, identified the Nilides in the African interior, and Pomponius Mela's recension of a similar tradition also states that the Nile was known as the Nunc as it passed through interior Africa.[104] Vitruvius' Agger may also have some parallel in the Gir of the Elder Pliny, although the precise identification of these rivers, lakes, wadis and oases remains unclear.[105] This cacophony of names accentuates the confusion at the heart of the description. In his initial description of the Dyris, for example, which is probably to be identified with the Wadi Draa, Vitruvius states that its waters pass through the west (*per occidentem*) to Lake Eptagonos, an ambiguous

---

[98] Strabo 17.3.4; Plin. *HN.* 8.77. On Pliny's dissonant treatment of the Nile sources, see below 285–8.
[99] Strabo 17.1.2–3.
[100] Pomponius Mela 1.50–54.
[101] Cf. esp. Plin. *HN* 5.51; 6.181–7.
[102] Along with the discussions in 5.51 and 6.188 compare HN 8.77, which notes a possible source in the *fons Nigris* as part of his description of the *catobeplas*. For further discussion, see below 286.
[103] Cf. Strabo 17.1.2. with the comments of Yoyotte, Charvet and Gompertz (1997), 64.
[104] Pomponius Mela 3.96.    [105] Janvier (1994), 58.

statement which Vitruvius further confuses in his discussion of the animals found in the Mauretanian rivers. The connection between the Eptagonos and Eptabolus, and the role of the Agger in connecting them, are never made clear. And – perhaps most remarkably – Vitruvius never explains the southerly course that the river must have followed in order to flow from Mauretania to the relatively familiar territory of Meroe.

The emphases within Vitruvius' account, and particularly his focus upon the changing names of the river, suggest that his principal sources were texts. While this need not completely exclude a visual source – after all, 'maps' (of various kinds) may extensively deploy verbal signifiers in the form of labels or annotations – there is a strong suspicion that Vitruvius was engaging with a long-standing textual debate in this section of his work. If the images and texts of chorographers were distinct, in other words, Vitruvius was primarily concerned with the latter when he put his geography together. He confirms this in the conclusion to this discussion. Here, Vitruvius only refers to written works, which provides further support for the argument that he did not rely exclusively on a map:

> Therefore, because all the rivers of any size in accounts of the earth [*in orbis terrarum descriptionibus*] seem to flow forth from the north, and the lands of Africa, which are in the southern region and exposed to the course of the sun, have their moisture lying hidden deep beneath them, but infrequent springs and rare rivers, one is left to conclude that the sources of the springs that face north or north-east will be found to be much better . . . [106]

Vitruvius' reference to *descriptiones* is no more conclusive than his earlier allusion to chorographers.[107] Although a *descriptio* may have referred to a visual representation of some kind, it need not have done. Several writers of the time equate the term with Greek device of *enargeia* – the conjuring up of images in the minds of an audience through vivid language.[108] In the *Ars Poetica*, Horace specifically identifies overly-elaborate descriptions of the Rhine as a weakness in some poetry.[109] Horace's concern in this work was to explore the boundaries between text and image, but the describers here were undoubtedly poets. Given this, it is noteworthy that when Vitruvius names his principal sources at the end of this brief discussion, all of his authorities are textual, and he makes no reference at all to visual representations:

---

[106] Vitr. 8.2.8. tr. Rowland and Howe (1999), 99.
[107] Nicolet (1991), 113 interprets *descriptiones* as evidence of written cribs for cartographic material; Prontera (2006/2011), 98 and Janvier (1994), 59 argue that they must have been visual sources (suggesting that he may have known two maps, rather than one). Alpers (1983) discusses at length the ambiguities of the same term in the Dutch seventeenth century.
[108] Cf. for example *Ad Herr.* 4.39.51; Quint. *Inst.* 2.4.3, 8.3.66. See Zanker (1981), esp. 301–4.
[109] Hor. *Ars P.* 18.

> Of some of these things I have been an eye-witness; of others I have read in Greek books, whose authors are Theophrastus, Timæus, Posidonius, Hegesias, Herodotus, Aristides, and Metrodorus, who, with the greatest care and accuracy have described how the properties of places and the virtues of different waters, depend on the various climates of the earth. From these I have borrowed and copied into this book all that I thought necessary respecting the varieties of water, whereby, from the directions given, persons can more readily choose springs from which they may conduct water to cities and states, inasmuch as nothing is more necessary than water.[110]

This list clearly reveals the type of material that Vitruvius regarded as appropriate models for a geographical description. Greek sources are privileged here, as they are throughout his work, and his use of the Greek toponym Maurusia suggests that Vitruvius' immediate inspiration for the Nile geography was written in that language.[111] Impressive as this roll-call is, however, none of these authors is likely to have been Vitruvius' main source. The account of the Nile in Herodotus lacks the detail of Vitruvius' account, and preferred an ambiguous conclusion about the origins of the river; Posidonius' discussion of the Nile, while no longer extant, is likely to have been similar to that of Strabo, whom he influenced considerably, and so probably postulated a southern rather than western source for the river.[112] None of the other sources is extant, although it is at least possible that the Atlas Nile theory was expounded in the Hellenistic *History* of Timaeus of Tauromenion or (less probably) in the paradoxographies of Hegesias of Magnesia or Aristides.

It is worth drawing some provisional conclusions at this point. Vitruvius' description engaged with ongoing debates about the western origin of the Nile: he drew conclusions similar to those of Juba II regarding the course of the river, but may have written independently of the royal scholar. It seems clear he depended more upon written sources than maps or pictures when composing his own text. This is suggested both by the nature of his description – an episodic compilation of names with relatively little overall coherence – and by the prominence granted to Greek written authorities in his concluding summary of influences. In other words, Vitruvius' Nile was an emphatically textual production, which drew upon written sources for its details, and proudly paraded this verbal heritage before his readers.

Yet the obvious importance of written sources to Vitruvius' account need not imply that visual inspiration was irrelevant to the writer or his audience. After all, in the appeal to authority which opens this digression, Vitruvius

---

[110]  Vitr. 8.3.27. tr. Rowland and Howe (1999), 103.      [111]  Janvier (1994), 58.
[112]  See above 47.

appealed unambiguously to visual as well as written works, and this seems significant. We cannot say whether Vitruvius' point of reference here was a grand wall-map, a representation of a landscape scene in the manner of the Praeneste mosaic, or little more than an allusion to diagrams in a manuscript text. All of these images may have been familiar to Vitruvius' audience, and it is possible that the author intended to appeal to all of these representations in his account. Evidently, visual modes of representation seem not to have contributed to the details of Vitruvius' essentially textual response to the Nile (and other rivers), but they did provide a helpful point of reference for the author and his audience alike. Images of the world could thus have important cognitive associations for the inhabitants of early Rome, without representing a definitive medium for geographical information in their own right.

One possible implication of this is hinted at in the list of sources quoted above. Before his impressive parade of Greek and Hellenistic authorities, Vitruvius notes that he also drew upon his own experience in constructing his account of the world's rivers – *sunt nonnulla quae ego per me perspexi.*[113] This may refer to little more than Vitruvius' personal observations on the paradoxical qualities of the hot and cold springs of Italy, which are also discussed in this passage: insistence upon autopsy is not unknown in the paradoxographical writing of the period.[114] But the reference also raises the tantalizing possibility that images – whether maps, landscapes or some other form of representation – also provided a medium through which the inhabitant of the Roman city might experience the wider world more directly, apparently unmediated by text. The Praeneste mosaic provides a starting point for thinking about responses of this kind.

### The Praeneste Nile Mosaic

The Nile mosaic from Praeneste is perhaps the most impressive visual representation of the physical world to have survived from the classical Mediterranean.[115] [FIG 1.1] In its current form, it is the centrepiece of the Museo Archeologico Nazionale di Palestrina. The mosaic has an approximately apsidal shape, and is around 4.30 m at its highest point, around 5.85 m at its widest. In its upper register, the mosaic presents a sprawling rocky landscape, punctuated with exotic species of African animals, many of which are labelled in Greek. Three groups of naturalistic human hunters move among them, armed with bows and spears. The lower register is a

---

[113] Vitr. 8.3.27.    [114] On this material, see esp. Schepens and Delacroix (1996).
[115] Meyboom (1995) and Hinterhöller (2009) provide the clearest general introductions.

1.1. The Nile Mosaic from Praeneste in its current form
[Nimatallah/Art Resource, NY]

much more crowded panorama of the Lower Nile valley in flood. Egyptian temples, kiosks and pergolas jostle for space with reed boats, huts and more Nilotic fauna. There are multiple human figures in this part of the landscape, populating what would appear to be religious processions, drinking parties and fishermen. The mosaic has been much restored and reconstructed since the early-seventeenth century, and the precise configuration of the original has been extensively disputed, although it was certainly slightly larger than the work as it currently stands.

The mosaic originally occupied an apsidal nymphaeum one end of a long basilica in the city of Praeneste, 23 miles to the east of Rome.[116] At the opposite end of the hall from the Nile landscape was a second nymphaeum, containing the so-called Fish Mosaic, also a fine example of the form.[117] The walls of both of these apsidal chambers were covered with a rocky façade and artificial stalactites, giving each the appearance of a grotto.

---

[116] Fasolo and Gullini (1953); Meyboom (1995), 3–19 summarizes this clearly. Moffitt (1997) argues that the mosaic was also ornamented with a personification of the river. There is no evidence to support this assertion.

[117] On the pairing, see Dunbabin (2001), 49–51. Meyboom (1995), 173–6 discusses comparanda.

This conceit was accentuated by a small fountain, which allowed water to trickle down the walls of each apse, covering the pavements with a thin film of water. The *aula apsidata* itself was the lowest part of an extensive architectural terrace which overlooked the forum of the city, and extended up the hillside.[118] The complex was constructed in the second half of the second century BCE, but was extensively rebuilt during the dictatorship of Sulla in the 80s BCE – a programme of restoration that is attested in the epigraphy, as well as in literary sources.[119] Thereafter, it certainly remained in use throughout the imperial period. We know from later texts that the upper part of the complex was dominated by the Sanctuary of Fortuna Primigenia, and access to these buildings may thus have been restricted.[120] It seems likely that the lower sections – including the basilical hall in which the Nile mosaic was place – were public buildings, and it has even been suggested that the *aula* was a library.[121]

The dating of the Nile mosaic is far from clear, but both it and the Fish mosaic were probably installed shortly after the construction of the basilica in the later second century BCE.[122] It is difficult to find close stylistic parallels between the Nile mosaic and other works in later Republican Italy, but there are certain similarities between the rendering of the Egyptian animals at Praeneste and those from the House of the Faun at Pompeii, which were certainly installed in the early first century at the latest. The Fish mosaic also bears comparison with works of a similar date from Pompeii, and it has been suggested that the same workshop produced the two works from Praeneste and some of the more impressive early examples from the Campanian city.[123] While this case is far from conclusive, arguments for later dating are still less convincing. The Elder Pliny does state that Sulla redecorated the Praeneste complex at the time of his restoration, and adopted a new form of *lithostraton* technique as part of this programme, but this probably alludes to lost mosaics in the upper complex, rather than the apsidal decorations.[124] Arguments for still later dating for the

---

[118]  Fasolo and Gullini (1953), 338–69.     [119]  Plin. *HN* 36.189.

[120]  Cic. *Div.* 2.41.85–6; Plin. *HN* 36.189.

[121]  Meyboom (1995), 11–13 convincingly argues the case for public buildings, and see also Versluys (2002), 54. Tammisto (2005), 7 concurs but with more caution. Ferrari (1999), 371–6 on the identification as a library. This is refuted by Hinterhöller (2009), 22–4, who notes that the water from the apsidal nymphaea may have created too much moisture to make the *aula* an appropriate place for keeping scrolls.

[122]  This is the most widely accepted dating: Coarelli (1990), 237–9; Meyboom (1995), 14–19; Versluys (2002), 52–4; Hinterhöller (2009), 36–9.

[123]  Meyboom (1995), 18–19, 91–6; Siebert (1999), 255; Dunbabin (2001), 51.

[124]  Plin. *HN* 36.189. Hinterhöller (2009), 34–6 argues against the interpretation of Gullini (1956), 12. Cf. also Siebert (1999), 257–8.

mosaic – primarily to the reigns of Augustus or Hadrian – tend to rest on the explosion of Egyptianizing artworks in these periods and the political and aesthetic resonance that a work like the Praeneste mosaic might have had.[125] But Egyptian themes and motifs remained a recurring fascination throughout later Republican and early imperial Italy, and broader cultural currents do not provide a particularly persuasive context in themselves for an individual work. As we shall see, moreover, the 'Egyptianizing' domestic art of the early imperial period rapidly gave way to conventionalized or caricatured form which seems a long way from the precision of the Praeneste mosaic.[126] In some sense of course the mosaic did have an early imperial resonance: it remained a prominent work of public art for several centuries, but its initial installation can probably be dated to the later second century BCE.

The precise form of the original Nile mosaic cannot now be known thanks to successive episodes of fragmentation, reconstruction and restoration in its later history.[127] It seems clear from the context in the basilical hall that the pavement was approximately apsidal in shape, and was probably slightly larger than the reconstruction as it stands today. Small rectangular panels probably projected from the upper part of the mosaic, in order to fill niches in the apse wall. The decorative scheme of the mosaic may be reconstructed from nineteen separate fragments of varying sizes. Seventeen of these have been incorporated in the current reconstruction, and an eighteenth is known from the Pergamonmuseum in Berlin – a replica of this section, which depicts a drinking party under a reed pergola, is also included in the current Praeneste mosaic. The nineteenth section has since been lost, but is known to scholars from a series of watercolours that were commissioned by Cassiano dal Pozzo in the early-seventeenth century, and which survive in the royal collection at Windsor.[128] This watercolour depicts a red parasol, which presumably originally shaded a group of important figures, and which many recent reconstructions have suggested probably occupied a focal position at the front of the mosaic.

The form of the Nile Mosaic and its subject matter clearly betray its origins in the artistic traditions of the eastern Mediterranean. The work has justifiably been celebrated as a triumph of late Hellenistic mosaic art,

[125] Sonnabend (1986), 151; Schrijvers (2007) (Augustan); Bonneau (1964), 91–2; Parlasca (1994) (Tiberian); Dawson (1965), 40, n.184; Panayides (1994), 44–6 (Hadrianic). Hinterhöller (2009), 39, n.66 provides a helpful survey with further bibliography.
[126] Discussed more fully in Chapter 3.     [127] Hinterhöller (2009), 15 for a summary.
[128] Meyboom (1995), 37. Whitehouse (1976) provides a thorough study of the so-called Dal Pozzo copies.

but the channels by which these cultural currents influenced the artists of later Republican Praeneste have been much disputed. A unique work – one scholar has justifiably termed it a *hapax* – the Nile Mosaic defies straightforward elucidation.[129] The work has frequently been associated with the spread of the Isis cult, and probably testifies to religious and mercantile links between central Italy and the eastern Mediterranean.[130] It has also been associated with diaspora artists, including one Demetrios *Topographos*, who is known to have travelled to Italy from Alexandria in 164 BCE.[131] Although this date is rather early for the Praeneste complex, the happy coincidence of Demetrios' cognomen, the subject matter of the mosaic and its unique mode of representing space have led many to suggest that the extant work was directly inspired by the Alexandrian artist at the remove of a generation or two.[132] Others have discussed the other media by which Ptolemaic influences could be felt in Italy, including illustrated manuscripts of natural philosophy, or large landscapes painted on papyrus. Paul Meyboom, for example, has persuasively suggested that the mosaic as it stands was inspired by two such landscapes, one of the Ethiopian south, the other of the Egyptian north, which were then brought together in successful juxtaposition by the mosaicists.[133] The identification of the influences behind the mosaic has important implications for the understanding of its reception within later Republican Italy, as we shall see, but it is important not to lose track of the work itself in this ongoing search for origins. In investigating the ephemeral influences thought to lie behind the Nile Mosaic, we run the risk of neglecting what the extant work itself can tell us about Roman modes of responding to the wider world.

One defining feature of the Praeneste mosaic is the frequently unsettling relationship between the image as a whole and its constituent parts. This 'gestalt effect' remains apparent, even after successive programmes of restoration and reorganization throughout the recent history of the mosaic. The reconstruction preserves the essential separation between the rocky, Nubian or Ethiopian landscape in the upper part, and the more familiar Egyptian motifs of the Nile in flood in the lower. Equally, although the modern restorers may well have somewhat liberal in their use of bridging sections of rocks or water to tie the different fragments together, it seems clear that the second-century original also consisted of a series of

---

[129] Siebert (1999), 251.    [130] On which, see below, 178–83.
[131] Diod. Sic. 31.18.2; cf. Val. Max 5.1.1.
[132] Meyboom (1995), 100–101; Holliday (2002), 107–8. And cf. Rouveret (2004), 333–4.
[133] Meyboom (1995), 103–4.

individual vignettes that were bound together in a larger whole by juxta-position, rather than by a coherent plan.

Monica Hinterhöller's recent study of the different systems of pro-jection employed within the mosaic has underscored this structural ambivalence.[134] She notes that the mosaic as a whole is – or was – lent a panoramic coherence through the relatively consistent application of a number of distinct visual strategies. In Hinterhöller's study these are identified as 'bird's-eye view' for the landscape as a whole, an oblique axonometric projection for the buildings, and a more familiar flat projec-tion for the human and animal figures.[135] In Vitruvius' discussion of modes of architectural drawing, comparable projections are termed respectively ichnographic, scenographic and orthographic, although these rarely seem to have been deployed alongside one another in Roman pictorial art as they are here.[136] On the Nile Mosaic, the presence of an artificial horizon at the top of the mosaic is the clearest example of the artists' attempt to lend a visual coherence to the panorama as a whole: by showing where land meets sky, the work approximates the experience of gazing upon a single landscape. This is accentuated by the consistent rendering of light within the mosaic – which always falls from left to right – and by patterns of diminution throughout the work.[137] Although this is not done to any precise scale, the figures in the Egyptian foreground are appreciably larger than the rather hazy outlines in the Ethiopian background. Similarly, the buildings and boats of the very bottom register are considerably larger than those in the middle ground. The consistency with which these rules were applied in the design of the mosaic have greatly helped in its reconstruc-tion, and the restorers have also augmented this effect by adding stretched of land and water which lend the whole work a naturalistic feel.

Yet the individual sections of the mosaic stand out vividly from this dec-orative field. Hinterhöller notes that the architectural vignettes within the mosaic are presented in a form of relief somewhere between an axonomet-ric projection and simple vanishing-point perspective – the 'scenographic' in Vitruvius' terminology.[138] Regarded in isolation, the individual scenes approximate the gaze of a single viewer, but this coherence collapses in the broader setting: vanishing points are not shared between the separate sec-tions of the mosaic, and also contrast with the projection adopted for the background landscape as a whole.[139] As Hinterhöller notes, the human and animal figures in the mosaic are generally rendered in a third perspective,

[134] Hinterhöller (2009), 73–100.    [135] Hinterhöller (2009), 75.
[136] Vitr. 1.2.2.    [137] Hinterhöller (2009), 83–9.
[138] Hinterhöller (2009), 77–83.    [139] *pace* Leach (1988), 95.

in which they are depicted on a similar level to the viewer.[140] As a result, the buildings and figures on the mosaic do stand out in striking relief, but the overall visual coherence of the work is disrupted. What appears at first glance as a spectacular panorama of the Nile Valley, presented before the eye of a single viewer, is revealed on closer inspection to be a series of episodic fragments, which both challenge and frustrate the spectator's gaze.

This tension between the mosaic as a panoramic whole and as a collection of disparate parts provides an important starting point for reflecting on its position within the wider geographical understanding of the period. It is now generally accepted that the mosaic was broadly conceived as a depiction of the Nile valley on a very substantial scale: the rocky landscape at the top of the mosaic must have been intended to represent Ethiopia, and evokes quite closely the peculiar topography of Lower Nubia.[141] The lower half of the image is clearly a representation of Egypt, and a strong case has been made that the very front of the mosaic was intended to recall the settlements of the Delta specifically – particularly Alexandria and perhaps Canopus.[142] Regarded in these terms, then, the image might be thought to have an essentially 'cartographic' quality, as a view of the whole Nile valley looking south, encompassing a vast swathe of territory far beyond the possible gaze of any individual.[143]

Quite how the separate vignettes fit into this 'cartographic' outline is rather less clear. Here, of course, the crucial issue is whether the temples, kiosks and other architectural features of the lower section were intended to represent specific Egyptian buildings, or were simply generic types. Predictably, there has been little consensus on this issue, and attempts to make sense of these exquisite vignettes have been as varied as they have been ingenious. The round well in section 8, for example, [FIG 1.2] is generally assumed to be a stylized representation of a Nilometer – one of the sacred pools which played such an important role in the rituals associated with the flood of the river, from the Pharaonic period on.[144] Precisely which Nilometer this was, however, is rather less clear, and the matter is made more confusing still by the Hellenistic prostyle temple

---

[140]  Hinterhöller (2009), 75–6.     [141]  Meyboom (1995), 41–2, 44.
[142]  Meyboom (1995), 70; Steinmeyer-Schareika (1978), 82.
[143]  Meyboom (1995), 43; Coarelli (1990), 238. Two other interpretations have been broadly discredited. Maspero (1879) argues from comparison with Egyptian tomb paintings that the mosaic depicts a cross section of the Nile valley, ranging from river, to bank to western desert. Vörös (2001) postulates that the mosaic was intended to replicate the view from the Pharos Lighthouse. These arguments are convincingly demolished by Meyboom (1995), 43 and Tammisto (2005), 21, n.39, respectively.
[144]  On which see esp. Bonneau (1964), and 174–97 below.

1.2. The 'Nilometer' well and Temple in Section 8 of the Praeneste Mosaic
[Nimatallah/Art Resource, NY]

and the two obelisks that are situated immediately behind it. The ritual complex at Syene may provide the most convincing model for this group. The well Nilometer there is relatively close to that depicted on the mosaic, in contrast to the pillar and step Nilometers known elsewhere. Hinterhöller has also argued that the rocks depicted nearby were intended to represent the First Cataract, and Meyboom has suggested that the fishermen sitting near these rocks were an allusion to the Egyptian grey mullet, which first appeared at Syene at the start of the flood.[145] Yet important Nilometers also existed at Philae, Elephantine, Hermopolis Magna and Memphis (as well as Alexandria itself), and the temple and obelisks may recall the Isis Temple at Philae.[146]

The large Egyptian temple in section 11 may also have been intended to represent a specific structure. [FIG 1.3] This part of the image was clearly created by an artist who knew Egypt at first hand, or who worked from a model book which originated in the province.[147] The large propylons

[145] Hinterhöller (2009), 60–1; Meyboom (1995), 51–3 cf. Plut. *De Is et Os.* 7. Coarelli (1990), 243 also identifies this as Syene.
[146] Strabo 17.1.48. Cf. Coarelli (1990), 243; Bakhoum (1999), 92.
[147] Hinterhöller (2009), 63.

1.3. The Propylon Temple in section II of the Praeneste Mosaic
[Nimatallah/Art Resource, NY]

of the temple are reminiscent of Ptolemaic temples of the Nile valley, as are the four large statues of pharaohs at the front of the structure. Viewed solely on these criteria, this could represent any one of a number of temples, between Philae and the Delta. A large statue of a bird of prey is situated prominently above the main entrance to the temple and promises a more precise identification. This statue was clearly not drawn from life – Egyptian temples did not display representations of zoomorphic gods in this way – but the addition of the motif could have been intended to identify the god to whom the temple was dedicated. Meyboom suggested that this was an eagle and was an allusion to Osiris; he argues further that the temple was probably that of Osiris Kanobos on the Delta.[148] Steinmeyer-Schareika argued that the image was of a falcon or hawk and proposed that the temple may have represented either Philae or Edfu in Upper Egypt.[149] Filippo Coarelli and Eleanor Windsor Leach maintained that the royal temple of Memphis was a more convincing archetype, based on the cargo vessel and mule caravans depicted nearby, which may signify

[148] Meyboom (1995), 53–5.
[149] Steinmeyer-Schareika (1978), 90–7. She ultimately concludes that the temple was probably Philae.

the commercial importance of the site.[150] In her recent study, Monika Hinterhöller tentatively proposed that the temple was probably Philae, based partly on its position on the boundary between the Egyptian and Ethiopian sections of the mosaic.[151] The details within the image do suggest that a specific archetype was intended, but it is impossible to identify what this might have been with any confidence.

Other specific sections of the mosaic pose similar challenges to interpretation. The most prominent feature in the lower section is a large columned building, partially covered by a velum, beneath which a group of soldiers are depicted at a banquet. In the current reconstruction of the mosaic, there is a quayside to the right of this structure, and it is generally assumed that a similar harbour appeared on the original. This section of the mosaic is almost always identified as Alexandria, but the absence of distinct landmarks makes such a reading difficult.[152] From this, the celebrations within the complex have been identified as allusions to specific historical events, including the *ptolemaieia* of Ptolemy II Philadelphus in 280–279 BCE, or the coronation of Ptolemy Alexander II in 80 BCE.[153] The drinking party sheltered beneath the pergola in the foreground of the mosaic might have been linked to these historical celebrations, or may simply have evoked the infamous excesses of nearby Canopus, but neither allusion is explicit.[154] Egypt as a whole was closely associated with leisured indolence, particularly during the high waters of the flood, and this fragment may have been intended to stand in for annual festivities throughout the country, rather than to a specific event or a single place. Much the same must be said of the smaller temples and minor structures scattered throughout the lower half of the mosaic. Specific points of reference might have been intended, then, but it is impossible for modern scholars to suggest what they might have been with any confidence, and the suspicion must be entertained that many viewers in Republican and imperial Praeneste would have shared this bemusement.

This uncertainty over the precise identification of the specific scenes has important implications for our understanding of structure of the mosaic as a whole, and hence for its status as 'cartography'. If we assume that

---

[150] Coarelli (1990), 241. Leach (1988), 93.

[151] Hinterhöller (2009), 64 and compare Martin (2005), 424.

[152] Steinmeyer-Schareika (1978), 82; Coarelli (1990), 238–41 confidently states that the image closely parallels the written description of Alexandria in Strabo 17.1.9.

[153] On the association with 280–279 BCE, see esp Steinmeyer-Schareika (1978) and Coarelli (1990). On the festival itself, see the helpful study of Rice (1983).

[154] Meyboom (1995), 70; Steinmeyer-Schareika (1978), 82. And cf. Strabo 17.1.16–17; Juv. 6.82–4, 15.44–6; Sen. *Ep.* 51.3–4.

the mosaic was organized according to cartographic principles, and that individual vignettes were positioned in order to approximate their position on the Nile, this would of course allow them to be identified much more easily, but this may not be the case. Both Filippo Coarelli and Monica Hinterhöller have suggested that the mosaic demanded a 'boustrephedon' reading, in which the gaze of the viewer was taken from Alexandria in the bottom right of the pavement, tracing multiple zig-zags and switchbacks through the Delta, Syene and the Cataracts before reaching its source in the upper left section of the mosaic.[155] While this would indeed be an elegant solution to the problem of depicting a linear river on an apsidal mosaic, the interpretation does have difficulties: conspicuously, the two scholars follow different visual paths, Coarelli suggesting that the temple in section 11 is Memphis (and hence to the north of Syene), and Hinterhöller that it is Philae (and thus to the south).

Other interpretations have suggested that the mosaic was structured according to the narrative conventions of texts, rather than cartographic space in the strictest sense. Angela Steinmeyer-Schareika, for example, suggested that the mosaic was ultimately inspired by the written reports, and perhaps paintings, associated with the Nubian expedition of Ptolemy II Philadelphus.[156] The similarities between the animals depicted in the upper section of the mosaic and the various menageries described in the texts of Agatharchides and Aelian support a link between the expedition and the mosaic and may well have been drawn from an illustrated text.[157] She further argues that the celebrations in the lower register were inspired by the triumphal celebrations that followed the expedition, perhaps in 279 BCE.[158] For Gloria Ferrari, the mosaic presented its spectators with an almost aetiological anatomy of the Nile Valley, in which the viewer's gaze would be drawn from Hellenistic Alexandria in the foreground, through Pharaonic Egypt to the timelessness of Ethiopia and wild nature in the upper reaches.[159] According to these readings, the mosaic was not organized cartographically, but rather adopted a narrative structure associated with real or imagined voyages upriver. For all of these scholars, the viewer was taken on a voyage upriver, as the eye wandered across the mosaic from the dramatic vignettes in the foreground to the misty landscapes at the back.

---

[155]  Coarelli (1990), 238; Hinterhöller (2009), 50–52, 66–7.
[156]  This expedition was certainly remembered within the Roman world: Strabo 17.1.5; Diod. Sic. 1.32, 37.
[157]  Steinmeyer-Schareika (1978), 102–6 and cf. Meyboom (1995), 97–107.
[158]  Steinmeyer-Schareika (1978), and see Coarelli (1990).    [159]  Ferrari (1999), 365–7.

The sheer diversity of these interpretations vividly illustrates their shared shortcomings. Similarly, efforts to 'read' the Nile mosaic in the light of textual geographies like those of Agatharchides or Strabo – to view text and image as manifestations of the same 'chorographic' or 'cartographic' conceptualization of space – create substantial difficulties. Perhaps most obviously, they concentrate on the small handful of vignettes which might be thought to represent specific sites at the cost of occluding large sections of the mosaic, which do not. The boats, smaller temples, wall-sections and animals, which occupy half of the extant fragments of the lower register, can hardly be thought to refer to identifiable locations. Nor can any of the upper section of the mosaic, in which carefully-labelled animals were clearly intended to represent types rather than specific creatures. Equally, the absence of the most important Egyptian landmarks within the Praeneste mosaic makes a strict 'cartographical' reading of the work rather difficult. No textual description of the Nile course would be complete without reference to Meroe, the First Cataract, the major civic settlements of Thebes and Memphis, or the separation of the waters at the Delta.[160] Despite Hinterhöller's best efforts, it is difficult to view the small rocky outcrop next to the Nilometer well as a representation of the First Cataract – a feature which was discussed with awe by Greek and Roman commentators alike, and viewed as one of the natural wonders of the world, but which seems like little more than a large boulder on the mosaic.[161] If this fragment is discounted, none of the other major geographical sites along the river is represented in any way. Nor are the familiar tourist landmarks of the Nile valley. The 'singing' statues of Memnon, the Labyrinth, the Pyramids and the Pharos Lighthouse would all have been familiar symbols of the region for an audience from the Northern Mediterranean, and commonly appear in narrative accounts of the Nile Valley, but none appears in the Praeneste mosaic in any form.[162]

For most ancient viewers of the mosaic, the individual sections can only have been regarded as evocations of typical Egyptian scenes, rather than of specific places. In this, the work anticipated the visual conventions of Egyptianizing art over the next 200 years. The representations of Egypt that became popular throughout Italy during the later Republic and

---

[160] The differing presentations of these landmarks are discussed in Chapter 5.

[161] Cf. Strabo 17.1.49; Pomponius Mela 1.51; Cic. *Rep.* 6.19; Sen. *Q Nat* 4a.1.3; Plin. *HN* 5.54; Heliod. *Aeth.* 2.29.5.

[162] Coarelli (1990), 240–1 suggests that the Pharos lighthouse may have originally appeared in the bottom right of the mosaic, perhaps in a state of partial construction (as would have been the case in 279 BCE). Vörös (2001) explains its absence by suggesting that the mosaic depicted the view *from* the Lighthouse. Neither seems convincing.

early Empire depended far more heavily upon generic scenes than specific locales.[163] Indeed, across the substantial swathe of Egyptian or Egyptianizing landscapes down to the later first century CE, there are innumerable representations of generic temples, symposia, hunting episodes and scenes of everyday life, but no images that can be identified with specific places. For viewers in Italy, reed huts were much more common as symbols of Egypt than were pyramids – which never appear in these images. It is worth reiterating immediately that the Praeneste mosaic vignettes are of a much higher quality than is apparent elsewhere in later Republican art.[164] The temples and scenes of Egyptian life are much closer to their archetypes than the stylized caricatures from the walls of Rome or Pompeii. In this sense, they certainly took inspiration from specific exemplars. But this need not mean that they were invariably interpreted in these terms by their various audiences. The temple in section II could very well have been inspired by the Temple at Edfu (or Memphis, or Philae), but there can have been little expectation that viewers in Praeneste would appreciate this correspondence, or would conclude very much from it.

Viewed in these terms, the mosaic becomes almost anti-cartographic in its depiction of space. The synoptic impression of the country in flood disrupts what would otherwise be an ordered landscape and fragments it into parts. Egypt is no longer a readily comprehensible territory, but a succession of islands separated by water.[165] In some ways this impression corresponds to two rather different traditions of textual geography, each of which is explored in more detail in later chapters. First, and perhaps most obvious, is the image of Egypt in flood as it appears in some natural philosophy – an impression of a disrupted world which anticipates the watery cataclysm, believed by the Stoics to mark the end of the world, even as it recalls the primordial floods.[166] Seneca's description in the *Natural Questions* is the most vivid account:

> It is a most beautiful sight once the Nile has poured across the fields. The plains are hidden, the valleys are covered and the towns stand out like islands. There are no communications between people living inland, except by boat, and the less people see of the land the more delighted they are.[167]

The somewhat jumbled image of the Nile as a confused succession of temples, animals and scenes of exotic excess also corresponds in some respects to representations of the river in itineraries and tourist accounts. In these

---

[163] Versluys (2002) provides an overview. For further discussion, see 146–8 below.
[164] Dunbabin (2001), 51.
[165] On Nilotic islands as a literary *topos*, see Chiai (2014), 101–3 and Borca (1998).
[166] On this tradition, see Chapter 4, below.      [167] Sen. *Q Nat* 4a.2.11. tr. Hine (2010), 60.

distorted accounts of the river valley as routeway, the Nile appears as a succession of essentially interchangeable stopping points, which approximate the subjective experience of travel along the river, rather than the essentially impersonal experience of gazing upon a (modern) map.[168] The precise nature of these accounts – and their uneasy relationship to other forms of geographical representation – will be explored in considerably more detail in Chapter 5. What is significant here, however, is the observation that these texts occupy a fundamentally different cognitive role to the systematic geographical descriptions which are often linked most closely to the mosaic. It is this sense of Egypt as a confused melange of images and associations that the Praeneste mosaic seems to reflect most closely.

## A World to Be Gazed upon and Talked About

Ultimately, the most important feature of the Praeneste mosaic was its extraordinary visual impact. It is in these terms, rather than as a pictorial pendant for textual descriptions, that it needs to be assessed. Viewers would not have contemplated the mosaic with a text in hand, mainly because they would not need to: the image is quite arresting enough in its own right. Two aspects are crucial here. First is the that the work was positioned on the floor. The pavement was laid down horizontally, the spectators standing at the 'northern' edge of the mosaic, gazing across the floor to the rocky lands of Ethiopia as they blurred into the artificial wall covering of the apsidal grotto itself. It is clear that the designers of the mosaic embraced the implications of this peculiar gaze – both through the *trompe l'oeil* effects of the blurring between image and reality through rocks and water, and through the combination of visual projections which ensure that the architecture and particularly human and animal figures spring out from the background. In this sense, the pavement presents a sequence of visual games to its viewers, as it repeatedly draws them in and challenges their gaze. Equally significant is the corporeal engagement between viewer and image that the mosaic simultaneously encourages and frustrates. As a floor mosaic, spread out beneath the gaze of the viewer, the work seems to encourage physical movement; yet the apsidal setting and water that covered the mosaic discourage this engagement, and sublimate the corporeal movement of the spectator into the restless movement of the roving eye – in one of the many 'itineraries' enabled by the structure of the landscape.[169]

---

[168] This phenomenon is discussed more fully in Chapter 5.
[169] On the impulse to movement generated by floor mosaics, see Molholt (2011).

The fact that the pavement was intended to be viewed publicly – and hence collectively – magnifies the polysemic capacity of the image, especially in contrast to the texts with which it is so frequently compared. Clearly the Praeneste mosaic was an image that could provoke and sustain multiple readings – if nothing else the innumerable recent interpretations on the work demonstrate precisely this. Modern scholars may well be right in seeing this as a representation of the Khoniak festival, the rebirth of Osiris, or the historic ceremonies of different Ptolemies, but even if one of these interpretations is correct – and they cannot all be – it seems unlikely that all spectators would have read these cues, or have been expected to, or indeed that alternative readings were repressed. Some ancient spectators may have looked at the temple in section II and have seen Edfu, Philae or Memphis, and have argued about it, others simply markers of the exotic world of the orient. Some may have been led by the image of the Nilometer in section 8 to discuss the different theories about the flooding of the river, others the political authorities that controlled the rich lands of Egypt, or the benevolent powers of Isis and Osiris that kept it in check.[170] The sheer accumulation of detail within the image would have encouraged speculation of this kind, its fragmented visual syntax demand different forms of interpretation. And it is likely of course that these interpretations would have multiplied and fragmented over the lifetime of the mosaic. This, after all, was a work that remained visible to the public for decades, and perhaps centuries, after its installation and would have been viewed afresh by successive generations of citizens. As Egypt was brought into the Roman political aegis, as Isiac cults were introduced or outlawed, as images from Strabo, Ovid or Seneca circulated in popular understanding, the resonance of the mosaic would have shifted successively. In one study, Klaus Parlasca has argued that the scorpions which decorate the shields of the soldiers gathered in one of the foreground vignettes would have had a particular significance in the early imperial period: this was the emperor Tiberius' birth-sign, and viewers in Praeneste would doubtless have known this.[171] While Parlasca probably goes too far in concluding from this that the mosaic must have been created under that emperor, as a celebration of his authority over Egypt, his reading is an important reminder that changing historical circumstances could alter the way in which a work like this was viewed and interpreted.

The Praeneste mosaic is a vivid reminder of the great differences between pictorial, cartographic and textual modes of representing space. The work would certainly have made an important contribution to the geographical

---

[170]  Meyboom (1995), 62–3, 77–8.          [171]  Parlasca (1994). And cf. Bonneau (1964), 91, n.3.

understanding of all of those spectators who viewed it over its long history: they would have interpreted it through the lenses of their existing knowledge of the world, but the experience of viewing the mosaic would have added a new dimension to this understanding. The Praeneste mosaic was an extraordinarily vivid representation of Egypt, much of it was clearly drawn more or less from life, and it may even have been structured along cartographic principles, and yet there is little here that would lend itself easily to textual reproduction. The carefully labelled animals of the upper register correspond relatively closely to the menageries known from travel writing and natural histories, but beyond this the nuances and paradoxes of this extraordinary work would be lost in any attempt to render it verbally. The Praeneste mosaic is unlikely to have been similar in form to the Agrippa map or the *pinakes* of Strabo, but it is a salutary reminder of the impossibility of reconstructing such works – and equally of appreciating the impact of visual products like these on their viewers – from textual allusions alone.

## Conclusions: Visual Geographies on a Grand Scale

Ultimately, we cannot know what Agrippa's survey of the world in the Porticus Vipsania looked like. We cannot say how many similar projects were displayed within the city, where they appeared or how they chose to represent the world. No amount of speculative reconstruction can fill this enormous gap at the heart of our knowledge of Roman geography at the turn of the common era. Works like the Praeneste Mosaic, the *Forma Urbis Romae* or representations of smaller areas like the Pompeian riot fresco give us some sense of the different modes of spatial depiction that were available within this period, but they also demonstrate the extraordinary diversity of these forms of representation. The most prominent public 'maps' are likely to have been very different from all of these works, and perhaps from one another: certainly, their precise form cannot be reconstructed with any confidence from these comparanda or from the brief allusions in contemporary texts. Nevertheless, the likelihood remains that a variety of different types of pictorial representation would have been known to the inhabitants of Rome in this period, and were commonly appreciated as a means of contemplating and even comprehending the developing empire.

While grand pictorial geographies may well have been a familiar feature of the imperial cityscape, there is little to suggest that such works were valued primarily as repositories of factual information, or were privileged over other modes of representation. We can state with some confidence that the 'maps' of this period were not particularly valued as sources of specific information, at least among those inhabitants of the city who cared about such things. Instead, texts proved to be far more stable sources for writers of geographical descriptions: when Vitruvius sought to establish the course of the Nile, he may have taken inspiration from chorographers' images (whatever they were), but his empirical information was clearly drawn from textual accounts. Similarly, when Pliny turned to 'Agrippa' for data on the measurements of provinces, his point of reference was almost certainly a written text, which was associated with the Porticus project, and not a visual display alone. We cannot know whether this text was Agrippa's preparatory *commentarii*, notes taken from the visual survey itself, or even a text inscribed upon the wall as part of the survey, but this was clearly a verbal rather than visual compilation, and was valued as such by Pliny and his audience.

There were practical limitations to the value of visual representations as definitive archives of geographical knowledge. Grand 'mapping' projects must have been challenging to construct and would certainly have been exceptionally difficult to reproduce and circulate with any fidelity. While there is some evidence to suggest that cadastral *formae* were stored in municipal or provincial archives, maps were not a particularly efficient means of storing geographical information of larger areas prior to the invention of printing.[172] As media for the transmission of empirical information about the world, visual representations also left much to be desired: placenames, dimensions of provinces or distances between places could all have been included on maps, but would have circulated far more readily by textual media. We should not conclude from this that visual surveys did not exist, or were unimportant within the developing imperialism of late Republican and early imperial Rome. Indeed, to assess the value of visual geographies solely on the data that they transmitted is to obscure their essential value. All of the textual accounts which allude to these works suggest that they were impressive and even architectural in their scope – they were designed to be gazed upon in admiration, rather than minutely scrutinized. While writers like Pliny and Vitruvius may not have turned to *tabulae* and *picturae* for discrete points of factual information, then, and their contemporaries did probably not regard these public projects as the absolute arbiters of geographical knowledge, they remained important in shaping the cognitive assumptions of the Roman *populus*.

There are two crucial points which we cannot overlook. The first (and perhaps most surprising) is that visual displays of this kind retained a

---

[172] On the impact of printing on the epistemological status (and practical value) of maps, see esp. Jacob (2006), 54–66.

considerable cognitive importance in spite of the practical difficulties associated with their use. Pliny may have used texts when he invoked 'Agrippa',
rather than a vast map, but he still appealed to the project in the Porticus as
the authority that ratified this information. For Pliny the authority of 'Marcus Agrippa' – one of his most frequently cited sources – was guaranteed by
the spectacular imperial display in the Campus Martius, regardless of the
precise medium from which he derived his information, and its palpable
shortcomings. Evidently, the very visibility of the project helped to establish its value to the writer.[173] Vitruvius creates a more difficult problem,
not least because it is not completely clear that he is referring to a display
map at all. Nevertheless, it is still striking that when he turned to the problematic topic of the watercourses of the world and the mysterious course of
the river, he appealed to images as well as texts to establish his point, even
though his information would seem to have been drawn entirely from the
latter. Great visual mapping projects (or great visual displays of the world
whatever form they took) may have been indifferent repositories of specific
information, but they were still viewed with respect by the inhabitants of
the imperial city and represented a stable point of reference for the writers
of the time.

Less frequently noted – because somewhat more difficult to unpick –
are the responses of audiences to these mapping projects. What is striking
across all of our textual accounts is that these representations seem to have
been regarded both as works to be viewed collectively, and as jumping-
off points for discussion or didactic explanation: these were works for
public consumption, not private contemplation. This is hinted at in Pliny's
reference to the position of the Agrippa map 'before the gaze of the world',
and Vitruvius' description of the Nile could be read as a long verbal gloss
on the images known to his audience. Similarly, Mancinus established his
plan of Carthage as a point of departure for his war stories, and Varro
presents his readers with the sort of speculative discussion that the *Picta
Italia* on the wall of the Temple of Tellus may have generated. Even
Propertius' elegiac allusion to 'painted worlds' drifts into the language of
Hellenistic geometry, as a reflection either of the lover's thoughts, or the
poet's. Survey projects could not simply speak for themselves, as 'invisible'
media for the representation of the world in the manner of modern maps,
and none of our texts refer to them as if they could.[174] Instead, spectators'
readings of them were determined by other forms of geographical discourse,

---

[173] On the value of the collective gaze as authentication in this period, see Bartsch (2006), 118–21,
Rutledge (2012), 103–21 and the discussion below 86–97.

[174] In broad terms, this is true of almost all references to maps in classical antiquity. Compare for
example: and *Pan Lat* 5.20–1 (on the Late Antique 'wall map' in Autun).

whether this was knowledge of textual geographies, historical narrative, natural philosophical speculation or the mathematical work of Eratosthenes and his contemporaries.[175] Prominent as these surveys may have been, in other words – and it does seem like the grand 'mapping' projects were quite visible – they only became meaningful as a part of the wider knowledge that their viewers brought to them.

These discussions and debates are also a reminder of the essentially public nature of projects like Agrippa's. Crucially, representations of this kind rarely seem to have been objects of private scrutiny, and were instead intended for the communal gaze. We see all of these elements come together quite clearly in the Praeneste mosaic. This was a work that was evidently spectacular, and remains an object of aesthetic as well as intellectual curiosity today. It held the gaze of its viewers, but it too demanded exposition. The multiple possible 'readings' that modern scholars have proposed for the mosaic may very well have been anticipated in the later Republic – and many other possible interpretations doubtless also circulated among the inhabitants of first-century Praeneste – but all would have depended upon didactic or discursive exposition. At different times, the mosaic may well have been read as reflection of Osiric ritual, as a boustrephedon 'map' of the Nile valley or as a celebration of Imperial conquest, but each of these interpretations depended upon the viewers themselves to bring them into focus. The physical constraints of the apsidal nymphaeum in Praeneste would have meant that the work would only have been visible to half-a-dozen or so spectators at any one time, but the collective nature of this gaze remains important. It is a truism of modern scholarship to state that images and texts depended upon their readers for meaning, but this is particularly relevant when it comes to the mapping projects of late Republican and early imperial Rome. Works like the Agrippa project, the chorographers' images known to Vitruvius, or the Praeneste mosaic were designed to be viewed collectively. And it was this communal gaze that lent these representations their peculiar authority. In this, they worked in parallel with other modes of geographical representation, as we shall see.

[175]  Jacob (2006), 343–60.

# CHAPTER 2

# The Dismembered Nile
## The Geography of Triumphs and Monuments

By all accounts, the triple triumph of Octavian in 29 BCE was a remarkable ceremony. For three days, the new ruler celebrated his victories of the previous years in a spectacular display of Roman military power. After two days devoted to the successful conquest of Illyricum and the victory over Mark Antony at Actium, the climactic part of the celebration commemorated the *Anschluss* of Egypt, which had taken place the previous year.[1] While this triumph is best remembered now for the great trophy that was missing from Augustus' parade – Cleopatra's suicide in Alexandria had deprived the Roman ruler of an obvious centrepiece for his display – viewers were impressed nevertheless.[2] According to our sources, the parade of wealth within the triumph was a staggering assertion of authority, and of the personal power of the man who would shortly afterwards declare himself Augustus and Princeps. For Sextus Propertius, a contemporary poet who alludes to the triumph repeatedly, a particularly striking feature was the paradoxical presentation of so much of Egypt within the walls of Rome:

> ... or I should sing of Egypt and the Nile, when, dragged into Rome, it flowed flagging with its seven streams captive; or the necks of kings encircled with chains of gold and Actian prows speeding along the Via Sacra ...[3]

This was not the first appearance of the Nile within a Roman triumph. Some nineteen years earlier, the river had been paraded in the splendid

---

[1] The triumph is described by Vell Pat. 2.89.1–2; Dio Cass 51.21.5–9 and alluded to at *Res Gestae* 4; Flor 2.21.10 Suet. *Aug.* 22 and 41.1; Suet. *Tib.* 6; Liv. *Per* 133; Serv. *Aen* 8.714; Oros. 6.20.1; Macrobius 1.12.35. On the ceremony see esp. Gurval (1998), 19–85.

[2] Dio Cass 51.14.6 implies that Octavian wished Cleopatra to appear in person in the triumph. Plut. *Vit Ant.* 86.3 and Dio Cass 51.21.8 state that an effigy of Cleopatra was carried in the triumph in her place. Prop. 4.6.65–6 pointedly celebrates her absence from the ceremony. See Gurval (1998), 30–1 and 160; Beard (2007), 114–22; Östenberg (2009), 143–4. Wyke (2002), 227–32 notes that the image of Cleopatra was probably not central in the original ceremony, but became so as a result of the poetic accounts. On this shift see further 239–46 below.

[3] Prop. 2.1.31–4 after Goold (1990), 105. On Propertius' use of triumphal motifs, see Chapter 6 below.

triumph for Julius Caesar's own victory in Egypt, this time recorded in the account of the historian Florus:

> Caesar returned home victorious and celebrated a triumph, first over Gaul, in which figured the Rhine and the Rhone and the captive Ocean represented in gold. A second triumph was celebrated for the conquest of Egypt; on this occasion the Nile, Arsinoe and the Pharos lighted with a semblance of flames were displayed on moving platforms.[4]

Other triumphs of the period saw the other great rivers of the world tamed and brought within the imperial city: the Rhine, Rhone, Tigris, Euphrates and even the great circumferential *Oceanus* were all included among the captives of victorious generals. Alongside them stood representations of countless cities, both captured and destroyed, and a seemingly endless parade of newly-subjected peoples. Through the military triumphs of the late Republic, the world came to Rome, and successive triumvirs articulated their claims to have brought the whole inhabited world (*oikoumene*) under Roman power.

For the vast majority of the Roman *populus*, ceremonies like these were a window upon the vast world outside the city. These transitory displays combined with permanent forms of commemoration – in inscriptions, statuary and the monuments of the city – to establish a uniquely imperial perspective on the world that was located firmly within Rome. The inclusion of the River Nile among the spoils of victory in late Republican triumphs may seem unremarkable: it seems an unimpressive allegorical footnote amid the more tangible treasures of Ptolemaic Egypt. Yet it was through the systematic display of newly conquered rivers, mountains, regions and people that the empire wrote its own geography. Maps and other visualizations may have allowed some inhabitants of the city to conceptualize the wider world in abstract terms, but did not provide definitive archives of geographical knowledge, as we have seen. Instead, Romans instead learned much about the world from the urban topography of their city and the processions which took place on its streets. Victory displays like Octavian's triple triumph broke the wider world into its constituent parts, and then rebuilt it in a new syntax of imperial conquest, systematically presenting the world as a series of discrete moments of military conquest. Equally importantly, these different processions moved through spaces which themselves bore the marks of imperial geography, and made their own contributions in turn to the fabric of the city. The processions

---

[4] Flor. 2.13.88. after Forster (1929), 297. And note the possible allusion to the same triumph in Ov. *Met.* 15.752–9.

successively rewrote new geographies onto the streets that they passed.[5] Such traces of imperial conquest were widespread. Plunder was prominently displayed in great public spaces, architectural motifs were borrowed (or stolen) from newly-conquered provinces, and even the cosmopolitan population of the city itself testified to Roman expansion; all of these media fed into one another and gave each other meaning. When the *populus* of the city reflected on the scale and scope of their new empire, it was these discrete points of detail which provided the foundations for their understanding.

## Triumphs

The military triumph was fundamental to the development and definition of the Roman Republic.[6] Traditionally awarded to a victorious general by the Senate, the ceremony marked the successful end of a campaign, asserted Rome's dominance over its vanquished foes, and symbolically reintegrated the returning troops within civilian society. The broad outlines of the ritual can be traced easily enough: the victorious general (*triumphator*) and his troops passed through Rome in a long parade, typically starting in the Campus Martius and finishing up at the Temple of Jupiter Capitolinus, where sacrifices of thanks would be made. The parade itself was carefully organized and symbolically resonant. The first half of every triumph displayed the spoils of victory. These told the story of the campaign itself to the audience: captured weapons were paraded, along with placards describing great victories and important episodes on the campaign, visual representations of the cities that had been captured, war booty in a succession of wagons and *fercula*, as well as representatives of defeated peoples, and vanquished generals. This plunder was escorted into the city by the victorious army, whose massed ranks filled the second half of the parade. Between the two halves, and providing the obvious focus of the event as a whole, came the *triumphator* himself who straddled the frontier between the two worlds, at once the guardian of Rome, and the victor over the world without.[7]

While the basic structure of the triumph seems clear enough, the specific choreography, symbolism and ideological significance of the ritual changed substantially over time, as several important recent studies have

---

[5] On the importance of monuments and the traces of rituals to the navigation of the city, see Rutledge (2012), 86 and esp. Favro (1994) and (1996).

[6] There has been extensive recent scholarship on triumphs. See esp. Itgenhorst (2005), Beard (2007) and the bibliographies therein. Hölscher (2006) sets the triumph within its broader socio-political context. Pittenger (2008) surveys its Republican origins.

[7] Establishing the choreography of a 'typical' triumph any more precisely than this is impossible. Cf. Beard (2007), 167–8 on these difficulties.

demonstrated.[8] The central problem that we face when attempting to reconstruct (and deconstruct) the ritual and its individual parts is the uneven nature of our source material. Our fullest narrative sources are somewhat late and need to be read with caution: Josephus provides an admirably full account of the triumph of Titus after the Jewish War, for example, but even he is more allusive in his discussion than we might like. Equally, it is important to remember that the ritual as it was performed at the time of the Flavians cannot easily be retrojected onto earlier periods.[9] In his *Parallel Lives* of the early-second century CE, Plutarch includes evocative descriptions of Republican triumphs, which provide us with crucial information, but which must also be read with caution due to his distance from the events that he describes.[10] Fortunately, the triumphs of the later Republic are among the better documented ceremonies, but again care needs to be taken when piecing together the sources available. The literate commentators who allow us to glimpse these events, even at several removes, were scarcely typical spectators in their own right. Poets like Virgil and Propertius, crucial sources for reconstructing the form and function of triumphs, undercut and parody the ceremonies even as they describe them. Ovid provides some of the richest evidence for triumphs during the reign of Augustus, but his allusions were frequently to entirely fictional events. While these 'typical' ceremonies may reveal a great deal about the expectations of the poet and his audience, they cannot always be taken on trust as a reflection of the practices of the period. Pliny and Mela, and historians like Velleius Paterculus, may have been more sympathetic to the ideology of the rituals, and readily appropriated triumphal geographies to their own ends, but in doing so manipulated this material to the demands of new (or old) generic form.

Because of this, the study of what we might term 'triumphal geography' demands considerable sensitivity, and not a little imagination. It has been something of a commonplace to assert that this was the way the unlettered inhabitants of Rome learned about the world: 'These were Rome's native geography lessons' in the words of one recent commentator.[11] In general terms, this is certainly true. Pompey's three great triumphs of the 70s and

---

[8] Chiefly Beard (2007) with (substantial) bibliography and Pittenger (2008), 278–9.
[9] Joseph. *BJ* 7.123–157. cf. Naas (2002), 460–7 and Beard (2003).
[10] Plut. *Vit. Pomp.* 45.1–5; *Vit. Aem.* 32–3.
[11] Murphy (2004), 160, and compare Östenberg (2009), 2: 'the ritually recurrent and visually emphatic triumphal processions both conveyed and constructed Roman views of self and other, and . . . can be studied as formative expressions of such conceptions.' For further examples of this in recent scholarship, cf. Desanges (1980), 398–9; Rawson (1985), 257; Brodersen (1995), 118–26; Beard (2007), 160–1; Holliday (2002), 29–30.

60s BCE – over Europe, Africa and Asia, as he framed them – were central to the articulation of the Roman domination over the *oikoumene*, even as the Republic collapsed into Civil War.[12] Octavian's triumph of 29 BCE, similarly, was fundamental in defining his own political power and in focusing the rhetoric of universal domination that underlay much of his developing political ideology.[13] Yet the precise relationship between the superabundant information provided by the triumphal processions and the other forms of geographical representation in this period deserve considerably closer investigation. While the public 'chorographies' and 'geographies' discussed in the previous chapter articulated a claim to universal rule that had obvious resonances in triumphal parades, and have conventionally been regarded as parts of the same imperialist discourse, their cognitive relationship was certainly more complex than these studies allow. The collective gaze of the *populus* determined the meaning of each form of display, but in radically different ways. The present chapter first examines the modes of geographical representation in the triumphs, and then considers the articulation of similar themes in some of the public monuments which adorned the city of Rome. It argues that in both cases, meaning was derived in part from the interaction of the audience with the different forms of display: these were essentially *shared* geographies, which were created by the spectators' collective gaze. As media for expressing detailed information about the world – for the specific material that we associate with modern geography lessons – these left a great deal to be desired. But as a way in which the inhabitants of Rome could conceptualize their own position in the world, with respect to distant territories like Egypt, to the generals or emperors of their state, and to one another, they had a crucial role to play.

## Geography in Procession

Representations of rivers were a common feature of triumphs in the late Republic and early empire.[14] We have already noted that the Nile was accorded a focal position in Caesar's triumph of 46 BCE, and in the third day of Octavian's triple triumph, and each of these appearances was long-remembered. From scattered allusions, we know that Caesar also included representations of the Rhine, Rhone and Ocean within his triumphs, and successfully established a reputation as the tamer of wild rivers.[15] Similarly,

[12] Nicolet (1991), 31–4.  [13] Gurval (1998); Nappa (2005).
[14] Östenberg (2009), 230–44 provides a helpful survey.
[15] Cic. *Marc.* 9.28–9; Ov. *Met.* 15.752–9; Luc. 10.76–8.

Octavian proclaimed his victory over the Euphrates, Rhine and Araxes in his own triumph, at least if the allusions in the *Aeneid* may be trusted.[16] Tacitus refers to the 'procession of spoils and prisoners, *simulacra* of mountains, rivers and battles' in Germanicus' triumph over the German tribes in 17 CE, and Gaius Caligula included Ocean and the Rhine in his own sham triumph after his campaign in 40 CE.[17] At least one personified river – probably the Jordan – was included in the Flavian triumph and preserved on the Arch of Titus, and other rivers may also have been represented.[18] Ovid provides further evidence of the importance of rivers to archetypal – if not historical – triumphs during the Augustan period. As shall be discussed, there are repeated references to Euphrates, Tigrises and Rhines in the imagined triumphs described within the *Tristia*, the *Ars Amatoria* and his verses from Pontus.[19]

The frieze on the entablature of the Arch of Titus depicts a personified river, carried on a platform known as a *ferculum*; this gives us some impression of how these captive rivers would have appeared to contemporary audiences, at least in that particular triumph. [FIG 2.1] The beard, hair and dress of the figure are recognizably those of river deities in art from the first century BCE onwards, and the reclining posture that he adopts was also to become standardized in coins and statuary from the early second century CE.[20] Given the immediate context of the Flavian triumph, it is generally assumed that the river here was the Jordan: the most famous relief on the same arch depicts the menorah amid the other plunder of the Jewish War, and there is little reason to assume that the other features of the frieze (and hence the triumph) were not just as specific.[21] Nevertheless, it is also possible that the river was intended as a generic statement of Titus' triumph over the world, and it is certainly likely that the artist, and indeed the choreographer of the original triumph, drew upon standardized form in the depiction of the subdued river.[22] Ovid's description of Euphrates, 'his forehead circled with reeds'; Tigris 'with dark blue hair' and elsewhere

---

[16]  Verg. *Aen* VIII.726–8.

[17]  Tac. *Ann* 2.41; On Caligula cf. Pers. 6.46–7. On the farcical campaign and the triumph that followed, see Suet. *Calig.* 44–7.

[18]  Joseph. *BJ*, 7.145 alludes to rivers in this triumph.

[19]  Ov. *Ars Am.* 1.217–28; *Tr.* 4.2.41–2; *Pont.* 3.4.107–112. For further discussion of these passages, see below 86–91.

[20]  Gais (1978) proposes a late Hellenistic inspiration behind the reclining river figures. Klementa (1993) provides a thorough study of these personifications.

[21]  Klementa (1993), 108–9, who also notes representations of Tiber and Ocean on the Arch of Constantine, and of Tigris on the Arch of Galerius; Beard (2007), 159; Murphy (2004), 155.

[22]  Suggested by Östenberg (2009), 237.

2.1. River personification (probably the Jordan) on the Arch of Titus
[photo: Jan Haywood]

the Rhine 'with locks trailing under broken reeds' all hint that personified rivers were commonplace in triumphs two generations earlier.[23] Neither Florus nor Propertius is conclusive about the form taken by the Nile in either Caesar's triumph or in Octavian's, and it is possible that staged dioramas or tableaux were preferred to personifications in this earlier period.[24] As we shall see in Chapter 6, however, Virgil's allusions to the triumph in *Aeneid* VIII strongly suggest that the Nile appeared as an anthropomorphic figure in the ceremony of 29 BCE, and the evidence from later ceremonies would seem to support this.[25]

Other geographical features also took human form in triumphs. Specific provinces or regions, for example, seem to have been represented either by

---

[23] Ov. *Ars Am* 1.223, 224; *Pont.* 3.4.107–8. And cf. *Tr.* 4.2.41–2 on a further personification of the Rhine.

[24] Klementa (1993), 108 is confident that Propertius' Nile was a personification; Östenberg (2009), 217 infers from Florus' reference to the 'golden' (*ex auro*) Ocean that Caesar's cannot have been, and is more likely to have been a painting.

[25] See 239–46 below.

'typical' inhabitants of these areas, or by personifications.[26] Archaeology provides our clearest evidence for these anthropomorphic representations, which were also familiar features of public and private art. The Sebasteion at Aphrodisias, for example, includes a number of female personifications of the regions of the empire, and a wall painting at the villa in Boscoreale depicts a figure who has been identified as Macedonia.[27] As we shall discuss, representations of this kind seem to have been familiar within the urban topography of Rome, not least in the so-called Porticus Ad Nationes.[28] Textual evidence suggests that triumphs exploited similar imagery. Tacitus alludes to a captive Germania in an imagined triumph in his *Tristia*, for example, which must also have taken human form.[29] Cassius Dio's descriptions of the funerals of Augustus and Pertinax further suggest that columns of grief-stricken provinces were a common feature of those rituals, and symbolically asserted the unity of the empire in periods of crisis.[30]

Captured towns were also a common feature of late Republican and early imperial triumphs, although here the conventions of representation appear to have been more varied. Unlike rivers, towns typically appeared towards the beginning of triumphal displays, apparently alongside the captured weaponry of defeated enemies, and often as part of the dramatic tableaux which recreated the key events of the campaign.[31] Again, some of our most vivid evidence for the display of these trophies related to the triumphs of the triumvirs: Caesar, famously, displayed ivory models of the captured cities in Gaul, a startling display which comprehensively outclassed earlier generals who sought to rival him. The rhetorician Quintilian later joked that these minor works of art made the wooden models presented by the triumphator Fabius Maximus seem like packing crates (*thecae*) in comparison.[32] In Caesar's case, spectators would have witnessed a double visual display – of images which were impressive in themselves, but also of the military victories that they were ostensibly intended to represent. This combination of celebration and display is well encapsulated in another of Ovid's fantastic triumphs, this time over Germania:

[26] Houghtalin (1993), esp. 481–515 provides a thorough catalogue and discussion. And see also Östenberg (2009), 219–30.

[27] Smith (1988); Nicolet (1991), 45–7. On the Boscoreale image, see Rutledge (2012), 88–90 and Holliday (2002), 114.

[28] On the Porticus, see 94 below.

[29] Ov. *Tr.* 4.2.37f on Germania. Cf. also Sil. *Pun.* 17.635–42 and Cic. *Phil.* 8.6.18 on a personification of Massilia.

[30] Dio Cass 56.34 (Augustus), 75.4 (Pertinax).

[31] These tableaux are alluded to at App. *Pun* 66; Liv. 26.21.7; and implied at Ov. *Am.* 2.12.7–8 and Joseph. *BJ* 7.139–45; Östenberg (2009), 199–215 provides a thorough overview.

[32] Quint. *Inst.* 6.3.61.

Before him, silver counterparts of the conquered walls, barbarian towns were carried with pictured men upon them, rivers and mountains and battles in deep forests, shields and spears in a confused pile, and from the gold of the trophies kindled by the sun, the buildings of the Roman Forum turned to gold.[33]

Here we see a fusion of the different elements of triumphal display – items that might be valued as art or as curios, which had an intrinsic value and which symbolized the Roman conquest of the world.

It is worth stating explicitly here that maps were not included among the abstracted symbols of conquest that adorned Roman triumphs. It has sometimes been suggested that the *forma* of Sardinia that T. Sempronius Gracchus displayed on the Temple of Magna Mater in 174 BCE was derived from a map that was originally carried in triumph, but there is no evidence to support this claim.[34] Others have suggested that the importance of topographical knowledge to Roman military success would have made maps appropriate symbols of power in displays of this kind.[35] By extension, it has been argued that triumphs provided the medium through which technological advances in the spatial representation of the battlefield or campaigning ground were translated into the civic sphere, and triggered a transformation in Roman cartography and landscape painting.[36] Appealing as this model is on an abstract level – it does, after all, bind the different strands of Roman imperialism together in an attractively concise bundle – it collapses under closer scrutiny. Roman approaches to geography and chorography were enormously varied, as we have seen, and 'landscape' painting has few obvious military analogues, as is discussed in the next chapter. Recent studies of Roman military intelligence, moreover, argue against habitual map-literacy, and any tools that commanders may have deployed to render battlefields comprehensible are unlikely to have made particularly impressive trophies in triumph.[37] As we have seen, 'maps' and other chorographies were intended to be contemplated and debated at length within the later Republican and early imperial world. There is little to suggest that examples of any kind were carried in triumph.

---

[33] Ov. *Pont.* 2.1.37–42. tr Wheeler (1924), 321. Ov. *Pont* 3.4.101–2 also refers to ivory models of towns in another imagined triumph. Compare Liv. 26.21.7 and esp. Cic. *Pis.* 60 who condemns triumphators for their vanity in peacocking with models of towns made of gold and silver.

[34] Holliday (2002), 106.

[35] Suggested for example by Holliday (2002), 105, that displays in triumphs 'appear to have made use of chorography and topography, types of cartographic illustration that were undoubtedly crucial to the military successes encoded by later paintings.' And see also 109.

[36] von Blanckenhagen (1957); Holliday (2002), 104–12 and most recently Schrijvers (2009), 172–3. Beard (2007), 180 terms this argument 'decidedly flimsy'.

[37] Cf. Austin and Rankov (1995). On surveyors in the Roman army, see also Morris (2016).

## Making Sense of Triumphal Geographies

The accounts of Ovid, Propertius, Appian and Plutarch all emphasize the visual aspects of the triumph, but they also reveal the fundamental role of the written word in establishing the meaning of this commemoration. Long lines of dejected captives; an endless procession of plunder-filled wagons; an interminable series of obscure geographical abstractions: such displays certainly demonstrated the general patterns of Roman conquest in emphatic style, but they were poorly suited to recounting the specific narrative of an individual campaign or the territory in which it took place. After all, one town, one river personification or one barbarian group might look very much like another. Consequently, displays which were exclusively visual might make a dramatic impression on their immediate audience, but their precise significance would be lost. These difficulties were overcome in part by the use of *tituli* – large signs which accompanied the procession and which informed the audience of the significance of what they were seeing.[38] Such surtitles were an essential reinforcement of the scale and spectacle of the triumph – it was through these that spectators might know just how much gold was contained in the countless wagons that rolled before them, or precisely which obscure towns had been brought to heel by the Roman army.[39] Propertius, in setting another of his verses against the background of an expected Augustan triumph over India and the east, describes how he will 'read (*legam*) the captured towns on *tituli*', alongside the more colourful sight of captive barbarians, and tamed rivers.[40] In one of the imagined triumphs in his long *Tristia*, Ovid similarly describes how the names of submissive leaders and provinces might be paraded before the people of Rome.[41] The functional value of these *tituli* as a means to inform the audience of the details of a victory, and to record a campaign for posterity, will be discussed in more detail shortly, but the ideological power of these signs is evident enough. Crucially, the Roman participants in the triumph – the triumphator and his victorious troops – were never identified in this manner: *tituli* were reserved for the foreign participants in the parade, which were being brought into the city from outside.[42] By naming these elements in Latin, the multifaceted splendour of the event was literally rendered legible to a Roman audience: the impressive

---

[38] Ov. *Tr.* 4.2.19–20. And cf. Ov. *Cons Liv.* 456–64 on *tituli* at (imagined) funerals.
[39] Plin. *HN* 33.54 notes that Claudius used *tituli* in his British triumph to draw the attention of the crowd to the considerable value of two gold crowns on display.
[40] Prop. 3.4.16. Propertius expects Tigris and Euphrates to be included in the triumph at line 3–4.
[41] Ov. *Tr.* 4.2.19–20.     [42] Östenberg (2009), 263.

piles of booty, countless captured towns and fortresses, and the confusing maelstrom of captive foreigners, were translated into the language of the conqueror, and thereby compartmentalized within the imperial city. No less importantly, these textual labels also represented the first stage in the lasting commemoration of the triumphs and the campaigns that they represented.

In some cases, the *tituli* were a noteworthy aspect of the triumph in their own right. They are visually commemorated on the Arch of Titus, and appear frequently in later accounts. The recording of this information is equally illuminating, however, and is well illustrated by looking at two of the best-known triumphs of the first-century BCE. First, we will look at Pompey's third triumph, which celebrated his victories over the Pirates and his eastern campaigns, and which took place over two days on 28 and 29 September 61 BCE. Second is the triumph of L. Cornelius Balbus in 19 BCE which commemorated his victories in North Africa, and which was the last triumph to be celebrated by an individual from outside the imperial family. This discussion will take us away from the Nile for a brief period, but should prove illuminating when we go on to consider the representations of the river in similar displays.

Pompey's third triumph is commemorated succinctly in the so-called *Fasti triumphales* – an inscription erected by Augustus in 12 BCE on the Capitoline Hill in Rome.[43] This inscription purported to list all of the triumphs ever to have been celebrated in the city, from Romulus down to Cornelius Balbus. The text itself is fragmentary, and was clearly shaped by the ideologies of the Augustan regime, but its entry on Pompey's third ceremony can be reconstructed with some confidence:

> [Cnaeus Pompeius Magnus III,] proconsul, [triumph over Asia, Pontus, Armenia, Paphla]gonia, Cappadocia, [Cilicia, Syria, the Scythians, the Jews, Alb]ania and the pirates, [for two days, *3 days before the Kalends of O*]ct. (28th & 29th September][44]

The list of conquered territories was partly lost, and the reconstruction draws upon later textual accounts of the triumph. In his *Life of Pompey*, Plutarch first lists the conquered regions included in the triumph, according to the names displayed on placards at the head of the procession:

---

[43] On the *Fasti triumphales*, see Degrassi (1954), 90–110 and the pertinent observations of Feeney (2007), 181.

[44] [*Cn. Pompeius. Cn. f. Sex.n. Magnus, III], pro co(n)s(ule), a. DCXCII.* | [*ex Asia, Ponto, Armenia, Paphla]gonia, Cappadoc(ia)* | [*Cilicia, Syira, Scytheis, Iudaeeis, Alb]ania, pirateis* | [*per. biduum III, pridie k. O]cto.* Degrassi (1954), 108.

Inscriptions borne in advance of the procession indicated the nations over which he triumphed. These were: Pontus, Armenia, Cappadocia, Paphlagonia, Media, Colchis, Iberia, Albania, Syria, Cilicia, Mesopotamia, Phoenicia and Palestine, Judaea, Arabia, and all the power of the pirates by sea and land which had been overthrown. Among these peoples no less than a thousand strongholds had been captured, according to the inscriptions, and cities not much under nine hundred in number, besides eight hundred piratical ships, while thirty-nine cities had been founded.[45]

A virtually identical list appears in the *Mithridatic War* of the second-century historian Appian, again followed by broad and hyperbolic statements about the sheer scale of Pompey's other spoils.[46] A similar order is also found in Pliny's account of the same triumph in Book VII of his *Natural History*:

> When he had freed the coast from pirates and had restored the rule of the sea to the Roman people, he triumphed over Asia, Pontus, Armenia, Paphlagonia, Cappadocia, Cilicia, Syria, the Scythians, Jews and Albanians, Iberia, the island of Crete, the Basternae and, above all these, over King Mithridates and Tigranes.[47]

Pliny returns to the same triumph in the last book of the *Natural History*.[48] The later passage is best known for the sumptuous splendour of the treasures that are included in the procession – a vast gaming board made of precious metals, gold dining couches and statues of the gods, and a portrait of Pompey himself rendered in pearls. Here, Pliny states explicitly that he based his account on statements taken from an official record of Pompey's triumph (*verba ex ipsis Pompei triumphorum actis*), and these acts are listed among his sources for both Book V and Book XXXVII in the opening section of the *Natural History*, and may also have been used elsewhere.[49]

The correspondence between these passages suggests how the most important features of specific triumphs were preserved in the literary record. Pliny's *Acta triumphorum* were evidently something rather fuller than the extant triumphal *Fasti* from the Capitoline: he states explicitly that his information about the treasures of Pompey's triumph came from these *Acta*, and the inscription includes no such information. We do not know what form Pliny's *Acta* took, where or by whom they were recorded, or how thorough they were. To judge from his summary of Pompey's conquests, however, and the recitation of similar material by both Appian

---

[45] Plut. *Vit. Pomp* 45.1–2.   [46] App. *Mith*, 116–7.   [47] Plin. *HN* 7.98.   [48] Plin. *HN* 37.12–18.
[49] Plin. *HN* 1 (5); 1. (7); and cf. *HN* 37.13. Pliny may have used the same text in *HN* 12.20 and 33.151 (both of which provide supplementary detail on the triumph over Mithridates).

and Plutarch, Pliny's *Acta* did not include substantially more geographical information than that included in the *Fasti*, at least in this particular case. To judge from Plutarch, the distinction between the 'major' geographical conquests, which were recorded (Pontus, Armenia, Paphlagonia and so on), and the 'minor' victories, which were not, was established in the order of the triumphal procession: the more important *tituli* seem to have been placed at the head of the parade, the remainder scattered throughout it. As a result, the 'smaller' conquests are omitted entirely in the *Acta* used by Pliny, and he, Plutarch and Appian bury them in the hyperbole of Pompey's wider display – the nine hundred cities and one thousand forts are not named individually and have a quantitative rather than qualitative value as an illustration of the magnitude of Pompey's victory.

The significance of this distinction can be examined a little more closely through the accounts of Cornelius Balbus' triumph on 27 March 19 BCE. The triumphal *Fasti* offers little help in discussing this event – it notes only that Balbus celebrated his victories *ex Africa*, with no further detail – but Pliny's account is unusually rich.[50] He notes first that Balbus had celebrated a victory over the Phazanii in Cidamum (Ghadames) and the Garamantes in their capital at Garama, both located in what is now central Libya.[51] He then goes on to list the smaller places to be included within the triumph:

> There is a noteworthy thing (*mirum*), that our authors had recorded the above-mentioned towns captured by him, and in addition to Cidamum and Garama, the names and representations [*nomina ac simulacra*] of the other peoples and towns were led forth and in his triumph, and came in this order: the town of Tabudium, the *natio* of Niteris, the town of Milgis Gemella, the *natio* or town of Bubeium, the *natio* of the Enipi, the town of Tuben, the mountain called Niger, Nitibrum, the town of Rapsa, the *natio* of Viscera, the town of Decri, the river Nathabur, the town of Thapsagum, the *natio* of Tamiagi, the town of Boin, the town of Pege, the river Dasibari; then following towns: Baracum, Bulba, Halasit, Galsa, Balla, Maxalla, Cizania; and *mons* Gyri, and a *titulus* stating that precious stones came from there.[52]

Pliny drew upon at least two distinct sources in putting together this list.[53] The first referred only to Cidamum and Garama, the political centres of the Phazanii and the Garamantes, and the two most important sites to be taken by Cornelius Balbus in his campaigning season of 20 BCE. This

---

[50] Degrassi (1954), 110.
[51] Plin. *HN* 5.35–6. Desanges (1978), 189–95 and Mattingly (1995), 70 put this campaign in its historical context.
[52] Plin. *HN* 5.36–7.      [53] Desanges (1980), 398.

source was presumably the same *acta triumphorum* that Pliny employed when describing Pompey's third triumph – that is, a text that summarized the key features of Roman triumphs in more detail than the Capitoline *fasti*, but which recorded only the principal points of interest for each ceremony. For Balbus' triumph, however, Pliny also had the benefit of a second source, which recorded the smaller geographical features which had also appeared in the procession. For once, a contemporary observer recorded the towns, mountains, rivers and battles included in the parade, and Pliny happily includes this material in his description of the African periphery, noting as he does so how wonderful it was that this information was preserved. Pliny states explicitly that all of this material is recounted in the order in which it appeared in the procession (*hoc ordine*); this provides us with a unique glimpse of the ordering principles within the triumphs themselves.[54]

The parade of names that Pliny provides is surprisingly complex, but clearly was not organized according to geographical location. Decri and Baracum may be located with some confidence in the Fezzan and its immediate environs – between Garama and Cidamum and hence presumably to be associated with the expedition of 20 BCE.[55] The *oppidum* Boin may well have been located near Gholaia in Tripolitania, and might conceivably have been taken in the same expedition.[56] The mountains Niger and Gyris are very difficult to locate; both incorporate the Berber stem *Ger* ('water'), and might be identified with the highlands of the Fezzan, and hence be plausible trophies from the campaign, but this is not certain.[57] Similarly, the River Dasibari might be associated with the Wadi el-Agial in central Libya, but this is also speculative.[58] Tabudium, Milgis Gemella and Rapsa, the Enipi and Viscera peoples and the River Nathbares have been most convincingly located elsewhere on the African frontier, in the area around the Chotts in southern Tunisia and in the Wadi Djedi region

[54] Desanges (2008), 136, n.3 notes that Pliny's reference at *HN* 6.180–1 to the settlements in Nubia taken by Petronius in the campaign of c.24 BCE *quo dicemus ordine* may also allude to triumphal information, but this is far from clear. Nilotic reports evidently followed different principles of organization, as is discussed in Chapter 5, below.

[55] Desanges (1980), 404–5, 407. *Decri* is probably to be associated with Debris, a settlement near Garama noted for its hot springs in Plin. *HN* 5.36.

[56] Desanges (1980), 406–7 is cautious. Mattingly (2000), 549 tentatively suggests either a location near Bu Njem, or in one of the Giofra oases.

[57] Desanges (1980), 403, 409–10. And cf. Plin. *HN* 37.104 which praises the precious stones from the mountains in the lands of the Nasamones. Mattingly (2000), 548 is more confident about the location of *Mons Niger* (which he places north of the Fezzan).

[58] Mattingly (2000), 549. cf. Desanges (1980), 407.

of Algeria.[59] The other toponyms are more difficult to place, but may also have been located in the Mauretanias rather than in the regions to the south of Tripolitania.[60] The list as it stands can only have resulted from the conflation of two or more military campaigns, one in the Fezzan and the others elsewhere on the African frontier, primarily in south-western Numidia.[61] Given that Pliny is explicit that his order followed that of the *simulacra ac nomina*, we must conclude that the *auctores nostros* upon whom Pliny drew in putting together his account, and hence presumably the *tituli* of Balbus' triumph itself, conflated a number of separate campaigns together in a single jumbled celebration of Roman conquests in North Africa. Two locations were assigned particular significance: Cidamum and Garama appeared at the front of the procession, and were certainly dutifully recorded in an official text. Thereafter, however, African *oppida*, *flumina*, *montes* and *nationes* followed in a spectacular (but geographically chaotic) parade.

The ceremonies celebrated by Pompey in 61 BCE and Cornelius Balbus in 19 BCE imply a great deal about the presentation of geographical information in Roman triumphs. In both cases, there was evidently a distinction between the handful of prominent geographical features, and the large number of smaller placenames which filled out the parade. Although we have less specific detail about other ceremonies, it seems reasonable to suppose that this reflected common practice. It might be assumed that triumphators would place particular emphasis upon the most prominent geographical features to be 'conquered', and this would have included the Niles, Rhines, Rhones and Oceans, as well as Asia Pontus, Armenia, or Cidamum and Garama. These were the places which seemed to have been recorded in the *acta triumphorum*, which sometimes made it to the Capitoline *Fasti*, and which (typically) were remembered by poets and letter writers. Minor geographical features were also included in triumphs, but in less prominent positions. These 'conquests' could number in hundreds (if not in thousands), and may have been represented in a variety of different forms, whether as models, personifications or simple placards. Typical of this is Livy's reference to the 134 representations of towns (*oppidorum simulacra*) carried in Lucius Scipio Asiaticus' triumph of 189 BCE, which he does not bother to list.[62] Here, the number was evidently more important

[59] Desanges (1978), 191–2; Desanges (1980), 400–410.
[60] Desanges (1980), 400–410 for specific discussion. [61] Mattingly (1995), 18, 70.
[62] Liv. 37.59.3–5. He does, however, note the parade of: 224 military standards, 1231 ivory tusks, 234 golden crowns, 137,420 pounds of silver, 224,000 Attic coins, 321,700 Attalid coins, 140,000 coins of

than the names of the captured cities or the record of how exactly they were displayed.

The evidence from Pliny's account of Balbus' triumph indicates that the smaller geographical tokens were paraded and recorded without reference to a wider spatial or historical organization. Just as elsewhere, the arms captured on campaign were often piled high on the ceremonial wagons, without thought for order or organization, so the same seems to have been true of the minor regions whose subservience to Rome was also displayed in the triumph.[63] As a 'geography lesson' for the people of Rome, this would have been rudimentary to say the least. Given how long it has taken modern scholars to unpick the precise ordering of Pliny's account through reference to modern mapping, toponymics and philology, it is inconceivable that the parade of 'Baracum, Bulba, Halasit, Galsa' and the rest can have meant anything at all to the spectators of the first century – at least as the basis for a sophisticated understanding of African physical geography. Instead, the triumphs adopted rhetoric of redundancy – the provision of a superabundance of information in order to impress upon the viewer the sheer scale of the operations commemorated, and not their detail.[64] Whatever form these *nomina ac simulacra* took – whether they were *tituli*, paintings, personifications, models or a combination of all of these – their ultimate impact was simply the assertion of Roman power through the rhetoric of the list.[65]

What is equally crucial is that triumphs also provided an interpretative and cognitive context for this information, and did not depend on the prior geographical understanding of their audience for their meaning. When modern commentators read Pliny's account of the place names of interior Africa, our natural response is to turn to the *Barrington Atlas* or *Google Earth* to locate the places that he mentions and to interpret the narrative of Balbus' conquests from there – indeed, the last few paragraphs of this chapter have been put together in precisely that way. Pliny neither had the tools to do this, nor the need. When Pliny states that he took his ordering from the *auctores nostros*, and hence from the triumph, this was not by way of apology, it was simply an explanation of his methodology, just as elsewhere his alphabetical lists of the places of Roman Italy were derived

---

Philip I, 1423 pounds of embossed silver vases and 123 pounds of gold. The inventory was rounded off with 32 royal generals, prefects and aristocrats.

[63] The chaotic display of weapons and plunder in triumphs is noted by several texts. Cf. Ov. *Pont.* 2.1.37–42 and esp. Plut. *Vit. Aem* 32.5–7: 'The arms themselves glittered with freshly polished bronze and steel, and were carefully and artfully arranged to look exactly as though they had been piled together in heaps and at random.'

[64] Cf. Veyne (2005), 379–418.     [65] Brodersen (1995), 126.

from his source material.[66] Pliny has been criticized for not reformulating this material along spatial lines – for his failure to clarify the jumbled order of the triumph in a manner that seems more natural to modern readers.[67] Yet this is anachronistic. Not only could Pliny could not do this, he did not have to: the 'names and representations' already had a historical – or triumphal – context, which was just as valid as a means of making sense of them for the encyclopaedist and his immediate audience as a spatial organization. The triumph was authoritative as a framework for geographical understanding. In this way, the medium was the message.

In many cases, the placenames and subject peoples displayed in triumphs derived their significance from the very fact that they had never been witnessed before. When the crowd in 19 BCE viewed the twenty-five or so peoples and places that Cornelius Balbus had conquered in North Africa, it must have been the strangeness of their names, as much as the names themselves, which made them important. Presumably it was this novelty that led Pliny's informants to note them down. We can see a similar process in Augustus' monument at La Turbie in the Alps, on which he listed the 46 peoples that he had defeated in the region, and in Pompey's similar boasts about sixty Pyrenaean tribes on his own inscription there.[68] Crucially, the builders of these monuments were not crossing names off on authoritative checklist of peoples of the world that remained to be conquered, but were rather engaged in the very process of *writing* that list. As the Roman army discovered places, it conquered them, and the very act of conquest – perhaps more accurately the very act of commemorating that conquest – effectively inscribed those new subjects into the accepted geography of the Roman world. Pliny's deference to the monuments, rather than the records on which they are frequently supposed to have been based, reveals that the public monument had a far greater geographical authority in this mind than any bureaucratic archive, and it was the act of inscription which helped to establish its significance.[69] Examples abound in the pages of Pliny's *Natural*

---

[66] Pliny, *HN* 4, *passim*. Discussed in detail by Bispham (2007).

[67] Mattingly (1995), 18: 'That Pliny did not always understand the significance and geographical indications of his own sources is clear from his account of the campaign of Cornelius Balbus c.20 BC'; and 35: 'disappointingly, Mela and Pliny give no up-to-date information although it must have existed following the campaigns of Balbus.' Sherk (1974), 539 simply ignores the problem, stating that the places captured by Balbus were 'apparently new to European geographers of the time. In his published memoirs he undoubtedly gave full details of all aspects of his venture.'

[68] Plin. *HN* 3.136–8 (The monument at La Turbie); 7.96 (Pompey's monument). Cf. Carey (2003), 47–53.

[69] Cf. Also Strabo 4.3.2 for a similar deference. This reading differs importantly in emphasis from that of Carey (2003), 55: 'Monuments such as the trophy at La Turbie, and Augustus' *Res Gestae* must have themselves drawn on this collection of public records [censuses and surveys kept in Rome].'

*History*, but perhaps the most striking is his paradoxical discussion of the Roman expedition to Arabia under Aelius Gallus in around 25 BCE:

> Only Aelius Gallus, from the Equestrian Order, has carried Roman arms into that land, for Gaius Caesar, the son of Augustus, only gazed upon Arabia. Gallus destroyed the towns which had not been named by the authors who had written previously: Negrana, Nestus, Nesca, Magausus, Caminacus, Labaetia; and Mariba, mentioned above, six miles in circumference, and also Caripeta, which was the farthest he reached.[70]

A striking example of imperialistic geography, Aelius Gallus' campaign wrote these seven towns into existence even as it destroyed them.[71] While Gallus was not granted a triumph for this campaign (which was a failure), Pliny's treatment of it remains noteworthy. This reconciliation of different geographical traditions is discussed in more detail below, but in this passage his deference to the imperial geography of conquest seems clear. So authoritative is the triumphal discourse that Pliny includes towns which no longer existed within his *Natural History*. It was only through their destruction that they attained the identity necessary for their inscription within the Roman geographical record.[72]

## The Wisdom of Crowds

It is important to consider the ways in which the audiences of triumphs might process the different kinds of geographical information presented to them. While countless smaller conquests might pass with little specific scrutiny, the crowd would encounter rather different issues when contemplating the larger geographical features that appeared before them – the 'headline' victories which would be accorded a prominent position, and dutifully recorded for posterity. In these cases, it was not the presentation of new geographical information which made the triumphs important: few of the spectators of Pompey's triumph can have been ignorant of the very existence of Mesopotamia or Syria, and none of those who watched the Actian celebrations would have been entirely unfamiliar with the Nile. Yet in many ways they were still defined by this rhetoric of superabundance,

---

But, crucially, they do not simply replicate the information. They monumentalize it, recognizing and exploiting the capacity of the list to make a visual statement of power.'

[70] Plin. *HN* 6.160.

[71] Murphy (2004), 130. On Aelius Gallus' Arabian campaign, see Dio Cass 53.29.3–8 and the discussion of Jameson (1968); Sherk (1974), 538; Sidebotham (1986); Beard (2007), 184–5 detects a similar message in the unsettling use of tenses in Ov. *Ars Am* 1.217–28.

[72] For a different interpretation of Pliny's lost towns, see Laehn (2013), 49–50.

and the geographical grammar in which they were presented was similar to that which defined the smaller *tituli*.

We will come back to the issue of the comprehensibility of the triumph, and the extent to which the geographical symbolism, of even its best-known trophies, was meaningful to the vast crowds of spectators. Before we do so, though, we need to acknowledge just how important these crowds themselves were to the triumph – not only as the passive consumers of this military triumphalism, but as active participants in a ritual which helped to establish the position of the city within the wider world.[73] The case study most frequently used to illustrate this point relates to Caesar's North African triumph of 46 BC. According to Florus, the focus of the first half of the triumph, and hence the visual and symbolic counterpoint to the triumphator himself, was the Egyptian princess Arsinoë, the younger sister of Cleopatra VII. As later traditions have it, the crowd was moved to pity by the sight of a young girl forced into a very public humiliation and so responded with hostility to the parade. While the details of this reaction might have got blurred over time – it is at least possible that the crowd simply objected to the fact that a young woman, a rather unimpressive conquest, should have been given so central a position in the parade – the anecdote illustrates the importance of the scrutiny of the Roman crowd.[74] To a certain degree, the audience had an important role as the arbiter of the success of a triumph, as was the case for other spectacles of the period. While the stakes may not have been as high as is sometimes suggested – even somewhat inauspicious and unpopular episodes rarely resulted in the humiliation of the triumphator – the fact that these moments were remembered testifies to the role played by the crowd in the orchestration of the ceremony itself.[75]

Equally important, if rather less well-documented, were the experiences of the audience members themselves: by witnessing a triumph, they were confirming their position as members of the Roman civic community, with respect to one another and to the world beyond. We witness this particularly clearly in the poetry of the Augustan period. Propertius, for

---

[73] The role of viewers in determining meaning compare the discussion of art more broadly in Bal and Bryson (1991), the varied discussions in Elsner (1996) especially Huet (1996) and Stewart (2008), 14–5. All helpfully set in context in Rutledge (2012), 1–29. Cf. also Duncan (1991) on the role of museums in creating a 'dramatic field' which demands viewer performance and the comments of Rutledge (2012), 92–3.

[74] Östenberg (2009), 141–2. Cf. Plut. *Vit. Aem.* 33.6–7 (for similar sympathy towards children in triumphal processions) and 34.1–2 (on sympathy even for Perseus).

[75] Beard (2007), 34–6 stresses the dangers of humiliation for the triumphant general. Jenkyns (2013), 4–5 challenges this.

example, describes watching a triumph from the bed of his mistress –
a succinct illustration of his own separation from the wider community,
and an elegant *recusatio* of the charge of writing an epic poem.[76] Where
a virtuous citizen and subject would be cheering the triumph alongside
his neighbours, and a worthy poet would be composing verses in honour
of these victories, Propertius pointedly eschews both responsibilities, and
thereby reaffirms his poetic persona as a political outsider. Ovid provides
a still clearer illustration of the value of the triumph as a marker of social
belonging in his repeated accounts of the ceremonies that he imagines he
is missing from his exile on the Black Sea.[77] As we shall see, the specific
details of Ovid's accounts reveal a great deal about the ways in which this
community identity might be performed, but the overarching function
of the triumph as a symbol of belonging is clear enough. Ovid claims to
feel his exile most acutely when he is denied his place among the cheering
throng.[78] The triumph was essentially something to be watched as part of
a group, and attained its meaning because of this shared experience.

The importance of this communal experience casts the personifications,
models and *tituli* of the triumph in a rather different light. These representations both directed viewers in their interpretation of the procession,
and contributed to the spectacle in their own right. At times, similar functions could be fulfilled by other methods. It seems likely, for example, that
professional claquers were sometimes employed to explain the procession
for those sections of the crowd uncertain of the significance of what they
were seeing, unable to read, or too far away from the procession to do
so.[79] This form of commentary has no direct textual attestation, but has
some parallel in early imperial theatrical display. Such media cannot have
been perfect, but this in itself may not be important. Ovid illustrates this
point, in all of its ambiguity, in another account of an imaginary triumph.
In his *Ars Amatoria*, Ovid provided a long treatise on courtship to the
young men (and women) of the new imperial capital: a 'songs for swinging
lovers' for the Augustan age.[80] Triumphs, he argues, provide the perfect

---

[76] Propertius 3.4. On his *recusationes*, see 242–4 and 249–51 below. Galinsky (1969), 80–90.

[77] Ov. *Tr.* 4.2 and *Pont.* 2.1 and 3.4. Ovid also deploys triumphal imagery extensively in his *Amores*,
on which see Galinsky (1969), 91–7 and 244–6 below.

[78] Edwards (1996), 116–22.

[79] Argued by Holliday (1997), 146 and Brilliant (1999), 225–7. On responses to the triumph see Stewart
(2003), 123–6. On levels of literacy in the period see Bowman and Woolf (1994), 1–16.

[80] For obvious reasons, this passage has become something of a commonplace in discussions of the
triumph, although the essential point – that audiences determine meaning, and multiple audiences
generate multiple meanings – has frequently been understated. Cf. Galinsky (1969), 97–9; Holliday
(2002), 218; Beard (2007), 49–51. On the generic context of the *Ars* and the companion *Remedia
Amoris*, see esp. Volk (2002), 157–95.

opportunity for the young Roman man to assert himself before the object of his desire:

> Joyous youths shall look on and maidens with them, and that say shall make all hearts overflow. And when some girl among them asks the names of the monarchs, or what places, what mountains, what rivers are borne along, do you answer everything, nor only if she ask you; aye, even if you know not, tell her as if you knew it well. That is Euphrates, his forehead fringed with reeds; he with the dark blue locks hanging down must be Tigris. These, say, are Armenians, here is Persia, sprung from Danae; that was a city in the Achaemenian valleys. That one, or that, are chieftains; and you will have names to give them, correct, if you can, but if not, yet names that are fitting.[81]

This comic sketch of a geographically ignorant yet quick-witted suitor reveals far more than the simple confusion of many of the viewers gathered at a triumph. Above all, it is an acknowledgement of the central involvement of the spectators in generating the meaning of the ceremony, and is a reminder that the heterogeneous nature of this audience lends a complexity to the significance of the triumph itself: spectators would view the geographical information presented to them in different ways, and these discrepancies were recognized at the time. Here, gender is the most obvious differentiating factor. Ovid's demonstration that the ambiguities of the ceremony might be exploited to erotic ends makes a clear point. Essential to the humour of the passage (and it was obviously intended as a joke) is the recognition that a man might be expected to understand triumphal symbolism of this kind, whereas ignorance might be acceptable in a woman: this stereotype of gendered roles is crucial to the poet's 'advice'. Participation in a triumphal crowd was yet another milieu in which the men and women of Rome could assert their essential identities as part of their community. Crucially, this was a performance that could only take place in a crowd, which itself provided the stage on which the *iuvenes* and *puellae* could play their respective roles. Ovid implies that accurate knowledge would be helpful for the amorous young man, but scarcely essential: it is his performance of his expected role that is the main thing. The opaque geography of the ceremony, whether 'truly' understood or not, provided the setting against which the spectators defined themselves – as men, as women and as Romans.

Ovid also draws a more subtle distinction, that between the priapic *iuvenes* to whom the *Ars Amatoria* is ostensibly addressed, and the other

---

[81] Ov. *Ars Am.* 1.217–28. tr. Mozley (1929), 29.

possible audiences of his treatise. Here, it is the poet who exploits the ambiguities of the triumph, not for erotic ends, but for poetic, comic or political reasons. The geographical features that are identified or misidentified by the lover – Euphrates, Tigris, Armenia – had considerable political resonance at the time of Ovid's composition. Parthia and the East had been an ongoing diplomatic problem for Augustus, even as he claimed authority over the whole *oikoumene*. This had only been magnified by the death of the *princeps*' presumptive heir Gaius Caesar while campaigning on the eastern frontier in 2–4 CE.[82] This part of the *Ars* was certainly composed before Gaius' death, but the poet's decision to include such sensitive regions within his whimsical vignette may well have had a deeper political implications: these were, after all, regions which remained firmly beyond the reaches of direct Roman control.[83] This lends another layer of ambivalence to the episode. While the imagined audience of the *triumph* impose meanings upon it for their own aphrodisiac ends, at least some of the audience of the *poem* would be aware that the episode is Ovid's own invention, and may have read it as a pointed jibe at the contemporary state.[84] For this section of the 'crowd', the triumph does not distinguish between man and woman, or between the successful and the unsuccessful lover, but between those who are well-informed politically and those who are not, or (perhaps) between young suitors and old political cynics. Once again, Ovid shows that the triumph is dependent upon the crowd for its meaning, and that the separate parts of the audience are reliant upon one another to give meaning to their own 'readings'.

Ovid returned to the image of the misinterpreted triumph in his poetry from exile. As he laments his absence from Rome, and his exclusion from the political community, Ovid describes the celebrations that he fears he is missing, and imagines himself among the crowd in the city's streets:

> So then all the people will be able to view the triumph, reading the names of captured towns and the titles of leaders, beholding the kings with chains upon their captive throats marching before the garlanded horses, seeing some countenances turned to earth as becomes captives, others grim and forgetful of their lot. Some of the people will inquire the causes, the objects, the names, and others will answer though they know all too little.[85]

---

[82] Tac. *Ann.* 1.3.

[83] Syme (1974/1984), 17 suggests that this may have been a later interpolation, and regards the allusion as 'a singular if not perverse want of tact.' Compare also Nicolet (1991), 44–5. Williams (1978), 78–9 suggests that the anticipation of an eastern triumph had a eulogistic function (which Nicolet convincingly refutes). Cf. Beard (2007), 184 for a more cynical reading of some of Ovid's imagined triumphs.

[84] Jenkyns (2013), 107 is sceptical.    [85] Ov. *Tr.* 4.2.19–26. tr. Wheeler (1924), 167.

There is much less humour here than in the earlier image, but the two poems make similar points about the importance of the crowd in imparting meaning to the triumph, and the importance of the triumph in allowing Romans to express and enact their inclusion within society. Significantly, Ovid goes on to narrate the remainder of this (imagined) triumph in direct speech, with the result that the reader is uncertain whether the reported triumph is in the poet's own voice or (more probably) in that of a misinformed commentator. The account, which includes descriptions of the personified Rhine and an abject Germania, thereby effectively clouds the distinction between the official 'meaning' of a triumph, and that provided by spectators to aid their own comprehension. None of Ovid's many imagined triumphs ever actually took place, but the implication of these multiple readings remain important. Because Ovid's triumph *is* imaginary, and because he offers no alternative reading, the explicitly subversive narrative provided by his commentator effectively becomes *the* meaning of the triumph, and thereby demands serious questions of the audience to the poem, both of the reading of the poet's own work, and of the wider interpretation of imperial display.[86]

## Making Maps from Metonyms

Viewed collectively, the succession of Roman triumphs broke down the wider *oikoumene* into discrete parts and presented each of these parts in an entirely new – and imperial – context. Just as the smaller placenames were defined only by their inclusion in a jumbled list of conquests, so too the larger regions, provinces and rivers of the world found their place in the *Acta* and the triumphal *Fasti*. This fundamentally repositioned the Nile in the eyes of the *populus*. The captive river that was brought symbolically into the streets of Rome – and more than once it might be noted – was cognitively transformed by this process into a discrete geographical entity that was entirely defined by its imperial captivity. The Nile presented in the Roman triumph was not the liminal river that separated Asia from Africa, nor was it the stream that rose in the unknown regions of the Ethiopian south. It was not the stream that Vitruvius carefully traced from its supposed origins in the Atlas mountains, or the stylized river in flood known to viewers of the Praeneste Mosaic. Instead, it was an identifiable object, labelled singly (as Propertius notes, even its seven separate streams are conveniently bound together), and defined solely in relation to the

---

[86] Cf. Kuttner (1999), 118.

imperial city, and not to its original surroundings.[87] In his description of
the *oikoumene*, Strabo was emphatic that a geography of the world could
not be separated artificially into its component parts, and that to define
and describe regions without sensitivity to their spatial context was akin
to severing limbs from an organic body.[88] In breaking up the world, and
parading its component parts before the gaze of its citizens, the Roman
triumphal geography did precisely that.

This significance of this reframing is accentuated by Ovid's repeated
joke that the different rivers, provinces and cities that appeared in triumphs were essentially interchangeable. It would be simplistic to view
this as evidence that the Roman populace did not pay attention during
their 'geography lessons', but his verses do help to unpack the nature of
these lessons themselves. Rivers like the Euphrates, Tigris and Nile, and
provinces like Pontus and Africa were evocative geographical signifiers that
lent authority to Roman triumphs, were dutifully recorded in the *Fasti* and
*Acta*, and very occasionally noted down by contemporary observers. These
in turn were commemorated in literary texts. But Ovid's joke about their
interchangeable nature is essentially true: by taking diverse geographical
features and reducing them to single labels, models or anthropomorphic
representations, the choreographers of the triumphs collapsed spatial distinctions, eliminated their unique aspects and rendered them all equal in
the eyes of Rome.

The representation of the Nile as a single, subordinate object was not
definitive: this certainly did not preclude the circulation of a variety of other
Niles within the varied geographical discourses of the period, as the other
chapters in this book discuss. Strabo, Mela and Pliny continued to identify
the Nile as the boundary between Africa and Asia; natural philosophers
puzzled on the mysterious flooding patterns of the river, and poets referred
habitually to the hidden sources of the river, and its seven mouths –
features which are unlikely to have featured in the triumphal displays.[89]
Roman thinkers continued to speculate on the mysterious origins of the
river and poets on its uncanny generative capabilities, even as they recalled
its subordinate position within the hierarchy of imperial rule. But it is
equally important to recognize that Roman triumphal geography – the
visceral representation of the world in its dismembered parts – was not
subordinate to these other forms of representation. Viewers of the triumph
did not turn to a map or text to 'make sense' of what they saw, and Pliny

---

[87] Prop. 2.1.32.      [88] Strabo 2.1.30.
[89] On Propertius' reference to the seven mouths of the Actian Nile as a possible poetic interpolation,
see below 248.

saw no particular need to reconcile the jumbled lists provided by Cornelius Balbus with a broader system of cartographic conceptualization.[90] The triumphs wrote a meaningful and coherent geography of their own, and one that proved to be enormously influential.[91]

## The World in the City

It is worth reflecting briefly on the effects that this process of geographical disarticulation might have had on the way in which the *populus* of Rome viewed the world around them, and how this related to other forms of representation. After all, while triumphs were important moments of collective celebration, they were essentially transient, and it was the preservation of these events – and specifically of the image of the world that they projected – that did most to shape the geographical understanding of the period. This was particularly marked in contemporary poetry, a factor that is explored in more detail in Chapter 6. As we have seen, the Augustan poets reflected at length upon the experience of viewing triumphs as a manifestation of citizenship, but they complemented this by appropriating many of the tropes of these processions in their own poetry. In Augustan epic and elegy, Egypt was commonly represented metonymically, as the personified and dejected Nile, as Cleopatra or through the trappings of Isiac religion, and all of these symbols would seem to have derived from the triple triumph. In presenting the region in these terms, collapsed into emblematic symbols and primarily defined through the rituals of imperial power, rather than by physical spatial context, the poets helped authenticate and naturalize this particular heuristic. Viewed in these terms, the triumphs were far more important than chorographies, or formal descriptive treatises, in shaping poets' responses to the new empire.

The physical fabric of the city also accelerated this dismemberment of the wider world, and helped its reconfiguration in multiple new forms in the minds of Roman inhabitants. The remainder of this chapter discusses how this was manifested in the public spaces of the city, but private spaces were also essential to this, as we shall see in Chapter 3. In some cases,

---

[90] Contra Clarke (2008), 213 [to make sense of a triumph the spectators] 'needed the geographer, the mapmakers, the constant rearticulations in different media of what it meant to rule the world'.

[91] Rutledge (2012) provides a vivid image for the analogous process of Roman collecting of natural and artistic wonders at 216: '. . . like Frankenstein and his bride, it was only in the end an incomplete patchwork monster, stitched together by a collection of objects that "creates an illusion of adequate representation of the world by first cutting objects out of specific contexts (whether cultural, historical, or inter-subjective) and making them 'stand for' the abstract whole"' citing Clifford (1985), 239.

monumentalization of the city can be linked directly to the triumphs themselves, or to the ideology of conquest that gave rise to them.[92] Under Augustus, this pattern of commemoration was particularly clear. We have already seen that the erection of the *fasti triumphales* on the Capitoline Hill in 12 BCE was a permanent record of the history of Republican triumphs and so formally inscribed Rome's domination of the world into its public spaces, even as it asserted Augustus' association with the great victories of the past.[93] Although the *fasti* seem not to have included the princeps' own triumphs, these were commemorated physically in their own way. Velleius Paterculus states that the *tituli* carried in Augustus' triumph over the Hispani 'and other *gentes*' were deposited in the forum, where they were permanently on display, and this may have been common practice in the aftermath of the celebrations.[94] Cassius Dio also states that some of the plunder from the triple triumph was formally deposited in the Cura Julia, although whether this included the allegorical representations is not clear.[95] Nevertheless, the triumphs certainly left their mark upon the city.

Pliny refers to two other structures which also formalized Roman authority in similar ways, though their precise relation to specific triumphs is unclear. At some point in the mid-first century BCE, the sculptor Coponius created statues of fourteen conquered *nationes* or peoples, which were put on display around Pompey's Theatre in the southern Campus Martius.[96] The identity of these *nationes* is unknown, but the representation of the subjected peoples were evidently so evocative that they haunted Nero's nightmares in the following century.[97] Not to be outdone, Augustus constructed the *Porticus ad Nationes*, which was located nearby.[98] Servius states that this structure contained 'images of all the peoples' (*simulacra omnium gentium*), and it is generally assumed that these were personifications of the conquered regions and provinces.[99] The fact that this appears in Servius' discussion of Virgil's account of the Actian triumph may betray a formal link to the celebrations of 29 BCE, but this is not certain.

---

[92]  Rutledge (2012) provides a stimulating overview of the broader discourse of Roman museums, which traces similar patterns to those discussed here. See esp. his opening chapter and the bibliography therein.

[93]  Feeney (2007), 181; Beard (2007), 61–7.

[94]  Vell Pat. 2.39.2. Cf. Hickson (1991), 133–4. This passage does imply that Egypt was not included among the *tituli* included in the triumph, so the practice may not have been consistent. On the dispersal of other plunder throughout the city, see Rutledge (2012), ch.2.

[95]  Dio Cass. 51.22.1–3.      [96]  Plin. *HN* 36.41. Jenkyns (2013), 50.      [97]  Suet. *Nero* 46.

[98]  Plin. *HN* 36.39. On the location, see the summary in Haselberger et al. (2002), 200–1 and cf. Coarelli (1999).

[99]  Serv. *Aen.* 8.721.

2.2. The so-called Vatican Nile statue
[Album/Art Resource, NY]

The Nile also featured prominently in Rome's monumental architecture. While these representations are commonly interpreted in isolation, or as part of wider decorative programmes, their importance in creating new cognitive geographies should not be underestimated: as triumphs broke the world down into its constituent parts, the topography of the city enabled its multiple reconfigurations. This is illustrated quite well by the anthropomorphic statues of the Nile, which ossified the conventions of triumphal imagery with permanent commemorations in public spaces. The most famous extant example is the so-called Vatican Nile, which was erected in the Iseum Campense probably during the early-second century CE. [FIG 2.2] It was originally intended to be viewed alongside a similar statue of the Tiber, which now stands in the Louvre, and the statues were clearly intended as pendants.[100] River statues seem to have been a common sight. Over twenty personifications of the Egyptian river are known from throughout the empire, and several texts refer to other

---

[100] See Klementa (1993), 24–9; and cf. 16–17 on another Nile/Tiber pair, perhaps from the Esquiline Iseum. Swetnam-Burland (2009), 443–7 and (2015) 155–67 discuss the setting (with bibliography). On the Iseum Campense, see esp. Lembke (1994) and the important surveys of Versluys (1997) and Brenk (1999).

works of this kind.[101] In the penultimate book of his *Natural History*, Pliny refers to a statue of the river that Vespasian placed in the Temple of Peace, in the early 70s.[102] Philostratus also discusses a comparable anthropomorphic in his *Imagines*, which may not have been intended as a description of a specific figure, but rather a response to a type that had become familiar at the time when he was writing.[103] The second-century rhetor Lucian would seem to confirm this in an ecphrastic description of his own, which purports to describe a painted figure of the personified Nile, but which also meditates on other forms of representation, including statuary.[104]

The Vatican Nile, the extant statues from elsewhere in the empire, and the three textual accounts of Pliny, Philostratus and Lucian demonstrate both the range of forms these sculptures could have taken, and the characteristics that they shared. Most seem to have depicted the Nile as a reclining, male figure – a convention that some commentators have traced to late Hellenistic Alexandria, but can be securely dated only to the later first or early second century CE.[105] The statues commonly seem to have been ornamented with representations of Nilotic animals, especially the crocodile and hippopotamus, with sphinxes and with *cornucopiae*, acknowledging the fertility of Egypt. Many of these motifs have also been found on anthropomorphic river figures on coins and other media, which became particularly common from the later-first century.[106] Pliny, Philostratus and Lucian all pay particular attention to the *pecheis* which commonly appeared on Nile statues – the sixteen cherubs or *putti*, intended to represent the ideal flood levels of the river. We see the same convention in the Vatican Nile, where they provide a visual counterpoint to the representations of the infant Romulus and Remus on the accompanying Tiber statue. It is important to stress that these sculptures could also vary considerably in form: Pliny states explicitly that the statue in the Temple of Peace was carved from dark Ethiopian basinites. He presents this as a further example of the commercial reach of Rome – even stone as far afield as the Upper Nile could be quarried and brought to the capital – but this is likely to have been a deliberate choice.[107] A century later, the Greek commentator Pausanias noted that statues of the Nile were commonly carved out of

---

[101] Klementa (1993), 9–51 provides a full catalogue.     [102] Klementa (1993), 43–5; Plin. *HN* 36.58.

[103] Philostr. *Imag.* 1.5.     [104] Lucian, *Rhet Praec.* 17–30.

[105] Gais (1978); On variety in the Nile figures, see Klementa (1993), 9–10.

[106] Bakhoum (1999). And cf. Dwyer (1992) and Pollini (1992) on a possible Nile personification on the Tazza Farnese libation bowl (which may be Augustan in provenance).

[107] On Pliny's emphasis here, see further, 293–4 below.

black stone, to represent the fertile soils of the annual flood, and an extant example of the type is known from Rome.[108]

These statues were richly laden with meaning, and reflect the complexity of the Roman reactions to the conquered territory of Egypt, even when regarded as isolated sculptures.[109] But the statues were also important within the kaleidoscopic cognitive cartographies that were enabled by the fragmented syntax of 'triumphal' geographies. Monuments like this became important features of the new 'maps of the world' that the citizens of Rome might reassemble from the fragments of their cosmopolitan city. The Vatican Nile enjoyed particular resonance thanks to its thematic interaction with the neighbouring Tiber statue – this juxtaposition connected the two rivers, and visual parallels accentuated this. The statues seem to have gazed at one another across the interior of the Iseum Campense. In so doing, they asserted the confluence of the Roman river and the Egyptian, and implied their shared deference to Isis and Serapis, and to imperial power. As Molly Swetnam-Burland has argued, moreover, representations of riverside life on the bases of each statue, and images of Aeneas and Ascanius on the Tiber plinth, also bound the mythic traditions of each river together into a polyvalent celebration of the city and its empire, both through the distant past and in a perennial present.[110] The pendant pair had enormous rhetorical resonance, then, but this was enabled in part by the well-established presentation of the Nile (and the Tiber) as contained and familiar geographical figures, which had significance beyond their original geographical location. The pairing of the Nile and Tiber was a common enough conceit in the early imperial period, and became an important motif in Latin epic, as we shall see in Chapter 6, but it was the geographical syntax of the military triumphs that facilitated this process. By simplifying geographical features into discrete conceptual units, detached from their original setting, triumphs enabled their redeployment in new cognitive contexts.

We see something similar with Vespasian's Nile statue. As Pliny explains, the statue was displayed in the Temple of Peace, a substantial complex which the new emperor had constructed close to the Forum of Augustus. In spite of its name, the Temple housed a considerable mass of plunder and artistic treasures that had been assembled from throughout the world,

---

[108] Paus. 8.24.12 refers to the particular conventions of representing the Nile in Black Stone. cf. P. Jones (2005), 40. On the Nile from the Atrio del Torso Bevedere (in dark stone), see Klementa (1993), 22–4.

[109] See esp. Swetnam-Burland (2009), 453–5 and (2015), 155–67.

[110] Swetnam-Burland (2009) and (2015), 164–7.

and Pliny drew upon this collection extensively in composing the latter
books of the *Natural History*.[111] According to one recent interpretation,
moreover, the Temple also housed an imperial botanical garden, in which
the varied flora of the known world were on display, and which had also
proved invaluable inspiration for the encyclopaedist.[112] At the very least,
the Temple was viewed as a marvellous assemblage of the world's wonders,
as Josephus states:

> Not only did he have unlimited wealth at his disposal; he also adorned it
> with paintings and statues by the greatest of the old masters. In fact, in that
> temple were collected and deposited all the works that men had hitherto
> travelled all over the world to see, longing to set eyes on them, even when
> scattered in different lands.[113]

This spectacular and varied abundance provided a significant setting for the
figure of the river. Presented among the trophies of empire, the Nile statue
was at once a reminder of countless triumphal ceremonies, an allusion to
the benevolence of the Egyptian gods, an example of the world's wonders,
and a point of departure for the discussion of the mineral wealth of Rome
and its empire.[114] The contents of the temple presented multiple 'maps' of
the empire to the inhabitants of the city, and the Nile had a prominent role
in all of them. None of these new constellations would have related in any
cartographic sense to the wider world, but they were no less important for
that. The tradition of triumph disarticulated the geography of the world
in the eyes of Roman citizens, but it was the architecture of the city, and
the textual responses to this, that pieced it back together in a variety of
surprising new forms.[115]

It is important to stress that this urban 'geography' of disaggregated
fragments differs from our own more cartographic conceptions of the
world. In an intriguing article, Filipo Coarelli traced an ephemeral 'Nile'
across the Severan Marble plan of Rome, and argued that the monuments
of the imperial city had been constructed with this conceit in mind.[116]
His argument centres upon an enigmatic triangular structure apparently
labelled 'Delta', immediately to the south of the Iseum Campense in
the southern part of the Campus Martius.[117] Most commentators have

[111]   Isager (1991), 168; Darwall-Smith (1996), 58–68; Naas (2002), 440–4 and 467.
[112]   Pollard (2009), noting parallels with De Vos (2007); Cf. Plin. *HN* 27.1 on the rhetoric of universality
         inspired by these plants. On plants more broadly as symbols of the breadth of empire, see Rutledge
         (2012), 213–5.
[113]   Joseph. *BJ* 7.159–60. tr, Williamson and Smallwood (1979), 386. Cf. Beard (2003), 555.
[114]   Cf. Carey (2003), 91.      [115]   Cf. Murphy (2004), 160–4.      [116]   Coarelli (1996).
[117]   Trimble (2008) provides a helpful discussion of the Severan marble plan, and cf. also Talbert (2012),
         172–7. On this tradition of cartography, see esp. Rodriguez-Almeida (2002).

assumed from the apparent form of this building that it was a monumental basin, perhaps related to the Temples of Isis and Serapis nearby.[118] Coarelli argues instead that the basin was filled with waters from the so-called Aqua Sallustiana, an underground watercourse which ran from the Gardens of Sallust between the Quirinal Hill and the Collis Hortulum, and that the complex was probably completed under Julius Caesar.[119] From decorations in the Garden buildings, the peculiarly Egyptian associations of the name 'Delta', and the suggested ritual function of the waters themselves, he posits that this entire system was intended as a physical recreation of the whole course of the Nile through north-eastern Rome.[120]

This interpretation has been rejected on archaeological grounds, but it also misrepresents the ways in which urban topography represented and re-presented the features of the wider world. The 'Delta' cannot be dated with confidence to the late Republic or Augustan period, and is more likely to have been a Flavian construction.[121] Equally seriously, the Aqua Sallustia is unlikely to have followed the course proposed by Coarelli, and the connections between the Horti Sallustiani and the Delta are otherwise unclear.[122] Rather more important here is the recognition that the planners and *flâneurs* of Rome could readily evoke the Nile in their city, with no need to recreate the whole of its course from source to mouth. When they conceptualized the Nile, it was not through the abstracted cartographic conventions so familiar from the modern schoolroom: as we have seen, there is no evidence to suggest that the river was represented in these terms in any of the public chorographies of imperial Rome, and even the prose descriptions of the river are surprisingly fragmented in their accounts of it. Instead, the Nile could have been meaningfully evoked in the trophies of the triumphs, and among the city's statues. 'The whole of the Nile is in the word "Nile"', as Jorge-Luis Borges put it in *El Golem*, or in this case in the statues, basins and obelisks of the imperial city.[123]

Certainly, some features within the Augustan city did take the names of well-known geographical features, and ornamental 'Niles' also became familiar architectural motifs, albeit without the complex hydrography suggested by Coarelli. The best-known example of this is the so-called 'Euripus' of the southern Campus Martius, a canal which ran through the centre of

[118] Lembke (1994), 27–32; Brenk (1999), 141.     [119] Coarelli (1996).
[120] Coarelli (1996), 194: 'una grande riproduzione simbolica del Nilo'.
[121] Elegantly demonstrated in Haselberger et al. (2002), 48–9 and 100.
[122] See also Versluys (2002), 356. Note Versluys (1997), 164 on the assumption that the complex as a whole was intended broadly to evoke Egypt (which seems incontrovertible).
[123] Borges (1989), 206.

the bathing complex established by Agrippa.[124] In due course, the canal was linked to the Aqua Virgo and became a central attraction of the new Augustan water park.[125] The name 'Euripus' derived of course from the strait between Euboea and Boeotia in mainland Greece, and in due course smaller Euripi and Nili became common features of private gardens throughout Italy, perhaps most obviously in Hadrian's famous complex at Tivoli.[126] The precise implications of these domesticated 'Nili', and how these fit into wider discourses of imperialism in this period, are explored in more detail in the next chapter, but their conceptual relationship to the fragmented geographies of the triumphs is worth emphasizing. By separating the world into its component parts, Roman imperial geography enabled the appropriation and reformulation of the world in precisely these ways.

This also provides a context in which we can consider the geographical resonance of other monuments within the city, regardless of their other associations. From the later first century BCE, Egyptian and 'Egyptian-izing' objects became increasingly widespread in Italy. These have been widely discussed in recent scholarship, particularly in relation to contemporary culture, politics, religion and aesthetics, as they were absorbed into new, Roman contexts. But they also catalyzed this tendency to view the world in terms of convenient metonyms, which might then be reassembled into new geographies by the collective gaze of the city.[127] This is illustrated well by the many Egyptian obelisks which were shipped into Rome by Augustus and his successors, and re-erected across the imperial city.[128] Perhaps the most famous of these was the obelisk of Psametik II, which was brought from Heliopolis in around 10 BCE, erected in the Campus Martius, and which now stands in the Piazza Montecitorio, but there were many more.[129] These monoliths clearly had significant resonances of their own. Pliny's famous account of the Campus Martius obelisk describes its function as the gnomon of a giant meridian – a structure intended to mark the changing hours of sunlight throughout the year – and it was clearly an important landmark in the Northern Campus

[124] Favro (1996), 115.     [125] Strabo 9.2.2 and 10.1.2

[126] Cic. *Leg.*2.2. laments the proliferation of these canals.

[127] On Egyptian and Egyptianizing artefacts: Swetnam-Burland (2015) is now fundamental. Versluys (2002), 325–83 and Swetnam-Burland (2007) provide recent surveys with bibliography. Davies (2011) discusses the cultural integration. Malaise (1972a), (1972b) and Roullet (1972) are important catalogues.

[128] Iversen (1968–72) provides a thorough introduction.

[129] Favro (1993), 241–3 and see also the rather neat interpretation of the monument in Favro (1996), 260–4. Cf. also Parker (2007), esp. 217–9.

Martius.[130] The practical function of this obelisk – whether it formed the focus of a great sundial or (as Pliny states) a meridian, have been much debated.[131] Equally controversial is the likely ideological function of this obelisk, and the others known throughout the city. They have plausibly been read as assertions of imperial power over the cosmos, and as appropriations of Pharaonic kingship.[132] The inscription on the base of a second Augustan obelisk from the Circus Maximus identifies it as a gift to the sun, while the hieroglyphic text carved into obelisks in the rule of Domitian assert the divine standing of the new Flavian dynasty.[133] Yet rich as these associations clearly were, obelisks could also simply stand for Egypt – a region that had been conquered, reduced to familiar symbols in triumphal displays, and which enabled new cartographies to be created in the topography of the city.[134]

The peculiar pyramid of Gaius Cestius was surely motivated by very different impulses, but contributed to a similar conceptual geography. This massive tomb, which is still standing on the route of the via Ostiensis, was built between 18 and 12 BCE and was erected in honour of a prominent Augustan aristocrat.[135] Cestius had no formal connection to the Roman occupation of Egypt and had a somewhat ambivalent relationship to the new Principate; as a consequence, the pyramid should probably be read as a reflection of his idiosyncratic taste (and considerable personal wealth), or of the ready absorption of Egyptian motifs into Roman funerary architecture, rather than a contribution to an over-arching political ideology of the period.[136] As we shall see in the next chapter, the popular appropriation of Egyptian and Egyptianizing motifs in private contexts could have important political resonances, even beyond the 'official' ideology of the regime: it was through engagement with the exotic imagery of the east that regional aristocracies could assert their own investment in the practice of empire, even if their direct contributions to it were minimal.[137] Yet even private

---

[130] Plin. *HN* 36.7–73. Pliny incorrectly attributes the Campus Martius obelisk to 'Sesosthis'. On which confusion, see Rouveret (2003), 181 and Swetnam-Burland (2015), 93. On the setting, see Zanker (1988), 144; Heslin (2007); Swetnam-Burland (2015), 98–100.

[131] Haselberger (2011) defends Edmund Buchner's interpretation of the monument as a sundial (see Buchner (1976) and the summary in Buchner (1996)). This is convincingly challenged by Heslin (2007) and cf. Heslin (2011) (with bibliography).

[132] Parker (2007), 217–9.

[133] Swetnam-Burland (2015), 41–5; Heslin (2007) discusses the Flavian appropriation of the Campus Martius obelisk, arguing that the associated pavement probably dates to the reign of Domitian.

[134] Swetnam-Burland (2010), 149 suggests that the two obelisks brought to Rome in 10 BCE may have been intended to commemorate recent military activity in Lower Nubia.

[135] On the pyramid, see Sonnabend (1986), 148–50; Ridley (1992); Neudecker (2005).

[136] Convincingly argued by Kramer (2000). See also Vout (2003) and Swetnam-Burland (2015), 84–5.

[137] See Chapter 3.

constructions like the Cestius Pyramid could contribute substantially to the public space shared by the citizens of Rome, and to the geographical resonances articulated by the cosmopolitan city-scape. Generations of imperial triumphs had created a context in which Cestius' tomb, like the obelisks scattered throughout the city, could contribute to a new imperial geography. Although neither obelisks nor pyramids are likely to have featured prominently in the triumphs of the previous decades, both conveniently encapsulated the territory as isolated symbols, and hence appropriated and relocated Egypt within the physical and ritual topography of Rome.

This disaggregation of the world, and the simultaneous objectification of its constituent parts, ultimately enabled its reassembly into an almost infinite variety of other geographies.[138] If 'Egypt' could be distilled into portable symbols that were increasingly divorced from their original physical referents, this effectively enabled a constant reformulation of new cartographies in a practically limitless range of different media. We have briefly seen how Vespasian used plants to create a legible archive of the world in the Templum Pacis, and how Pliny used plants, artistic treasures and marble to similar ends in his own massive text.[139] Other conceptual cartographies might be created from paint pigments, or (perhaps most remarkably of all), from food.[140] Suetonius, for example, hints that the Emperor Vitellius, who ruled briefly in AD 69, fashioned a food 'map' through his favourite meal, which he affectionately christened the 'Shield of Minerva':

> In this he mingled the livers of pike, the brains of pheasants and peacocks, the tongues of flamingos and the milt of lampreys, brought by his captains and triremes from the whole empire, from Parthia to the Spanish strait.[141]

In naming his meal the *clipeum Minervae*, Vitellius (or perhaps Suetonius) recalled a common poetic metaphor for representing the wider world. The shield of Achilles in the eighteenth book of the *Iliad* encompassed the whole of the *oikoumene* and beyond, from the circumferential ocean at its rim to the depicted struggles between men and gods. Famously, this conceit was later picked up by Virgil and Ovid in their own accounts of shields with deeper cosmological resonances, and it is likely that Suetonius was

---

[138] Cf. for example, Vasaly (1993) on Cicero's similar appropriation of monuments within the civic landscape within new rhetorical constellations.
[139] Cf. Naas (2002), 470–1.
[140] Compare Vitr. 7.9.7–14 (on an ecumenical array of pigments).
[141] Suet. *Vit.* 13.2. tr. Rolfe (1979), 267.

alluding to this tradition here.[142] By naming his dish in this way, and by creating a meal deliberately drawn from every part of the empire, Vitellius was effectively consuming the world in an edible ekphrasis – an assertion of imperial power that was not lost on his contemporaries.[143] Nor was this viewed in wholly hostile terms by contemporary writers. Pliny was among Vitellius' critics, but he too noted that each region could make its own unique contribution to the diet of the imperial city, and thereby create a sort of gastronomic map:

> Truly, the tracts of the heaven and the earth are mixed together, in one type of food India is recalled, in another Egypt, Crete, Cyrene and every land.[144]

It may seem something of a leap from the formal *tituli* and tableaux of the imperial triumphs to the fabulous excesses of imperial feasting, but there are important ways in which these practices were all based upon a shared conceptualizaion of the world. All contributed to a geographical under-standing that was at once profoundly Roman and utterly un-cartographic. This was a form of imperial geography that delighted not in the panoptic survey of the world as it was – the accumulation of data in the man-ner of the Royal Geographical Society or the Ordnance Survey – but of the reconfiguration of its constituent parts in whichever form might be desired. Once 'the Nile' was separated from its spatial context, was reified as a label, or an anthropomorphic figure, and familiarized in ceremonies and monuments, it could be recontextualized in an infinite variety of ways.

## Conclusions: Fragments and Assemblages

Triumphs were exceptionally important as a means of geographical cog-nition for the people of Rome. As has long been recognized, they were a medium through which the peoples and plunder of the conquered world could be presented to the gathered citizens of the city, and in which dif-ferent towns, rivers, mountains and territories would appear to them in a variety of forms. Crucially these dismembered parts of the world were not presented according to a geographical order in the triumphs; that is to say, they were not organized according to the spatial distribution of the referents in the real world, or according to the narrative of the cam-paigns that they commemorated. On one level, of course, information

[142] Hom. *Il.* 18.468–617; Verg. *Aen*, 8.626–728. Cf, Ov. *Met.* 5.187–92 on the Nile on Nileus' shield. On the cosmic implications of these passages, see esp. Hardie (1986).
[143] Cf. Plin. *HN* 35.163–4 for condemnation of the excesses of Vitellius' feasting. On this passage see esp. Gowers (1993), 1–49. For an earlier edible *oikoumene*, in similar form, compare Sall. *Fr.* 2.70.
[144] Plin. *HN* 15.105.

contained within a given triumph was determined by some geographical considerations – Cornelius Balbus' campaign in Africa delimited the region presented to the *populus* in the celebration of 19 BCE – but within the ceremony itself, different peoples, places and things were ordered according to relative importance rather than location.

Equally important – indeed, rather more important within the argument of the present study – is that the viewers of the triumphs did not require a deeper foundation of geographical knowledge to 'make sense' of what they were seeing. Again, some small qualification is necessary: the audience to the triple triumph of 29 BCE, or Caesar's celebrations of two decades earlier, would have been aware in general terms of the location of the Nile within Egypt when they saw that figure paraded before them. And it is possible that those whose knowledge was more limited found *tituli* or the running commentary of other citizens helpful in making sense of what they were seeing, but in some senses this was immaterial to the wider impact of the displays themselves. No spectator would have watched the triumph with a map or geographical description in hand; nor would any viewer require specific knowledge to make sense of the parade, even when presented with a panoply of toponyms that were utterly unfamiliar. Instead, the superabundance of information within the triumphs created the conceptual framework in which it was to be understood. Placenames on *tituli*, models of towns or personifications of rivers and provinces were invested with a new significance through their relationship to one another, to the spectators, and to the conquering power of Rome.

Baffled as many spectators may have been by the cavalcade of information that passed before them, their collective engagement with this display remained an important aspect of the triumphs' function. If the public 'chorographies' introduced in Chapter 1 were intended to be gazed upon by groups of citizens together, were lent meaning through discussion and debate, and derived their authority from this form of shared engagement, we can see something essentially similar in the triumphs. The trophies borne in procession could only be identified through collective effort – with the aid of sharp-eyed or sharp-witted spectators – but only became meaningful when viewed as part of the citizen body. This was a form of geographical display that depended on collective engagement for its meaning, but which also situated its viewers in an essentially subordinate position – of political subjecthood. As we shall see in Chapter 3, this contrasts sharply with the more active geographical gaze articulated in the wall-paintings of Italian houses.

This chapter has also argued that the rhetoric of the triumphs – what has here been termed the 'grammar' of these ceremonies – also changed the way in which a well-known feature like the Nile might be conceptualized. The repeated representation of an abject (and subject) river appearing as a discrete geographical entity solidified an imperial image of the Nile as an emblem of a conquered region. The reiterations of this image in a variety of media – from the statues and monuments of the imperial city to the *topoi* of the Augustan poets – helped emphasize this point. And the fact that the Nile may frequently have been mistaken for the other Rhines, Jordans and Tigrises that came within the city is a further illustration of its power. Triumphs and monuments performed their geographies before a collective audience, and in so doing helped to define the position of those viewers within the world. We see a similar process – albeit one enacted on a very different stage, and in strikingly different form – when we look at the domestic 'Niles' on the walls and floors of Rome and Pompeii.

# CHAPTER 3

# Gazing on the Nile
## The Domestication of the River

Egypt became known to the Roman populace collectively through triumphal processions, honorific inscriptions and monumental architecture. Yet unusually among the provinces of the new empire, the region also appeared widely in domestic contexts. From the end of the second century BCE, when the great Nile Mosaic was established in Praeneste, visual representations of the Egyptian landscape and its inhabitants became known in Italy. By the time of the Battle of Actium, these representations had increased dramatically in number and included not only mosaics but also frescoes and portable art, a pattern that can be traced both in the imperial buildings of the capital and in the private homes of the provinces. By the time of the eruption of Vesuvius in 79 CE, Nilotic motifs or 'Aegyptiaca' were exceptionally common in public and domestic settings throughout Pompeii and Campania and were also to be found in a number of tombs.[1] Encompassing a wide range of decorative forms, from small floor mosaics and tiny vignettes within complex wall-schemes to substantial vistas and complete decorative systems, this material provides an extraordinary – indeed unique – opportunity to reflect upon the conceptualization of a distant colony within the emergent Empire.[2]

The exoticism of this art, and its sheer variety of form and content, have generated a fascinatingly varied scholarship. These motifs have been viewed as a manifestation of the spread of the Egyptian cults throughout Italy, but also as the visual souvenirs of householders who had travelled to Egypt as tourists or servants of the empire.[3] The striking and even comic nature of this art has been explained in apotropaic terms, that is as a means

---

[1] Swetnam-Burland (2007) and now (2015), 18–65 on the terminology and interpretation, and cf. Humbert (1994) and Malaise (2007).

[2] Versluys (2002) is essential on this material. His text includes a detailed catalogue and discussion. For ease of cross-referencing, Versluys's catalogue numbers are included in the footnotes for each work discussed. Tybout (2003) provides an important commentary on Versluys' work. Earlier treatments of the same subject include Whitehouse (1979); De Vos (1980); McKay (1985); Cappel (1994).

[3] McKay (1985) for bibliography and discussion. Cf. also Leclant (1976).

of averting the unwanted attentions of demons or the evil eye by provoking laughter.[4] But it has also cheerfully been dismissed as little more than a passing fashion – a pseudo-cosmopolitan affectation by metropolitan or provincial elites, akin to the periodic aesthetic fads of modern Europe and America.[5] There is little doubt that Egypt was a familiar visual trope within Roman houses of the Julio-Claudian period, but the precise significance of this has been much debated.

The importance of these images in shaping the geographical under-standing of later Republican and early imperial society also deserves closer investigation. The present chapter explores how domestic decoration rang-ing from small vignettes to substantial landscape panoramas relates to other forms of representation in the same period. It considers how the 'Egypt' known from the walls and gardens of Pompeii related to the region that appeared in public 'chorographical' monuments discussed in Chapter 1, and to the abstract geographical syntax of the triumphs that were analyzed in Chapter 2. Although all of these forms of display were clearly influenced by the expansion of Roman political and military authority over Egypt, and so must be regarded in some senses as products of a wider imperial or proto-colonial discourse, the precise manifestations of this differ in impor-tant respects. This chapter also reflects on the relationship between these images of Egypt, which frequently collapsed into caricature, and the textual descriptions which circulated at the same time. While many householders who gazed on painted 'Niles' would have been familiar with the accounts of Lucan, Seneca or Pliny, we should not assume that either text or image took priority in shaping conceptions of the distant eastern region. If we are to understand the polyvalent nature of geographical thought at the time, this is a crucial observation.

## The House of the Ephebe and the *Praedia* of Julia Felix

The House of the Ephebe, also known as the House of Publius Cor-nelius Tragus [I.7.10-12/19] was a relatively large building, situated on a central block in Pompeii, just to the south of the Via dell'Abondanza thoroughfare.[6] The excavators have concluded from the unusual ground-plan that it was essentially an agglomeration of four or five smaller houses, which had been bought up by a single owner and knocked together at some

---

[4] Discussed extensively by John Clarke. See esp. Clarke (2007a) and (2007b).
[5] Most famously by Rostovtzeff (1911), 71 in his survey of Roman landscape painting. See also Leach (2004), 140.
[6] A. De Vos (1990); Zanker (1998), 175–80.

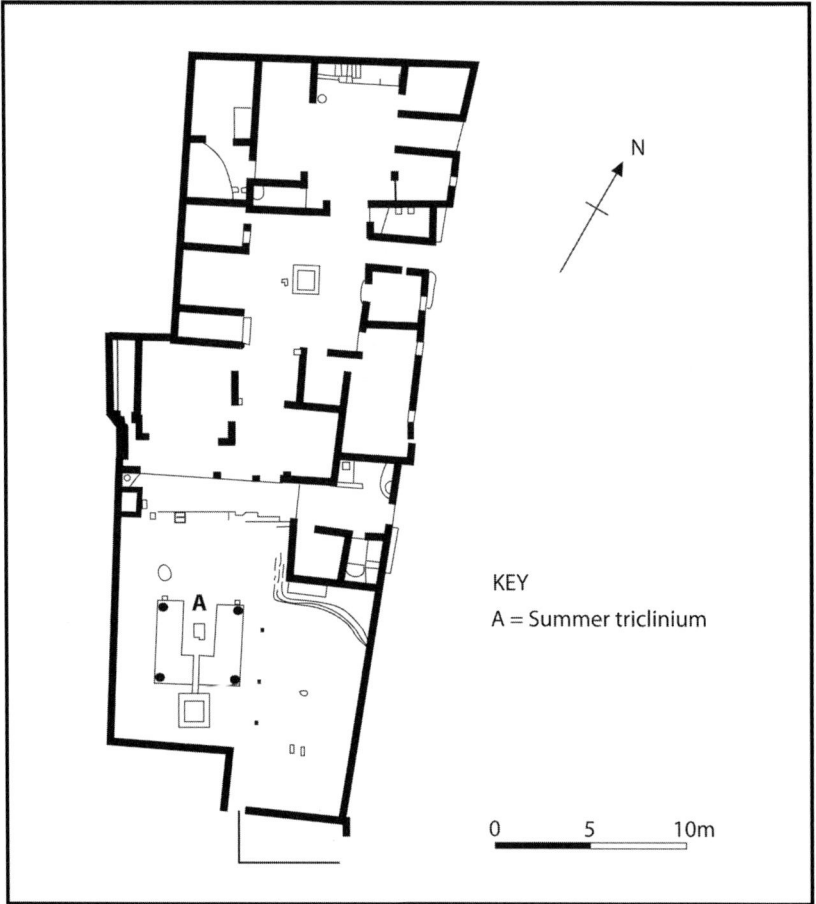

3.1. Groundplan of I.7.9-12
[© Debbie Miles-Williams 2016]

point during the 60s or 70s CE. [FIG 3.1] The householder responsible for this rebuilding programme has been identified as Publius Cornelius Tragus, who was probably a freedman, and who first appears (albeit in a rather undistinguished context) as a signatory in the archive of the banker Lucius Caecilius Iucundus in the 50s. After this, his fortunes seem to have improved, perhaps through his involvement in the wine industry, and his new, extended townhouse was in the process of extensive refurbishment at the time of the eruption of Vesuvius in 79.[7]

[7] A. De Vos (1990), 619–20; Maiuri (1927), 32–9.

3.2. The garden triclinium in I.7.9-12 from the north
[photo: Penelope Allison]

The garden is the best-known feature of the House of the Ephebe.
Located at the southern end of the house, it is moderately sized by the
standards of Pompeii, and is dominated by a substantial masonry triclinium – a three-sided couch on which diners could repose while taking an al
fresco meal.[8] [FIG 3.2] This triclinium, which remains in situ, was originally shaded by a wooden pergola, and further cooled by a channel which
ran between the couches, carrying water from a fountain on the south
wall of the garden to a pool in the centre of the dining area. Surrounding
the couches was a variety of statuary, including the bronze ephebe which
gave the house its modern name, as well as a variety of plants. Diners
would thus enjoy their meals in a sensuous environment, as the gentle
sounds of the water combined with the smells and visual impact of the
plants and food.[9] This was a setting consciously located between nature
and culture: as guests ate and savoured their surroundings, they could
look out from their benches to the covered ambulatory to the north of the

---

[8] A. De Vos (1990), 708–27; Jashemski (1993), 37–41.
[9] On gardens and the manipulation of 'nature' see Purcell (1987), Ricotti (1987) and esp. von Stackelberg (2004), 49–72 on the creation of these mythic 'heterotopias'. Littlewood (1987) provides a
helpful survey of the textual material.

3.3. Detail of the Eastern external panel, I.7.9-12 triclinium
[From Maiuri 1938. Reproduced with permission]

garden, and beyond to an indoor triclinium, the best-decorated room in the house.[10]

The immediate attention of the diners would have been drawn to the decoration which ran around the masonry base of the triclinium.[11] A long frieze depicted a variety of scenes combining a grotesque fantasy of life on the banks of the Nile with some striking representations of Egyptian worship and leisure. The most frequently reproduced sections of this decoration are the two panels on the north side of the triclinium – that is, on the outside of the masonry bench. The eastern panel depicts an architectural complex and associated figures. [FIG 3.3] At its centre is a shrine with a pediment and an arched niche, apparently containing a statue of Isis-Fortuna and surmounted by a sphinx. Immediately next to this is a small pillar supporting a statue of the god Horus in the form of a falcon. A number of trees and built screens surround this central complex, and a figure is shown making a sacrifice on an altar in the immediate foreground. To the right is a shrine within an ogival arch, to the left a

[10]  Bek (1983) on this 'dining experience'.
[11]  Versluys cat. 035; Maiuri (1927), 53–63; Maiuri (1938), 23–7; Peters (1963), 181–2; McKay (1985), 129–30. And see also A. De Vos (1990), 713–27 (with images in colour).

3.4. Detail of the Western external panel, I.7.9-12 triclinium
[From Maiuri 1938. Reproduced with permission]

slender obelisk. Two ibises and a number of human figures complete the
scene. The western panel, at the other side of the triclinium, also includes
architectural elements, here a small kiosk with awnings on either side and
another small altar. [FIG 3.4] But it is the activities taking place beneath the
awnings which demand the attention of the viewer. On the right, a couple
is engaged in an erotic *symplegma*, with the woman sitting astride the man,
and facing away from him. The couple are surrounded by observers and
musicians, including one playing a double flute. Under the awning on the
left, a further figure is shown working a water screw or *coclea* with his feet –
the earliest visual representation of this particular technology. There is a
river bank in front of these figures, and a number of ducks in pairs. It is
at once apparent that these are Nile scenes: the ibises, ducks and specific
religious details of the statuary make this clear.

These two panels evoke a world of Egyptian worship and leisure that is
played out still more vividly in the continuation of the frieze that runs along
the inside of the couches. [FIG 3.5–8] These are the parts of the decoration
which would have been visible to the diners as they ate. These viewers
were presented with a parade of different temple complexes and awnings,
in a more or less continuous display, including a further obelisk and a bull
statue atop a pillar – presumably an allusion to the god Apis. There is also
a variety of Nilotic animal life. Ducks and ibises again appear, along with

3.5. Interior frieze, I.7.9-12 triclinium (detail)
[From Maiuri 1938. Reproduced with permission]

3.6. Interior frieze, I.7.9-12 triclinium (detail)
[From Maiuri 1938. Reproduced with permission]

3.7. Interior frieze, I.7.9-12 triclinium (detail)
[From Maiuri 1938. Reproduced with permission]

3.8. Interior frieze, I.7.9-12 triclinium (detail)
[From Maiuri 1938. Reproduced with permission]

a hippopotamus and at least three crocodiles, all of which are threatening the human inhabitants of this river bank. These figures are engaged in a variety of different activities. Individuals are fishing, spinning, praying and worshipping, as well as fighting the crocodiles. Elsewhere, there are two separate dining scenes, in which several figures are shown sitting around semi-circular *stibadia* – scenes that were crucial to the way the frieze was viewed, as shall be discussed.

The House (or *Praedia*) of Julia Felix [II.4] stands about ten blocks to the west of the House of the Ephebe on the Via dell'Abondanza, and immediately to the north of the amphitheatre and the Grand Palaestra.[12] [FIG 3.9] Like the House of the Ephebe, this building was substantially remodelled during the last years before the eruption of Vesuvius, and combined a number of separate structures into a single complex, including at least one private house and a small public bathhouse. This has been variously interpreted by modern scholars as an inn or as some sort of semi-public 'clubhouse'.[13] The baths remained in use in the new building, and were certainly important, but a substantial chunk of the groundplan of the building was given over to its large central garden. This in turn was dominated by a number of ornamental fishponds, connected into a single *euripus* or ornamental canal – a popular feature in villas, private houses and inns of the period.[14] The garden also contained some elaborate statuary, and a series of decorated planting beds which run along its eastern side. To the west of the garden was a covered portico and a single summer triclinium, which was ideally positioned to allow a few fortunate diners to gaze upon the delights of the garden and its canal.[15]

---

[12] Sampaolo (1991).     [13] Sampaolo (1991), 184–6.     [14] See below, n.69
[15] Sampaolo (1991), p.185; Jashemski (1993), 86–7.

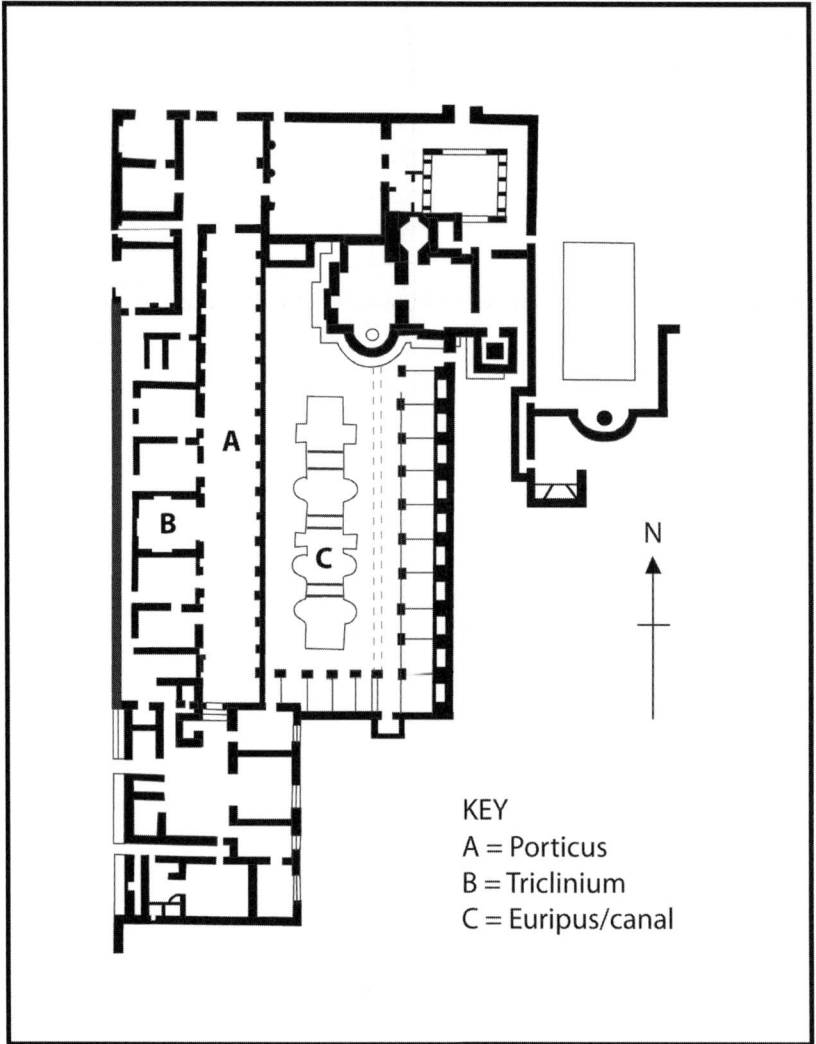

3.9. Groundplan of the Praedia of Julia Felix
[© Debbie Miles-Williams 2016]

This triclinium was decorated with Nilotic scenes, similar to those in the House of the Ephebe.[16] Here, however, images of Egypt covered the walls

---

[16] Versluys cat. 038; Sampaolo (1991), 260–77. Tran tam Tinh (1964), 55–6 briefly discusses the Isiac motifs in the *Praedia*.

3.10. Triclinium in the Praedia of Julia Felix
[Gianni Dagli Orti/The Art Archive at Art Resource, NY]

of the alcove, rather than the masonry couches themselves. [FIG 3.10] Regrettably, the preservation of these images is poor, and they can only be partially reconstructed. Nevertheless, we can deduce from the few fragments that survive in situ, and from the larger sections that were removed and taken to the Archaeological Museum in Naples, that the walls were covered with a substantial Egyptian frieze. Three fragments depict dwarfs in boats, one group threatened by a crocodile, the others apparently engaged in a fishing trip. Other crocodiles, hippos, ducks and large fish also appeared on the frieze along with several isolated figures and at least one colonnaded building complex. The whole of this frieze was supplemented by an ornamental waterfall, which poured down the steps on the back wall of the room, and which flooded the space between the diners with water.[17] When combined with the images, and the garden canal laid in front of them, the effect must have been extraordinary.

[17]  Ricotti (1987), 133–5.

## Pompeian Aegyptiaca

These buildings provide particularly striking examples of Nilotic decoration within Pompeii, but represent only a tiny fragment of the Egyptianizing themes adopted in the city, and in sites throughout Italy. Many gardens and open spaces include Nilotic imagery of some kind, including garden decoration in the House of Apollo (VI.7.23), peristyle decoration in the House of Sallust (VI.2.4), the House of the Chariots (VII.2.25) and the House of the Sculptor (VIII.7.24), the decoration of a fountain in the terrace of House VIII.2.34–5 and two decorated masonry triclinia in a block near to the amphitheatre (II.9.2 and 4).[18] The small, half peristyle garden of the House of the Surgeon (VIII.5.24) is ornamented with an unusually rich selection of Nilotic paintings, including a sympotic scene, a remarkable tableau depicting the Judgement of Solomon, and one of the best-known panels depicting combat with hippos and crocodiles.[19]

The strong association between Nilotic imagery and water also meant that this was a common motif in bath houses, both public and private. The Stabian, Sarno and Suburban Baths all contain some Nilotic imagery, as do baths in the House of the Cryptoporticus (I.6.2).[20] Nile imagery was also employed in reception rooms, including the tablinum in the Villa of the Mysteries, and the triclinium in the House of the Bracelet (VI.occid.42).[21] Most remarkable of all, perhaps, is the anomalous little room in the House of the Pygmies (IX.5.9) – a small space just to the north of the peristyle, which is richly adorned with fabulous Egyptian landscapes similar to those in the House of the Ephebe.[22] The popularity of this decorative conceit is extraordinary. If we can assume that Pompeii was more or less typical of provincial Italian cities in its taste in decorative art – and comparanda from Brescia, Rome and Ostia suggest that this is reasonable – it is clear that Egyptian motifs must have been an exceptionally common sight throughout Italy, during the first century.

The human figures are the most arresting features of many of these images, and which have defined this whole genre of Campanian painting.

---

[18] Versluys cat. 045, 042; 050; 060; 057; 039; 040. See also the detailed discussions in Spano (1955) and Maiuri (1956).

[19] Versluys cat. 059. These images have been discussed extensively, and a detailed bibliography can be found in Versluys (2002), 139–40. See esp. McDaniel (1932) and Bragantini (1998). Clarke (2007), 98–104 provides an exemplary discussion of these paintings in their architectural context (which is crucial).

[20] Versluys cat. 049; 055; 066; 032; Sampaolo (1998a). Cf. Clarke (1996).

[21] Versluys cat. 067; 048. Allison and Sear (2002), 68–77.

[22] Versluys cat. 062. Bragantini (1999); Clarke (2007a), 106–7.

The figures from the House of the Ephebe and the House of Julia Felix are marked by stocky, truncated limbs and disproportionately large heads. Many of them also have very dark skin. Often, these figures appear in mortal combat with the crocodiles and hippos of the Nile; at other times they are either engaged in leisure, religious worship or sexual activities. The same characteristics are apparent in many of the other paintings, perhaps most famously in the House of the Pygmies and in the friezes from the House of the Surgeon. This caricature of the inhabitants of the Nile valley first became common in the Augustan period, and disappeared for a generation or so thereafter.[23] By the second half of the first century CE, however, these grotesques proliferated and almost entirely eclipsed more naturalistic representations of Egypt's inhabitants within Italy. By the 60s and 70s CE, this was an exceptionally common motif in Pompeian domestic art.

Understandably, these caricatures have made many modern commentators uneasy. At the very least, they seem to represent a striking denigration of alien groups on the part of Roman viewers, and they also introduce some intriguing issues of category confusion by their artists. At first blush, it seems likely that these figures were intended to represent the mythical pygmies, said by some classical writers to inhabit the upper stretches of the Nile, and which also appear in a number of mythological paintings.[24] As several commentators have pointed out, however, the caricatures of the later first century would seem to have been inspired primarily by images (or by first-hand observation) of achondroplastic dwarfs.[25] Consequently, these figures are referred to as 'pygmies' and 'dwarfs' in the scholarly literature, more or less interchangeably, although it should be acknowledged that this convention rather obscures the complex association between Roman visual art and contemporary ethnography and myth. The 'pygmies' in the House of the Ephebe or the Praedia of Julia Felix (or indeed in the House of the Pygmies) have an uneasy relationship with the 'pygmies' who appear in the pages of Pliny, Strabo or Homer: this is a point which is discussed in more detail towards the end of the chapter.

The peculiarity of the human figures should not distract us from other remarkable aspects of these friezes. Collectively they reveal the key visual signifiers of Egypt and the Nile within the Italian provinces at this time. The architectural elements within these images are recognizably Egyptian

---

[23] Contra Tybout (2003), 510–12.    [24] Dasen (1993) provides a general introduction.

[25] McKay (1985), 12–25; Meyboom (1995), 151–4; Versluys (2002), 275–9. Daszewski (1985), 139, 167–8 presents some mosaic parallels from Egypt, which probably date from the first century BC. They are considerably more sensitive treatments than the caricatures that were later to become familiar in Italy.

and include temples, kiosks and reed huts, but never refer directly to specific buildings. As we saw in the discussion of the Praeneste mosaic, the familiar landmarks of the Nile valley do not appear in the visual repertoire of Roman art.[26] The river was also associated with particular animals (the crocodile, hippo, ibis and duck above all, but also the camel and ichneumon in some early pictures, and frequently the ass), and plants (the date palm and the lotus). In many cases, these motifs also rapidly became conventionalized. The Nilotic fauna of the earliest mosaic images is more or less recognizable. The hippos and crocodiles on the mosaics from Praeneste and the House of the Faun may well have been executed by Hellenistic artists who either knew the animals from life, or worked from detailed preparatory sketches, but this precision rapidly degenerated into caricature.[27] Later artists might well have seen these animals in theatrical spectacles, but such appearances were exceptional and of little immediate help. Consequently, by the later-first century, hippos were conventionally represented as rather slender, aggressive man-eaters and crocodiles as chubby lizards, sometimes with dorsal fins. Representations of flora also followed a similar trajectory: images of lotuses rapidly became conventionalized, not as the distinctive Egyptian plant, but as the *nelumbo nucifera* or *nelumbium speciosum* species.[28]

In this sense, the language employed by art historians in assessing later phases of 'Egyptomania' and 'Egyptophilia' in the seventeenth, eighteenth and twentieth centuries is convenient.[29] What we see in Pompeii is 'Egyptianizing' art, rather than 'Egyptian' art – that is, a decorative scheme which took Egypt as its inspiration and theme, but which presented the country through an essentially parochial prism. These works were certainly intended to evoke Egypt, but did this in an Italian register. What was significant was not the accurate, encyclopaedic depiction of Egyptian animal, human and plant life 'as it actually was', but the rehearsal of established semiotic tropes derived from familiar exemplars and set in a domestic context. In part, this may be explained by the recycling of motifs by artists working in Pompeii and other cities, in part by a standardization of tastes among their patrons, particularly as 'Egyptian' themes became more and more common, and were no longer limited to the very highest strata of society. In either case, we may regard the images as a 'translation' of Pharaonic and Hellenistic Egypt for an expanding Latin audience, to use a metaphor recently adopted for the study of other forms of cultural interaction in this period.[30]

---

[26] See above 61–2.    [27] Meyboom (1995), 91–8.    [28] Whitehouse (1979), 9.

[29] Curl (1994) provides a helpful overview of changing fashions in Egyptomania. For definitions, see Humbert (1994). Swetnam-Burland (2007) sounds a cautionary note on the dangers of distinguishing too rigidly between different types of Aegyptiaca.

[30] Wallace-Hadrill (2008), esp. 3–38.

This context was itself important. In the House of the Ephebe, in the Praedia of Julia Felix and in several other sites in Pompeii, Nilotic art was simply one element in an immersive decorative scheme which blended Egyptian and Italian themes in a variety of media. The water of the paintings reflected and blended with the water from the fountains in each house, which burbled behind, between and beneath the triclinia and provided a soundtrack for the Egyptian setting. The plants from the gardens and the food and wine served to the diners would add further sensory aspects to the experience of these Nilotic landscapes. And crucially all of these elements – sound, taste and smell as well as sight – were centred upon the viewers themselves. These diners could gaze upon a distant world that was open to their scrutiny – a fundamental aspect of this Nilotic art, as shall be discussed.

## Egypt in Context: The House of the Ceii

Context was crucial to the impact of this Egyptianizing art, not only in terms of the physical positioning within a house or garden, but also in the juxtaposition of different decorative schemes within the same room or building. Here, a third case study is particularly illuminating. At the House of the Ceii (I.6.15), a block to the west of the House of the Ephebe, the small garden was decorated with a series of massive painted vistas, probably in the 70s CE.[31] The most dramatic (and the most frequently reproduced) is the fresco of wild animals which dominates the north wall – that is the wall which would immediately confront the viewer when he or she entered the garden from the south. [FIG 3.11] This prospect is set in a rich painted frame of red and yellow, plants and birds ornament the lower register, and a number of decorative cartouches run up the two sides of the wall. Two elaborately-painted fountains are located to the lower right and left of the wall, each supported on a painted female sphinx, and each immediately standing before the masonry channels, which carried run-off water from the roofs of the adjacent houses through the garden.

A hunting scene dominates the central part of the fresco, which is the largest of its kind from Pompeii. This is divided into two registers. In the lower, a lion chases a bull in front of a circular building; in the upper, a leopard chases two rams to the right, while two wolves set upon two boar and a deer to the left. The upper register is rendered in softer colours than the foreground. This creates some visual space between the two parts

---

[31] M. De Vos (1980); Jashemski (1993), 36; Michel (1990), 73 on the dating of the paintings (to Vespasianic fourth style). For a helpful comparandum, see Fröhlich (1993).

3.11. House of the Ceii – Garden. Hunting scene
[© University of Maryland College Park W.F. Jashemski Archive. J61f0345 I.6.15 Pompeii.
1961. Room 9]

of the painting, and thereby emphasizes the illusory distance between the registers. There are no human figures. This painting which has variously been interpreted as an echo of the *paradiseos* scenes which depicted idealized nature on the walls of Hellenistic palaces, and (more persuasively) as a fantastic visual elaboration of the hunting shows or *venationes* which would have been familiar from the amphitheatre nearby.[32] If a political graffito on the external wall of the house is to be trusted, the probable owner at the time of the decoration was one Lucius Caius Secundus, who was successively elected civic aedile and duovir in Pompeii, probably in the late 70s, and who may have been directly responsible for the organization of the shows.[33] The garden painting may thus have commemorated (and glorified) his great moment of civic prominence.[34]

---

[32] Leach (2004), 130–2 and 211–8.

[33] *CIL* IV 7194. M. De Vos (1990), 407. On the dating of L. Caius Secundus' magistracies (conventionally given as 76 CE and 78 CE, respectively), see Mouritsen (1988), 41. The ownership of the building is discussed in Michel (1990), 88–90.

[34] Although not necessarily. Cf. Petron. *Sat.* 29 on Trimalchio's celebration of another's *munus* on his own walls.

3.12. House of the Ceii – Garden. Sacral-idyllic landscape
[© University of Maryland College Park W.F. Jashemski Archive. J61f0347 I.6.15 Pompeii.
1961. Room 9]

Of more immediate interest here, though, are the prospects which dominate the other walls of the same garden, and which combine to form
a coherent decorative whole. The east wall is dominated by a dreamlike
Egyptian landscape, populated by recognizably human figures.[35] [FIG 3.12]
Again, the image is divided into two, but this time vertically, with a dramatic rocky river bank separating the scenes on the left from the similar
vignettes on the right. The picture surface is further disrupted by three
large windows that are physically cut through it, but which would seem to
predate the completion of the fresco, given the facility with which the artist
navigated around these gaps.[36] On the left-hand side of the landscape, three
figures sit on an island grove in front of an Egyptian funerary structure or
*osireon*. That this scene is set on the Nile is made clear by a sailed riverboat which passes behind the complex. In front of the *osireon*, two further
figures stand at the river-bank, immediately in front of a large statue of

---

[35] Versluys cat. 033. Detailed discussion (and reproduction) at M. De Vos (1990), 476–82; Michel
(1990), 84–7.
[36] This is a particularly clear example of the way in which Pompeian artists exploited and explored the
physical surface to be painted in their works (the triclinium in the House of the Ephebe is another).
This has interesting parallels to early Dutch *landskip* art, as discussed by Casey (2002), 14–15.

3.13. House of the Ceii – Garden. Pygmy landscape
[© University of Maryland College Park W.F. Jashemski Archive. J59f0135 I.6.15 Pompeii.
1959. Room 9]

Priapus. The right side of the mural is dominated by a temple complex, and seated worshippers. The main temple building is barrel-vaulted, and is further ornamented by an awning, and by two statues of sphinxes, one of which sits atop a column, the other on a large plinth. An isolated wayfarer or shepherd wearing the hooded *cucullus* of a low-status traveller stands in front of this vignette, accompanied only by his goat. Like the *venatio* scene on the north wall, this 'sacral-idyllic' landscape is framed with a painted border, including a red dado, with climbing plants depicted on it.

Facing this mural is a fine example of a large 'pygmy' landscape on the west wall.[37] [FIG 3.13] This prospect also depicts life on the Nile banks, and again Egyptianizing temples and a riverboat make this identification clear. The inhabitants are very different from those on the wall opposite, however. Here, caricatured pygmies replace the elegant figures of the sacral-idyllic landscape. This prospect is dominated by a prominent river-bank on which dwarfs engage in fighting, fishing and conversation before the

---

[37] Mentioned only briefly in Versluys cat. 033, and without reproduction. The best general discussion and reproduction is at M. De Vos (1990), 470–2. And cf. Michel (1990).

sacred buildings. A second island and a second temple appear in the lower right-hand section. Nearby a dwarf is engaged in ineffectual combat with a hippopotamus. Behind him is a rather soporific crocodile who would seem to have escaped the attentions of the local inhabitants. Again, the mural is elaborately framed and was clearly designed as part of a consistent decorative scheme with the other images. Most scholars concur that the paintings represent an accomplished example of Pompeian wall painting in its final phase.[38]

These three paintings were intended to be viewed together as a complete decorative system, and not in isolation. It is also evident that the garden itself contributed to this composite effect. As is the case in the House of the Ephebe and the Praedia of Julia Felix, the depiction of 'watery' landscapes is complemented by the physical presence of water: here, both the sacral-idyllic landscape of the east wall and the pygmy painting of the west wall had a water channel running in front of them.[39] This emphasizes the marked 'Egyptian' theme within the garden (which is certainly important) and lends the *venatio* scene an additional exoticism. The obvious pairing of the sacral-idyllic landscape and the pygmy painting on facing walls also affects the impact of each of these prospects on the viewer. The contrast with the comic excesses and figural distortions of the pygmy painting partly emphasizes the other-worldly calm of the sacral-idyllic landscape, but also punctures it: the statue of Priapus and the strong sexual associations of the pygmies draws one link between the two worlds, and the caricatured philosophical posturing of some of the dwarfs another. More dramatic still is the effect that this sombre landscape has upon the appearance of the pygmy landscape. Every action of the dwarfs is either a distorted reflection of the hieratic seriousness of the painting opposite, or a violent refutation of the image of stately peace that it projects. Even for eyes long familiar with the painted caperings of the Nilotic grotesques – as L. Caius Secundus and the visitors to his house must surely have been, given the dozens of examples scattered around their home town – the juxtaposition is startling as the provocative nature of these figures is accentuated. By including different varieties of 'Egypt' within the garden, the homeowner magnified the message of each. Egypt was both a place of idealized religious seriousness and a world of comic idiosyncrasy. And both of these worlds could be gazed upon by the visitor to the garden of the House of the Ceii.

[38] Peters (1963), 172–6; Michel (1990), 84.     [39] On these watery themes, see Andersson (1991).

## Nile Landscapes and Roman Visual Culture in the Private Sphere

The Nilotic landscapes of the Pompeian townhouses offer us a unique view of Roman responses to the wider world. They also provide some sense of the active involvement of provincial aristocrats and freedmen in the wider discourses of Roman imperialism.[40] These images are a reminder that emotional and cultural investment in the new empire was not limited to those at the very highest levels of society, or to those engaged in the active administration of the new provinces: it might also be felt at home. These may seem like bold claims for a minor form of decorative art most commonly compared to the fussy fripperies of European Chinoiserie in the seventeenth and eighteenth centuries or Japonisme in the nineteenth (or indeed to successive waves of Egyptomania throughout the modern period), but it is as well to remember that these later orientalisms were themselves drawn by the deeper cultural and political currents of their time, both at home and abroad.[41] As trade, diplomacy and military pressure created new relations with China, India, Egypt and Japan, the domestic tastes of the European (and American) west often followed in their wake. Equally, by prominently adopting such esoteric fashions, individuals could establish their own cultural capital within contemporary western society. The relationship between politics and orientalist aesthetics was not precise, of course: after all, not every new imperial project was reflected directly in the drawing rooms of the metropolis, but when exotic tastes were adopted, they were frequently bound in to wider geopolitical events. We can see something very similar happening in Roman representations of Egypt.

The conspicuous popularity of Nilotic frescoes in the Julio-Claudian period represents a direct – even competitive – engagement with the Roman imperial project on the level of the provincial aristocracy and freedmen. This is most obviously true in the case of the painted prospects described above, but may also be detected on a reduced level in smaller examples of Egyptianizing art. What we see in these painted representations of Egypt is the replication and appropriation of the ideology of conquest in a variety of domestic settings, and hence an assertion of involvement within this project on the level of the individual. These paintings were a complement to – and in many ways were symbiotic with – the more formal representations and ideologies that were propounded by the imperial administration, and put

---

[40] Hinted at (but not fully developed) in Swetnam-Burland (2007), 126–30.
[41] On these later trends, see Curl (1994); Humbert (1994). On Chinoiserie see Honour (1961); Impey (1977) and Jacobson (1993).

forward in texts, triumphs and spectacles; indeed, these images partly relied upon the familiarity with the descriptive conventions of these media for their impact.[42] But they also imposed an agency on behalf of the viewing subjects. This was not the vicarious celebration of conquest in the abstract that we see in triumphs or panegyrics, but a formal engagement with it. The patrons who commissioned these paintings, and admired them on the walls of their *viridaria* or on the sides of their *stibadia*, were not passive replicators of an official ideology, but rather were active appropriators of it and turned it to their own ends. They wished to stage their own representations of the world, gaze upon their political inheritance, and thereby claim their own role in the empire. The subjectivity evinced in these paintings is different in kind from the 'subject-hood' manifested as the same individuals stood in crowds and authenticated triumphal geography as a part of the collective.

These Egyptianizing landscapes have been interpreted in a variety of different ways, and the essentially political reading proposed here need not preclude these. Although recent scholarship has challenged the straightforward assumption that the taste for such visual motifs was directly associated with devotion to the Egyptian cults, religious concerns must have played a part in their interpretation and appreciation – a point that is explored in more detail in the next chapter.[43] Antithetical to this explanation, but in some ways just as convincing, is John Clarke's argument that the pygmy scenes had an apotropaic function – that is, they were intended to provoke laughter from the viewer and hence provide protection against the evil eye.[44] This threat was perceived to be at its greatest in liminal spaces between inside and outside or between life and death – in thresholds, gardens, bathhouses and tombs – which is precisely where we find many pygmy images. According to this reading Egyptianizing landscapes were comic, rather than devotional, intended to provoke a bark of surprised laughter, rather than a reverential silence.

Specific sign-systems certainly are important, and are discussed at the end of this chapter, but so too is the wider visual context in which these symbols are presented. Regardless of whether a specific vignette was intended to make the viewer laugh, or to reflect upon the rebirth of Isis, the manner in

---

[42] My thinking on this topic has been profoundly influenced by Alpers (1983) on Dutch art of the seventeenth century, and Edney (1990), 53–63 on the links between Imperial politics and the 'picturesque' gaze upon British India.

[43] Takács (1995b), 32–4 clearly summarizes the sceptical position. But cf. Meyboom and Versluys (2007), who have identified possible ritual significance in some of the Pompeian friezes.

[44] Most clearly applied to the Egyptianizing landscapes in Clarke (2007a), 63–108. See also Clarke (1996), (2003), 191–6 and (2007b).

which it appears may still tell us a great deal about the cultural assumptions of the artist and the viewer. Crucial to my argument is the recognition that landscape prospects of the kind we see here only became a popular visual medium within the last few decades of the Republic and were unknown before that period. Large-scale landscape vistas only appear in the later Julio-Claudian period, moreover, and it was also in this period that decorative art of this kind began to appear in the town-houses of freedmen and provincial upper classes. Admittedly, this is the period which also provides us with the richest body of evidence, and we know rather less about the decorative conventions of later centuries. Nevertheless, the extraordinary proliferation of landscape art – and specifically Egyptian landscapes – deserves some comment, particularly when viewed alongside other forms of geographical representation.

In some ways it is anachronistic to regard the pygmy paintings or sacral-idyllic images as 'landscapes' in the modern sense of the term, and thought-less application of theoretical positions better adopted to the Dutch seventeenth century or the American nineteenth can obscure as much as they illuminate. Indeed, several prominent modern art critics have been reluctant to place the origins of recognizable landscape painting any earlier than the sixteenth century because of these very differences.[45] But there are important points of comparison to be made too. Like these later representations of the landscape, the Roman images of the Nile present a view of the physical world that privileged a single point of view, and hence reconfigured the natural world around a static viewing subject. In other words, they articulated a very different relationship between the viewer and the wider world than those constructed by maps or monumental chorographies (whatever form they may have taken), triumphal geographies or textual descriptions. These were images of the world that were presented to the viewer as an individual, not as a member of a crowd. Like post-Renaissance landscapes, moreover, the Julio-Claudian frescoes emerged as part of a much wider discourse on visuality, which extended far beyond the painted surface of the wall to encompass physiological reflection, poetry, prose and even political action. As such, these were not simply mute manifestations of a particular mode of viewing, but were a form which was consciously developed within a far larger cultural discussion of the meaning and significance of seeing as a whole. There are differences, to be sure: the Roman landscapes tend to

---

[45]  Clark (1953), 1–15, which frames the 'landscapes' of the period down to c.1400 in terms very different from those after. Cf. also Casey (2002), 3. The implications of this conviction are examined (with different results) in both Steinmeyer-Schareika (1978), and Rouveret (2004).

be formulaic and dominated by certain familiar visual *topoi*, they rely more heavily upon figural representation than their western successors, and their use of perspective lacks the conventional order of the post-Renaissance west. Nevertheless, the Nile landscapes do betray a changing engagement with the physical world in the early imperial period. The flourishing of 'landscape art' in the first century deserves some explanation, both as a phenomenon in its own right, and as a complement to other forms of geographical representation in the period.

Central to the understanding of the Nilotic landscape frescoes is the Roman view of visuality itself – the contemporary sense of what it actually was to see, and how the act of seeing reflected and reinforced one's position in society.[46] We have already briefly encountered some issues of spectatorship and viewing in the discussion of Roman triumphs, and have witnessed the normalizing power of the communal gaze within the streets of the city. But the act of seeing defined the spectator as much as the object of his (or her) gaze. If we take an individual male citizen as an example – the kind of Roman who served as the audience for imperial triumphs and spectacles, yet who was wealthy enough to commission domestic decoration according to his own informed tastes – this is immediately apparent. Once this citizen moved out from the kinetic spectacle of the city to the controlled environment of the house, he moved onto a stage that he was more readily able to manipulate.[47] This was a stage upon which he might present himself to others – guests, *clientes*, family members and slaves – but also one in which he could assert his social position through his own active gaze. Put simply, representation and spectatorship meant different things in different settings.[48] Viewing the great beast-hunts or *venationes* in the amphitheatre was important to the practice of social belonging, and in the assertion of communal civic power over nature: it helped to define the shared 'subject-hood' of the viewers. The analogous experience of contemplating a painted fresco of wild animals in one's own garden might prompt similar reflections – of human dominance over the animals, for example, or Rome's dominance over the world – but it also forced the spectator to

---

[46] Elsner (1995), 49–87 expounds on the visual ambiguities and uncertainties inherent in Roman domestic wall decoration. The bibliography on sight and subjectivity in the Roman world more broadly is immense, and constantly growing. See esp. Leach (1988), Bergmann (1999), Bartsch (2006), Beagon (2011) and the collected papers in Elsner (2007). Alston and Spentzou (2011) esp. 193–224 offer a provocative recent discussion of Roman subjectivity.

[47] Wallace-Hadrill (1994), 1–15; Holliday (2002), 16; Leach (2004), 18–54.

[48] Jacob (2006), 92–3 discusses the different significance of display maps in domestic (as opposed to public) settings. No 'maps' are known from Pompeii, but the observation remains important.

reflect on his own position as a viewer: it helped to define his subjectivity.[49] The interlocking gazes which lent amphitheatrical spectacles their profound social meaning were replaced by a single gaze, which was important in a different way. The various strategies of perspective and diminution employed within the picture helped simulate a naturalistic spectacle, but simultaneously drew attention to this artificiality, thereby challenging the viewer to reflect upon the significance of his contemplation. For male viewers – the citizens who commissioned, enjoyed and shared these frescoes – the political implications of this privileged gaze were crucial. As we shall see, however, women, children and slaves must also have looked out onto these painted vistas, and have generated their own responses to the new empire.

Domestic wall-paintings did not have the visceral brutality of the amphitheatre or the triumphalism of imperial ceremonial, but where civic spectacles channelled the collective gaze, and defined those experiencing it with respect to their peers and compatriots, this art privileged the more private contemplation of the individual viewer and that of his invited guests. It demanded contemplation and encouraged self-reflection. In many ways, all Romano-Campanian wall painting was predicated on issues of visuality and seeing. This is just as apparent in the smaller domestic friezes, as in substantial works like the Praeneste mosaic discussed in Chapter 1. Such themes, which were almost universal in Campanian wall decoration, both purport to fool the eye of the viewer, and delight in the very impossibility of this process. Architectonic frames are too slender to support the illusion of depth for long, depictions of lifelike animals and plants are frozen impossibly in place.[50]

Landscape paintings were equally influenced by contemporary concerns about visuality and the power of sight. After all, such images promised a glimpse into a world far beyond the house or garden wall. They might employ perspective and different types of diminution to replicate the experience of gazing at a receding landscape and could exploit the framing of the pictures to evoke windows or to explode such illusions.[51] Similar visual themes have been explored eagerly by the artists of the modern period, and provided an invaluable medium for the examination of the changing relationship between art and viewer. As several recent studies have shown,

---

[49] My interpretation here is influenced (inevitably) by Mulvey (1975) and the work that has followed in her wake. On the impact of her ideas on classical scholarship, see esp. Richlin (1992), Fredrick (2002b) and Bartsch (2006).

[50] Vitruv. 6.2.2; 7.Praef 11, 7.5.2.

[51] cf. Casey (2002), 16–17 and 119–26, on similar themes in a different context.

landscape vistas are also deeply political images.[52] Above all else, they imply and effect a relationship between the viewer and the land (or the viewer's society and the land) that could be expressed through this static, contemplative gaze, rather than through movement across it or other actions within it.[53] Yet illusionistic landscape prospects were by no means universal within classical painting, and the vast majority of our extant examples date from the first centuries BCE and CE – precisely the period which concerns us here. There was nothing remotely resembling the Pompeian garden prospects in either classical Greece or in late Antiquity. In the former case, admittedly, we are substantially hampered by an absence of conclusive evidence, although the textual evocations of the natural world in this period do suggest that static contemplation of the view was rare.[54]

For late Antiquity, we are blessed with an abundance of visual evidence, which almost never replicates the 'first-person' perspective of the earlier imperial art. Instead, natural scenes were more commonly represented as a series of discrete visual signifiers, intended to be read or decoded, rather than contemplated as a coherent visual field. This contrast between forms of landscape representation is particularly well illustrated by comparing briefly the Pompeian Egyptian frescoes discussed here with the later representations of the same subject matter which appear on mosaics between the third and the sixth centuries.[55] In the third-century mosaic from El Alia in Tunisia, or in the sixth-century Sepphoris Mosaic from northern Israel, there is no attempt to approximate a landscape 'view' as we would understand it today.[56] Crucially, the details of these mosaics are at once familiar, but their syntactic arrangement is wholly different. At El Alia, the familiar motifs of pygmies, buildings and Nilotic fauna appear in a completely neutral visual field, with no orientation whatsoever. Rather than presenting the spectator with an ordered vista, it projected a chaotic jumble, which might be viewed or read from any direction. The Sepphoris mosaic was clearly intended to be viewed from a particular direction, but the Nile here is represented by an anthropomorphic God, as well as schematic representations of Alexandria, the Nilometer and the river itself.[57] [FIG 3.14] This is no longer an Egyptian landscape to be gazed upon, but a collection of

---

[52] Politics and the landscape: see for example Adams and Greutzner Robins (2000) (and the gender politics of the gaze). Cf. Alpers (1983), 144–53.

[53] Cf. Casey (2002).    [54] See esp. Fitter (1995).

[55] Elsner (1995) is fundamental. On late antique Nile mosaics, see Balty (1984/1995) and the specific discussions in Foucher (1965); Alföldi-Rosenbaum (1975); Leclant (1984); Daviault, Lancha and Lopez Palomo (1987); Hachili (1998); Hamarneh (1999).

[56] Versluys cat. 086; 130. Foucher (1965), 138–40; Balty (1995), 251–2.

[57] Discussion in Hachili (1998) and Maguire (1999).

3.14. The Nile and Nilometer on the sixth-century Sepphoris Mosaic (detail)
[Alamy BP27PP]

discrete visual glyphs to be read and interpreted. This point is particularly well illustrated by the status of the dwarf figures: no longer caricatured approximations of the river's inhabitants, by the sixth century they had been formally reconfigured as *pecheis*, who represented the different levels of the Nile flood.[58] The decorative conventions of these mosaics were not new, but the perspectival landscapes which are so familiar from the Pompeian gardens had disappeared almost entirely by late Antiquity. What had changed was not the particular artistic skill of the mosaicists, but rather the political and social circumstances which might have led them to represent Egypt as an illusionistic prospect in the first place.[59] For them, and for later medieval artists, the natural world was a complex text, to be decoded and elucidated piece by piece, not a panorama to be admired.

The recognition that the landscape vista is not a 'natural' medium for representing the natural world, but was in fact extremely rare in European art before the Renaissance, places the study of early imperial art in a new light. Motivated equally by a fascination with the complex philosophy and

[58] Hachili (1998), 109; Whitehouse (1979), 194–6. Lucian *Rhet Praec.* 17–30 and Philostr. *Imag.* 1.5 both allude to *pecheis* as features of Nile images, although their *ekphraseis* clearly drew upon the conventions of statuary.
[59] Elsner (1995) is fundamental. Cf. also Fitter (1995), 84–155.

physiology of vision and by an aggressive political impulse which has always motivated such art, the landscape representations of Egypt had a central role to play in the articulation of early imperial ideologies.

## The Development of Roman Nilotica

In many ways, the study of Roman landscape art is inseparable from the study of Roman representations of Egypt. Egyptian elements are prominent in these vistas from the very earliest stages, and it is likely that the first landscape artists in Italy either were exiles from the Hellenistic east or took their inspiration from these regions.[60] Many of the earliest extant examples of Roman landscape art display conspicuously Egyptian themes. The Nile mosaic at Palestrina is certainly the most famous example of Nilotic art in Italy, and is discussed in some detail in Chapter 1, but several other high-status mosaics on the same theme are known from the late Republic. The mosaic of Nilotic animals in the House of the Faun (VI.12.2) has frequently been compared to the example from Palestrina, and as we have seen is often thought to have been produced by the same workshop.[61] This is a striking visual catalogue which includes a hippopotamus, crocodile, snake and ichneumon, set against a watery field filled with ducks, ibises and other birds and a number of lotuses and other plants, but no human figures. This mosaic was found in front of the entrance to the columned *exedra*, which originally contained with the famous Alexander Mosaic – perhaps the most remarkable example of Hellenistic mosaic art in Italy. A further Nile mosaic fragment was found during the construction of the Palazzo delle Esposizioni in Rome, and which may originally have ornamented the Serapeum on the Quirinal in Rome.[62] Measuring approximately 45 cm × 45 cm, the fragment depicts a number of figures on the banks of the Nile. To judge from the actions and dress of the figures, and the presence of Nilotic wildlife, it was originally intended to represent the feeding of the sacred crocodiles at Arsinoe or Crocodilopolis – an event also described by Strabo.[63]

Landscapes also appear in frescoes from the early part of the first century BCE, and Egyptian themes are immediately apparent, particularly in the friezes which decorate the upper registers of several well-known rooms. The earliest dated example of one of these 'sacral-idyllic' landscapes is a frieze from the Great Atrium in the Villa of the Mysteries in Pompeii.[64]

---

[60] De Vos (1980), 88–95; Ling (1991), 140–4; McKay (1985), 62–74.  [61] Versluys cat. 047.
[62] Versluys cat. 013; Whitehouse (1979), 29–31.  [63] Strabo 17.1.38.  [64] Versluys cat. 067.

The extant fragments suggest a river scene with a number of figures, boats and buildings, which hint at an Egyptian association. For the most part these fabulous landscapes played only a supplementary decorative role within late Republican wall decorations, typically as friezes in the upper or lower registers. The world that they evoked was generically hieratic or pastoral, rather than specifically Egyptian, although familiar Nilotic motifs are present in the ala and cubiculum of the House of Livia in Rome, and from a wall-panel from the so-called 'Aula Isiaca' in the same city.[65] Both of these landscapes probably date from the earlier Augustan period, and both were certainly part of exceptionally high-status domestic decoration (smaller Egyptianizing motifs are also known from other imperial palaces of the period). The originals of the Aula Isiaca paintings have since been lost, but eighteenth-century drawings depict a hippo and other familiar Nilotic fauna, and two dwarfs (not yet the caricatures which would so dominate the later art).[66] The Livia friezes present a more spectral landscape in yellow monochrome, including a familiar repertoire of temples, animals and Egyptian figures.[67]

All of these works were undoubtedly of very high status: their workmanship is exceptionally accomplished and, where their context can be determined definitively, they came from major sacred sites, imperial buildings or some of the largest and most prestigious houses in Pompeii. They have been confidently identified as illustrations of the diffusion of Hellenistic tastes throughout the peninsula, and perhaps of the immigration of skilled artists from Egypt and the eastern Mediterranean.[68] In many ways, this is to be expected. The Roman fashion for ornamental garden canals, which we see in the Praedia of Julia Felix and in the House of Octavius Quarto (II.2.2), and which reached a spectacular climax in Hadrian's 'Canopus' complex at Tivoli, was viewed with disdain by some contemporary commentators as an effete Hellenistic affectation.[69] But in the face of this chauvinism, Alexandrian craftsmanship and Egyptian subject matter seemed to fuse in a new genre of decorative art. This rarefied taste was rapidly and very visibly diffused, and one of the most fascinating aspects of Augustan and Julio-Claudian Nilotic art is the extent to which it was adopted even in relatively small houses and semi-public spaces.

---

[65] Versluys cat. 017; 016. On this material see esp. De Vos (1980), 76–8; Iacopi (1997).
[66] McKay (1985), 87–99.    [67] Ling (1991), 142–3.    [68] Meyboom (1995), 85–6.
[69] Sen. *Ep.* 90.15; Cic. *Leg.* 2.2. See Spencer (2005), 68–9. The fashion was clearly widespread; Euripi are mentioned as an attractive feature of the cityscape at Ov. *Pont.* 1.8,38; Plin. *HN* 36.123 and of the rural villa at Sen. *Ep.* 55.6. For speculative interpretations of these garden complexes, see (for example) Brenk (1999), esp. 139 and Capriotti Vittozzi (2000), 129–38 on Pompeii II.2.2.

As early as the Augustan period, we can see the traces of the full appropriation and absorption of this Nilotic art into indigenous Italian forms.[70] Significantly, this diffusion also represents the first appearance of the pygmy caricatures in this tradition: in many ways the dwarfs mark the point at which the art became 'Egyptianizing' rather than simply 'Egyptian'. In Pompeii, the stereotyped dwarfs first appear in their characteristic form in the emblemata of two floor mosaics, one in the triclinium of the House of Paquius Proculus (I.7.1), the other in the Green *oecus* of the House of Menander (I.10.4).[71] These mosaics are both seventeen or eighteen inches across and are virtually identical in detail and execution, although the former is a circular design, the latter rectangular. Both prominently feature a Nile fishing boat, crewed by four pygmies. In each case an Egyptian temple is in the background, and a smaller boat in the foreground, along with a variety of Nilotic animals. While each of these mosaics was evidently viewed with some pride by its owner – both remained visible at the time of the eruption three generations after their initial installation, and both were carefully preserved even during the extensive restoration of the rooms around them – the similarities are important.[72] These mosaics were almost certainly the work of the same craftsman or craftsmen, who may well have replicated their work in many other houses in the city.[73] Attractive as these mosaics were deemed to be, the very similarities between them reveal the extent to which scenes like this had become generic in Pompeii during the Augustan period. Evidently the work of craftsmen from the region, they represent a local adaptation of this decorative form.

This pattern is still more striking in the adoption of Nilotic scenes in decorative terracotta plaques at around the same time.[74] Named the 'Campana' reliefs after their first modern collector, these plaques derived from an Etruscan practice, but were produced in their greatest numbers in the Augustan period and early empire. They were a common decorative feature of senatorial and imperial villas, public buildings, temples and baths, particularly in Rome and its immediate environs. They were ornamented with a great variety of mythological scenes, Dionysiac episodes and scenes of quotidian life, but almost 150 extant reliefs from the later first century BCE bear recognizably Nilotic scenes. The vast majority were produced

---

[70] Versluys (2002), 288 rightly identifies the early Augustan period as the key shift in the production and form of this art, and see also 303–8.

[71] Versluys cat. 034; 037.     [72] Badoni and De Vos (1990), 534–43; Ling (1990), 296–304.

[73] De Vos (1980), 81 suggests that they may have been produced by the same workshop as the Palestrina mosaic. This seems unlikely.

[74] Versluys cat. 027. Kern (1958). Rauch (1999) provides a full discussion.

3.15. Campana Relief
[Alamy DHKAAB]

from the same family of moulds and show two dwarfs in a canoe with an ass-head prow. [FIG 3.15] They are surrounded by two crocodiles, a hippo and a pair of ducks, and behind them is a river bank with two straw huts. Three ibises (or cranes) are sitting on top of the huts. The whole scene is framed by two large arches and some architectural decoration. The likelihood is that the Campana reliefs were largely used in relatively high-status contexts, and hence for an audience which may already have been familiar with the

Hellenistic mosaic art discussed above. Nevertheless, the translation of these key motifs into the quintessentially Italian medium of moulded terracotta, the mass production of these plaques, and the simplification of the key figures into a number of simple yet memorable caricatures demonstrate an active absorption of Alexandrian artistic traditions into an Italian milieu.

The same is true of the sudden appearance of the pygmy art in Augustan funerary contexts. Around a dozen small painted panels with Egyptian themes were recovered from the columbarium of the Villa Doria Pamphili in Rome.[75] Around 130 decorated panels were recovered, each of which ornamented a single burial niche in the chamber. The majority are images of birds or other animals, and several other landscapes have also survived, but the dozen or so Egyptian panels do represent a respectable proportion. Many of these are sacral-idyllic waterscapes with a certain Egyptian flavour, but we also encounter several pygmy scenes, including one depicting combat with a crocodile and a second showing a dwarf defecating on a hippopotamus. Quite what the precise significance of these images may have been is unclear, although the sheer variety of this art may indicate that simple decoration was the primary motivation. At the very least, the illustrations of the Villa Doria Pamphili, when combined with the prestigious mosaics in Pompeii and the Campana reliefs, illustrate the extent to which Egyptianizing themes, and specifically pygmy images, had become a familiar (and perhaps unremarkable) visual motif by the Augustan period.[76]

By the end of the first century BCE, landscape vignettes and friezes of the kind we found in the Villa of the Mysteries had become increasingly familiar. When Pliny the Elder looked back on the origins of decorative art in his *Natural History*, he placed the origins of this form of landscape painting as he understood it in the Augustan period:

> Nor must Studius be neglected, from the age of the divine Augustus, who first introduced the most delightful images – villas and porticoes and landscaped gardens, groves, woods, hills, fishponds, euripus canals, rivers coasts and whatever else might be desired, along with representations of people walking, sailing or on land, or coming to villas, on donkeys or in carriages, people fishing, fowling, hunting or even harvesting grapes.[77]

[75] Ling (1993), McKay (1985), 123–7.
[76] There is no particular reason to follow the suggestion of Bendinelli (1941), 37 that the subject matter of these panels indicates that the painters were Egyptian.
[77] Plin. *HN* 35.116–7.

The importance of this brief passage to the history of Roman art has been much disputed.[78] Pliny's artistic aetiologies can be eccentric to say the least, and few scholars have been confident in ascribing extant works from Pompeii or Rome to the genre of painting supposedly established by Studius. Nevertheless, Pliny's statement does remind us of two important points. First, that the landscapes of this period were essentially formulaic, and consisted of the combination of different specific tropes – gardens groves woods, fishing, fowling and hunting – in aesthetically pleasing form. Vitruvius also noticed this in his own celebration of contemporary practice.[79] This was certainly true of the sacral-idyllic landscapes of the time, both Egyptianizing and otherwise. While the execution of these paintings varies dramatically, similar buildings, human actions and natural motifs do recur regularly. In commenting on Virgil's evocation of the north African coast in the *Aeneid*, the scholiast Servius notes that a similar pattern was also evident in contemporary poetry. He identified Virgil's exquisite description of the North African coast as *topothesia* as distinct from *topographia* – the poetic description of an imagined place from the imagination, rather than from life.[80] The term is equally appropriate for the visual arts of the early empire. Visually as well as textually the landscapes of the early empire were topothesic, that is they were not representations of specific places, but were derived instead from the combination of familiar formulaic elements in a manner that approximated a believable natural scene. It is at once apparent, moreover, that these works drew upon a relatively limited visual vocabulary in their depiction of the world.[81]

Pliny's second point is that these frescoes were judged in large part for the effect that they had on spectators, and that 'Studius'' paintings consciously emulated the experience of gazing upon a physical landscape. Pliny's celebration of Studius deliberately elides the viewing positions of the individual in the physical landscape and the individual standing before a painting. In this, it draws upon and develops the conventions of rhetorical *ekphrasis* and consciously blurs the distinctions between landscape, painting of landscape, and description of painting of landscape. This is not to suggest that the paintings were intended as accurate representations of specific vistas – of

[78] Discussion at Ling (1977); Isager (1991), 132; Ling (1991), 140–2; Beagon (1996), 286.

[79] Vitr. 7.5.2. Bergmann (1991), 49–51.

[80] Serv. *Aen.* I.159. Cf. Leach (1988), 30. Pratt (2008), 44 notes that Turner lamented the conventional nature of eighteenth-century landscape painting in similar terms.

[81] In itself, of course, this isn't especially unusual within landscape art of any period. Cf. Casey (2002), 74–90 on Constable's selective representations (or rather 'presentations') of the East Anglian landscape and McClintock (1995), 122–5 on the semiotics of 'exotic' photographs and postcards in Victorian London.

course, the familiar *topoi* of the painting show clearly that this cannot have been the case. What Pliny does imply, however, is that these paintings prompted the viewer into reflection upon his own relationship with the wider world. Like all Roman wall painting of the period, representations of the landscape demanded that the viewer interrogate his own relationship to the image. This was just as true of the smaller panel paintings and subordinate friezes as it was of the full-scale landscape murals which will be discussed shortly. Each of these wall paintings simultaneously affords the viewer a glimpse into this imagined world, drawing him or her in, and then immediately frustrating this absorption by reiterating to the very artificiality of the image itself. This is accomplished in a number of ways. Most obvious is the framing of the painted vignettes. Each of the landscapes is organized focally around the viewing subject: the cluster of figures, trees and other structures forms an aesthetically pleasing group; a simple form of vanishing point perspective further ensures that buildings recede from the viewing plane in a more or less convincing manner, and other strategies of diminution also focalize the gaze, including the haziness added to the edges of the image.[82] The paintings that result are not abstracted visual motifs, therefore, but a collection of images presented together in a manner that more or less replicates the gaze of a spectator on a physical landscape. No viewer would imagine himself actually transported to this imagined world. Instead, the attention of the viewer is drawn to the framing itself, and to the visual trickery employed there, quite as much as to the painted landscape.

## Larger Prospects. Gardens and Villas

The larger landscape prospects which began to appear in the second half of the first century CE placed the viewing subject in a rather different position. As these vistas moved to occupy a complete wall surface, or the whole of a decorated object, the decorative schemes in which they were set were increasingly geared towards the maintenance of this single illusion. The heavy painted borders around the landscapes of the House of the Ceii approximated a great window frame, which surrounded this glimpse into the Egyptian world. Other conceits like the combination of painted water scenes and physical water channels further immersed the viewer into this spectacle. Deprived of other visual cues and distractions, and confronted

---

[82] Roman approaches to perspective are usefully discussed by Stinson (2011).

with what were often very large landscape vistas, the spectator had no choice but to engage with the landscape display as it was presented.

The Roman fascination for the grand view is best known through the celebration of villa landscapes in the later first century CE, but is equally relevant to the more modest garden paintings of Pompeii. In the writing of Statius and the Younger Pliny, we see the great country estates of the Bay of Naples praised for the perfection of their appearance, but also for the prospects that they commanded over the surrounding countryside.[83] In this creation of what Chris Fitter has termed the 'managerial landscape', the boundaries between appearance and reality, between painted prospect and genuine view are systematically blurred.[84] Pliny's description of his own villa at Laurentum repeatedly defines the position of its house by the views that that it afforded, both on the journey there from Rome, and from the villa itself. Statius' poetic celebration of the villa of Pollius Felix at Surrentum also stresses the exquisite setting of the building, and its position of visual dominance over the surrounding countryside:

> Why should I rehearse the thousand rooftops and the changing views? Every room has its own delight, each its particular sea; and beyond the expanse of Nereus each separate window commands its own landscape.[85]

As Bettina Bergmann's study has demonstrated, moreover, Statius' subsequent celebration of marble wall-decorations 'mimicking soft grass' in their greenness and so blue as 'to match the waves', further blurs the distinction between the view from the villa window, the decoration on the wall, and the poetic description of each. In doing this, Statius underscored Pollius Felix's command of both the natural and domestic worlds, even as he demonstrated his own poetic skill.[86]

This managerial gaze had important political implications. On one level, it may simply be seen as the articulation of familiar aristocratic self-aggrandizement through a new medium.[87] The celebration of the private estate had been widespread since the middle of the first century BCE and can be seen clearly enough in the poetry and prose of the period.[88] If certain affectations were viewed in earlier periods with distaste by contemporary commentators, the underlying idea that the landscape might be controlled through direct physical interaction underpins many of the great

---

[83] See esp. Spencer (2005), 104–34.     [84] Fitter (1995), 25–31 for the definition of 'managerial' space.

[85] Stat. *Silv* 2.2.72–5. tr. Shackleton-Bailey (2003), 129.

[86] Bergmann (1991), 62–3. Stat. *Silv.* 2.2.91, 93.

[87] Fitter (1995), 40–5, notes that the aristocratic taste for these 'dominated' landscapes may be linked to their loss of political power in the same period.

[88] Varr. *Rust.* 3.5.9–17; Cato *Agr.* 1.1–7; Columella *Rust* 1.4–6; Plin. *Ep.* 2.17.

literary works of the period. As such, the novel celebration of a villa for its static views might be seen as just one more area in which rich landowners could boast about their power and influence.

Landscapes of this kind are a reminder of the authority of the static landlord, who expresses his control by gazing upon territory, and not moving through it. This assertion of individual or cultural dominance through surveillance is implicit in all modern western landscape painting, whether in Breughel's ordered Dutch farmscapes or in the sublime representations of the American west by Thomas Cole or Ansel Adams.[89] Such images imply an active gaze, not only upon the painted surface, but on the world beyond. The same processes have important implications for the study of the Egyptianizing landscapes in the gardens of Pompeii. The large frescoes of the House of the Ceii, the all-encompassing decorative scheme of the Praedia of Julia Felix and the covered triclinium in the House of the Ephebe, all promote the illusion of a privileged gaze over a submissive landscape and thereby elevate their viewers over the objectified world. The figures within these landscapes are implicitly placed in a subordinate position to the spectator – strikingly so in the case of the pygmy frescoes, where their physical bodies are torn, penetrated and mocked for the entertainment of the viewer – but also in the sacral-idyllic landscapes, where an otherworldly environment is also controlled and subordinated to the viewer's gaze.[90] For the spectators in the House of the Ceii, the diners in the House of the Ephebe or the guests of Julia Felix, Egypt was the object of their confident, lordly contemplation.

Equally significant is the particular setting of many of these images in gardens. Gardens were extraordinarily charged places within the Roman house.[91] In part domestic, in part public, simultaneously inside and outside, natural and cultured spaces, gardens represented a liminal point of contact with the outside world. As such, they were not only the threshold between the house and the city, but also between the familiar world of Italy and the expanding political world that lay beyond. Moreover, the paintings of the wider world were themselves liminal – like all paintings they played on the oppositions between what was painted and what was represented, but they were also split between water and land, between an idealized world of perfect *otium* or leisure, and a world of profound dangers. As such, gardens were the perfect controlled space in which the Roman

[89] See, for example, Casey (2002) and the images and discussion in Wilton and Barringer (2002).
[90] For parallels to this violent gaze in the arena, see Brown (1992).
[91] Leach (1988), 123–32; Hales (2003), 153–7; von Stackelberg (2004).

city dweller could establish and articulate an individual response to the wider world.

This brings us back to the decorated summer *triclinium* in the House of the Ephebe. As discussed, the images of sex and violence which immediately catch the eye of modern visitors are complemented by a number of less violent scenes – a woman weaving, priests making offerings at a temple, and so on. Crucially, these include two scenes in which a number of pygmy diners sit at semi-circular dining benches (*stibadia*) – a type of furniture analogous to the *triclinium* on which they were painted.[92] In one of these scenes, the pygmies are continuing their party happily; in the other, they seem vaguely threatened by the presence of a crocodile in near vicinity. What is particularly important is where these *stibadia* appear within the frieze. One appears on the inside left of the *triclinium*, immediately in front of the place where the head of the household would be dining, according to the standard seating plans of the time.[93] The other was immediately opposite him, in front of his most respected guests. In other words, these images occupy the spaces that would be most frequently scrutinized by all of the diners in the normal course of a (socially deferential) evening meal. As a consequence, the paired *stibadium* scenes would have been the most visible, and the diners would immediately have been confronted by a distorted image of their own situation in the Nilotic art before them. The precision of this *mise-en abîme* meant that at every level, the diners would not only have looked out at the imperial world beyond Italy, but have peered back at themselves in the distorting fun-house mirror of these images.[94]

Where the Egyptianizing prospects of Pompeii differed from the villa landscapes of Statius and Pliny was in the exoticism of the subject matter. While the villa landscapes and texts evoked an ordered countryside with the viewing subject at its heart – an ideology, after all, which had motivated a great deal of Roman culture of the Augustan 'Revolution' – the Nilotic art expanded that gaze to the newly-conquered provinces of the east. The landlords of the Bay of Naples celebrated or imagined the seignurial view from their own villa windows, but the householders of Pompeii were evidently more ambitious and dreamt of gazing over the distant Nile valley. In part, these aspirations may be dismissed as conventional fantasy: the Egyptian paintings were simply a stock series of visual tropes which were no more intended to evoke a specific provincial landscapes than were

---

[92]  Maiuri (1938), 24–5.     [93]  On *triclinia* and dining conventions, see Bek (1983).

[94]  For other images of dining in Roman dining areas, see D'Arms (1999). For a similar response to a similar scene, see Clarke (2003), 191–2.

the sacral-idyllic vignettes that Pliny associated with Studius. As such, the immediate function of these vistas was to convey a sense of Hellenistic *paideia* to an audience with aspirations to aristocratic cosmopolitanism. Yet this was also a political assertion in itself. By the first century CE, Roman aristocratic power was no longer framed within a purely Italian context, but could be expressed through claims to authority over a far wider area. In embedding themselves in this landscape, Roman viewers could implicitly declare their membership of an impeccably Mediterranean elite.[95]

The other key difference between the Egyptianizing paintings of Pompeii and the villa landscapes of Pliny and Statius is the identity of the viewers themselves. Throughout this chapter, I have discussed these paintings as manifestations of an essentially male, aristocratic relationship to the expanding empire. This is entirely justifiable on one level – after all, these paintings are likely to have been commissioned by [male] heads of household, primarily for their own contemplation, or for the pleasure of their guests. As we have seen, moreover, there are strong correspondences between the representation of subordinate landscapes in these frescoes and that in the poetry and prose of our aristocratic (and male) authors. Yet we should not occlude other viewers so readily. There is good reason to suppose that landscapes were commissioned and enjoyed by an increasingly broad audience by the third quarter of the first century BC, at least in Pompeii. If this primary audience was still largely restricted to a relatively small number of male patrons, moreover, in most cases, the paintings would have been equally visible to the women, children and slaves who made up the considerable households of early imperial Italy. Landscape paintings may have placed the individual viewer in an extraordinary position of power, but this was a privilege which could be assumed by many different spectators at different times.

We should deal with the question of social standing first. Unpicking the demographics of Pompeii remains a challenging proposition, but we can draw very broad conclusions about the viewers of the friezes in the House of the Ceii, the House of the Ephebe and the Praedia of Julia Felix – the three principal examples within this chapter.[96] Crucially, the

---

[95] *Pace* Fitter (1995), 44, who argues that the prevalence of 'imagined' sacral-idyllic landscapes was a function of the loss of genuine aristocratic power in the early Principate and represented a retreat into a world that *could* be dominated. The specific details of the Egyptian landscape, the prominence of other Egyptian geographical discourses (discussed elsewhere in this book), and the rising (rather than falling) social status of many of the householders with grand Nilotic prospects seem to argue against this interpretation.

[96] On demographic changes in decorative conventions in Pompeii's last years, see Leach (2004), 186–240.

viewers in these buildings were not from the very upper crust of Pompeian society (although some of them may have had ambitions in that direction). To judge from the electoral graffiti outside his door, Lucius Secundus Caius was a municipal office-holder in Pompeii, probably shortly before the eruption of Vesuvius, although the moderate size of his house may imply that his rise to prominence had been relatively recent. Most scholars have suggested from independent textual evidence that Publius Cornelius Tragus was a freedman, although the ambition of his building project in knocking together several houses to make the House of the Ephebe may suggest that he was also on his uppers. Finally, the *triclinium* in the Praedia of Julia Felix was very probably occupied, not by a single privileged man or woman (and guests), but by the members or guests of the inn itself. We may assume from the relative splendour of the room's setting that this remained a relatively restricted privilege, and it was clearly one of the focal dining areas within the whole complex, but the point remains telling. These views were not restricted to the wealthy owners of Neapolitan villas, as were those described by Statius and Pliny, but were rather enjoyed by an upwardly mobile section of a small municipal elite. Equally, these views were not prescribed by the imperial state as an aspect of official propaganda, but were decorative schemes chosen by the patrons themselves.[97] Cornelius Tragus, Secundus Caius and the guests at Happy Julia's were not thoughtlessly absorbing imperial culture, they were actively appropriating it and asserting their own position at its centre.[98]

Precisely how the same landscapes were regarded by the other inhabitants of Pompeian households is less clear.[99] To a large degree, the women of the household must have been invited to share in the 'seignurial' gaze, even if this contemplation is never recorded textually. The same cannot have been true of slaves and servants: even if they could see the same paintings as the home-owners, they were in some senses excluded from the full implications of this contemplation. This is a contentious point, given the evidence available to us, but is perhaps best illustrated by returning to our opening examples. The internal frieze on the couches in House of the Ephebe would have been all but invisible to spectators who were not themselves seated within the garden. Similarly, the Nilotic decorations of the Praedia of Julia Felix would only be apparent to those positioned within the *triclinium* itself: servants could have seen the waterfall and the decorations on the back wall,

---

[97] Cf. Tybout (2003), 514 who notes the association of these artistic motifs with an upwardly mobile social class, but rejects the argument that they had a political dimension.

[98] Cf. Hales (2003), 135–66 on comparable examples of the 'trickle down' of artistic motifs.

[99] Clarke (2003) provides a starting point.

but would not have enjoyed the immersive experience that the decorators envisaged. In many other cases, the visual humour of the Egyptianizing art – the interplay of water and paint, the representations of sympotic debate and excessive consumption – were meaningful only when viewed at leisure by an audience who were themselves eating, drinking in a manner similar to the depicted figures. Servants and slaves may well have concurred in the view that the excesses of the Hellenistic world had been successfully translated to the Italian peninsula, but they were not themselves invited to participate fully in this. Even as the free men (and women) of Pompeii appropriated the ideology and imagery of imperialism for themselves, they excluded others from this discourse.

## Text and Image

By the end of the Julio-Claudian period, 'Nilotic' scenes would have been familiar to a substantial proportion of the Italian population. If Pompeii was at all typical of Italian towns at this time, then Egyptianizing art must have been widespread throughout the peninsula, and complete decorative systems such as those in the House of the Ephebe, the Praedia of Julia Felix and the House of the Ceii must have numbered in the hundreds, if not thousands. Crucially, these representations of Egypt appeared in a variety of different contexts – small, private rooms, reception rooms, gardens, baths and pubs – and it seems reasonable to regard this imagery as domesticated through its familiarity. These frescoes rapidly came to symbolize the *truphe* and *paideia* of the Nile valley at the time of the floods, and when Romans looked upon them from their own *stibadia*, *triclinia* or bath benches, they would have seen this Egyptian world transposed into a new and domestic cultural context. It is difficult to assess what impact this familiarity had upon the geographical 'poetics' of the period – the extent to which reference to the Nile in a history, poem or geographical text would immediately evoke images familiar from the bathroom, garden or inn for the reader – but it must have been considerable. For a man like L. Caius Secundus, the Nile was not just a river in Egypt or a name in a text, it was a combination of familiar – and domestic – images.

We can say rather more about the other side of this equation – how images like these shaped writers' understanding of the wider world, and the production of texts. For many audiences, domestic landscapes are likely to have been much more familiar points of geographical reference than were monumental chorographies or the triumphal trophies discussed in the earlier chapters. Writers of more formal geographical accounts seem to have been sensitive to this and tailored their accounts appropriately. The point is illustrated especially clearly by Strabo's exasperated statement on the pygmies of Egypt and Ethiopia:

> Perhaps because they are naturally small, Pygmaians have been conceived of and fabricated, since no man worthy of belief has recorded seeing them.[100]

Strabo composed his work during the latter years of Augustus' rule and into the reign of Tiberius, when the pygmy caricatures of later decades were only starting to become widely known. Yet it seems likely that the popular misconception that he alludes to here can only have come from such paintings and mosaics. Textual authorities did refer to the diminutive inhabitants of the upper reaches of the river, of course, among them Herodotus and Homer.[101] But Strabo rarely took Herodotus to task, and normally defended Homer with considerable zeal: the myth he was challenging here was a contemporary one, and must have been prompted by the images that were so popular in the Augustan period.

By the time that Pliny composed his *Natural History*, visual Aegyptiaca was far more widespread. Like Strabo, Pliny was sceptical about traditions which identified groups of pygmies near the headwaters of the Nile:

> Some have situated a race of Pygmies among the swamps from which the Nile rises.[102]

Pliny may have had certain Greek authors in mind here, but this allusion also neatly evokes the popular images of domestic Aegyptiaca.[103] A more striking example is apparent in his account of the Tentyritae – the inhabitants of Middle Egypt – who are said to have harboured an unusual hatred of crocodiles.[104] Here again we can see visual convention informing geographical description, as much as the other way around. Pliny's account is especially illuminating:

> Moreover, there is also a group of people right on the Nile who are hostile to this monster; they take their name from the island of Tentyrus on which it dwells. They are of small stature but in this one thing only they have a spirit that is wonderful. The creature in question is terrible against those who run away but runs away from those who pursue it. But these men alone dare to go against them; they actually dive into the river and mounting on their

---

[100]  Strabo 17.2.1. tr. Roller (2014), 760.
[101]  Hom. *Il.* 3.2–6; Hdt. 2.31–2; 4.43. On these and other literary descriptions of pygmies, see esp. Dasen (1993), 175–82.
[102]  Plin. *HN* 6.188.
[103]  On possible Greek influences, cf. Desanges (2008), 168.
[104]  Cf. Also Strabo 17.1.44 and Sen. *QNat* 4a.2.15.

back as if riding a horse, when they yawn with the head thrown backward to bite, insert a staff into the mouth, and holding the staff at both ends with their right and left hands, drive the prisoners to the land as if with bridles, and by terrifying them even merely with their shouts compel them to disgorge the recently swallowed bodies for burial.[105]

This description sounds very much like the frescoes that we see in the House of the Surgeon, the House of the Pygmies or the Columbarium at Villa Doria Paphili. Indeed, Pliny's evocation of a single moment in the course of a hunt is so close to these images that a direct debt seems very likely. It is possible, of course, that certain texts described the hunting techniques that were common in the Nile valley, and that these accounts inspired both Pliny and the fresco painters, but this seems unlikely.[106] Instead, the striking detail of Pliny's account suggests that his account of the *Tentyritae* was inspired by the long-familiar visual convention.[107] The audience of the *Natural History* already had an image of Egypt in their minds when they encountered the text, and Pliny simply drew upon this and expanded it when creating his own representation of the river.[108]

A brief, final illustration may underscore the point. Juvenal's fifteenth *Satire* is a rather complex text, written in the early second century CE, and ostensibly concerned with a reported struggle between the Tentyritae and their neighbours the inhabitants of Ombi.[109] The *Satire* adopts an intriguing spatial organization, which owes a great deal to linear conceptions of the Nile, as we shall see in Chapter 5, but here it is a passing allusion which is most significant. Juvenal asserts the gravity of the events he is describing in striking fashion:

> Neither the dreaded Cimbrian hordes, nor the barbarous Britons,
> Nor the grim Sarmatians, nor yet the wild Agathyrsi raged
> With the utter frenzy displayed by that soft and worthless rabble
> Who are used to setting their tiny sails on earthenware vessels,
> And to bending over their miniature oars in painted potsherds.[110]

The humour of this hyperbole derives, of course, from the contrast between the unwarlike inhabitants of the Nile and the fearsome barbarians

---

[105] Plin. *HN* 8.92–3. after Rackham 1940: 67–9.   [106] Contra McDaniel (1932), 265–6.

[107] Whitehouse (1979), 34 notes that the elaboration of this account by Solin. *Collect.* 32–37 may also have been made with reference to a painting.

[108] Cf. also Herodian 1.15.45 on the *venationes* that Commodus organized between strange animals from India and Ethiopia 'known only from pictures', and the familiarity with elephants implied in Achilles Tatius, *Leucippe and Clitophon* IV.4. which refers to both 'experts' and 'pictures' when two individuals are comparing a hippo (in front of them) with elephants (known only at second hand).

[109] Swetnam-Burland (2015), 167–81.   [110] Juv. 15.124–8. tr. Rudd (1991), 135.

of the popular imagination, and that between the diminutive figures of from Tentyra and Ombi and the famously gigantic northerners. But the proliferation of pygmy scenes in early imperial Italy provided Juvenal with a ready stock of images upon which to draw, and the poet evidently intended to acknowledge this. The tiny sails (*parvula . . . vela*) and miniature oars (*brevibus . . . remis*) are familiar tropes in the paintings and mosaics of Pompeii and emphatically identify the Egyptians of the poem as caricatured pygmies. This clear visual parallel also creates a pun out of Juvenal's 'earthenware vessels' (*fictilibus . . . phaselis*) and 'painted potsherds' (*pictae . . . testae*). There is little doubt that these were intended as an allusion to the 'painted vessels' (*pictis . . . phaselis*) of the fourth *Georgic*, and Pentheus' 'painted ship' (*pictae carinae*) in the *Metamorphoses*, and hence perhaps as a comic deflation of Virgil's celebration of the fecund Nile, but they also evoke the material depiction of these familiar scenes in Roman domestic contexts.[111] The boats of Juvenal's pygmies were a familiar and comic sight to his readers precisely because they had been so widely painted.

What impressions of the Nile, then, would this visual culture encourage, and how would this compare to the authoritative textual geographies of the period? To judge from Strabo and Pliny, the proliferation of wall-paintings and other imagery led at least some viewers to believe that many of the inhabitants of the region were dwarfs or pygmies. In itself, this is not surprising, but less literal interpretations of these landscapes are likely to have been still more pervasive. The political understanding which motivated the commissioning of these paintings, and which they in turn supported, was that this was an essentially *Roman* territory. That is, it lay beneath the benevolent imperial gaze of the city and its inhabitants. The representation of Egyptians as dwarfs, and the brutal depiction of their painful suffering, lent a new dimension to this view of the wider empire. Roman and Pompeian citizens would be familiar enough with the images of the captive Nile from triumphs, or of its abject and defeated gods from poetry, but wall-paintings helped to affirm this subjection in their very domestic spaces. It also allowed them to assume a role for themselves in this imperial domination.

The very proliferation of this form of landscape art occluded some other forms of geographical representation, and complemented others. The visual stereotype of Egypt in domestic interiors was of a fabulous, but essentially repetitive territory – a region which could be economically represented by

---

[111] Verg. *Georg.* 4.289; Ov. *Met* 3.639. On the borrowing, cf. Courtney (1980), 607 who identifies this as 'a purely literary flascule taken from Vergil (who intends a different type of vessel) and Ovid.'

a typical landscape scene on the banks of the Nile. In some senses, this corresponds to the geographical metonymy propounded by the triumphs – that 'Egypt' could be collapsed into a single toponym or symbol, and be redeployed in new, Roman settings. As Pliny tells us in an anecdote about the Hellenistic painter Nealkes, a Nilotic scene could easily be signified by a vignette of a crocodile and an ass, and so save the artist the effort of distinguishing between the waters of the Nile and those of the Ocean.[112] Significantly, there is no room in any of these domestic representations for identifiable geographical locations or for recognizable individual figures. Egypt was never signified in the domestic sphere by a pyramid as it was in later periods of European Egyptomania. Occasionally an *osireon* may be identified or a temple is shown to be dedicated to Sobek or to Horus, but again these are generic temples and not specific buildings. Much the same is true of the occasional obelisks. As far as we can tell, there are no representations of Alexandria, Memphis or the Cataracts in Pompeii, there are no pyramids and no Nilometers. Crucially, this also extends to many of the most familiar textual *topoi* that were associated with the river. The Nile is always shown in flood, but there is no direct allusion to the causes of this phenomenon, or to the unknown origins of the river. Nothing is shown of the Nile Delta (except obliquely), or of the famed seven mouths of the river. Some of these aspects of the Nile would have been difficult to represent visually, of course, but it is as well to remember that literary tropes were not the only cultural commonplaces in this period.

Perhaps the most striking aspect of these early imperial representations of Egypt is that artists could confidently represent the Nile without recourse to the personifications so familiar from other media. As we have seen, statues of the Nile God were probably a well-known sight by the end of the first century: the Vatican Nile provides one example, and similar (smaller) figures are also known from Pompeii.[113] It is also likely that the many individuals who viewed these paintings were familiar with the triumphal representations of the river. And yet these forms were never – or almost never – employed in interior decoration until the high imperial period.[114] When in their own domestic environments, spectators in Italian towns were less interested in the Nile as an abstracted geographical concept, or as

---

[112] Plin. *HN* 35.142.

[113] This was situated on the ornamental canal in the large garden of the House of Octavius Quarto (also referred to as the House of Loreius Tiburtinus) (II.2.2). On which see Zanker (1998), 145–56; and (on the statue) Klementa (1993), 13–16.

[114] The exceptions are the representation of the Nile in the Temple of Isis in Pompeii, and the similar image from the House of the Duke D'Aumale (VI.7.15) on which see below, 185–8.

a puzzle to be solved, than as a foreign landscape to be contained and laid before them as evidence of their own self-confident power.

In other ways, the visual representations of the Nile corresponded to textual assumptions. Perhaps the most consistently represented aspect of Egyptian life in text and image was its intense religiosity. Almost every large fresco depicts at least one temple, and in many cases the specific statuary or architecture of the temples allows the viewer to identify the Egyptian god being honoured. The strong religious associations of the Nile are very well known and are discussed in more detail in the next chapter: at the very least, this was a caricature of the riverlands which remained central. The enthusiasm with which Nilotic fauna were depicted in many images may also be connected to this. Although Roman consensus seemed to view Nilotic religion with a bemused tolerance, and there were many adherents of these cults within Italy, the denigration of Egyptian religion as the practice of unhinged animal-worshippers did not lie far below the surface, as Juvenal's satires and certain passages of the *Aeneid* may show.[115] It may have been for this reason, then, as well as their inherent curiosity, that the fauna of the Nile are also a common feature of this Egyptianizing art. This, too, was crucial to much geographical writing on the river – indeed, the presence of Nilotic animals was adduced by a number of writers as proof that different watercourses were in fact connected to the river.[116] In this sense, the animals did not so much inhabit the Nile as define it: and this point is well supported by the visual evidence.

## Conclusions: The Power of the Gaze

Domestic landscapes of Egypt were widespread in Pompeii from the last decades of the first century BCE, and would seem to have enjoyed comparable popularity elsewhere in late Republican and early imperial Italy. This peculiar decorative convention has been variously explained by modern scholars, who have suggested that the images were intended for entertainment, as markers of religious affiliation, or as apotropaic symbols. Given the variety of contexts in which these images appeared – and their surprising longevity – it is likely that these images were prompted by a variety of stimuli and fulfilled many different functions. Irrespective of their primary function, however, it seems clear that images of this kind provided an

---

[115]  The scholarly consensus has long been that the Romans viewed the Egyptians with hostile disdain. See, for example, Smelik and Hemelrijk (1984), Alston (1996) and Versluys (2002), 428–34. Gruen (2010), 76–114 demonstrates that this caricature was not all-pervasive.

[116]  See 45 above.

important means by which a diverse population in Roman Italy engaged with the newly-conquered territories of the empire and enacted their own position in response to it.

This chapter has argued that these perspectival landscape paintings were intended to place their viewers in a privileged position, and that this was part of their appeal. Audiences to these works gazed upon a dominated world, even one that was far distant from them. This was a more complex operation than might be thought – landscapes could be idealized and caricatured, and part of the appeal was the knowing collapsing of boundaries between the viewer and the viewed. But what we see here is a strikingly direct engagement with the practical political power of the empire, even on the part of minor provincial aristocracies. These landscapes testify to a view of the world that was not mediated by official forms of geographical writing or display, and indeed took its power from the immediacy of the engagement that it promised with the world. Far more people would have seen landscapes like these than would have seen public chorographies, and some sense of the impact that they had is evident through textual responses to them. Strabo and Pliny struggled to correct some of the misconceptions that these images generated, even as they deferred to them in certain contexts. Viewed collectively – and alongside other forms of geographical representation in use at the time – these landscapes were an important medium by which members of an imperial society could establish their own position within the world.

# CHAPTER 4

# Creatio ex Nilo

## *Metaphysics and the Unknowable River*

So when the seven-mouthed Nile has left at last
The sodden acres and withdrawn its flow
Back to its ancient bed, and the fresh mud
Is warmed by the bright sunshine, farmers find,
Turning the clods, so many forms of life,
Some just begun, still in the stage of birth,
Others unfinished, short of proper parts,
And often, in one creature, part alive,
Part still raw soil. Because when heat and moisture
Blend in due balance, they conceive; these two,
These are the origin of everything.
Though fire and water fight, humidity
And warmth create all things; that harmony,
So inharmonious, suits the springs of life.[1]

Ovid's allusion to the Nile in the opening book of his *Metamorphoses* surpasses even the familiar tropes of Egyptian fertility. As the flood waters of the river recede, the farmers of Egypt discover creatures on the very cusp of animate life, a visceral anticipation of the kind of physical transformations that Ovid will later celebrate at length over the course of his great poem. But this is an uneasy, even uncanny, transformative power, which recalls each year the origins of life on earth. When the farmers, the poet and his audience contemplate the 'inharmonious harmony' – *discors concordia* – of the unique Egyptian river, they also confront the vertiginous prospect of something much, much bigger.

The significance of this Nile analogy can only be appreciated by considering Ovid's peculiar fusion of scientific and mythic motivations in the *Metamorphoses* more broadly, and to the varied cosmological tenets in circulation at that time. Composed in around 8 CE, the *Metamorphoses* sits

---

[1] Ov. *Met.* 1.422–32. tr. Melville (1986), 19.

among the most brilliant works of the Augustan period.[2] It is widely known as an appropriation of Greek and Near Eastern myths within a Latin epic framework, in which the familiar gods and heroes of the Mediterranean world are presented in a collage of mutation and transformation. But Ovid was not only interested in reinventing classical aetiologies for a new audience, and the first few hundred lines of the *Metamorphoses* directly address the origins of the universe itself. In the opening sections of the poem, Ovid describes the original creation of matter from chaos, the fusing together of the four elements of fire, water, earth and air, and the gradual emergence of life.[3] He describes the creation of mankind, and its subsequent history, from the paradise of the golden age down to the conflict and corruption of the age of bronze.[4] Eventually, the sins of mankind become too great: the religious transgressions of the shepherd Lycaon incur the wrath of Jove, who is first tempted to destroy the world, and then submerges it beneath a great flood – an episode replete with paradoxes which Ovid describes with particular delight.[5] Only Deucalion and Pyrrha survive the flood, but they repopulate the world through the ritual casting of stones, from which a new race of humanity is born.[6] It is in this second narrative of human creation that Ovid invokes the Nile, not simply as a noteworthy phenomenon in its own right but as a comprehensible analogy to the colossal organic rebirth that he relates. By contemplating the Nile floods, Ovid implies, the contemporary reader might begin to understand the great physical processes which created the world as a whole.[7]

The association between the regenerative properties of the annual Nile floods and the original creation of the world was not unique to the *Metamorphoses*. Ovid's own imagery was substantially shaped by earlier natural philosophy. His opening description of the fusion of the elements and the creation of order from Chaos was clearly indebted to earlier Stoic philosophy and would find an echo in the writing of the Younger Seneca two generations later.[8] His somewhat unsettling image of the almost haphazard coming together of living beings also bears comparison with the work of the pre-Socratic philosopher Empedocles, and the later compositions

---

[2] The bibliography on the *Metamorphoses* is substantial. Fantham (2004) provides an accessible introduction.
[3] Ov. *Met.* 1.5–75. Bömer (1969); Myers (1994).     [4] Ov. *Met.* 1.76–150.
[5] Ov. *Met.* 1.163–312.     [6] Ov. *Met.* 1.348–437.     [7] Ahl (1985), 119–123; Myers (1994), 42–5.
[8] Cf. Ov. *Fast.* 1.105–110 for a similar cosmology. On Stoic cosmologies, see esp. Mader (1983), Long (1985), Todd (1989) and the discussion of Seneca's *Natural Questions*, below. On Ovid's debts see esp. Wheeler (1995).

of the Epicureans.[9] Even the specific invocation of the Nile has some precedent. The historian Diodorus Siculus, writing in the middle decades of the first century BCE, opened his own vast *Library of History* with a survey of Egypt, in large part because he assumed it to be the most ancient region of the world.[10] Diodorus drew upon a variety of Hellenistic sources in this section of his work, primarily the writings of Hecataeus of Abdera and Agatharchides.[11] These accounts are not always consistent, but together they provide a compelling collective case for the primacy of Egyptian history, based on the unique nature of the Nile Valley itself. Diodorus argues that animals must have emerged first in Egypt because the Nile easily nourished the plants which animals required for food; he then adds that the intense fertility of the soils of the Thebaid still exhibit the spontaneous generation of animal life, in the manner of original creation.[12] Changing tack slightly, Diodorus suggests that Egypt may well have been spared the worst excesses of Deucalion's flood (and hence might have preserved the few remnants of human life), thanks to the lack of rain in upper Egypt.[13] Even if it did not, he argues, the creation of life through the fusion of heat and moisture must have taken place in Egypt originally, because it still does each year. Here, we see in Diodorus' Greek prose a comparable image to the Latin verse of the *Metamorphoses*:

> For when the moisture from the abundant rains, which fell among other peoples, was mingled with the intense heat which prevails in Egypt itself, it is reasonable to suppose that the air became very well-tempered for the first generation of all living things. Indeed, even in our day, during the inundations of Egypt the generation of forms of animal life can clearly be seen taking place in the pools which remain the longest; for, whenever the river has begun to recede and the sun has thoroughly dried the surface of the slime, living animals, they say, take shape, some of them fully formed, but some of them only half so and still actually united with the very earth.[14]

Diodorus probably took this image from Hecataeus, but it proved to be a popular one within the Roman world.[15] Pomponius Mela relates how the Nile 'even pours out the breath of life in clumps of silt and from

---

[9]  Nelis (2009), 254. Gregory (2007), 78–101 provides a convenient summary of Empedocles' cosmogony. On Epicurean writing, see also the discussion of Lucretius, below.

[10]  On this work, see esp. Burton (1972); Spoerri (1959), 34–5, 117–8 discusses specific comparisons between Ovid and Diodorus.

[11]  Diodorus' debts have been much disputed. Murray (1970), 144–5 argues for extensive dependence on Hecataeus, Burton (1972), for a more varied group of influences.

[12]  Diod. Sic. 1.10.1–3.     [13]  Diod. Sic. 1.10.4.

[14]  Diod. Sic. 1.10.6–7. tr. Oldfather (1933), 37.     [15]  Murray (1970), 150.

the very soil fashions living creatures.'[16] Pliny describes the mice that are found when the Nile flood retreats – half alive from the generative water, and half still formed of the soil.[17] Perhaps the most revealing case is Virgil. In his fourth *Georgic*, the poet takes the common motif of the *bugonia* – the process by which a farmer might create a new swarm of bees from the carefully-treated carcass of a bullock – and presents it in the world of the flooded Nile, where 'the black sands fertilize green Egypt'.[18] This can hardly have been useful practical advice for the typical Roman beekeeper, but it fitted well with the contemporary view of the uncanny fertility of the Egyptian river and its links to the grand cycles of cosmic time.[19]

The present chapter explores the metaphysical associations of the Nile from two different directions. The first part of the chapter explores the appearances of the river in the natural philosophy of the later Republic and early empire, through particular focus on Lucretius' *On the Nature of Things* (*De Rerum Natura*) and the *Natural Questions (Naturales Quaestiones)* of the Younger Seneca. For both writers, the Nile was interesting chiefly because it defied straightforward explanation. Although they devoted varying amounts of space to the problem of the floods, Lucretius and Seneca essentially approached it in the same way: rather than rule definitively on the likely cause of the inundation, each took the opportunity to explain the processes of reasoning by which a philosopher might tackle such seemingly insoluble problems. To accomplish this, each adopted a doxographical approach, listing the different theories that earlier scholars had proposed. This had the obvious advantage of establishing the scholarly authority of the philosophers, but it also succinctly defined the limits of human scientific knowledge and allowed each to lead his audience on to the contemplation of issues still greater – and more troubling. For Lucretius, these included human mortality, the absence of divine providence and the scale of the cosmos; for Seneca, the transience of worldly experience and the notion of the great cosmic cycles by which the universe would eventually be destroyed.

---

[16]  Pomponius Mela 1.52. tr. Romer (1998), 49.

[17]  Plin. *HN* 9.179; McCartney (1920), 109 sets these passages within their wider context.

[18]  Verg. *Georg.* 4.281–332, esp. 287–94. The line *et viridem Aegyptum nigra fecundat harena* is line 292. On the sequence, see Lambert (2003).

[19]  Cf. Wild (1981), 95–7. The trope proved to be a long-standing one. Burton (1972), 52–4 cites an exchange between Alexander Ross and Sir Thomas Browne in the eighteenth century. Faced by the latter's scepticism on spontaneous generation, Ross declared: 'Let him go to Egypt, and there he will find fields swarming with mice, begot of the mud of the Nylus to the great calamity of the inhabitants.'

Natural philosophy was not the only medium through which the Nile was connected to grander, metaphysical themes. The second part of the chapter examines the impact that Egyptian religion and theology had on the early imperial world, particularly outside the Nile Valley. To do this, it looks first at the attempts made to reconcile the cosmology of the region with Graeco-Roman thought. The fragmentary writings of Chaeremon, an Alexandrian priest at the court of Nero, provide one starting point for this investigation, and Plutarch's treatise *On Isis and Osiris* another. In each case, Egyptian mythology was clarified through comparison with Stoic and Platonic physics. Equally important, however, were the religious associations of the river, in both ritual and theological terms. The final section of the chapter considers Nilotic theology in Plutarch's text, an imperfect reflection of the religions as they were practiced in Egypt, but an illuminating perspective on a very different form of Nilotic sublime from those articulated by Lucretius and Seneca. Plutarch notes the Egyptian conviction that the flood waters were a direct connection to the primordial substance of creation, were the divine Osiris made manifest, and hence were worthy of worship in their own right. This provides a point of departure for an analysis of the different representations of the river that appear in the Temple of Isis in Pompeii. Crucial here is a small rainwater cistern within the temple complex, which was evidently intended to collect water for ritual and other uses. In the light of Plutarch's theological discussion, and similar structures known elsewhere in the empire, this reveals a mode of containing and reproducing the Nile that is quite unlike any other medium. Considered alongside other features in the same temple, moreover, which include a well-accomplished personification of the Nile in a high-status fresco, a series of smaller landscapes and a somewhat schematic rendering of an episode from the myth of Isis, this is a reminder of the multitude of different associations that Roman audiences might draw with the river. Where other media represented the river as a domesticated landscape to be gazed upon, the object of prosaic or poetic description, or a personification of a captured region, such waters formed a living geography that was much less easily contained.

## Lucretius, the Nile and the Nature of Knowledge

The *De rerum natura* of Titus Lucretius Carus was foundational in the development of Roman natural philosophy. It also helped establish the value of the Nile as an object for contemplation in the Latin west. Written in around 60 BCE, Lucretius' text was justly celebrated as a clear articulation of the philosophy of the Hellenistic thinker Epicurus of Samos, and as a seminal work of Latin verse in its own right.[20] The separate books of the poem systematically lay out the physical and metaphysical underpinnings of Epicureanism, the form and movement of atoms, human mortality, the nature of human perception, the creation and ultimate destruction of the universe and finally (the book that will concern us most here), the physical explanations for some of the more unusual and terrifying phenomena within the terrestrial world.[21] Lucretius' fundamental moral concern in his work was to demonstrate the irrationality of belief in the gods, and to encourage his audience to attain emotional tranquillity through an appreciation of the deeper rhythms of natural philosophy. The Nile had a subtle but significant role to play within each of these ambitions.

It is worth stating immediately that Lucretius did not regard the flooding of the Nile as a model for understanding the origins of the world, or for the creation of terrestrial life, in the manner of Ovid or (as we shall see) Seneca. Where the later writers suggested that these new life-forms, annually struggling forward from the Nile mud, were evidence for the workings of benevolent natural forces, Lucretius includes no such reassurance. His cosmogony was determined by chance and had no place for the phenomena witnessed each year along the banks of the Egyptian river. Indeed, when he describes the spasmodic origins of animate life, in a passage which closely anticipates the later authors, Lucretius includes no reference at all to the annual Nile floods.[22] Instead, the Nile surfaces only in the last book of *On the Nature of Things*.[23] Here, Lucretius recapitulates the essential contention of the epic as a whole – that only a firm understanding of nature would dispel human fears. The poet argued that an ignorant observer could be driven to anxiety by many things. These might include the bleak mysteries of death, but also cataclysmic events that could befall the physical world at random, or even by puzzling natural phenomena that defied straightforward explanation, and so unsettle the unwary thinker. To this end, Lucretius addresses several of these issues, in order to demonstrate that systematic reason might confront even the most intractable of problems and provide intellectual reassurance in the face of terror of the unknown. The best-known of these are the discussions of thunder

---

[20] The collected papers in Gillespie and Hardie (2007) provide a valuable introduction to *De rerum natura*.

[21] Gregory (2007), 173–86 neatly summarizes Epicurean ideals of Creation. On Lucretius' view of the 'laws' of nature, see also Lehoux (2012), 47–76.

[22] Cf. Lucr. 5.449–508,        [23] Lucr. 6.712–37.

and magnets, but Lucretius' account of the Nile flood also occupies an important place within the book, not least because of the deeper methodological point that it makes.[24]

Crucially, Lucretius does not simply state what he believed the causes of the Nile flood to have been, but rather sets about exploring the means by which the problem might be approached. To this end, he lists in turn the different explanations that had been proposed to explain the inundation.[25] First, he suggests that the floods may have been caused by the retarding effects of the Etesian winds, slowing the current of the Nile, and thus manifesting a grander struggle between the ice-bound north and the sun-baked south:

> It waters Egypt when the Days are hottest | Maybe because in the summer north winds blow, | in the season when so-called 'Etesians' rush | south, gusting against the current, slowing it, forcing | the waves to well upstream, to stand and flood. | Don't doubt, these storm-winds sweep against the current, | Roused by the icy stars of the North Pole, | While the Nile comes from the sweltering lands, the South, | Arising from the Black and sun-baked men, | deep in the region of the equal days.[26]

Lucretius' second suggestion is that the same winds combined with changing currents at sea to create sand-banks in the mouth of the Delta, and hence obstruct the debouchement of the river:

> Or it may be that a great clogging of sand | in the crosscurrents chokes the mouth of the river, | Sand that the wind-whipped ocean washes against it, | Making the outlet of the river less | Free, less of a ready downward glide for the water.[27]

Third, he suggests that the winds caused clouds to amass in the deep south during the summer and led to rains around the Nile headwaters:

> Or maybe too much rain at the headwaters | Falls in the summer, as the northern winds | Hurl all the clouds together to those parts. | Sure: when at the land of noon these far-hurled clouds | Arrive, they are pushed and packed together against | The mountain peaks, where they're wrung out by force.[28]

The final (brief) explanation is that it was only during the intense heat of this season that the snows of the region melted, and it was this water which caused the Nile floods:

---

[24] Lucr. 6.80–422 (Thunder); 6.909–1063 (Magnets).
[25] Bonneau (1964) and Postl (1970) provide thorough discussions of ancient theories of the Nile floods.
[26] Lucr. 6.714–23. tr. Esolen (1995), 220.      [27] Lucr. 6.724–8. tr. Esolen (1995), 220.
[28] Lucr. 6.729–34. tr. Esolen (1995), 220

Or in the heart of the Ethiopian mountains | Nile swells, where snow in the warmth of the gliding sun | Dissolves and runs cascading to the plains.[29]

None of these suggestions was original to Lucretius, and the origins of each can now be traced with a little effort, thanks to the tireless work of several modern scholars.[30] The first explanation, on the effects of the Etesian winds, for example, probably originated with Thales of Miletos, a philosopher of the sixth century BCE, whose theory was also followed by Herodotus and probably Agatharchides, who influenced Diodorus Siculus in turn.[31] The second and third of Lucretius' explanations are a little more difficult to trace. The clogging sands have been variously read as a variation of Thales' theory, as an Egyptian tradition, or as an original explanation of the mathematician Eudoxus of Cnidus.[32] The Atomist Democritus of Abdera may have deduced that the Ethiopian snows were responsible for the Nile floods, or this explanation may have come from autopsy as a result of expeditions into the Ethiopian interior, and circulated by Hellenistic writers.[33] Lucretius' final *doxa* can certainly be attributed to the fifth-century writer Anaxagoras, who is cited by name by Diodorus, and who also influenced Herodotus.[34]

This methodology of approaching a problem by listing the different theories that earlier scholars had proposed was a common feature of ancient natural history and philosophy, and was labelled 'doxography' by the nineteenth-century scholar Hermann Diels.[35] Lucretius was not the first writer to include a doxography on the Nile floods, and it remains possible that this section of *On the Nature of Things* was taken wholesale from a single Greek source, which the poet then translated and rendered in verse. In due course, Lucretius' summary was itself cannibalized by later writers. Consequently, much scholarship on this section of the poem has been concerned with locating Lucretius within this scholarly genealogy and has rather neglected the function of this passage within the work as a whole.[36] Various solutions have been put forward to explain and identify the poet's source for the Nile passage. Democritus, Eudoxus of Cnidus and Theophrastus have all been identified as possible influences, although it has also been argued that Lucretius drew directly on a summary of these works

---

[29] Lucr. 6.735–7. tr. Esolen (1995), 220.     [30] Bonneau (1964) discusses this tradition.

[31] Hdt. 2.20.2; Diod Sic. 1.38.2; Diog Laert. 1.37. Cf. Bonneau (1964), 151–60 and Feraco (2008), 586–8.

[32] Godwin (1991), 145; Feraco (2008), 589–601.     [33] Feraco (2008), 593–7.

[34] Diod. Sic. 1.38.4 and Hdt 2.22. Bonneau (1964), 161–8; Feraco (2008), 603.

[35] Diels (1879). On the origins of the term, and its application to ancient scientific practice, see Runia (1999), and cf. Van der Eijk (1999).

[36] Feraco (2008) provides a thorough critical survey of this scholarship.

by Epicurus.[37] It has also been suggested that Lucretius was influenced by the *On the Ocean* (*Peri Okeanos*) of Posidonius.[38] Most recently, Fabrizio Feraco has persuasively argued that Lucretius' principal influence was a lost Aristotelian work on the flooding of the Nile.[39] The most important piece of evidence for this is a medieval Latin treatise on the Nile floods, a later translation of what may well have been the work of Aristotle, but which has also been attributed to Theophrastus of Eresus.[40] While there are noteworthy similarities between the material presented in the anonymous treatise and the discussion in *On the Nature of Things*, it should also be remembered that Lucretius influenced the later Latin tradition considerably, as we shall see.

However derivative his doxography may have been, Lucretius' decision to include this material within *On the Nature of Things* remains significant, and the elegant versification was certainly the poet's own. Here we have to look beyond the specific theories that the poet puts forward and focus instead on his refusal to differentiate between them and make a clear statement about the explanation that he found most plausible. This was a common feature of doxographies of this kind, particularly where an accepted solution to a philosophical problem remained elusive, as was the case here. But the strategy also explains Lucretius' inclusion of this material, which would otherwise be tangential within his final book. The poet's essential point is to demonstrate that the process of investigation is more important than the identification of a definitive solution when confronting the mysteries of nature. His doxography – whether borrowed or otherwise – illustrates this clearly. Human reason, Lucretius implies, can provide illumination and moral consolation, even when firm conclusions remain elusive. He underscores this point with a surprising analogy in the short introduction to the Nile passage:

> There are some things for which it's not sufficient | to ascribe one cause – it's better to give many | and have one be right; as when you see far off | a corpse stretched on the ground, you guess each cause | of death, so that you'll hit upon the truth. | for you can't prove that he died by cold, or the sword, | or by disease or poison even – still | That he was caught by something of this sort | we know. The rule applies to many things.[41]

[37]  Suggested by Woltjer (1877), 153–4 and Pascal (1903), 184–94 and discussed by Feraco (2008), 583.
[38]  Rusch (1882).        [39]  Feraco (2008), cf. Bonneau (1964), 180.
[40]  Bonneau (1971b) provides an edition and translation of the text with a brief commentary, and states confidently that the work was Aristotelian. Sharples (1998), 197–9 outlines the scholarship which has associated the text with Theophrastus.
[41]  Lucr. 6.703–12. tr. Esolen (1995), 219–20

The crucial point here is that human reason might identify multiple causes for phenomena, even when it cannot discriminate between them. This was an important principle in Epicurean physics.[42] The knowledge that human reason could deduce an explanation even to the most intractable of problems – and the confidence that such an explanation certainly existed – offers Lucretius and his audience relief from anxiety about the mysteries of the natural world, and hence saved them from the need to turn to the gods in superstition.[43] Lucretius makes a similar point in his discussion of the movement of the stars in Book V, but the Nile passage is particularly emphatic.[44] Here, the doxography is tantalizingly open-ended, but each of the possibilities proposed by Lucretius draws upon basic principles of meteorological understanding that have already been developed elsewhere in *On the Nature of Things*. This makes the doxographical discussion more convincing in its own right, but it also integrates the Nile puzzle within the wider argument of the text and underscores Lucretius' essential point: the reader can draw confidence from the basic tools of philosophical enquiry, even when a particular issue seems to elude definitive explanation. Lucretius' seemingly inconclusive Nile doxography was not an evasion of the need to explain the inexplicable, it was an articulation of his own fundamental confidence in causal explanation, even in the face of seemingly impossible problems. It also established an implicit but persuasive image of the natural world in which the Egyptian river was subtly linked to celestial movements on the one hand, and human mortality on the other – a point that we explore in more detail below.

Lucretius was certainly not the first writer to adduce earlier scholarship in his response to the Nile flood, but the popularity of his work in the Latin west helped to underscore the image of the river as an essentially elusive geographical puzzle. The strategy was a relatively common one in Greek writing on the river in a variety of different genres, from Herodotus onwards.[45] Allusions in Diodorus and Strabo suggest that these discussions continued throughout the Hellenistic period, and it is likely that they shaped Lucretius' writing, as we have seen.[46] But regardless of this intellectual heritage, the image of the Nile as an essentially unknowable river proved to be a popular one in the Latin west, even in works that

---

[42] Long and Sedley (1987), 90–7; Godwin (1991), 143; Hardie (2008), 69–71.
[43] Lucr. 6.54–6.  [44] Lucr. 5.509–34 and cf. esp. 531–4. cf. Bailey (1947), 1660–2.
[45] Hdt. 2.19–26. Bonneau (1964), 135–214 on this tradition. For an example of the same practice in a rather different cultural context, compare Philo, *VM* 1.114–7 and the discussion in Pearce (2007), 219–22.
[46] Strabo 17.1.5; Diod Sic. 1.37–41; cf. Yoyotte, Charvet and Gompertz (1997), 74, n.58 Burton (1972), 137–41.

were not otherwise noted for their imaginative range. A long passage in the work of Pomponius Mela shows this well. In the first book of his prose *Chorographia*, Mela outlines four key explanations for the Nile floods fairly clearly – a long digression given the fairly brisk pace at which the work moves. In a competent and concise summary, Mela discusses theories about Ethiopian snowfall, the relative position of the sun in the summer, and the effects of the Etesian winds.[47] But the most intriguing interpretation is left to last. Here, Mela suggests that the origins of the river might perhaps be sought in the southern hemisphere:

> If however, there is a second world, and there are Antichthones located directly opposite to us in the south, that first explanation will not have departed too far from the truth. The river, originating in those Antichthonian lands, emerges again in ours, after it has penetrated beneath the ocean in an unseen channel, and therefore increased at the summer solstice because at that time it is winter where the river originates.[48]

This thesis is intriguing, but seems not to have been original to Pomponius Mela; Diodorus Siculus includes a similar passage in his own doxography, which some commentators have traced to Eratosthenes or the fourth-century astronomer Eudoxus of Cnidus.[49] It probably came to Mela through an intermediate source, although this text is impossible to identify. Mela is unusual, however, in the prominence that he grants to the thesis. In placing it last in his survey of the different explanations for the Nile flood, the chorographer emphasizes it most. Indeed, later attempts to render Mela's account as a map have frequently privileged this explanation in their representations of his world.[50]

Nile doxographies never became absolutely formulaic, but were widely adopted as a rhetorical strategy for charting the unsettling characteristics of the river in a variety of genres. In essence, the perpetuation of this tradition reveals a fascination with the ambivalence and uncertainty of the Nile floods and the river course, even in brief or derivative descriptions of the world. While the different solutions proposed were occasionally varied or confused, the acknowledgement that this was an area for natural philosophical speculation, rather than simple geographical description, remained important. The Nile gave writers the chance to advertise their

---

[47] Pomponius Mela 1.53.    [48] Pomponius Mela 1.54 tr. Romer (1998), 50.
[49] Diod. Sic. 1.40.3. Burton (1972), 140; Parroni (1984), 221. The theory is briefly discussed by Bonneau (1964), 176; Postl (1970), 29–30.
[50] Compare Bunbury (1883), II, 368, which traces the Nile to the Oceanic coast adjacent to the Antichthones; Silberman (1988), endpapers, map 1 and the various maps included in Brodersen (1994).

own intellectual authority, as the heirs to the classical and Hellenistic natural philosophers. Equally, it provided a subtle means to articulate their own particular sympathies – in Strabo's deference to Homer over more esoteric speculation for example, or Mela's ambitions to transcend however briefly the stage of the *oikoumene*.[51] But these themes depended upon the essentially unknowable nature of the Nile for their resonance. These accounts propound an essentially indeterminate image of the Nile: a river that *could* have its origins in the Atlas or the Anthichthones, that *may* have been flooded by the actions of the Etesians or the inflow of the Ocean, was at once imbued with all of these characteristics and none of them. The doxographic approach delighted in this geographical multiplicity, effectively shifting the unknowability of the river in the present, to the timeless speculations of the past. The Nile was important for its very uncertainty.

The Egyptian river fit Lucretius' arguments in several ways. It was a well-known puzzle of the natural world, which was increasingly familiar within Roman Italy in the middle of the first century; it had been discussed at length by generations of scholars, including some of the best-known philosophers, historians and poets of antiquity, and it was satisfyingly enormous in its dimensions: like Etna, or Ocean, the Nile was a vast geographical feature, made greater still by its mysterious aspects.[52] In this light, Lucretius' comparison of the study of the Nile to the examination of a corpse seems particularly significant. This connection is further underscored in the harrowing closing section of his work, in which he describes the terrible effects of the Athenian plague and identifies Upper Egypt as its likely source.[53] And yet in spite of their scale and the unsettling associations that they prompted, these phenomena were primarily important to Lucretius as mental stepping-stones to the contemplation of yet larger topics, rather than simply as objects of speculation in their own right. By looking first at the spectacular wonders of the terrestrial world, the viewer could prepare himself for the leap to a cosmic grandeur, and true enlightenment. This is the driving ambition of *On the Nature of Things* as a whole, and of its final book in particular. Lucretius makes the point clearly in opening his discussion of Etna 6.648–80:

> You must look deeply into these affairs, | long ponder every part, keep your scope wide, | remembering the vastness of the All, To see what a tiny

[51]  Strabo 17.1.5; cf. Bonneau (1964), 196–8.
[52]  The importance of the Nile as a particularly noteworthy object for appreciation of the natural sublime is briefly noted by Longinus, *Subl.* 35.4, alongside Etna and Ocean. On which see Porter (2007), 172–4.
[53]  Lucr. 6.1137–1285 at 1140–2.

proportion of the whole | is this one sky, what a trivial thing it is, | Less to the All than one man is to the earth.[54]

The Nile, too, could aid the initiate in making such a leap, first in its recognized status as one of the unique features of the world, *unicus in terris*, but also through Lucretius' repeated association between the river and death.[55] Like Etna or Ocean, the Nile is a big thing in itself; like the terrible Athenian plague, it forces its audience to contemplate human mortality, a still bigger thing. And yet Lucretius' demanded that his audience go still further – beyond the microscopic concerns of the terrestrial world or a single human life to infinity (and beyond). The Nile had always been an important subject for scholarly enquiry, but Lucretius' principal concern was to show just how insignificant it really was.

## Seneca and the Limits of Knowing

The fullest Latin doxography of the Nile – indeed the longest discussion of the river to have survived from classical antiquity – appears in the *Natural Questions (Naturales Quaestiones)* of the Younger Seneca. This work was composed towards the end of the philosopher's life in the early 60s CE.[56] Remembered in equal parts as the major champion of Latin Stoicism, and as tutor and advisor to the Emperor Nero, Seneca navigated between these seemingly irreconcilable positions in his natural philosophy.[57] Like Lucretius, Seneca wished to show how the calm contemplation of the natural world could provide consolation from the troubles of life, but the later writer was more concerned by the enervating effects of contemporary politics than superstitious fears of the gods. The details of Seneca's Stoic cosmology also differed markedly from Lucretius' Epicurean philosophy, and his much fuller discussion of the Nile was used to rather different ends.

The contemplation of the physical world was a central branch of Stoic philosophy, along with logic and ethics, with which it was intimately linked. Stoic cosmology was founded on the principle of cosmic sympathy and interconnectedness.[58] The whole of the universe was thought to be permeated with a divine spirit (*anima* or *pneuma*), often connected to a fiery

---

[54] Lucr. 6.647–52. tr. Esolen (1995), 218.     [55] Lucr. 6.713.

[56] Williams (2012) is an important recent study. See also Lehoux (2012), 77–105 on the influence of forensic rhetoric on Seneca's writing and Berno (2003) on the moralizing ambitions in the work.

[57] Griffin (1976) is the classic political biography in English. See also Griffin (2008) and Wilson (2014). On the political paradox in particular, compare Sullivan (1985), 115–44 and Roller (2001), 64–124.

[58] Todd (1989). Williams (2012), esp. 17–28 sets Seneca in this context (with more recent bibliography).

essence, and bound together in an essentially organic manner.[59] Cosmic time was cyclical in this Stoic world-view: the universe was created by the fusion of the elements, acting with divine inspiration, and would then grow and flourish organically, before reaching its end and subsequent rebirth in the watery cataclysm and fiery *ekpyrosis*.[60] According to this understanding, the universe, nature and the gods were simply different names for the same thing.[61] Contemplation of the workings of the cosmos was thus an ethical practice, which would lend the viewer an appropriate perspective on his place in the world.[62] This cosmology developed over time, and Seneca's inheritance of it was idiosyncratic – his own work readily combined Epicurean and other elements in order to make sense of the world.[63] Nevertheless, his presentation of the Nile was fundamentally shaped by these concerns: like Lucretius, he regarded the attempt to comprehend the physical world as a morally laudable activity, and the Nile provided an admirable focus for these efforts. Like Ovid, moreover – a poet whose evocative language he readily borrowed – Seneca also recognized that the Nile floods could help illuminate the grander cycles of cosmic time that might otherwise elude human understanding.[64]

The *Natural Questions* comprises seven (or eight) books, devoted to the major meteorological questions of the time. As such it adhered to a genre of scientific enquiry which was formalized by Aristotle, and popularized in the Hellenistic period, particularly by Stoic and Epicurean writers, and which Lucretius had already appropriated for a Roman audience.[65] Seneca did not stray far from the conventions of this tradition in the subjects that he chose to address, but he did so by combining an impressively wide reading in Greek philosophy with a direct engagement with Lucretius and other Latin poets. Although Seneca evidently cites some of his named authorities at second hand – particularly in his long doxographies – there is good reason to assume that the composition was not the slavish reproduction of earlier works, but represents a coherent philosophical and rhetorical composition of the writer's own.[66] Thanks to the vicissitudes of the medieval manuscript

---

[59] Cf. for example Manilius 1.247–54. On the changing vocabulary of Stoic physics, see esp. Lapidge (1989), 1381–6.

[60] See Cic. *Rep.* 6.23; Sen. *QNat* 3.13.1. On Stoic cosmologies see esp. Mader (1983); Long (1985); Todd (1989).

[61] Succinctly stated at, for example, Sen. *QNat* 2.45.1–3.

[62] See, for example, Sen. *Ep.* 88.26–7; 117.19; *De Otio* 5 with comments of Lapidge (1989), 1398.

[63] Lapidge (1989), 1397–1401; Gill (2003), 39–40.

[64] Sen. *QNat* 3.27.3–28.2 citing Ov. *Met* 1.272–3, 285–90, 304. On which see esp. Williams (2008), 239–40.

[65] Inwood (2002/2005); Taub (2003); Hine (2006). On this tradition more broadly, see Taub (2003).

[66] Williams (2012), 8–11; on the coherence of Seneca's rhetoric, see Lehoux (2012), 77–105.

tradition, the original order of the books of the *Natural Questions* has become confused, but a convincing consensus has now emerged. Most scholars now agree that Book III ('On Terrestrial Waters') was the first book of the *Natural Questions*, followed by Books IVa ('On the Nile' – a book which has been partially lost); IVb ('On Clouds, Rain, Hail and Snow'); V ('On Winds'); VI ('On Earthquakes'); VII ('On Comets'); I ('On . . . Fires') and II ('On Lightning and Thunder').[67] This interpretation of the structure of the *Natural Questions* is followed here, but in the interests of clarity, and for ease of reference to the standard editions, the conventional system of book-numbering is kept.

Sadly, Book IVa, 'On the Nile', only survives in part, but the section that has come down to us is still substantial.[68] This includes a long opening preface to Lucilius Junior, to whom the work as a whole is dedicated, a discussion of the origins and course of the river, and the first part of his account of the floods. Seneca's treatment of the Nile was much fuller than Lucretius', and the cosmology into which it fitted was rather different, but there are important similarities between the two accounts which are worth highlighting immediately. Like Lucretius, Seneca addressed the puzzle of the Nile floods through doxographical discussion and seems not to have identified their ultimate cause. It is likely that the philosopher had his own opinion on the matter, and there are hints that he understood the Nile to be connected to other rivers by subterranean channels, but this is never explicitly articulated in the extant sections of his work.[69] This reticence is particularly striking, given contemporary interest in the river. Nero had sent a small expedition upriver, which returned to Rome in the early 60s bearing new information on the course of the Nile as far as Meroe and the territories beyond. Seneca was certainly aware of this operation, and drew upon its report elsewhere in his work, but there was no place for autopsy in his discussion of the Nile.[70] Instead, his concern was to demonstrate the moral value of reasoning and disinterested reflection. Seneca wished the great puzzle of the Nile to be a jumping-off point for a contemplation of yet greater aspects of nature in much the same way as Lucretius did. Yet the eschatological underpinnings of Seneca's account were very different from those of his predecessor. These were effected primarily through the structural and thematic parallels which bound the discussion of the Nile in Book IVa to the account of terrestrial waters more broadly in Book III,

---

[67] Codoñer (1989); Hine (1996). Summarized in Inwood (2002/2005), 161–2 and Williams (2012), 13.

[68] Rossi (2012) surveys the scholarship on the book, and see also the bibliographical discussion in Pellacani (2012).

[69] Bonneau (1964), 173–4.

[70] Sen. *QNat* 6.8.3 on the expedition, and see below 206–15 and 270–3.

which immediately preceded it, and hence to much grander themes of cataclysm and *ekpyrosis*. Book III reflects at length on the different waters of the
world and culminates in an extraordinary account of the apocalyptic floods
which the Stoics believed would end life on earth. Seneca clearly intended
these two books to be read together, and thereby to draw the associations
between the grand cycles of cosmic time and the annual rhythms of the
Egyptian river. Like Lucretius, Seneca regarded the Nile as a starting point
for the contemplation of far grander themes; like Ovid (whom he quotes
with approval), he identified a particular connection between the floods
and creation itself.

Seneca's Nile doxography occupies the focal section of Book IVa and
provides the best place to start a closer reading of the text. The extant
text identifies four possible explanations for the flood, although it is likely
that the original account included a number of others. Conspicuously,
Seneca is also at some pains to identify the philosophers to whom each
of these proposals was attributed, although several of these names he may
only have known at second hand.[71] First is the theory that the Nile was
filled with melting snows from Ethiopia – a theory that Seneca associates
with Anaxagoras and the Greek tragedians, but which he refutes through
reference to other rivers and the known heat of the torrid zone.[72] The
next discusses the various theories associated with the Etesian Winds –
first Thales' arguments that the southerly winds retarded the outflow of
the Nile at the Delta, and then the claim of Euthymenes of Massilia that
he had seen the same winds blow waters into an Oceanic mouth of the
Nile during his voyage into the Atlantic.[73] Seneca's refutation notes the
contradictions between these arguments, the poor correspondence of
the Nile floods with the Etesians, and the copious evidence that the Nile is
a freshwater river.[74] The third explanation is that of Oenopides of Chios,
who argued that the river was fed from underground caverns, and that
the heat of the summer caused this water to expand and flood out into
the world; this was an explanation, as Seneca notes, which does not correspond to the behaviour of other rivers.[75] His fourth explanation is that
the heat of the southern summer sun draws the waters contained within
the earth towards it. Seneca ascribes this to Diogenes of Apollonia, but
again refutes it through reference to the behaviour of other rivers in the
world.[76]

---

[71] Pellacani (2012) provides a thorough discussion.
[72] Sen. *QNat* 4a.2.17–21. Cf. Bonneau (1964), 161–8; Diels (1969), 384–5.
[73] Sen. *QNat* 4a.2.22–3. Cf. Bonneau (1964), 143–6, 151–7.
[74] Sen. *QNat* 4a.2.22–5. Cf. Bonneau (1964), 143–6; Diels (1969), 387–92.
[75] Sen. *QNat* 4a.2.26–7. Cf. Bonneau (1964), 182–3.      [76] Sen. *QNat* 4a.2.28–30.

While the latter sections of Seneca's discussion have been lost, the broad outline of these passages may be inferred from two later redactions. Seneca's nephew Lucan drew upon the *Natural Questions* in his own treatment of the river in the last book of his epic *Civil War* – a text that is explored in much more detail in Chapter 6. A brief summary of Seneca's text had also survived in the treatise *On Months* (*De Mensibus*) of the sixth-century antiquarian John Lydus.[77] Lydus paraphrases each of the extant explanations, without dwelling upon their refutations. He also adds the theory that winds drove rain-bearing clouds down to the Ethiopian highlands, a suggestion that he attributes to 'Egyptians' and Thrasyalces of Thasos. The same source also notes Ephorus of Cyme's suggestion that the summer sun baked the soils of Egypt, and that the floods were a terrestrial 'sweat' of water, which would otherwise have been absorbed, and attributes to Dicearchus the identification of an Atlantic source for the Nile, which Seneca associated with Euthymenes.[78] Lucan is rather less systematic in his treatment of Seneca, and understandably tailored his account to the needs of his poem. Nevertheless, it seems clear that the *Natural Questions* was his immediate influence.[79] Like Seneca, he identifies several possible causes of the floods: Ethiopian snows, the power of winds (erroneously and probably deliberately labelled Zephyrs, rather than Etesians), fissures in the earth, an Oceanic mouth and finally Ethiopian rains. Neither Lydus nor Lucan states firmly which explanation he preferred.

Seneca does not seem to have been greatly concerned with the 'solution' to the puzzle of the Nile, although the loss of the latter part of Book IVa makes a definitive statement on this point impossible. It has been argued, for example, that he followed Aristotle's Nile treatise and left his preferred explanation until last, although Lucretius provides an equally compelling precedent for the opposite conclusion.[80] More immediately, the open-ended doxographies at the end of Book III, and his passing reference to the unknown source of the Nile, reveal that Seneca was not overly concerned to reach a definitive conclusion on every point, and was content to discuss different theories that others had put forward without making a final statement of his own.[81] Seneca may have regarded a report produced by Alexander's lieutenant Callisthenes as the last word on the Nile

---

[77] Diels (1969); Gross (1989), 170–82.

[78] Lydus, *De Mens* 4.107. These passages are helpfully translated in Hine (2010), 63–4.

[79] Diels (1969); Gross (1989), 170–4. For full discussion of Lucan's Nilotic geography, see Chapter 6, below.

[80] Hine (2006), 56–8 and Doody (2013), 290.

[81] Sen. *QNat* 4a.2.3. 'If the place from which it begins to rise could be discovered, the causes of its rising would be found.' tr. Hine (2006), 58. Note Williams (2012), 135: 'Given his lack of original

floods, as some have argued, but this seems particularly unlikely, given the his outspoken hostility to the Macedonian king.[82] Rather more convincing is the argument that Seneca's obvious fascination for the underground passage of waters betrays his preferred explanation for the Nile floods, but if this was the case he remains surprisingly silent on his conclusions in the extant portions of the text where that theory is discussed.[83] Regardless, what remains most noteworthy is that Seneca seems to have been much more concerned with establishing the methodologies of reasoning and explanation than he was with his final conclusions. This is particularly remarkable in the light of the information that was available to him.

The most conspicuous feature of Seneca's discussion of the Nile is the information that he chose not to include. Shortly before the completion of the *Natural Questions*, Nero's court celebrated the return of a military expedition that had travelled upriver at least as far as the imperial capital of Meroe, and may well have penetrated much further. These explorers had brought back reports on the upper course of the river, which were later incorporated at some length into Pliny's *Natural History*, and which are also noted in the sixth book of the *Natural Questions* (in Seneca's discussion of earthquakes).[84] The form that this expedition report took is important and is discussed in much more detail in the next chapter. Yet Seneca includes nothing on Nero's expedition in his discussion of the Nile floods. It is possible that the reports of the explorers came to Seneca only after he had completed his discussion of the Nile in Book IVa, and before he turned his attention to earthquakes in Book VI, but this is unlikely: it is difficult to imagine him not updating his earlier analysis when the new information became available, even if he had temporarily put it aside.[85] It could also be argued that this material was discussed in one of the sections of Seneca's doxography that has since been lost, but again this seems improbable. When the explorers' observations are finally introduced in Book VI, they are linked quite closely to the theory of underground caverns which Seneca associates with Oenopides of Chios in the extant section of his doxography.[86] Had Seneca included the explorers' reports in Book IVa, it would surely have been here: the fact that he did not, and that both Lucan and John Lydus are also silent on the expedition, is telling.

---

theorizing elsewhere in the *Natural Questions* . . . it is hardly likely that in the last portion of Book 4a he ventured a strikingly original explanation of the Nile's summer flood'.

[82] As argued by Pellacani (2012), 90–1. Seneca's hostility to Alexander is evident in Sen. *Ben* 7.2.5–3; *Ep.* 91.17, and cf. Ozanam (1990), 285–6.

[83] Gross (1989), 170 and 180 followed by Tracy (2014), 159–61.     [84] Sen. *QNat* 6.8.3.

[85] Suggested by Diels (1969), 406, n.1.     [86] Sen. *QNat* 6.8.3. And see also Sen. *QNat* 6.8.5.

Instead, Seneca's silence needs to be explained in other ways – first with reference to the wider didactic programme of the *Natural Questions*, and a form of philosophical enquiry that corresponded closely to Lucretius' earlier model, and second (and more cautiously) to the wider political points that Seneca may have wished to make.

Like Lucretius, Seneca regarded the practice of natural philosophy in essentially moralistic terms: physics and ethics were intimately related in Stoic thought, even if this was sometimes downplayed in the work of Roman writers.[87] By reflecting upon the grand rhythms of the natural world, he argued, an individual might find a metaphysical tranquility that could not be created by worldly success. Equally, the contemplation of nature could free the philosopher from the transient temptations of political life. Seneca establishes these points in the prefaces to Books III and IVa, respectively, and returns to these moral principles throughout his work:

> What is most important in human life? Not filling the seas with fleets, nor setting up standards on the shore of the Red Sea, nor, when the earth runs out of sources of harm, wandering the Ocean to seek the unknown; rather it is seeing everything with one's mind, and conquering one's faults, which is the greatest victory possible. There are countless people who have been in control of nations and cities, very few who have been in control of themselves.[88]

A similar travel metaphor recurs in different contexts elsewhere in Seneca's philosophical writing. In several passages, Seneca employs the image of the curious traveller in positive terms as an analogue for the restless enquiry of the philosophical mind: this is the sense intended in the very opening sentences of the *Natural Questions*.[89] Elsewhere, he adopts the well-worn *topos* of the journey as a metaphor for human life, particularly a life that has been well-lived; again, this is evident in the preface of the *Natural Questions*, and elsewhere in his work.[90] Yet the passage above is a reminder that travel could also stand for aimless and even counter-productive activity, which lacked the concentrated focus of the philosopher.[91] Where the philosopher was content to stand still and reflect, the endless kinesis of the wanderer

---

[87] Lapidge (1989), 1379–81; Ozanam (1990). On the moral ambitions of the *Natural Questions*, particularly as expressed through the Nile passages, see Berno (2003).

[88] Sen. *QNat* 3.Praef 10. tr. Hine (2010), 26–7.

[89] Sen. *QNat* 3.Praef.1. tr. Hine (2010), 25. Cf. *De Otio* 5, and the discussion in Montiglio (2006).

[90] Sen. *QNat* 3. Praef.4. tr. Hine (2010), 25. Cf. *Marc* 18, and again discussion in Montiglio (2006).

[91] Compare Sen. *Ep.* 2.1–3; 94.67–9; 101.6. (and, in a more positive vein, *Cons Helv* 8.1–9.8). Discussed by Veyne (2003) and Montiglio (2006).

(or soldier) frustrated true understanding. To Seneca, travel certainly had its advantages, but it was not unambiguously beneficial.

Seneca was concerned to value travel and exploration merely as a starting point for enquiry rather than as a laudable activity in its own right. Even his warmest celebrations of movement within the world are coupled with the firm imperative that the wanderer should allow time for internal reflection upon the marvels that he encountered. Perhaps the clearest illustration of this point is in one of his *Moral Letters*, and relates to the Nile:

> What travel will give is familiarity with other nations: it will reveal to you mountains of strange shape, or unfamiliar tracts of plain, or valleys that are watered by ever-flowing springs, or the characteristics of some river that comes to our attention. We observe how the Nile rises and swells in summer, or how the Tigris disappears, runs underground through hidden spaces, and then appears with unabated sweep . . . But this sort of information won't make better or sounder men of us. We ought rather to spend our time in study, and to cultivate those who are masters of wisdom, learning something which has been investigated, but not settled; by this means the mind can be relieved of a most wretched servitude, and won over to freedom.[92]

This tension between travel as a worthy stimulus for contemplation and as a distraction from the true concerns of the Stoic thinker is played out fully in the striking description of the Nile in the *Natural Questions*. Book IVa is introduced with the conceit that Seneca will help Lucilius escape from the political realities of his life in Sicily by taking him on an imaginary 'tour' of Egypt:

> So that I can get you completely away from there, even though there are many marvels within Sicily and nearby, for the moment I shall bypass all the questions associated with your province and shall draw your thoughts elsewhere. For I shall investigate with you the topic I postponed in the previous book, why the Nile floods as it does in the summer months.[93]

Seneca immediately makes good on this promise by transporting his reader to Egypt. His account of the region opens with a passing acknowledgement that the sources of the river are unknown, and a short account of the river itself. This description is somewhat notorious for Seneca's evident confusion of the islands of Philae and Meroe, an error that is all the more confusing in light of his personal familiarity with the country.[94]

---

[92] Sen. *Ep.* 104.15–16 after Gummere (1962), 199.    [93] Sen. *QNat* 4a.1.1. tr. Hine (2010), 57.
[94] Sen. *QNat* 4a2.3–5, the mistake is at 3. Cf. Williams (2012), 121 with bibliography. The afterlife of this error is briefly discussed at 264 below.

Equally important, however, is the evocative language that deployed in this section. The long description of the Nile that follows is a striking example of Senecan *enargeia* – of the conscious creation of evocative images through text.[95] This is apparent through the concentration of visual metaphors. The Nile is introduced as 'the most famous river that nature has exhibited to the eyes of man' (*nobilissimum amnium natura extulit ante humani generis oculos*), and the flooded river is described as a 'most beautiful sight' (*Illa facies pulcherrima est*) in a passage which also recalls the familiar wall paintings of Pompeii and Rome.[96] The Cataracts are a *spectacula*, its boatmen perform *miracula*, and their antics are watched by *spectatores*. Towards the end of his description, Seneca refers to the account of the prefect Cornelius Balbillus who witnessed a battle between dolphins and crocodiles in the Heracleotic Mouth of the river. This is framed like an amphitheatrical display, and it too is termed a *spectacula*.[97] Finally, the conflict between the Tentyritae and more crocodiles also recalls the imperial theatrical displays and wall-paintings of the time.[98] Throughout, the implication is that the identity of the Nile is strongly bound up in its appearance. The violent course through the Cataracts mean that the Nile 'no longer resembles itself',[99] and Seneca states that it is the invisibility of the Nile sources which mean that the causes of its unique behaviour cannot fully be understood.[100]

This is the Nile as an exotic visual distraction; it is sumptuously described, but Seneca's evocation of the river's *mirabilia* will not make a 'better or saner man' of Lucilius. This imaginative journey is just the first step in the programme of philosophical instruction, one which promises to break Lucilius free from the temporal world in which he is trapped, but only as a single stage on his route to enlightenment. The true substance of Book IVa is in the interrogation of the different explanations for the causes of the floods – a pattern of scientific enquiry that transcended the merely visual and depended ultimately on a grasp of the deeper patterns within the universe. Like Balbus, Cicero's fictional Stoic interlocutor in *On the Nature of the Gods*, Seneca recognized that true understanding transcended the limits of ordinary sight.[101] The point is underscored in the preface to Book I, in which Seneca notes that the contemplation of the divine in true

---

[95] On *enargeia*, see esp. Zanker (1981). On similar themes in Seneca's account of the cataclysm in *QNat* 3, see Williams (2012) 113–4.

[96] Sen. *QNat* 4a 2.1. tr. Hine (2010), 57–8.

[97] Sen. *QNat* 4a.2.13–4; cf. Plin. *HN* 8.91 on the same episode and Beagon (1996), 298.

[98] See André (2003), 183 on the visual nature of Seneca's description here; on this material, see 144–5 above.

[99] Sen. *QNat* 4a.2.5: *dissimilis sibi*.    [100] Sen. *QNat* 4a.2.3.    [101] Cic. *Nat D.* 2.45.

cosmology surpassed other branches of philosophy simply because it considered the beauties beyond ordinary sight.[102] The same was true on a more mundane level when it came to the Nile. The structural parallels between Books III and IVa underscore what was at stake in this. For all the appeal of the 'most beautiful sight' of the flooded Nile and towns standing out like islands, the attentive audience to the *Natural Questions* is encouraged to recall the image of similar settlements stranded on the brink of their destruction.

For Seneca, only the most authoritative autopsy could be accepted as evidence for the workings of the natural world; in other cases, only philosophical contemplation could offer satisfaction.[103] This also explains his reticence on Nero's Ethiopian expedition within this section of the *Natural Questions*. Seneca could never have said, as Pliny was later to do, that the explorers' reports had essentially brought speculation on the origins of the river to an end, and that theirs provided a definitive account on the upper reaches of the Nile Valley.[104] Instead, Seneca's epistemology demanded that his account remain open ended. The moralizing prefaces of Books III and IVa, in which grandiose imperialist conquest was contrasted unfavourably with philosophical contemplation, effectively invalidated the adduction of information gathered in such a manner. Equally, the implicit tension within Book IVa itself, between the superficial visual splendour of the Nile as seen, and the deeper cosmological implications that appropriate contemplation might bring forth, also effectively ruled out autopsy as a definitive mode of scientific enquiry. Indeed, it is significant that when Seneca does refer directly to the reports of the Neronian explorers, it is for what they suggest about the underground caverns of the world, and their effects on earthquakes, rather than for what they directly report about the origins of the Nile.

## Seneca's Nile and the Cycles of Cosmic Time

The fact that Seneca devoted the whole of the second book of the *Natural Questions* to the Nile gives some indication of its importance, but the river reappears throughout his text. Books III and IVa of the *Natural Questions* – the first two books in Seneca's original sequence – were certainly conceived

---

[102]  Sen. *QNat* 1.Praef.1–2; Williams (2012), 22.
[103]  On the value of autopsy within Seneca's methodology, see esp. Lehoux (2012), 77–105.
[104]  Pliny *HN* 6.184. See 210, below. On the political contrast between Pliny and Seneca in their treatment of the natural world, see esp. Hine (2006). On Seneca's hostility to other mundane rulers in *QNat*, see esp. Williams (2012), 33–5.

as a pair and need to be read in parallel.[105] At the start of his opening book, Seneca states explicitly that it will be concerned with all of the terrestrial waters apart from the Nile, and that the Egyptian river will be treated separately in the following book.[106] Yet this distinction is only ever nominal. At various points in Book III, Seneca notes the power of the Nile to improve human fertility, discusses the theorizing of Egyptian scholars on the hydrological cycle and – significantly – introduces the popular theory that great rivers like the Nile and the Danube were primordial waters.[107] For all of his assertions to the contrary, then, Seneca could not prevent these waters from mingling. When we assess the opening of the *Natural Questions*, we need to consider the first two books together.

The structural parallels between Books III and IVa are most obvious in Seneca's concern to connect the annual floods of the Nile and the cyclical destruction of the cosmos.[108] Book III ends with a long description of the watery cataclysm – or rather a series of possible cataclysms – which present nature at its most devastating.[109] Seneca admits that he is uncertain whether the deluge will start with excessive rains, the floods of rivers, the overflowing of the sea or all of these things – 'for such a great catastrophe does not have a single origin'[110] – but the devastating effects upon the familiar markers of human geography will be clear enough:

> So many famous names will disappear, the Caspian and Red Seas, the Ambracian and Cretan Gulfs, the Propontis and the Black Sea, when that deluge spreads a single sea over everything. All distinctions will disappear; everything that has its own place assigned by nature will disappear. No-one will be protected by city walls or by towers. Temples will be of no use to worshippers, nor the highest points of cities, for the waves will overtake them as they flee and pull them down even from the citadels.[111]

This horrific apocalypse contrasts directly with the effects of the Nile flood on Egypt explained in the following book:

> So the character of this river is remarkable, because, while other rivers wash away and gut the land, the Nile, so much larger than the rest, far from eating away or eroding the ground, on the contrary adds strength to it, and the least significant thing about it is that it controls the moisture of the

---

[105]  Demonstrated clearly by Waiblinger (1977) and see also Williams (2012), 93–135.
[106]  Sen. *QNat* 3.1.2. tr. Hine (2010), 28. And cf. *QNat* 3.26.1.
[107]  Sen. *QNat* 3.25.11 (fertility), 3.14.2 (Egyptian scholars' theories), 3.22 (primordial waters). The parallel between the Nile and Danube is further elaborated at *QNat* 4a.1.1–2.
[108]  Waiblinger (1979), 45–50; Williams (2012), 124–35.
[109]  Cf. also Sen. *Cons Marc* 26.6 and discussion in Mader (1983).
[110]  Sen. *QNat* 3.29.2. tr. Hine (2010), 49.     [111]  Sen. *QNat* 3.29.8. tr. Hine (2010), 50–1.

soil; for by importing mud it soaks and binds together the sand, and Egypt owes to it not just the fertility of the land but the land itself. It is a most beautiful sight once the Nile has poured across the fields. The plains are hidden, the valleys are covered and the towns stand out like islands. There are no communications between people living inland, except by boat, and the less people see of the land the more delighted they are.[112]

Ovid provides one fulcrum around which this opposition turns: the poet's evocation of Deucalion's flood is cited approvingly in Book III and, as we have seen this passage, also drew an important parallel with the Nile inundation.[113] But the thematic correspondences between the passages are also striking: where the global cataclysm will destroy the land, the alluvial silts of the Nile actively create it; where one flood brings anguish, removes human order, and makes momentary islands of towns and forts only to destroy them, the other leaves its observers delighted in an almost pre-lapsarian state of joy and idyllic isolation. Where one represents a return to primordial chaos, the other recalls nothing so much as the reassuring motifs on the domestic interiors of rich Roman houses. On the most immediate level, Seneca certainly intended this contrast to reassure his audience of the essentially benevolent nature of providence after the extraordinarily bleak picture at the close of Book III. While Seneca's picture of nature's sublime has obvious parallels to Lucretius' chilling image of an impersonal universe, the reassuring geography of Egypt reminds the reader that there is some order within this chaos, and that this is something to be celebrated.[114]

The annual Nile floods and the world cataclysm were also connected by their cyclical recurrence, and this plunges us back into the darker undercurrents within the structure of Seneca's text. Although one phenomenon recurred annually, the other only after innumerable centuries, this temporal relation is fundamental to the connection between the opening books. In the closing section of Book III, Seneca recasts his description of the terrestrial waters in order to show that the coming cataclysm has always been immanent in the waters themselves:

> Already from the first day of the world, when it separated out from formless unity into its present structure, the date when the earth would be drowned was decreed; and so that in the future the effort should not be difficult, as with an unfamiliar task, the seas have been practising for it . . . So the causes

[112]　Sen. *QNat* 4a.2.10–11. tr. Hine (2010), 59–60.

[113]　See Sen. *QNat* 3.27.3–28.2 citing Ov. *Met* 1.272–3, 285–90, 304. Cf. Williams (2012), 101 on Seneca's use of Ovid in the *QNat* see esp. Mazzoli (1970), 240–2.

[114]　Waiblinger (1989), 53–8.

of the deluge will come from all sides, since some waters flow under the earth, others flow around it; they have long been restrained, but they will be victorious, and will merge rivers with rivers, lakes with swamps.[115]

Time present and time past are perhaps present in time future: the behaviour of waters in the present both anticipates the cataclysm to come, and recalls the earliest origins of the world.[116] Equally, the formless unity of the future will be nothing more than a recreation of the chaos of origins. Crucially, the Nile is also situated within these cycles of deep time.[117] Elsewhere in Book III, in further contravention of his insistence that the Nile will be excluded from that section of the text, Seneca addresses this point directly:

> Some people also think that the rivers whose nature is inexplicable originated along with the world itself, for instance the Danube and the Nile, enormous rivers, too remarkable to allow us to say they have the same origin as the rest.[118]

Seneca does not state explicitly whether he accepted this theory that the Danube and Nile were primordial waters, but the association between the Egyptian river and the deeper cycles of cosmic time are strengthened by the allusion. Consequently, we can read Seneca's Nile as both a fragment of the larger whole (both terrestrial and cosmic) and a functional microcosm of it. The floods of the river may be couched as a reminder of the benevolence of providence, after the shock of this cataclysm, but they remain a firm reminder that the cataclysm is coming.

## Egyptian Cosmology and Roman Geography

The Nile descriptions of Lucretius, Seneca and Ovid deliberately flirt with grand and unsettling themes – suggestions of almost incomprehensible spans of time, of unplumbed depths within the interior of the earth and of the vast extent of the cosmos.[119] Comparable hints of the sublime can also be found in accounts of Egyptian wisdom by other Greek and Roman writers, particularly regarding the arcane cosmological knowledge thought to have been preserved for impossibly long stretches in the cryptic form of the hieroglyphs.[120] Given this parallel, it is noteworthy that the natural

---

[115] Sen. *QNat* 3.30.1, 4. tr. Hine (2010), 51.    [116] Waiblinger (1989), 52.
[117] Williams (2008), 235 and (2012), 126–7.    [118] Sen. *QNat* 3.22.1. tr. Hine (2010), 39.
[119] Bottomless holes – Strabo 17.1.52 following Hdt 2.28. cf. *QNat* 3.16.4–5 (not specifically Nilotic, but undeniably sublime).
[120] Cf. Pl. *Phdr.* 274C-275A and cf. *Philb* 18 B-C; Hdt. 2.109; Cic. *Rep.* 3.14; Diod Sic 1.81; Strabo 17.1.3; Tacitus also asserts Egyptian origins of writing in *Ann* 11.14. On this tradition, see esp.

philosophical tradition paid so little reference to how this Egyptian wisdom responded to the puzzle of the river. The doxographies of Greek and Roman scholars rarely engaged at any length with local speculation about the Nile. Herodotus gave Egyptian explanations short shrift in his own summary, simply because he found their discussions to be irrelevant.[121] Hellenistic writers within Egypt seem to have followed this precedent: Diodorus alludes to the wise men of Memphis, and may have drawn this material from Hecataeus of Abdera, but he did not discuss these theories in any detail.[122] Similarly, Seneca's account of the circulation of the world's waters makes reference to the elemental theories of the *Aegyptii*, but does not elucidate further. As we have seen, this was one of several points at which the Nile intrudes into the opening book of the *Natural Questions*, but it is conspicuous that this passage is not included in the account of the Egyptian river proper.[123] That Seneca, in particular, was aware of Egyptian philosophy is not to be doubted; as a young man, he had travelled to Alexandria for his health, and while there composed a treatise *On the Location and Rites of the Egyptians* (*De situ et sacris Aegyptiorum*), which has since been lost.[124] To judge from the one known fragment, this work included sensitive analysis of Egyptian religious rituals, which he may also have drawn upon in the *Natural Questions*, yet Seneca seems to have had little interest in the intellectual activity of the region.

This is not to suggest that Egyptian responses to the Nile were entirely ignored within the wider Greek and Roman worlds. Indeed, the metaphysical understanding of the river that had developed in Egypt had a profound influence throughout the Mediterranean, albeit in some rather unexpected forms. The failure of natural philosophers to engage with these traditions more directly can partly be attributed to ignorance, and partly

---

Iversen (1993); Klotz (2012); Hornung (2001), 1–68 (who terms this interest in Egyptian arcana 'Egyptosophy'); Tait (2003). Lindsay (1968), 97–104 surveys the territory. Irwin (1980) provides extraordinary comparanda from the nineteenth century.

[121]  Hdt. 2.19.

[122]  Diod Sic. 1.40.1 and cf. 1.37.7 (which is openly sceptical about the value of such sources). Cf. Burton (1972), 140. Bonneau (1964), 151–2 proposes that the Etesian Winds theory had Egyptian antecedents, but it is conspicuous that it is never presented as such in the doxographies.

[123]  Sen. *QNat* 3.14.2. At 7.3.2 Seneca discusses Egyptian astronomy and its (limited) influence on the Greeks. See also Frankfurter (1994). John Lydus' summary of Seneca's Nile doxography suggests that the philosopher did eventually turn to the Egyptians in his discussion of the role of the Etesian winds in pushing rain clouds south to Ethiopia, in a section of Book IVa that has since been lost, but this supplemented an existing Greek theory and was not presented as an authoritative explanation in its own right.

[124]  Serv. *Aen.* 6.154, and note the parallels to the material in *QNat* 4a.2.7. On the treatise, and Seneca's hostility to Egyptian superstition in later life, see esp. Turcan (1967) and Grimal (1979), 66–77. On the sojourn see Faider (1930).

to the irreconcilable ontologies of the Egyptian and the Graeco-Roman worlds. The Nile, of course, was fundamental to all aspects of Egyptian cosmogony and theology, indeed was so utterly central to all aspects of life on its banks, that understanding of the river cannot be separated from far broader metaphysical speculation. The earliest cosmogonies from Egypt closely associated the Nile and the *Nun* – the undifferentiated primordial waters from which matter was held to have emerged.[125] While the Nile was not exactly equivalent to the *Nun*, the annual floods of the river were regarded as one of a nested series of periodic renewals of this creation, along with the rising and setting of the sun each day.[126] This process bears a superficial similarity to Stoic cosmology, as several ancient commentators noted, but the forms in which it was articulated were radically different.[127] Creation was comprehended through a range of different metaphors – of the expectoration, or masturbation, the sweat or tears – attributed to many gods. Typically, each region of Egypt articulated different versions of these creation myths, although the Nile floods were viewed as an integral to most, and the waters of the inundation had important libation and ritual functions throughout the valley.

From the early Pharaonic period, the floods were commonly represented in temple reliefs as anthropomorphic fertility figures. The best-known of these was certainly the androgynous Hâpi, but larger groups of these figures are also common, often paying homage to Pharaohs.[128] The pendulous breasts and ample stomach-spill of these figures symbolized the intense fecundity and originative power of the river floods, although there was some variety in their rendering.[129] It is important to stress that Hâpi was not the focus of worship in himself, and did not have temples dedicated to him, but instead was closely associated with a variety of other gods and the Pharaonic (and later Ptolemaic) ruler cults. Although the Nile later assumed the trappings of other River gods, the figure of Hâpi continued to appear into the Roman period, and also seems to have been known outside Egypt. Similar fecundity figures appear on the *mensa Isiaca*, an Egyptianizing work from Claudian Rome that presumably drew upon Egyptian iconography circulating in Italy at that time.[130]

---

[125] Variously explored in the edited volume of Amenta, Luiselli and Sordi (2005), especially the contributions of Bickel (2005), Laborinho (2005) and Rotsch (2005).

[126] Hornung (1992), 39–54; Knigge (2005), 61–3. Cf. Diod Sic. 1.10.1–3; 1.12.6.

[127] See below 181–2.

[128] On religious attitudes to the Nile in Roman Egypt, see Malaise (1985), 126–33; Bonneau (1995); Frankfurter (1998), 42–6.

[129] Baines (2001) is fundamental.     [130] Roullet (1972), no. 324; cf. Baines (2001), 83.

Personified Niles were, of course, familiar figures in Rome by the later first century, and we have already discussed several examples in an earlier chapter.[131] Important as these figures came to be in the triumphal architecture of the imperial city, however, they are a considerable simplification of Egyptian theology as it was practiced, both prior to the Roman occupation, and as it was adopted throughout the empire. Simply put, the Nile was very rarely worshipped in its own right in Egypt, and was never exclusively associated with any individual god prior to the period of the Roman occupation. Instead, hymns to the Nile linked the flooded river with different gods, which were themselves often more fluid than the figures of the Greek and Roman pantheon.[132] The major divinities Amun, Re and Osiris were variously identified as creator gods in different theologies, and so were linked closely to the Nile, as a reflection of its cosmic importance. Other cults also appropriated river symbolism for different reasons: Nilotic associations were particularly pronounced in the worship of Khnum at the First Cataract, for example, of Sothis at the time of the rising of the Dog Star, and of those gods like Sobek who were particularly connected to the animals of the river.[133] It was only after the Ptolemaic occupation of Egypt that the theological understanding of the Nile began to change. Osiris was increasingly linked to the river as a manifestation of the primordial waters, and the rituals surrounding his worship clustered around the period of the end of the inundation.[134] As the cults spread beyond Egypt, moreover, the precise identity of the divinity associated with the Nile also changed: the god Serapis frequently assumed Osiris' role, and by the early-second century CE, *Neilos* (or *Nilus*) was occasionally worshipped as a distinct deity, particularly outside the Nile Valley.[135]

The multiplicity of Egyptian cosmologies eludes straightforward explanation, and this frustration was felt particularly acutely by those Hellenistic scholars who sought to make sense of Egyptian culture, even as it changed under the Ptolemies. Pharaonic cosmogony was not founded on coherent creation narratives, in the way that Greek and Roman myths were, and the relationship between the divine and physical worlds was difficult for outside thinkers to comprehend.[136] From the later-fourth century BCE, Greek scholars scrutinized Egyptian religion, just as they examined the physical peculiarities of the Nile, but these trajectories rarely intersected.[137] Our

---

[131] See above 95–8.    [132] Knigge (2005), 60–2.

[133] On regional diversity in Nile cults, see Hornung (1971), 79–80; de Buck (1948); Frankfurter (1998), 42–3.

[134] Griffiths (1980), on the separation of Osiris and the Nile in early texts. See also Claus (2005).

[135] Bonneau (1964), 354–60; Bonneau (1994).    [136] Hornung (1992), 39–54.

[137] On the context of this scholarship, see esp. Stephens (2002b); Burstein (1996).

understanding of this is substantially hampered by the imperfect survival of the most important works in this tradition, but the fragments suggest little in the way of genuine intellectual syncretism. Hecataeus of Abdera and the Egyptian priest Manetho of Sebonnutos both worked under the early Ptolemies and did much to correct some of the caricatures of the region propounded by Herodotus.[138] Their compositions included the systematic exposition of Egyptian theogony, and the discussion of the allegorical significance of the gods as a means for explaining the elemental processes of creation, but beyond passing allusions, they had little immediate impact on contemporary discussions of the Nile.[139] If local ideas on the river were adopted, these ideas were not taken up by later scholars. There is no evidence that Posidonius alluded to Egyptian theories of the primordial waters when he wrote in the first century BCE; similarly Eratosthenes seems not to have drawn upon local traditions in his own interpretation of the river and its source.[140] We know of other Hellenistic writers who also analyzed the Nile, including Bion, Eudorus and Ariston, but Strabo's dismissal of their compositions as unremarkable and derivative suggests that they also worked from a Greek tradition, rather than an Egyptian one.[141]

The true impact of Egyptian cosmology on the Greco-Roman world – and the most important role of the Nile as a conduit for this thought – came not through natural philosophy, but through the spread of 'Egyptian' cults. These were syncretistic religions which rose to prominence in Egypt during the early Ptolemaic period, and which fused Greek religious sensibilities with local traditions of long-standing significance. The expansion of these cults beyond Egypt intensified during the second and first centuries BCE, and continued throughout the early empire.[142] Isis was the most prominent of the gods, but she was by no means alone: the dissemination

---

[138] Burstein (1996) discusses the Hellenistic context, cf. also Murray (1970); Mendels (1990); Marincola (1997), 108–10; Dillery (1998); Dillery (1999); Stephens (2002b), 20–73. See also Fraser (1972) 520–52 on the cultural background to Hellenistic geography. Vasunia (2001) is exemplary on Greek knowledge of Egypt before Alexander.

[139] See for example Manetho in *FGrH* 3C 609, Fr. 17–18. On the difficulties of this syncretism, see Hornung (1971), 80.

[140] Bonneau (1964), 143–5.

[141] Strabo 17.1.5. This passage would seem to have been taken verbatim from Eratosthenes. *contra* Yoyotte, Chervet and Gompertz (1997), 74, n.58.

[142] The bibliography is immense. Bowden (2010), 156–80 sets the Egyptian religions within the context of other 'eastern' cults, and Burkert (1987) remains important. Takacs (1995b) provides a helpful introduction on Isis and Serapis in the Graeco-Roman world and cf. Bommas (2012). On the spread of the cults within the empire, see esp. Tran tam Tinh (1964), (1971), (1972), (1983), Malaise (1972a) and (1972b) and Orlin (2008). Vidman (1970) remains important on the transformations undergone by the cults. The papers in Bricault, Versluys and Meyboom (2007) are a major contribution to the literature.

of her cult was accompanied by other figures including Osiris, Serapis and Harpocrates, and a menagerie of zoomorphic gods like Anubis, Horus, Apis and Bubastis.[143] This extraordinary religious diaspora had a profound effect upon the way in which communities throughout the Mediterranean viewed Egypt and the Nile, particularly in those areas where the cults took particular hold. Simultaneously, this expansion witnessed the transformation of religious practice, both in response to changed local conditions, and to the existing metaphysical assumptions of new worshippers. As the religions adapted to their new surroundings, the Nile had an increasingly prominent symbolic role to play, as a setting for the worship of these gods, as an aid to ritual, as a connection to the original lands of the cults, and ultimately as a manifestation of the divine in its own right.

As Egyptian gods spread throughout the Roman world, so too did priests and philosophers.[144] The most prominent of these – and certainly the most influential in social as well as intellectual terms – was Chaeremon, an Alexandrian who had previously held an important position in the Great Library, and who deployed his first-hand knowledge of Egyptian philosophy, theology and social practice in a number of important texts.[145] Chaeremon first came to Rome as part of the embassy to Claudius in 41, and later became advisor to the young Nero.[146] Like Seneca, who held a similar position, Chaeremon was a Stoic, and distilled his knowledge of the Egyptian world through these filters.[147] Sadly, his writings survive only in the fragments of later authors, but we know from these allusions that they included works on Egyptian history, meteorology (specifically comets), hieroglyphs and a celebration of the asceticism of the Egyptian priesthood.[148] Within this work, Chaeremon was particularly concerned to reconcile his own philosophical understanding with the mythology of his homeland: he looked at the ancient religious traditions of Egypt and identified the outlines of Stoic cosmology.[149] There is nothing in the extant fragments of Chaeremon's writing on the River Nile, and little to suggest that his unique translation of Egyptian thought for a Roman audience was concerned with indigenous speculation on the river, but his project

---

[143] Malaise (2007).
[144] On Egyptian priests in early imperial Rome, see esp. Capriotti Vittozzi (2000), 126–7; Swetnam-Burland (2011).
[145] Frede (1989), 2075–81.   [146] Van der Horst (1984), ix–xi; Chaeremon *Test.* 5.
[147] The fullest discussion of Chaeremon's Stoicism is Frede (1989). On Chaeremon's appointment as tutor to Nero, see Chaeremon *Test.* 3, 4.
[148] Frede (1989), 2081; Van der Horst (1984), ix–xiv; Thissen (2006).
[149] Frede (1989), 2092–7. Cf. for example Chaeremon Fr.5. tr. Van der Horst (1984), 15. Cf. also *Test* 12, fr. 2, 4, 6, 7, 9, 17D.

remains important. One uncertain fragment may indicate that Chaeremon included a passage about the spontaneous generation of insect life in the Nile's waters, and extrapolated from this a wider analogy to the creation of the world, but this is far from certain.[150] A further possible fragment hints at Chaeremon's expectation (or that of his countrymen) that the world would be destroyed in a grand flood, but the passage in question is far from explicit.[151] Nor do the extant fragments display a concern with deductive speculation in the manner of Seneca's *Natural Questions* (or Lucretius' *On the Nature of Things*). Ultimately, while Chaeremon may have been an important figure in a court circle which discussed Egypt at length, we cannot know what his own contribution to these debates was. Nevertheless, Chaeremon represented an important bridge between the cosmological traditions of Egypt and Rome, even if this had little obvious effect upon contemporary philosophy.

The fullest extant attempt to clarify Egyptian theosophy for an outside audience was Plutarch's treatise *On Isis and Osiris*, which dates to the early part of the second century CE, and which survives in full.[152] While Plutarch's rendering of this cosmology differs greatly from the complex raft of texts known to modern Egyptologists, his work does give some indication of how these ontologies were interpreted and adapted outside the Nile valley. The stated intention of this treatise was to discuss the Egyptian gods (or *daimons*), as well as the mythology, ritual and cosmology associated with them, and to situate them within a Greek cognitive context. Plutarch drew heavily upon earlier Hellenistic accounts in this work, but it is also possible that he also had some familiarity with hieroglyphic texts, which he may have known from his own personal experience.[153] Whether or not this was the case, his principal inspiration seems to have come from Egypt, rather than the disparate theologies and rituals associated with the cults as they spread throughout the world.[154] For our purposes, the text serves well enough for reflecting on the importance of the Nile in Egyptian cosmography, and a helpful starting point for a more detailed study of the ways in which the river might be understood by different communities throughout the empire.

---

[150] Chaeremon Fr. 25D. cf. Chaeremon Fr. 21D; Fr. 2 and Van der Horst (1984), 72, n.7.
[151] Chaeremon Fr. 28D.     [152] See esp. Griffiths (1970), with introduction and notes.
[153] Note for example, the references to Hermaeus in Plut. *De Is et Os* 37, 42 on which see Griffiths (1970), 8–5; Aristagoras in Aelian *Nat Anim*. 11.10 (on Apis); Diog Laert. 1.11 (on cosmology). On this tradition, see also Diod Sic. 1.37.2–34 and Eus., *Prep Evang*. 3.2–5, 3.11. Griffiths (1970), 75–101; Malaise (1985), 129–31. Thissen (2009), notes that Plutarch may have drawn on Egyptian sources.
[154] Griffiths (1970), 46–8.

In writing *On Isis and Osiris*, Plutarch sought to establish a relatively straightforward aretology of the Egyptian gods. We can detect similar ambitions in the fragments of Chaeremon and the Hellenistic scholars, but coherent narrative theogonies of this kind were unknown in Egypt prior to the Ptolemaic occupation.[155] To this end, Plutarch devotes several early chapters of his treatise to telling the story of Osiris and Isis, in simplified form.[156] This relates the kidnap of the benevolent and semi-divine Osiris by his brother Typhon (Seth in the Egyptian rendering), and Isis' desperate search for the casket in which her lover and brother was trapped. First taken out to sea, and then washed up on shore, the casket was found by Isis and her son Horus. Typhon then stole the casket once more, chopped the body of Osiris into a number of pieces and scattered them throughout Egypt. Isis gathered together these parts, fashioning a phallus to replace what was missing when she reassembled her brother's body. Resurrected, Osiris returned to instruct Horus in his struggle with Typhon. Horus won this battle, but Isis showed mercy to her defeated brother, and so incurred the wrath of her son, who replaced her crown with a cow's horns. In a final act of generation, Isis bore a further son Harpocrates after a further union with the dead Osiris.

Plutarch's summary of this myth is deliberately brief and somewhat simplified, but it provided an important starting point for the author's work: he was evidently more concerned with unpacking the allegorical associations of these myths than with a rigorous examination of their innumerable variations.[157] In the chapters that follow, Plutarch argues that the Egyptians had an understanding of the elemental workings of nature which corresponded closely to the findings of philosophers elsewhere. Just as Egyptian gods could be worshipped under different names, in other words, so too could their cosmology be appreciated throughout the world.[158] These aspirations were evidently close to those of Chaeremon, and many of their conclusions seem to have been similar. Plutarch notes explicitly the Stoic and even Epicurean resonances that he detected in Egyptian cosmology, for example, before ultimately concluding that his own Platonic philosophy

---

[155] Chaeremon Fr. 2, 5, 17D. Cf. comparable passages preserved in Origen, *Contra Cels* 5.38; Diog Laert. 1.10–1 (which refers to Hecataeus and Aristagoras). On the absence of similar narratives in Pharaonic Egypt, see esp. Hornung (1992), 39–54.

[156] Plut. *De Is et Os.* 12–20. Cf. Chaeremon Fr. 17D.

[157] Griffiths (1980), 1–40 notes the mutability of these myths in the Egyptian context. Some of this variety – even in the Graeco-Roman rendering of the myth – is apparent in (for example), Diod Sic. 1.11; 1.13; 1.22.3; 1.25; 1.27.3–5; 1.85.5, in which different narratives compete. On which see Burton (1972), 56–67. And compare Paus. 10.32.18 for a contrasting tradition circulating in contemporary Greece.

[158] The *locus classicus* is Plut. *De Is et Os.* 66.

provided the most appropriate lens through which to view this material.[159] For our purposes, however, it is Plutarch's discussion of the cosmic significance of the Nile that is most important:

> The wiser of the priests not only call the Nile Osiris and the sea Typhon, but apply the name Osiris simply to the general principle and power of moisture, regarding it as the cause of generation and the essence of seed, while the name Typhon is applied to the whole dry and fiery and generally scorching element.[160]

The particular association of Osiris and the generative waters remains prominent throughout the work:

> They call not only the Nile but all moisture generally the efflux of Osiris, and in honour of the god the water-pitcher always leads the sacred ceremonies.[161]

As we have seen, the direct association of Osiris with the waters of the inundation was a considerable simplification of a Pharaonic theology, in which many different gods were associated with the floods of the Nile, and the primordial *Nun* remained an important metaphysical presence. Nevertheless, Plutarch's summary hints at the changing significance of the river in contemporary religious practice. Associated only in the most basic sense with the river, Osiris was more properly identified with the Nile inundation, and hence with the creative element in all of its forms. While this simplification enabled natural philosophers to read this theogony allegorically, as a model for the fusion of the elements, it also explained the central role of the river in much Egyptian religious observance. Many contemporary writers were content to state that the Egyptians worshipped the Nile as a god, or simply regarded Osiris and the Nile as equivalent, thereby obscuring the complexity of this tradition.[162] While this may represent the chauvinism of external observers, and later the hostility of Christian authors to the baffling practices of the established cults, these suggestions of divine immanence remain important.[163]

This brief survey demonstrates that the metaphysical associations of the Nile were kaleidoscopic in their variety, certainly within Egypt. Changing theology and ritual demanded that the Nile be appreciated differently in different contexts – in flood and in spate, inside and outside the sacred

---

[159] Plut. *De Is et Os.* 40, 41 [explicit reference to Stoics] On Platonic elements, compare Plut. *De Is et Os* 53–4, on the Creation narrative.

[160] Plut. *De Is et Os.* 33. tr. Griffiths (1970), 169.     [161] Plut. *De Is et Os.* 36. tr. Griffiths (1970), 173.

[162] Cf. for example Philo *VM* I.98; Athanasius, *Contr. Gen.* 24; Aelian *Nat Anim* 10.46; Origen, *Contra Cels* V.38; Heliod. *Aeth.* IX.9; Firm. Mat. 2.1, 2.6.

[163] Pearce (2007), 219–38.

bounds of the temple, inside and outside Egypt, and even in different parts of that country. Given this extraordinary diversity, it is perhaps understandable that natural philosophers of the Greek and Roman worlds contented themselves with passing allusions to the theories of the *Aegypti* without examining them in depth. Utterly contrasting ontologies between the Egyptian and Greek world made genuine intellectual syncretism exceptionally difficult, as Plutarch discovered. Yet these dissonances are perhaps worth exploring in a little more depth. The Nile continued to have a central symbolic and ritual function within the 'Egyptian' cults as they spread throughout the Mediterranean world. These functions may have been strikingly different from those that developed in the Nile valley itself, and may be impossible to explain in all their rich variety, but they remained important to an appreciable population of Roman citizens. The sensory centrality of the river waters to cultic practice, and hence to the cognitive understanding of the worshippers, should not be underestimated and is worth considering in more detail.

## Isis, Serapis and the Nile in Pompeii

For many inhabitants of the early empire, the cults of Egypt would be the stuff of everyday experience, and not simply the subject of erudite treatises. These were cognitive encounters that were effected on a daily basis, in the scattered temples of Isis, Serapis, Osiris and other Egyptian gods, and in the wider communities in which they flourished. To the inhabitants of the imperial heartlands, religious practices in the cult centres themselves are likely to have had a far greater significance than the commentaries of Plutarch and other writers. Within such communities, the 'Nile' was a focus of cultic activity and an object of veneration. Important work has been done on the social and cultural context of the Egyptian cults, most recently on the extraordinary variety of this worship within different provinces.[164] Several important sites have also received extensive attention, most obviously the triple temple complex at Delos, which seems to have been an important staging post for the development of these cults outside Egypt, and the Iseum Campense in Rome.[165] For the purposes of the present chapter, the Temple of Isis in Pompeii provides an appropriate focus. This is partly because the structure remains the best-known Egyptian temple outside the Nile Valley, and one of the best-studied communities of worshippers, but

---

[164] Takács (1995b), 130–205, and see the papers collected in Bricault, Versluys and Meyboom (2007).
[165] Iseum Campense cf. Lembke (1994) and the helpful discussions in Brenk (1999) and Versluys (1997). Wild (1984), 1811, n.166 provides the earlier bibliography; Delos: see Siard (2007).

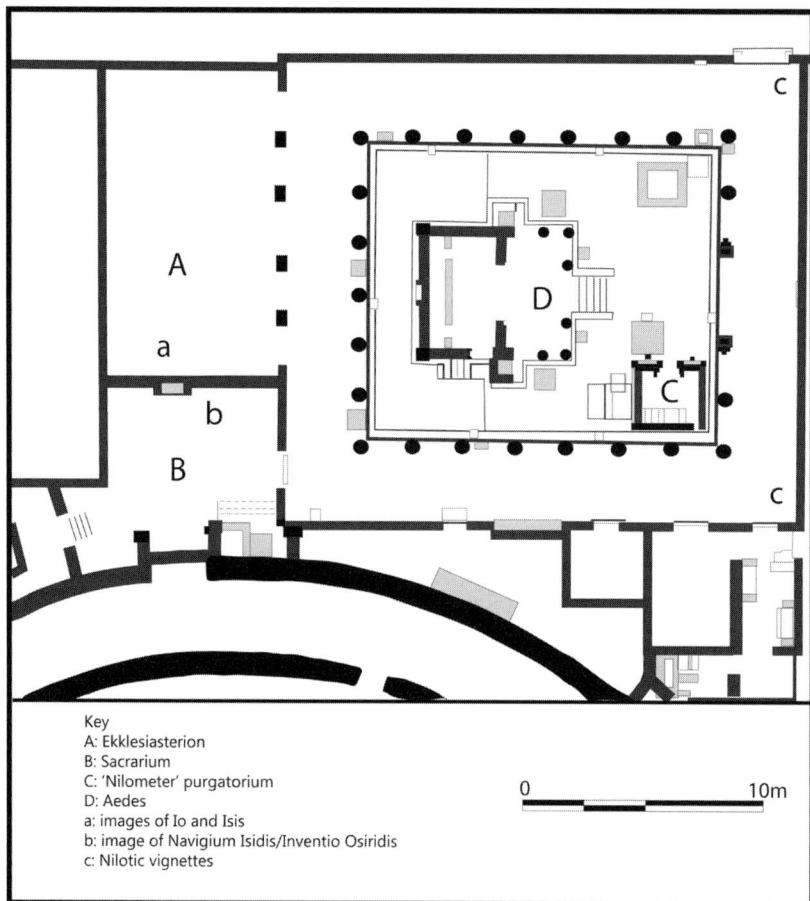

Key
A: Ekklesiasterion
B: Sacrarium
C: 'Nilometer' purgatorium
D: Aedes
a: images of Io and Isis
b: image of Navigium Isidis/Inventio Osiridis
c: Nilotic vignettes

0                    10m

4.1. Groundplan of the Temple of Isis
[© Debbie Miles-Williams 2016]

also because the discussion of Pompeian art in earlier chapters allows us to situate this structure in its immediate cultural context more easily.[166]

The small size of the Isis temple in Pompeii belies its enormous significance in the scholarship on the period.[167] Excavated in the 1760s, the temple caught the contemporary imagination, and remains one of the most

---

[166]  See esp. Tran tam Tinh (1964), Malaise (1972b), 67–85.

[167]  Hoffmann (1993) provides a basic overview. On the decoration, see esp. *Alla ricerca* (1992), Moormann (2007) and (2011), 149–61; Versluys (2002), 143–6, cat 061; Swetnam-Burland (2015), 105–37.

familiar landmarks in the city.[168] The enclosure stands in the south of the city, close to the Stabian Gate, in the shadow of the large theatre. The temple may have been founded as early as the late-second century BCE, and would seem to have been rebuilt during the Augustan period.[169] The whole complex was badly damaged in the earthquake of 62 CE, and epigraphy testifies to the substantial restoration in the decade and a half that followed. The focus of the site is the small podium temple or *aedes Isiacae*, in an open courtyard surrounded by a covered portico. The most unusual building within this portico, and for our purposes the most important, is a small water-crypt in the south-eastern corner, which has conventionally been labelled as a *purgatorium* or Nilometer.

Beyond the portico and occupying the whole of the west of the temple complex are two rooms which contrast markedly in their decoration and likely function, and it is worth addressing these briefly first. The so-called *ekklesiasterion* is the larger of the two. This was probably intended as a meeting space and dining area and was richly decorated in the Fourth Style.[170] Its wall paintings include two well-known mythological panels depicting episodes from the story of Io, and a series of large sacral-idyllic landscapes. The smaller room is conventionally termed the *sacrarium*. A large number of sacred objects were found in it, including an iron tripod, and a variety of lamps and figurines.[171] The room may have been used as a storage area, but the presence of a niche shrine and peculiar wall decorations may suggest a further purpose. Its paintings include a schematic representation of Isis's search for the casket of her brother Osiris – the *Inventio Osiridis* – an image of the enthroned Osiris, and several pictures of Egyptian animals, which may also have had a cultic significance.[172] [FIG 4.2] It is generally assumed that the room had a ritual function, which may have included the instruction of new adepts, as well as individual acts of devotion. The southern part of the Temple also includes a small number of rooms which may have been the living quarters of the priest, and which were decorated in a Fourth Style painting, without obvious Egyptian associations.

For most visitors to the Temple, the most visible depiction of the Nile would have been that on the south wall of the *ekklesiasterion*. This is one of two extant mythological panels from the room, which depict different

---

[168]  For full bibliography on the earliest excavations, see esp. Wild (1984), 1809, n.155.

[169]  On earlier dating, see Tran tam Tinh (1964), 30–1; Malaise (1972a), 275.

[170]  Swetnam-Burland (2015), 136.     [171]  D'Errico (1992); Hoffmann (1993), 96–100.

[172]  Sampaolo (1992), 59–60; Hoffmann (1993), 101–6; Meyboom (1995), 302–3, n.97; Moormann (2007), 148; Moormann (2011), 156–9; Swetnam-Burland (2015), 111–2.

4.2. The *invenitio Osiridis* from the sacrarium, Temple of Isis, Pompeii
[© Vanni Archive/Art Resource, NY]

stages in the story of Io. Here, Io is presented at the moment of her transformation back into human form, following her initial metamorphosis into a heifer at the hands of Jupiter.[173] [FIG 4.3] A seated Isis is the agent of this transformation, and is attended by a priest and a priestess of the cult, alongside the diminutive figure of Harpocrates. Io herself is held aloft by an anthropomorphic Nile, who looks up at her with concern. The Nile is dark skinned and bearded, and bears a certain resemblance to the painted busts on the north wall of the *sacrarium*, which are conventionally identified with Serapis.[174] This figure, however, is visible from the waist up and emerges from behind a pair of rocks. In front of these rocks, a small crocodile is swimming in a simply-rendered river. Io and Isis are clearly the focal characters of this vignette, as is made clear both by their visual prominence and by the narrative sequence of which the painting is

---

[173] Ov. *Met* 1.588–747 and cf. *Her.* 14.85–92. Swetnam-Burland (2015), 125–37.
[174] Cf. Sampaolo (1992), 60. Bonneau (1964), 336 suggests that the dark skin of the Nile may be associated with the Ethiopian source, but it could also reflect the alluvial silts of the inundation.

4.3. Io is received by Isis. From the *Ekklesiasterion* of the Temple of Isis, Pompeii
[Scala/Art Resource, NY]

part; another panel on the facing wall depicts Io, Argus and Mercury in an earlier episode from the same myth, and a lost panel may have depicted Jupiter's seduction of the nymph and her original metamorphosis.[175] The close association between Io and Isis was also well developed in Roman literature and visual art by the third quarter of the first century. But if Nile was only a supporting character in this visual drama, the representation remains important.

[175] Swetnam-Burland (2015), 127–30.

Several different artistic conventions meet in this depiction of an anthropomorphic Nile. Mythological subjects are common enough in first-century painting, of course, but the use of an allegorical figure of this kind remains noteworthy. As we saw in Chapter 3, the painted landscapes of this period tend to approximate the perspective of a single viewer, rather than deploy geographical abstractions or allegories.[176] Indeed, the rather unusual choice in the Io painting is highlighted by the presence of two large sacral-idyllic landscapes in the panels on either side of it. These are striking depictions in their own right, and may well allude to specific sacred sites in Egypt, but are more or less conventional in their depiction of physical space.[177] [FIG 4.4] The Io scene, by contrast, eschews the approximation of the single viewer's gaze, in favour of a metonymic rendering of the Nile. As we have seen, personified Niles were increasingly common in the sculpture of this period: Vespasian installed his basinites statue in the Temple of Peace in Rome at around the time that the *ekklesiasterion* Nile was painted, and both works probably drew upon motifs already long familiar from coins and triumphal display.

The Io painting represents a striking fusion of different modes of representation, but was not unique to the Isis Temple. A somewhat cruder rendering of the same vignette of Io, Isis and the Nile was found in the triclinium of the House of the Duke d'Aumale (VI.7.15), which again presents the river as a subordinate human figure.[178] [FIG 4.5] It seems clear from this that we should not attach any particular religious significance to the anthropomorphic river: indeed, worship of the Nile cult was not yet established at the time when the painting was completed. Viewed alongside the schematic rendering of the *Inventio Osiridis* in the *sacrarium*, however, the small landscapes in the porticus, and especially the Nilometer, what is most striking is the variety of modes in which the Nile was represented. Images of the Nile permeated the Isis Temple, but adopted a striking array of forms.

The small landscapes in the Iseum porticus seem rather more conventional in their representation of the Nile. The walls surrounding the temple are adorned with well-executed architectonic designs of the Fourth Style.[179] Small panels in the central register of each wall panel depict a variety of

---

[176]  Klementa (1993) is essential here. Cf. also Bakhoum (1999), 87–104; Gais (1978); Bonneau (1964), 329–51. Bonneau (1994), 54 identifies the *ekklesiasterion* figure as the earliest painting of an anthropomorphic river (leaving aside the precise chronological relationship to the painting in VI.7.15).

[177]  On which see esp. Croisille (1988); Moormann (2007), 144–6.

[178]  Tran tam Tinh (1964), 54, 128, cat. 14.

[179]  Sampaolo (1992); Sampaolo (1998b); Moormann (2007), 143.

4.4. Sacral-idyllic landscape from the *Ekklesiasterion* of the Temple of Isis, Pompeii
[© Vanni Archive/Art Resource, NY]

scenes, including still lifes, *naumachiae* and two pygmy landscapes, one on the north side of the east wall, the other on the south side.[180] These landscapes are by no means large – each is approximately 16 cm in height, and around 60 cm in breadth – but they are well executed, and include buildings, fauna and flora typical of the genre, as well as some noteworthy details. The panel on the south side, for example, includes a rather elaborate *shaduf* – an Egyptian crane for raising water – which is an unusual feature.[181] In broad terms, however, they are entirely typical of the small landscapes known from throughout Campania and beyond.

But these images also unsettle the established conventions of geographical representation, this time through the evidence that they provide for the

---

[180] Versluys (2002), 143–6, cat. 061 A and B.
[181] *Alla ricerca di Iside* (1992), 42–3, cat 1.10; cf. Versluys (2002), 285.

4.5. Io is received by Isis. From the House of the Duke D'Aumale
[Gianni Dagli Orti/The Art Archive at Art Resource, NY]

response of one specific viewer. One of the small landscapes is tagged with a graffito scrawled across the middle of the other panel that states *veni hoc*: 'I came here'.[182] [FIG 4.6] The intention behind this declaration is far from clear. As Molly Swetnam-Burland has noted, the writer may simply have been marking his passage through the temple, or his evident boredom: this could be the start of the popular tag *veni hoc cupidus multo magis ire cupi* – 'I came here eagerly, and now I wish much more to leave'.[183] It is also possible that there was a deliberate double entendre in the truncated tag (preserved in the translation). In this case, we might imagine an author making a wry comment on the erotic content of many pygmy landscapes of this kind, although the panel in question is not particularly sexualized by the standards of the genre.[184] Finally, it is possible that the message was not intended to advertise the presence of the writer in the Iseum porticus,

---

[182] *Alla ricerca di Iside* (1992), 40, cat 1.2. The inscription is reproduced at TAV VI.
[183] Swetnam-Burland (2015), 145–6.     [184] Swetnam-Burland (2015), 145.

4.6. Egyptian Landscape vignette, from the Porticus of the Temple of Isis, Pompeii
[© Vanni Archive/Art Resource, NY]

but rather an earlier visit to Egypt itself – a collapsing of the boundaries between representation and object, and a consummation of the spectacular power articulated in these landscapes. Where other inhabitants of the city merely gazed upon representations of the exotic world of Egypt, in other words, this individual may have boasted of having travelled.

A radically different response of the Nile is articulated in the water crypt that occupies the eastern corner of the temple portico.[185] [FIG 4.7] This small structure is approximately 3.2 m × 2.8 m above ground and has a small door in the centre of its northern side. The standing walls of the crypt are well-decorated on the outside with stucco reliefs, including prominent representations of Perseus and Andromeda and Venus and Mars. A frieze in the upper register depicts a series of figures in a religious procession, and a water pitcher prominently presented on the tympanum over the door. Inside, the building is largely undecorated. The interior is dominated by a small staircase, approximately 0.65 m wide, that leads down into the crypt proper. This lower level consists of a small room with a vaulted ceiling. Much of the floor space is occupied by a basin approximately 0.85 m × 1.5 m, although there is also a small platform, on which a ceremonial vessel may originally have been placed. Excavations revealed that the basin would have been filled by rainwater brought to the crypt through a cut channel

[185] Descriptions – Tran tam Tinh (1964), 43–5; Malaise (1972a), 239–40; Wild (1981), 44–7, 77–85; Hoffmann (1993), 206–7; Moormann (2007), 141–2, Moormann (2011), 151–2.

4.7. The Iseum water crypt or 'Nilometer'
[Alamy EB4WY9]

and pipes. The absence of a drain in the basin, and its relatively small size, would have meant that it frequently overflowed during periods of particularly heavy rainfall.[186]

Water-crypts and other reservoirs were relatively common features of temple architecture throughout the Mediterranean, of course, but these structures enjoyed a particular prominence in Isea and other Egyptian cult centres. As Robert Wild's systematic surveys have demonstrated, a variety of technologies were deployed to ensure that the canals and basins in these temples would periodically overflow, thereby replicating the Nile floods, and generating a supply of sacred water that could be associated particularly with the inundation.[187] The various water fixtures in 'Egyptian' temples throughout the Mediterranean were certainly inspired by the sacred Nilometers of Egypt, in which the flood levels of the river were formally measured, and which served economic as well as ritual functions in the region.[188] The form and function of these structures varied even within the Nile Valley: contemporary commentators spoke approvingly

---

[186]  Wild (1981), 46–7; Hoffmann (1993), 206.
[187]  Wild (1981), Wild (1984) and see also the helpful survey in Siard (2007).
[188]  The function of Nilometers in Egypt is discussed in Frankfurter (1998), 42–5; Bonneau (1991). Wild (1981), establishes essential typologies.

of the Nilometers at Philae, Syene and Memphis as particularly worthy of a visit, and the well at Syene may indeed have been depicted on the Praeneste mosaic.[189] But these structures had different architectural features, and their position within the Nile Valley suggests that their ritual and economic roles also varied. This is particularly true of the water crypt in the Alexandria Serapeum, which was filled by a canal running from the Nile rather than directly from the river itself.[190] While this Nilometer certainly had considerable ritual importance – and proved to be a major point of contention in the religious struggles of later centuries – it can hardly have had a practical function in charting the level of the flood. A similar variety is apparent outside Egypt. In the famous sanctuary at Delos, for example, three different reservoirs have been identified and were apparently employed in different ways in the worship of Isis, Serapis and Hydreios, perhaps an early manifestation of the Nile cult itself.[191]

In practical terms, the operation of the Pompeii crypt would seem to have been straightforward enough. During periods of rainfall, water would flow into the lower level of the crypt, eventually spilling over the sides once the limited capacity of the basin had been reached. It was this overflow that provided a reservoir of ritual water, for use in the temple and elsewhere. All of our accounts of Egyptian cults in the Roman Empire emphasize the importance of sacred water to temple rituals, and there can be little doubt that the crypt in Pompeii was intended for this purpose. Apuleius' coy descriptions of Isiac ceremonies in his *Metamorphoses* include references to a small golden vase (*aureum vasculum*), in the shape of a breast, and a large amphora which are borne in a formal procession; an *urnula*, highly-decorated with Egyptian motifs, which was a particularly focal position in the public Isiac procession; and an instrument called a *spondeo*, which seems to have been used for more private ceremonies.[192] Different allusions to cultic water vessels appear in the writing of Juvenal, Servius, Porphyry and Clement of Alexandria, and Plutarch also includes a substantial description.[193] Even Vitruvius, who betrays little interest in either Nilotic theology or the structure of Egyptian temples, makes a point of highlighting the devotion of priests to their sacred water and

---

[189] Strabo 17.1.48; Diod Sic. 1.36.11–12. On the Nile mosaic, see Meyboom (1995), 51–3, and the discussion in Chapter 1.

[190] Wild (1981), 29–34. The site as a whole is discussed with helpful bibliography in Wild (1984), 1755, n.24.

[191] Wild (1981), 34–43; Siard (2007).

[192] Apul. *Met* 11.10 (*vasculum* and *amphora*), 11 (*urnula*) and 20 (*spondeo*). With notes in Griffiths (1975), 213–4, 227–32, 275.

[193] Porphyry *De abst* 4.7; Serv. *Aen* 2.116, and cf. 4.512; Plut. *De Is Os* 39; Clem. *Strom.* 6.4.36 and cf. Nonnos, *Dion.* 11.509. Bonneau (1964), 283–4; Malaise (1985), 143–4.

identifies the crucial vessel as a *hydria*.[194] Various attempts have been made to establish a typology of these different vessels, based in the descriptions in the texts, extant archaeological examples, and a number of painted images.[195] These paintings include a well-known fresco from Herculaneum, which underscores the ritual significance of these vessels, and a number of different images in the Pompeian Iseum and elsewhere in the city. As we have seen, a pitcher appears prominently above the main door of the Nilometer; a barrel-shaped vessel, normally identified as a *cista*, is depicted among the images in the *sacrarium;* and a third container is among the decorations within the portico.[196] A further image of a water vessel with a very long spout appears in the triclinium of the Casa del Centenario, held by one of twenty-two figures in a further religious procession.[197]

Nor were these 'Nile' waters limited to the ritual confines of the temples themselves. During the excavations at Pompeii, six coarseware vessels were found within the *sacrarium*, and inscribed with the name of the priest, N. Popidius Natalis, which have plausibly been identified as containers for sacred waters.[198] With these was a silver situla inscribed with the legend 'Serapis dora' – 'Gift of Serapis' – which was discovered in 1813 and subsequently presented to Ludwig I of Bavaria.[199] Perhaps most significantly, the same inscription was found on thirteen amphorae or fragments of amphorae discovered throughout the city, including one at the Vesuvian Gate and a second at the Stabian Gate.[200] While it is possible that these vessels originally contained wine or other produce from a temple estate, the connection to the vessels found within the Iseum strongly imply that they were instead used for the transportation of 'Nile' flood water, and that this probably originated in the city itself.[201] This interpretation is supported by the fact that forty-four similar (but unlabelled) amphorae were discovered in the garden of the House of Octavius Quarto, where they can only have been used to contain the overflow from the elaborate decorative canal.[202] While it is possible that these amphorae were imported from Egypt, and

---

[194]  Vitruv. 8.Prol.4.
[195]  Malaise (1972a), 116–49; Wild (1981), 104–23; Malaise (1985), 149–55; cf. Siard (2007), 434–6.
[196]  Malaise (1972a), 279–80; Malaise (1985), 136; Moormann (2007), 148.
[197]  De Vos (1980), 34, fig 7. On this procession see eadem. 34–43.
[198]  Tran tam Tinh (1964), 42–3; Vidman (1969), 228–9; Malaise (1972a), 265 cat 6 (1985), 147.
[199]  Sampaolo (1992), 60, n.5.
[200]  Malaise (1972a), 265 cat 6–23; Tran tam Tinh (1964), 177–80, cat 150–55, 157, 160–2, 165–7; Vidman (1969), 230, n.495.
[201]  I am grateful to Dan Stewart for this observation.
[202]  Tran tam Tinh (1964), 44–5. For further discussion on the canal complex cf. Zanker (1998), 145–56; von Stackelberg (2004), 101–6; on the cultural complexity of the decorative scheme see Valladares (2012).

originally contained water from the Nile itself, this can hardly have been true of the situla.[203] Instead it seems much more likely that the 'Serapis Dora' vessels were filled from the Iseum Nilometer crypt and circulated through the city from there. The script on the amphorae is relatively consistent and has plausibly been identified as the work of the same writer, which would also imply a systematic distribution from a local base.[204] It is more difficult to identify the uses to which these waters were put by the inhabitants of Pompeii. One example is known from the Temple of Mercury, which may imply a ritual function in other cults, but others were also found in a taberna and in the Forum Baths. Although similar finds are exceptionally scarce from elsewhere in early imperial Italy, it seems that the 'Nile' was a relatively familiar sight in Pompeii.[205]

A remarkable number of 'Niles' flowed through the Pompeii Iseum, then. Each represented the river in a very different way, but collectively they give some impression of the wider metaphysical importance of the river within this sacred setting. The *ekklesiasterion* fresco was indebted to established traditions of domestic painting, but incorporated an image of the personified river that was unusual in such a context, if not completely unknown. The small Egyptianizing landscapes of the porticus are more obviously conventional in their spatial representation, but also seem to have triggered a direct response from at least one viewer. The images from the *sacrarium* are perhaps best viewed as a Campanian adoption of Egyptian religious imagery, and depict the Nile in a manner almost entirely alien to local traditions. And finally the waters drawn from the Nilometer cistern were a manifestation of the Nile itself, that could be incorporated in rituals, or exported throughout the city.

The Nile itself was not the focus of worship within this building, but provided the setting in which such worship might take place. The images in the porticus and *ekklesiasterion* evoked Egypt in the most vivid possible terms. They allowed spectators to gaze on the increasingly-familiar landscapes of the region, and drew upon the established visual rhetoric of coins and triumphs, thereby placing the subject province back into a privileged setting. Equally, the high status of these paintings, and their appropriation of a visual language familiar from elsewhere in Pompeii, asserted the local

---

[203] There are textual references to the export of Nile waters at Hdt 3.6 and Diod Sic. 1.97.1, as well as the familiar parody at Juv. 6.526–9 cf. also Epiphanius *Adv. Haer.* 51.30.3. But these are scarce. Nevertheless, Della Corte (in Vidman (1969), 228–9) argues that the *sacrarium* hydria were full of Egyptian Nile water, and cf. Malaise (1985), 147.

[204] Tran tam Tinh (1964), 85.

[205] One example is known from Aquileia. Malaise (1972b), 11 and cat 27.

importance of the temple and its worshippers. As we have seen, the Nile could be a marker of belonging to the Roman world, as well as of deference to the Egyptian cult. For those visitors privileged to see the *sacrarium* images, or to be involved in the rituals of the temple, the other Niles moved beyond familiar conventions of representation and acknowledged the mythic narratives surrounding the river, and the creative power of the worshipped gods. Here, the Nile was not the marker of a subject territory of empire, indeed was not defined as an earthly river at all, but rather was a direct physical reminder of the mysteries of Egyptian divinity, and the perennial reality of cosmic creation.

## Conclusions: Metaphysical Niles

The different Niles discussed in this chapter repeatedly intersect with the rivers known from other forms of geographical representation, but occupy a fundamentally different set of cognitive positions. Lucretius and Seneca, for example, exemplify a long tradition of natural philosophical speculation on the Nile floods, and the account of the river in the *Natural Questions*, in particular, bears obvious comparison to other prose geographies of the early imperial world. The images from the Pompeii Iseum similarly appropriate landscape imagery from contemporary domestic contexts and allude to the personified figures familiar from coins and statuary. Yet in spite of this deference to established forms, all of these representations emphasize the instability and ambivalence of the river – the very impossibility of containing the Nile within the traditional language of geographical representation. Lucretius and Seneca were fascinated by the Nile because its most important features were unknown, and because contemplation of these mysteries represented the first step in approaching wonders that far transcended the physical present, or the world as it could be experienced by a human observer. Worshippers in the Pompeii Iseum similarly appreciated how contemporary forms might approximate the Nile – in personifications, landscapes or amphorae filled with 'the gift of Serapis' – but here again it was the transcendent qualities of the river, and the divine creation that it represented, that were the cause of this appreciation.

The metaphysical Niles brought forth by Lucretius, Seneca and the Pompeian adepts – or by Ovid, Chaeremon and the inhabitants of Roman Egypt – were evidently very different from one another: they represented contrasting assumptions about the cosmos and the value of the Nile as a means to comprehend it. But we should not assume from this, or from the arcane themes drawn upon in these various invocations, that these were merely esoteric perspectives that had little impact on wider modes of geographical understanding in the period. Lucretius' *On the Nature of Things* was an enormously influential text, and Seneca was widely read; even the Niles of the Iseum would have been familiar to more than a small circle of adepts. Importantly, these influences can also be traced across a range of other texts. Pomponius Mela readily embraced doxography in his prose description of the world, and thereby lent a frisson of uncertainty to his account of interior Egypt; Pliny similarly discusses the theories of the Nile floods, and exhibits a remarkable agnosticism in his various attempts to identify the Nile source.[206] Even Strabo, whose patience with philosophical sophistry was notoriously thin, paused in his long account of the Nile in Egypt to reflect on the creation of the universe and the development of life.[207] Without its unsettling qualities, the Nile would have been much less of a trophy for Caesar or Augustus, and less of a challenge for Vitruvius' chorographers. The metaphysical qualities of the Nile – a river that replicated each year the origins of the world, and which overspilled its banks even into the bathhouses and taverns of Pompeii – were essential to its resonance in the Roman world.

[206] Pomponius Mela 1.52–4.; on Pliny see below 285–8.
[207] Strabo 17.1.36. His cynicism on philosophical speculation regarding the Nile floods is apparent in 17.1.5.

# CHAPTER 5

# *This River Is a Jumbled Line, Perhaps?*
## *Journeys and Lines*

Ancient writers and readers never forgot that a river was a living, moving thing. Pliny's evocative description of the western course of the Nile in the fifth book of his *Natural History* illustrates the point vividly.[1] Here, the course of the river is traced from its supposed origins in the Atlas Mountains, across the North African desert, to its confluence at Meroe and north to Egypt. But this is not an impersonal description. Throughout, it is the anthropomorphic behaviour of the Nile that animates the account. The whole journey of the river is shaded with agency and metaphors of sequential movement; indeed, the entire section is presented in essentially narrative terms, with the river itself as the protagonist. In the opening sentence the Nile is defined as a 'wandering' (*ambulans*) river, a metaphor of leisurely strolling which was central to Roman ideals of aristocratic identity in the first century.[2] This proud comparison continues, as the Nile 'disdains to flow' (*indignatur fluere*) through deserts, or 'hides' (*condit*) underground. Thereafter, its tortuous course 'surveys' mankind (*circumspicit*), eventually bursting forth from the so-called Black Spring when it senses (*sensit*) the presence of human habitation. The account of the passage through the Cataracts is replete with islands that the river 'scatters' (*spargit*). This is a tremendously tactile and kinetic account, in which the Nile becomes the sentient traveller who records an otherwise unknown landscape. The final passage into Egypt is worth recounting in full:

> It is carried by rushing waters to the place in Ethiopia called *Catadupi*; at the last Cataract it seems not to flow between the obstructing rocks, but to sweep headlong with an immense crash. Smooth thereafter, its waters are broken and its violence subdued, and, wearied from its long journey, it expels itself by many mouths into the Egyptian Sea. However, for some

---

[1] Plin. *HN* 5.51–4.
[2] Plin. *HN* 5.51. On the importance of walking in Roman culture see esp. the extraordinary study of O'Sullivan (2011).

days, greatly increased, it spreads over the whole of Egypt and fertilizes the land.[3]

Pliny reprises this elsewhere in his *Natural History* – in his eighteenth book, the Nile appears as an elderly farmer cultivating his fields – but it is in his geographical chapters that this image is most effectively employed.[4] At several different points in his accounts of Africa, Asia and Europe, Pliny organizes his descriptions of inland regions around rivers. Watercourses like the Tigris, Danube and Nile provided him with a baseline around which he could structure his descriptions of otherwise undifferentiated territory.[5] As Trevor Murphy succinctly puts it in his study of the *Natural History*, rivers 'are the rails on which his narrative slides', particularly when Pliny was confronted with the challenge of genuine *terra incognita*.[6]

This use of rivers as a means of comprehending large landmasses was not unique to Pliny; it reflected descriptive strategies that were widespread during this period. Although the charming wandering rivers of the *Natural History* have no direct parallel in the geographical texts of Strabo or Pomponius Mela, both of those writers routinely organized their descriptions of inland regions through the careful discussion of the rivers that passed through them, and we can see similar patterns in the *Germania* of Tacitus.[7] To a large degree, this was to be expected. Strabo, Mela and Pliny all depended on coastal surveys to lend structure to their accounts of the world and its various parts.[8] They traced these outlines through the careful enumeration of ports, capes and river mouths, and in so doing deferred to the copious body of *periplus* or itinerary literature that had been created by more or less constant travel through the Mediterranean world. Given such methodologies, it is unsurprising that writers would depend upon the familiar linear form of rivers to fulfil a similar function in their descriptions of wide spaces of land. While the practices employed in doing this were evidently rather different from the straightforward deference to *periplus* literature of the coasts – it is hard to imagine a traveller's account anticipating Pliny's amiably wandering Nile, for example – the conceptual link was certainly there. Faced with the challenge of representing a complex land-locked world, Strabo and his successors often turned to linear features like rivers to structure their accounts.

---

[3] Plin. *HN* 5.54.     [4] Plin. *HN* 18.167; cf. Beagon (1996), 289.
[5] Cf. Plin. *HN* 6.127–30 (Tigris); 3.146–8 (Danube and tributaries).
[6] Murphy (2003), 315 and Murphy (2004), 136–44. Pliny's narrative strategies are discussed in more depth in the Afterword, below.
[7] Cf. Tac. *Germ.* 30–4 and the brief discussion in Thomas (2010), 63.     [8] See above 39, n.61.

The dependence of geographical writers on narrative strategies of this kind, particularly in the description of rivers, draws attention to an essential epistemological tension at the heart of these accounts – the uneasy awareness that geographical texts purported to be disinterested, impersonal and timeless, and yet were necessarily dependent upon the accumulation of information drawn from discrete moments of travel and observation in the human past. This opposition was famously dissected by Michel de Certeau in *The Practice of Everyday Life*. Here, he identified the 'map' as a totalizing expression of omniscient state knowledge, which consciously obscured the individual journeys from which it had been created.[9] While ancient map-making could not enable the panoptic world-survey that he envisioned, as we saw in the first chapter, this remains a helpful starting-point for the present discussion. The more or less constant intrusion of metaphors of personal travel within texts like Pliny's and their extensive dependence upon itinerary and *periplus* sources demand more than an appreciation of the patchwork processes of compilation. They also hint at the imaginative engagement of audiences with these texts and are a reminder of the cognitive world that produced them. By acknowledging the intimate connection between travel and description – even for writers and readers who had no personal experience of the regions concerned – we can appreciate the further complexity of the cognitive geographies apparent in this period.

This chapter adopts a number of different approaches to explore the essential 'linearity' of the Nile, and hence the multi-faceted nature of Roman responses to the wider world. It starts with an investigation of the importance of written itineraries and *peripli*, both as technologies for navigation and as basic foundations for the understanding of space in the classical world. This has been the subject of considerable scholarly debate in recent years, but surprisingly little attention has been paid to the production and deployment of these itineraries in their wider cultural context. In an effort to examine these modes of representation on the ground, two accounts are then explored in detail – first the Neronian Nile expedition recorded by Seneca and Pliny, which was briefly introduced in the last chapter, and then the first-hand description of Egypt that dominates Book XVII of Strabo's *Geography*. Examination of these accounts, along with a range of other texts from the first, second and third centuries, reveals the development of a caricature of Egypt as a linear province, in which sites (and sights) rapidly became jumbled.

---

[9] De Certeau (1984), 121.

## Itineraries: A World Defined by Routes, Nodes and Lines

Travel was fundamental to ancient geographical understanding, and hence to the ways in which the world was represented. Although synoptic modern studies of 'ancient geography' have often focused on literary, mathematical or descriptive texts, the most widespread form of geographical writing to have survived from the classical world was undoubtedly the written *periplus* or itinerary, and a developing body of scholarship has recognized this.[10] The simplest extant examples of these texts are (or purport to be) basic narratives of individual journeys, often comprising little more than lists of nodal points along a given route, sometimes including the distances or journey times that separated them. These include both coastal and maritime *peripli* (or *periploi*), which largely survive in Greek, and terrestrial itineraries, which are known in both Greek and Latin.[11] At their most complex, these texts exhibit sophisticated narrative strategies and demand careful literary analysis.[12] Numerous as these texts are, they can only represent the tiniest proportion of the itineraries that were once produced either to aid navigation around the world, or to record specific journeys. Such accounts were essentially ephemeral, and for each time an individual like Cicero happened to record a specific journey, he made thousands of trips that are now lost to us – to say nothing of the millions of trips made by other travellers.[13] We know from fragmentary allusions that itineraries of some sort were employed by individuals travelling on military and imperial business.[14] The role of this technology in the *cursus publicus* – a transport and requisition infrastructure that spanned the empire – is also becoming increasingly clear.[15] Itineraries, it would seem, were everywhere.

---

[10] Marcotte (2000), lv–lxxi provides a useful summary of the different types of itinerary literature. Modern scholarship on the topic is extensive. See esp. Janni (1984) with discussion below. Salway (2007) provides a thorough recent overview; Purcell (1990) addresses their interaction with other forms of geographical knowledge, and see also Arnaud (2007–8), 34–9. For an important recent study of an important Greek *periplos*, see Shipley (2011). I am grateful to Graham for extensive discussions of this text (and of itinerary literature more generally).

[11] Arnaud (2004) discusses the interface between these forms in the maritime section of the *Antonine Itinerary*.

[12] This is illustrated most succinctly by recent work on the *Itinerarium Burdigalense* (the 'Bordeaux Itinerary') – an early fourth-century text ostensibly relating a single pilgrimage from the Gallic city to the Holy Land. Cf. Douglass (1996); Bowman (1999); Elsner (2000); Salway (2007), esp. 188–90.

[13] Cicero did record several journeys, all of them in more or less itinerary form: Cic. *Att* 5.12.1; 5.20.2; 8.11.7. For modern comparanda, see Akerman (2006b).

[14] Ambrose *Ex in Ps*. 118.5.2; SHA *Alex Sev* 45.2. On these sources, see Janni (1984), 31–2; Brodersen (2001), 12.

[15] On itineraries and the *cursus publicus*, see Mitchell (1976); Kolb (2001) and (2007).

There is also considerable evidence for the fossilization of this information in a variety of different contexts. Inscriptions were commonly erected at town gates, at crossroads or at bridges, listing the stopping points and relative distances along roads.[16] These *tabellaria* were established by the individuals responsible for the upkeep of the roads, but offered travellers a useful means of navigation around the empire.[17] Several of our texts also allude to the *milliarium aureum* – the 'golden milestone' which was erected by Augustus in the Republican Forum, and which celebrated Rome's position at the heart of this web.[18] Precisely what information was included on this monument has been the matter of some dispute: it may have calculated the distance to the different cities of Italy or the empire, in the manner of the whimsical 'world' signposts familiar from some modern tourist landmarks, but equally it may not have been inscribed at all. Comparable public inscriptions are known from different parts of the empire, including a monument from Patara in southern Turkey dating from the reign of Claudius, and epigraphy of the high imperial period from Tongeren and Autun in Gaul.[19] These monuments undoubtedly had a strong political resonance, and linked communities directly to the wider world of the empire, but did not represent the consistent application of a single body of geographical information across the Roman world as a whole.[20]

Less symbolically resonant, but equally significant, are the surprising appearances of 'itinerary' texts as decorative motifs on prestige objects. A set of four silver goblets deposited in a sacred spring near the Lago di Bracciano in southern Etruria were ornamented with detailed itineraries of the route from Gades at the Pillars of Heracles to Rome. These 'Vicarello goblets' can scarcely have been intended primarily as aids for navigation, since they would have made for an eccentric route-map to say the least, and their precise function remains unclear.[21] Similarly, three enamelled bronze bowls are known from Britain, France and northern Spain which include systematic lists of the stations on Hadrian's Wall along their rims.[22] These have plausibly been interpreted as souvenirs of officers once stationed on

---

[16]   Plut. *Vit. C Gracch.* 7. Salway (2001), 48–58 and (2007), 190–4 are fundamental on these *tabellaria*; cf. Elsner (2000), 184 and Brodersen (1995), 166–73, 181–4. Inscriptions of this kind are unknown from the Nile valley. On milestones see Adams (2001), 141–2 and Eide et al. (1998), 921–4.

[17]   The *elogium* of Polla provides the clearest example. Cf. Salway (2007), 190–2 and Kolb (2007), 179–80 on this monument.

[18]   Plut. *Vit. Galb.* 24; Plin. *HN* 3.66.

[19]   Salway (2007), 194–200 provides a useful overview and see also Kolb (2016), 229–31.

[20]   Kolb (2007), 176–7.

[21]   *CIL* XI 3281–4. Brodersen (1995), 178–9; Elsner (2000), 185; Salway (2007), 192; Kolb (2007), 175.

[22]   Brodersen (1995), 176.

the wall, and may well reflect a widespread fascination with the mechanics of travel and the representation of space during the high empire.

Precisely how this proliferation of varied itinerary literature affected the popular conceptualization of the world in antiquity has been the subject of surprisingly intense dispute over the last generation. It seems clear that the majority of independent travellers in the ancient world thought of their journeys in linear terms, and changes to modern practice have only increased sympathy for this view: the proliferation of in-car navigation systems, which frame and re-frame modern road journeys as satellite-controlled 'strip maps', illustrates vividly how technologies of navigation can shape cognitive understanding in precisely this way.[23] It is also noteworthy that two of the most important summative surveys of the late empire were plainly dependent upon itineraries and fashioned visions of the world articulated by the imperial road network. The so-called *Antonine Itinerary* was produced in the later third century CE and comprises ten interlocking itineraries that span the whole of the empire, with the exception of the trans-Danubian provinces.[24] This economical survey of the world seems to have been compiled from *tabellaria* in different regions and is now thought to have been the result of independent scholarship (or individual eccentricity), rather than an official text.[25] The Peutinger Table or 'Map' is a rather more complex work; a vast visual survey of the empire, the text itself dates from around 1200 but is clearly derived from a late antique exemplar.[26] Like the *Antonine Itinerary*, the Map is dominated by an exoskeleton of itineraries, but it also includes stylized representations of major rivers, seas and mountains: one recent interpretation has argued persuasively that it was these topographic features, rather than the road network, that were the intended focus of the map.[27]

One important school of scholarship has argued that linear 'routes' of this kind had a still greater significance within ancient geographical understanding. In an influential study published in 1984, Pietro Janni suggested that the inhabitants of the classical Mediterranean conceptualized the world as a network of interlocking routes of travel, rather than as a planar surface.[28] He acknowledged that elementary instruction in geometry allowed writers to conceive of the world as a globe, and that while

---

[23] MacEachren (1986); Delano-Smith (2006); Akerman (2006c); French (2006).

[24] Salway (2007), 182–7.    [25] Arnaud (1993); Salway (2001), 58–9; Talbert (2008), 119.

[26] Talbert (2010a) is an important assessment of the text. Compare Albu (2005) who argues for a Carolingian origin (derived from later Roman itineraries). The medieval context of the extant map (and its immediate influences) are explored in Albu (2014).

[27] Talbert (2010b), 262–3.

[28] Janni (1984); compare Kolb (2016) for a recent articulation of a similar view.

the commonplaces of the schoolroom associated specific provinces or features with particular shapes, geographies on a regional scale were almost always understood and expressed in linear terms. From this perspective, the dependence of literary geographers like Strabo, Mela and Pliny upon itineraries, or the widespread use of linear description in historical texts, reflected much more than the simple proliferation of itineraries as means of navigation. Janni argued not only that people thought in terms of lines when they travelled, but also that this dominated the spatial assumptions of the world at rest. Drawing upon the work of a number of cognitive psychologists, particularly those specializing in the development of spatial cognition in children, Janni termed this a 'hodological' mode of geographical understanding.[29] These arguments have since been elaborated by Kai Brodersen and Dick Whittaker, both of whom have examined the difficult conceptual boundary between 'geometrical' understanding on a global scale, the knowledge generated by land surveys on the local level, and this 'hodological' means of conceptualizing space in between.[30] These assumptions have been challenged extensively, but once more, detailed study of representations of the Nile can add something to this debate.

River travel has always had a somewhat ambivalent position within discussions of Roman geographical cognition.[31] On the one hand, rivers had been natural regional route-ways long before the arrival of Roman power and continued to be so for centuries afterwards.[32] Imperial authority could do little to control the more or less constant movement along the Nile, for example, and the somewhat artificial manner in which both the *Antonine Itinerary* and the Peutinger Map attempt to contain the river in their accounts illustrates this point. The relevant Egyptian sections of the *Antonine Itinerary* chart the major settlements along the west bank of the Nile as far south as Hiera Sycaminos in Lower Nubia and then return north along the east bank back to the Delta.[33] Significantly, this pattern is followed even when there are no settlements on the appropriate bank to serve as landmarks: several stopping points are simply defined as places 'opposite' (*contra*) settlements on the other side of the river.[34] While this

---

[29] Janni (1984), 79–154; note the comments of Isaac (1991), 511. Janni drew particularly on the work of Lewin (1936) and the important collection of Downs and Stea (1973). Golledge (1999) surveys recent work in this area, and see also O'Rourke (2013) for a provocative overview of contemporary artists' responses to similar impulses. Belyea (1998) identifies a similar approach in Native American maps (and draws a similar parallel to Beck's Tube Map at 141).

[30] Brodersen (1995), 166–94; Whittaker (2004), 69: 'when it came to wider spatial perceptions, Romans did not think like land surveyors'. Cf. Arnaud (1989), 22–5.

[31] Salway (2004).　　[32] Campbell (2012), 200–215.　　[33] *It Ant* 155.1–170.4.

[34] See, for example, *It Ant* 159.3, 160.4–5, 161.1, 164.1–4, 165.2–3.

implicitly (and economically) presents Egypt as thoroughly ordered and organized Roman province, the Nile itself is curiously absent from the text. There is no allowance here for the variations of wind and current that dictated travel along the river, or for the flexibility of stopping points that such travel allowed.[35] Instead, the *Antonine Itinerary* presents Egypt as an essentially linear province, artificially defined by routes which few long-distance travellers would ever have followed, and structured around nodal points which were at least partly the creation of the system of description.[36] Conspicuously, there is no direct reference to the very geographical feature that made Egypt a linear province. Much the same is true of the treatment of the river on the Peutinger Table. While the Nile does appear on the Map, from its mysterious origins to the intricate cobweb of the Delta, which is one of the most appealing visual features of the work, the correspondence between the river and the road network appended to it is ambiguous to say the least.[37] Once again, the linear roadwork is broadly independent of the great river. Where itineraries of river travel do exist – and there are several that survive on later Roman papyri – they reflect a much less ordered system of travel, as will be discussed shortly.[38]

Yet discussion of river travel allows us to examine Roman geographical cognition in a new light, and relate this to other modes of representing the world – to search for the 'beach beneath the street', to adopt an apposite metaphor of the Situationist movement. The proliferation of later works relating to river navigation – including Mark Twain's absorbing discussion of training as a steamboat pilot in *Life on the Mississippi*, and a plethora of modern tourist narratives of Nile travel – provide a more direct point of comparison than the classroom studies of environmental cognition preferred by Pietro Janni.[39] Equally important is the simple fact that a relatively generous body of ancient source material relates to travel along the Nile. While this material is far from comprehensive, Pliny and Seneca preserve a first-class account of the use and production of itineraries along the Nubian Nile, Strabo vividly reveals the centrality of travel in his own account of Egypt, and Tacitus, Juvenal and the ancient 'novelists' show how rapidly the ordered lines of Nilotic travel could be simplified in

---

[35] See below 223–8.

[36] Salway (2004), 74–6; Adams (2007) provides a more positive assessment of land travel within Egypt, and the roads along both banks. But long-distance journeys must still have been effected by river.

[37] Brodersen (2001), 18; cf. Cooper (2014), 38–9 on the ambiguous hydrography of the Delta in the Peutinger Map.

[38] On the suggestion that a fluvial itinerary was incorporated into the Peutinger Table for parts of Germany and Italy, see Salway (2001), 44.

[39] For further discussion, see the examples in Akerman (2006a).

the popular imagination. In this chapter we examine how all of these texts negotiated the shift between travel and textual representation in this period, and challenge some of the assumptions of Janni and his successors. One commonplace of proponents of the 'hodological' model is that inhabitants of the ancient world conceptualized routes of travel with reference only to the stopping points on their journeys, and the order in which they came. It may have been even simpler than that when moving by river. For many inhabitants of the ancient world, the Nile simply seems to have been comprehended as a line – the order of the locations on its banks being less significant than the fact that they were bound together by the essentially linear nature of the river. The stopping points themselves, it would seem, were frequently secondary to this, and were often presented in a confused order.

### The Ethiopian Expedition: To Meroe and Beyond?

In the mid 60s CE, the Emperor Nero sponsored an expedition up the Nile and into the Ethiopian interior. Commentators at the time debated whether this was intended as a preliminary to a full-scale campaign to the south, or was motivated by simple scientific curiosity, but the success of the exploration was widely acknowledged.[40] The Romans had travelled beyond Syene before, but never this far: during the reign of Augustus expeditions under Cornelius Gallus and Publius Petronius established a provisional military presence in Lower Nubia.[41] Only the Neronian explorers could plausibly claim to have travelled further. Upon their return to Rome, the two centurions who led the expedition reported a journey deep into what is now central Sudan, well past the capital at Meroe. Regardless of its original

---

[40] Plin. *HN* 6.181; Dio Cass. 62.8.1–2; Hinze (1959) first proposed that discrepancies between the accounts of Seneca and Pliny suggest that there were two expeditions rather than one. These were chiefly the motivations ascribed to the explorers (military reconnaissance in Pliny's account, scientific exploration in Seneca's), and the gender of the ruler of Meroe (Pliny identifies a queen Candace, Seneca a king). This is followed by Cesaretti (1989), 60–2. De Nardis (1989), 139–40 argues that a single expedition may have split into two, with Seneca's two centurions pressing beyond Meroe, and Pliny's praetorians staying in the city. For statement of the case for a single expedition see Desanges (2008), 133–5. The motivations of the explorers are discussed by Desanges (2008), 133, n.1. El-Sheikh (1992) sets the expedition in a wider context.

[41] Earlier expeditions: The inscriptions of Cornelius Gallus are conveniently collected with commentary in Eide et al. (1996), 689–95; the Publius Petronius expedition is recorded in *Res Gestae* 26.5, on which see Eide et al. (1996), 700–4; Strabo 17.1.53–4; Plin. *HN* 6.181–2; Dio Cass. 54.5.4–6. On Petronius (given the cognomen G[aius] by Dio, and P[ublius] by Pliny), see Bagnall (1985), who provides convincing support for Pliny's nomenclature based on papyrus evidence and Capponi (2005), 179–81 on the prefectures. On the expedition, see Jameson (1968); Desanges (1978), 308–17; El-Sheikh (1992), 157–9.

motive, the evidence that we have for the mission provides an invaluable perspective on how 'hodological' conceptions of the physical world worked within the Nile valley. The Neronian explorers took pre-existing itineraries with them to help them find their way, and produced a similar text of their own, which they presented in Rome, together with an oral report. These in turn fed into the understanding of the course of the river, yet augmented rather than replaced existing geographical knowledge.

Pliny preserves important details of the expedition in his *Natural History*, as we shall see, but the fullest description comes from the *Natural Questions* of the Younger Seneca. As we saw in the previous chapter Seneca was something of an *éminence grise* at the imperial court and may even have been the instigator of the journey.[42] He was also evidently fascinated with the Nile, which he regarded both as an admirable object for philosophical contemplation and reasoning, and as a medium for reflecting on the wider patterns of cosmic time. Seneca was evidently suspicious of the value of autopsy over reason in responding to the sorts of grand questions posed by the Nile floods, and consequently was silent on the findings of the Neronian expedition in the opening books of his treatise. In Book VI, however, as part of his analysis of earthquakes, the philosopher digresses at some length on the reports of the explorers:

> I heard two centurions whom Nero Caesar, great lover of the other virtues and especially of truth, had sent to search for the sources of the Nile. They told how they made a long journey, when they were provided with assistance by the King of Ethiopia, were given recommendations to the neighbouring kings, and penetrated further inland. "Then", they said, "we reached interminable marshlands. The local people had not discovered where they ended, nor can anyone hope to do so: weeds are so entangled the water and the water <with weeds>, they are impassable either on foot or by boat; only a small one-man craft can manage on the muddy, overgrown swamp. There," he said, "we saw two crags from which a huge volume of water cascaded down." Whether this is the source of the Nile or a tributary, whether it first emerges there or returns to the surface after being swallowed underground in its earlier course, do you not believe that this water, whatever it is, rises from a great lake within the earth? For the earth must contain liquid, both dispersed in many places and concentrated in a single place, to be able to disgorge it with such force.[43]

This brief account reveals how easily new information could be integrated into received geographical knowledge. Seneca's primary purpose here is to connect the testimony of the centurions to the common Stoic contention

---

[42] See above 162.     [43] Sen. *QNat* 6.8.3–4. tr. Hine (2006), 95.

that the Nile was fed from a vast underground reservoir: although the writer was at pains not to rule definitively on the causes of the inundation in the doxography of Book IVa, for the reasons outlined above, there is good reason to suspect that this was his preferred explanation.[44] Equally, the explorers themselves clearly integrated their own observations with their pre-existing geographical assumptions, and thereby made sense of an unfamiliar landscape, although this takes a little more unpacking.[45] It is unclear how far the expedition actually penetrated beyond Meroe. The great scholar of Nubia L. P. Kirwan noted that Seneca's reference to impenetrable grasses and 'interminable marshlands' (*immensas paludes*) would seem to be an accurate description of the Sudd – a sclerotic mass of floating vegetation that choked the White Nile around its confluence with the Sobat and which was finally only penetrated by European explorers in 1903.[46] More recently, Giovanni Vantini has suggested that the swamps refer to Lake No to the south of Malakal, and that the praetorians' identification of two rocks 'from which a violent stream of water gushed out' (*ex quibus ingens vis fluminis excidebat*) may reveal that they got as far south as Murchison Falls.[47]

There is little that can be read with complete confidence in this account. Viewed critically, Seneca's treatment of the praetorians' journey to the south of Meroe is so allusive as to be beyond critical interpretation and seems to have been inspired by geographical commonplaces as much as by first-hand observation.[48] As we shall see, the explorers followed Hellenistic itineraries in their journey between Syene and Meroe and produced an annotated itinerary of their own. Beyond Meroe, however, they seem to have written little, and Pliny's careful discussion of these regions includes reference to Hellenistic sources, but not to the explorers' account.[49] Given this, the allusion to the pair of rocks at the source of the river seems suspiciously similar to Herodotus' account of the rocks of Elephantine – a statement that had become something of a *topos* in accounts of the river.[50] This is not to deny that these descriptions ultimately reflected some practical knowledge of the Upper Nile, but simply to observe that the praetorians were influenced by these traditions in shaping their accounts

---

[44] See 166.

[45] For an illuminating modern comparison in Europeans' views of Australia, see Ryan (1996).

[46] Kirwan (1957), 16, developed in idem. (1982/2002), 73.

[47] Vantini (1994–5), and cf. De Nardis (1989), 140–1.      [48] De Nardis (1989), 134.

[49] Plin. *HN* 6.189–95. Contra Sherk (1974), 541, n.25 who wrongly states that Pliny's information came from the Neronian expedition.

[50] Hdt 2.28 cf. Aristid. *Or.* 36.47, 54. Cf. Kirwan (1982), 71–2.

for an expectant Roman audience.[51] Nero and his courtiers knew that the
Nile originated in 'very remote regions' and were familiar with the idea of
Nilotic swamps and the image of rocks at the source: the expedition simply
confirmed this knowledge.

Pliny and Seneca both had direct access to the written reports of the
Praetorians and made the most of them. Pliny referred to them repeatedly within his *Natural History*. His account also hints at the form that
these reports may have taken. In a brief discussion on Ethiopian ebony in
Book XII, and on Herodotus' account of tributes paid in that wood, Pliny
notes the information that had recently become available to him:

> The well-known *Aethiopiae forma* – brought recently to the emperor Nero as
> we have explained – revealed that trees are scarce for 996 miles from Syene,
> at the edge of the Empire, as far as Meroe, and none is known there except
> for the palm species.[52]

Pliny refers to the information provided by the Praetorians as *Aethiopiae
forma*, variously translated as 'a map of Ethiopia' or 'information about
Ethiopia' in modern commentaries.[53] In itself, Pliny's reference to a *forma* is
not especially illuminating: cartographic vocabulary is confusing in Latin,
to say the least, and this language does not simply indicate that Nero's
explorers produced a 'map' in the modern sense of the term.[54] Indeed the
nature of the Praetorians' task, the subject matter, established tradition
and the fragmentary allusions to the work preserved by Pliny, all suggest
that the *Aethiopiae forma* was either an annotated itinerary of the voyage
upriver, or an itinerary that was accompanied by a narrative gloss.

The most basic evidence for the nature of the *Aethiopiae forma* comes
from Pliny's use of the text in his discussion of the geography of Nubia in
Book VI of the *Natural History*. This passage follows a detailed analysis
of the Nubian geographies of Bion and Juba II, and his brief allusion to
the river itineraries of Dalion, Aristocreon, Bion, Basilis, Simonides and
Timosthenes, all writers of the Hellenistic period, who had varying degrees

---

[51] Diels (1969), 406 is more cynical.     [52] Plin. *HN* 12.19.

[53] Desanges (2008), 133, n.1. states simply that this was a 'carte' without discussion; Cary and Warmington (1929), 174 state that the report was accompanied by 'a map'; Arnaud (1983), 696: 'qui
semble avoir été un authentique cadastre'; De Nardis (1989), 139 concludes that the *forma* was
intended to update Agrippa's chorography; László Török in Eide et al. (1998), 887 concludes that
'Pliny collected the information from a structured cartographical source, i.e, a map, in which the
distances between significant places and points were exactly indicated'; Kolb (2016), 223: '[they]
returned to the Emperor with precise measurements of the distances between the towns as well as a
map of the country.' Sherk (1974), 541 also assumes that this must have been a map and speculates
on the specialists who would have accompanied the mission.

[54] See above, 41–3.

of personal familiarity with the upper Nile.[55] Throughout, Pliny expresses
frustration at the inconsistencies across these texts, but suggests that the
Neronian explorers may offer a solution of sorts to this scholarly tangle:

> But this debate has now ended, for the explorers sent by Nero have reported
> the distance from Syene [to Meroe] to be 975 miles, in this manner: from
> Syene to Hiera Sycaminos 54 miles, from there to Tama 72 miles, through
> the lands of the Ethiopian Euonymites, to Primi 120, Acina 64, Pitara 25,
> Tergedus 106. The Gagauden island was found to be in the middle of
> this section; from here parrots (*psittaci*) were seen for the first time, after
> another island called Artigula, they saw the *sphingion*, and after Tergedus
> the *Cynocephalos*. From there to Nabata is 80 miles; that small town is the
> only one of those mentioned [that still exists]. From there to the island of
> Meroe is 360 miles. The plants around Meroe are greener, and some trees
> can be seen, along with traces of rhinoceroses and elephants. This town of
> Meroe is 70 miles from the approach to the island, and next to it is another
> island, Tados, in the right-hand channel, as one goes upstream, which makes
> a harbour. The *oppidum* has few buildings.[56]

This passage can only have been derived from an itinerary. It is structured
around a succession of stopping points on the Nile; it is punctuated by the
distances between these points, and the whole section is framed in terms
of the total distance covered. This is exactly the form that we see in extant
itineraries.[57] The precision of Pliny's location of the parrots after Gagades
and monkeys or baboons after Articula also suggests a text structured
around specific nodal points.[58] To judge from their stopping points, the
Neronian explorers simply followed the Nile upriver: this was a journey
which would be rendered difficult by the cataracts and the current, but
which scarcely necessitated elaborate navigational instructions, or needed
to be rendered in anything but the most straightforward form.[59] The
centurions go on to discuss the Temple of Ammon in Meroe and its rule
by Queen Candace, and this detailed description of the city hints at some

---

[55] Plin. *HN* 6.183. For an introduction to these passages, and their authors, see Eide et al. (1996), 541–49, 552–7 and Desanges (2008), xvii–xix, 106–32. On their historical context, see Fraser (1972), 176–7. Brief biographies of each are helpfully collected in Keyser and Irby-Massie (2008).

[56] Plin. *HN* 6.184–5. The distances given vary between manuscripts. Cf. Brodersen (1996), 282.

[57] It is worth comparing here the information that Pliny derived from a report (*quidem eius*) of Suetonius Paulinus in the Atlas in *HN* 5.14–15. Pliny did not term this source a *forma*, and consequently modern commentators have rarely assumed it took cartographic form, but the material and its presentation seems more or less identical to that found in the account of the Neronian explorers.

[58] Desanges (2008), 152–3 discusses the animals in detail (with bibliography).

[59] Unlike Petronius, the centurions do not seem to have left the river to take the Korosko-Abu Hamad desert road. See Eide et al. (1998), 881.

narrative elaboration at this point.[60] Seneca implies that the praetorians added an oral gloss to their written report when they returned to court, and this information may well have been in popular circulation thereafter.[61] Finally, it is evident that the document which Pliny drew upon here is the same as the *Aethiopiae forma* in Book XII. The difference in the stated distance between Syene and Meroe in the two books may be explained by copyists' errors, and the fact that these figures are prominently presented in each account is surely significant.[62] Equally noteworthy is the emphasis that each places upon the presence (or absence) of animals, plants and trading commodities at different stages of the journey.

Pliny's account also reveals the type of information that the explorers took with them when they made their trip to the south. It is here that we get some sense of itineraries in action, and how they might be supplemented in the field. Of crucial importance here is a passing statement in the passage just quoted. Pliny states of Nabata: *oppidum id parvum inter praedicta solum* – 'this small *oppidum* is the only one of those mentioned [which survives]'. This reference to the apparent depopulation of the Nubian Nile is an important theme of this whole section of the *Natural History*. In the preceding passage, Pliny enumerates the settlements of Meroe and Lower Nubia as they appear in the itinerary of Bion and in the geography of Juba II – two Hellenistic sources that were evidently available to him.[63] He then undermines this careful topography by stating that only seven settlements were still in existence at the time of Petronius' campaign in 25 or 24 BCE, six of which were captured and the seventh (Napata) sacked.[64] Again, the Neronian centurions are introduced to drive the point home:

> These are the places reported as far as Meroe, but almost none of them is still known today, on either bank. The Praetorian soldiers under the command of a tribune recently sent by the emperor Nero for the purpose of exploring the region, reported nothing but desert . . . [65]

The fact that the Neronian explorers took care to record settlements that were no longer present can only imply that they were expecting to find them – clear proof that they travelled upriver with itineraries in hand. For our purposes, this reveals more about the continuity of textual practice than it does about changing settlement patterns in Lower Nubia, although historians and archaeologists of that region have sometimes argued otherwise. Pliny states that ongoing wars between the ruling powers of Ethiopia

---

[60] Plin. *HN* 6.186; Desanges (2008), 154–61.     [61] Sen. *QNat* 6.8.3.
[62] Desanges (2008), 147, 155, n.2.     [63] Plin. *HN* 6.178–183.     [64] Plin. *HN* 6.181.
[65] Plin. *HN* 6.181.

and Egypt had desolated the country long before the arrival of Rome.[66] One reason for this emphasis was Pliny's anxiety to show that imperial expansion was not an essentially destructive force, particularly in comparison with earlier border wars in the region: there was no place in the *Natural History* for Tacitus' famous declaration that the soldiers of empire 'create a desert and call it a peace'.[67] Yet the observation may also reflect the dissonance between occupation patterns in Lower Nubia, and the expectations of explorers who were expecting to encounter more substantial settlements. The locations listed in Hellenistic itineraries were likely to have been either temporary or seasonal and may well have been overlooked by Roman military personnel more used to orienting themselves by the substantial towns and cities of the Mediterranean world.[68]

The state of knowledge presented by Pliny could only have come about if Petronius and later the Neronian explorers took obsolescent itineraries with them on their expeditions to the south, and then used them as templates for their own descriptions of the region. They continued to use established stopping points as markers in their reports, even when these places were said to have been abandoned or otherwise destroyed. Precisely which texts were available to them is itself an important question. Given the military nature of the expedition, we might expect that the expedition would have been equipped with the reports of Petronius and of the other Augustan generals who campaigned in the region, although comparanda from later periods of commercial (especially maritime) mapping warn against glib assumptions on this score.[69] To judge from the *forma* produced by the Neronian explorers, they did not have access to an authoritative archive of recent military reports, and it seems likely that no such collection of intelligence existed in this period. Instead, their principal work of reference was a much earlier itinerary. A close reading of the different itineraries listed by Pliny suggests that the closest text to the Neronian *forma* was

---

[66] Plin. *HN* 6.182.

[67] Tac. *Agr.* 30. Cf. Beagon (1996), 293–4 and Thompson (1969), 43. On this destruction, see Desanges (2008), 141, n.1.

[68] *Pace* Desanges (2008), 132–3. I am grateful to Dave Edwards for this observation.

[69] This crucial question is passed over rather lightly in Sherk (1974), 543: 'Not only did Roman arms pacify, unite and open up vast territories for geographical exploration, but also Roman commanders were themselves often directly involved in the dissemination of the newly acquired facts. Their reports and memoirs formed permanent storehouses of raw material for the future use of geographers and other men of science.' Cook (2006) provides an illuminating discussion of the haphazard archival practices of a much more recent enterprise – the hydrography department of the East India Company. It seems likely that the Roman military was beset by similar problems of 'knowledge' production and preservation – a point explored further in Chapters 1 and 2, above.

the itinerary produced by Juba II, although the parallel is not precise.[70] The toponyms preserved in the two documents are not identical, but all of the points identified by the Praetorians are present in some form in the earlier text, even when they are identified as abandoned settlements.[71] The simplest explanation is that both Juba and the Praetorians worked from (or travelled with) the same Hellenistic itinerary that has since been lost – a tantalizing glimpse of a rich tradition of literature of this kind. The crucial point, though, is clear enough: when they set out into the interior, the centurions turned to a long tradition of itinerary literature to help them find their way.

Roman knowledge of the stretch of the Nile between Syene and Meroe was unstable in the period of the late Republic and early empire. Although the river was well-travelled in Lower Nubia, by merchants, seasonal work-ers and pilgrims to the temples of the region, it was not quite the regional highway represented by the Nile to the north.[72] The imperial presence in the region was manifested primarily in the military garrisons at Syene and sporadically further south in the Dodekaschoinos.[73] These garrisons doubt-less increased geographical intelligence on the region, and the campaigns of Petronius in Nubia certainly created more, but it remains noteworthy that when the Neronian explorers headed downriver, they were guided by itineraries that were centuries old, and not by more recent military intelli-gence. In annotating these itineraries, and creating a *forma* of their own, the centurions exemplified the way in which geographical texts of this kind were created and exploited throughout the empire. All of these itineraries are best regarded as palimpsests – as working texts which could be expanded and amended when employed in the field, but which never completely obscured the records of journeys made by earlier travellers. After all, as Pliny so vividly illustrates, the praetorians did not simply erase settlements and stopping places which they felt had been abandoned, they marked this change in their text, thereby preserving the records of the explorers who had gone before. By extension, we can see that these itineraries were normative, rather than prescriptive; that they shaped the expectations and views of the individuals who used them, but did not impose a definitive interpretation upon the landscape.

---

[70] These itineraries can conveniently be compared with reference to the tables in Eide et al. (1996), 555–7; Eide et al. (1998), 806–9 and 879. See also Desanges (2008), 108–33 on the toponyms.

[71] Eide et al. (1998), 879–80.     [72] On Nile travel in the north, see Rutherford (2012).

[73] Speidel (1988). On geographical knowledge from these campaigns, see Desanges (2008), xvi.

It is less clear how the Neronian *forma Aethiopiae* represented the river beyond Meroe, if indeed the explorers ever got as far as the Sudd or the territories beyond. The *Natural History* mentions the great marshes to the south of Meroe, and presumably took this information from the *forma*, but Pliny also states that pygmies had been placed in the region by 'certain' writers, implying that he supplemented this source with more imaginative material at this point.[74] A similar methodology shapes the remainder of Pliny's account of the upper Nile in Ethiopia: details and distances were taken from itineraries, but were supplemented with other sources where necessary.[75] This hints at the difficulties faced by geographers when they attempted to extrapolate broader images of a region from itinerary literature alone. Much of Pliny's description undoubtedly came from Hellenistic itineraries – Aristocreon, Bion and Dalion are cited by name, and the account is more or less structured around the river itself.[76] But it is also apparent that these texts were much less forthcoming on the area to the south of Meroe than they were on the more familiar regions to the north. Distances between stopping points appear much more rarely and are measured in days of travel, rather than in *milia*. Equally, the points themselves are increasingly geographical features or peoples, rather than well-defined stopping points. Pliny, moreover, wilfully coloured this section of his account with material derived, as he readily admitted, from *fabulosa* – fabulous stories.[77] Evidently, the Hellenistic texts lost their lucidity beyond Meroe and provided a less precise source for Pliny to exploit. The Neronian Praetorians surely faced similar problems. Deprived of a clear template from which to work, the explorers may well have abandoned the precision of their own *forma* at this time – certainly, they do not seem to have left a source from which Pliny or Seneca could work.

But Pliny had other narrative strategies to hand. It was this very paucity of itinerary information on the Upper Nile which led Pliny to construct the extended narrative account of the Nile's course with which this chapter opened. In place of detailed, discrete geographical information of specific points on the Nile banks, Pliny created a continuous account of a constantly flowing river. There are two Niles within the *Natural History* – one the personified spirit of Book V, which flows from the source to the mouth, the other the route for exploration and conquest, which is described in

---

[74] Plin. *HN* 6.188: *quidam et Pygmaeorum gentem prodiderunt inter paludes ex quibus Nilus oriretur.* Cf. the discussion above 144.

[75] Plin. *HN* 6.189–95.

[76] On Pliny's debts to these sources, see Eide et al. (1996), 541–57; Desanges (2008), 143–7.

[77] Plin. *HN* 6.195.

the opposite direction. Both are shaped profoundly by the conventions of itinerary literature, or by the conception of the world as the sum of a series of journeys, but together they highlight the complexity of classical 'hodological' geography. There was more than one way of defining a river, and more than one way of travelling along it.[78]

## Itineraries in Roman Egypt

Soldiers and explorers were not the only travellers who came to the Nile valley with established expectations about what they would see. The region between Alexandria and the First Cataract was visited by countless tourists and pilgrims during the Roman period.[79] Varied as their individual itineraries were, it is safe to say that there were two constants that determined the form of every trip. The first was the Nile itself, which was Egypt's most spectacular marvel, according to many travellers, and the object of wonder in its own right.[80] But even those who neglected the wonders of the river floods could not escape the fundamental importance of the Nile in directing their travel through Egypt. Egypt *was* the Nile, as innumerable commentators noted, and it was the means by which the country could be explored.

The second constant for tourists was literary and historical expectation. Educated Roman tourists travelled the Nile with copies of Herodotus or Homer to hand, just as their nineteenth-century successors did, and this fundamentally shaped their response to the country both culturally and geographically. When Julius, Augustus or Germanicus Caesar lingered on the Nile and admired the beauty of the country, they did so in part because Alexander had also done so, and all paid due deference to the supposed tomb of that king.[81] In turn, when Titus, Vespasian, Hadrian and Septimius Severus all visited Egypt and the Nile, theirs was a conscious emulation of the early Julio-Claudians, as well as the Macedonian king. These travellers also made sure to pay their respects at the supposed resting place of Pompey the Great, whose murder in Egypt had a continuing political resonance within the Roman imagination.[82] In so doing they further inscribed the historical and geographical line that firmly bound the Roman present to

---

[78] On these multiple Niles, see further the Afterword, below.

[79] Foertmeyer (1989) provides the best general introduction. See also Rutherford (2012) for a recent précis.

[80] Sen. *Ep.* 104.15; Diod Sic. 1.36.7; Aristid. *Or.* 36.119.   [81] Foertmeyer (1989), 110–13.

[82] Cf. Dio Cass. 69.11.1, Dio Cass 76.13; SHA *Sev.* 17.1; *Hadr.* 14.4; App. *BCiv.* 2.86. On visits to Pompey's tomb, see Foertmeyer (1989), 112–13. On the historical resonance of Pompey's murder, see Chapter 6, below.

the pre-Ptolemaic past, and Alexandria to the sights and cities of Upper Egypt.[83]

This process of travel and tourism as an affirmation of pre-existing knowledge is a well-known phenomenon from other periods, and several important studies have applied these approaches to Greek and Roman understanding of 'Egypt' in broad cultural and historical terms.[84] But this phenomenon also had a role in the articulation and solidification of specifically *geographical* knowledge. The increasingly familiar practice of Nilotic travel shaped the expectations of those who arrived in the region, and the assumptions of outsiders who were never to travel there at all. The equation of Egypt with the Nile was a long-standing trope in classical literature, whether in Homer's naming of the river itself as *Aegyptos*, or in Herodotus' well-known declaration that Egypt was the gift of the Nile.[85] But the popular touristic performance of this equivalence – the very experience of Egypt as a linear series of points of interest, strung out along the river, and the subsequent circulation of such reports in the form of itineraries or narrative tourist accounts – helped to solidify this association still further amongst armchair travellers across the classical world. Tourists still went to Alexandria and the Delta, of course, and the more adventurous journeyed to the Fayyum or even Siwa, but it was the Nile itself which provided the core around which all narratives of travel were built, and it was this travel which shaped in turn, the view of Egypt within the wider world.[86]

## Strabo

Strabo provides the clearest illustration of the role that physical journeys played in shaping geographical description, and hence in articulating a view of the Nile that was essentially linear. Written during the reign of the Tiberius, between 18 and 23 CE, but drawing upon the travels and observations of a long lifetime, Strabo's *Geographika* surveys the whole of the inhabited world in seventeen substantial books.[87] Like its author, a Greek from Asia Minor who had served the empire and lived the latter

---

[83]　Note Diod Sic 1.46.8 on tourists who subsequently wrote histories of Egypt.
[84]　See for example, Foertmeyer (1989); Takács (1995a).　　[85]　Hom. *Od.* 4.477; Hdt 2.5.
[86]　The second-century writer Aelius Aristides claims to have visited Egypt four times, and got as far as Philae at least once. His resulting description of the region is entirely structured around the Nile: Aristid. *Or.* 36.1; Behr (1981), 15–21, 62–3. Foertemeyer (1989), 10–84 discusses ancient tourist graffiti in Egypt (which is plentiful); cf. also Brennan (1998) for spectacular examples of graffiti on the Memnon statues, and Bernard and Bernard (1960) for a comprehensive survey.
[87]　On Strabo see: Clarke (1999), 193–7 Dueck (1999), Dueck (2000), 1–30; Koelsch (2004) and now Roller (2014).

part of his life in the imperial capital, the text itself was very much a product of two cultural worlds. Strabo drew proudly on different aspects of his Greek intellectual heritage, including the mathematical tradition of Eratosthenes and the weighty poetic legacy of Homer, but also revelled in the changed political realities of the new Roman Empire.[88] Strabo is commonly presented as an armchair geographer, but he took pride in his own extensive travels, and judiciously supplemented his learning with direct personal observation.[89] This combination is particularly evident in the penultimate book of the work, in which Strabo describes Egypt. As a young man, he had spent some time on the staff of the Roman provincial governor Aelius Gallus in the 20s BCE, and evidently knew Alexandria well.[90] This experience was to have a lasting effect upon the representation of Egypt when the *Geography* was finally published.

In the discussion of the Nile Delta, Strabo draws not only upon his own observations, but also upon the records of other travellers. His attempts to make sense of a subtly shifting landscape, and his frustration at opaque Egyptian methods of measurement, mean that this section of the *Geography* affords a rare glimpse of his engagement with different types of sources, and their recasting into new form. As is the case with the Neronian explorers, we get some impression here of an outside observer, travelling through unfamiliar territories and struggling to make sense of a landscape primarily through the texts available to him:

> This is the description from Alexandria to the head of the Delta. Artemidoros says that the sail up is 28 *schoinoi*, which is 840 stadia, calculating the *schoinos* at 30 stadia. When I made the voyage different measurements were made by different people, in giving the distance in *schoinoi*, so that 40 stadia or even more was agreed upon, according to the places. That the measure of the *schoinos* among the Egyptians is uncertain was made clear by Artemidoros himself in the following: he says that from Memphis to the Thebais each *schoinos* is 120 stadia, and from the Thebais to Syene 60. He also says that

---

[88] Clarke (1999) sets Strabo's work within its Hellenistic intellectual context; cf. Biraschi (2005) and Dueck (2000), 31–8 on the Homeric influences. The search for reconciliation between these two traditions occupies much of Books 1 and 2 of the work. Strabo's interest in contemporary political power is shown most clearly in the exaltation of Roman history and government at 6.4.1–2 and 17.3.24. And cf. the history of the occupation of Egypt in 17.1.11. On the celebration of Roman power see Clarke (1999), 210–19; Dueck (2000), 107–29. Van der Vliet (2003) discusses ethnographic order within Strabo's work.

[89] Jacob (1999), 26 terms the work 'a literary geography that did not rely at all on map-making but on the compilation of a library'. Strabo stresses the breadth of his own autopsy at 2.5.11, but also acknowledges his (inevitable) dependence on others.

[90] Strabo refers to his personal experience of Alexandria when discussing the harbour (2.3.5), the plants of the region (3.5.10) and the sight of Lake Mareotis during the Nile flood (5.1.7). On this material, see Dueck (2000), 20–1.

sailing up from Pelousion to the head [of the Delta] is 25 *schoinoi*, or 750 stadia using the same measurement.[91]

Strabo is on slightly firmer ground in his discussion of the relative positions of different towns within the Delta, but again specific journeys provide the framework for his account.

Strabo's Egyptian geography is dominated by his discussion of the Nile above the Delta, and his own journey upriver structures this narrative. This was the trip in around 27 BCE which he made while on the staff of Aelius Gallus, then prefect of Egypt.[92] Aelius Gallus was not the only Augustan prefect to make this journey: his predecessor Cornelius Gallus erected a hubristic inscription commemorating his own authority at Philae in around 30 BCE, before being whisked back to Rome in disgrace.[93] Graffiti left at the same temple by a poet in the entourage of Gaius Turranius in 14 CE hint at a more humble combination of wonder at the glories of the First Cataract landscape and exhaustion at the long trip from the north, but Strabo's is certainly the richest extant account.[94] The description of Egypt is structured around his own voyage, even where he digresses at considerable length. The different stopping points along the river are presented in order, and throughout the orientation is that of an individual travelling from north to south. In tone and detail, this has obvious similarities to the accounts of later travellers in the same region:

> Here the Nile is above the Delta. What is on the right, as one sails up, is called Libya – as is that around Alexandria and the Mareotis – and what is on the left Arabia . . . As one sails up, there is the fortress of Babylon, to which some Babylonians withdrew and then obtained a settlement here from the kings. Today it is the camp of one of the three legions that guard Egypt. There is a ridge reaching from the camp to the Nile, on which water comes up from the river by means of wheels and screws, and a hundred and fifty captive men work it. The pyramids are conspicuously seen from Memphis on the far side, and are nearby.[95]

Thereafter, the description settles into its rhythm. Strabo describes in turn Memphis and its sanctuaries; the Pyramids; Acanthus; Lake Moeris; Arsinoe or Crocodeilopolis; the City of Heracles; Cynopolis and Oxyry-hnchus; the garrison of Hermopolis (where the calculation of the length

---

[91]  Strabo 17.1.24. tr. Roller (2014), 746.
[92]  The voyage is mentioned at 2.5.12 and 11.11.5 as well as repeatedly in Book XVII.
[93]  Strabo 17.1.53 and cf. Suet. *Aug* 66.1–2 and Dio Cass. 53.23.5–7. Gallus famously erected a trilingual inscription at Philae establishing the imperial presence there. On which see Eide et al. (1996), 689–700 for texts, translations and commentaries, and Burstein (1988) for discussion.
[94]  Philae II.142, 143, 144.    [95]  Strabo 17.1.30. tr. Roller (2014), 748.

of the *schoenus* changes again); Ptolemais and the Labyrinth; Abydus, Little Diospolis and Tentyra; Thebes; Hermonthis, and cities dedicated to crocodiles, Aphrodite, Eileithuia and Apollonospolis.[96] The long narrative closes with a description of Syene, Elephantine and Philae.[97] Although the systematic order of this account is obscured by a number of long digressions – on the history of the Pyramids, the importance of oracles and the nature of Creation – Strabo remains bound by an essentially linear structure. Significantly, he also underscores the ultimate origin of his geography in his own autopsy through frequent reference to his personal observations in each of these places. Thus, he recalls his first view of the pyramids, his impressions of the construction of the Labyrinth, the feeding of the crocodiles at Arsinoe and the journey by wagon from Syene to Philae and back again.[98]

These digressions reveal a great deal about the practices of ancient tourism. Perhaps the best-known episode is the account of the spectacle provided by the boatmen at the First Cataract:

> A little above Elephantine is a little cataract on which the boatmen put on a performance for the commanders. The cataract is in the middle of the river and is the brow of a rock that is flat on top, so that it receives the river, but it ends in a dropoff, over which the water flows down. On either side toward the land there is a stream, which generally can be navigated up. They sail up here and then drift down the cataract, and are thrust with the boat over the dropoff but are saved without harm.[99]

Philae and the First Cataract was the point at which many Roman tourists turned back, either because they travelled for religious reasons and had reached their destination at the Isis Temple of Philae, or because the island and the rapids seemed to mark the end of one world and the beginning of another. Tourist graffiti at Philae expresses wonder and disquiet at the strange new landscapes of Lower Nubia, and even the ferocious sounds of the First Cataract were regarded as otherworldly by Classical commentators.[100]

---

[96]  Strabo 17.1.31–2 (Memphis); 33–4 (the Pyramids); 35–7 (Acanthus and Lake Moeris); 38 (Arsinoe); 39 (the City of Heracles); 40 (Cynopolis and Oxyryhnchus); 41 (the Hermopolitic garrison); 42 (Ptolemais); 44 (Abydus, Little Diospolis and Tentyra); 46 (Thebes); 47 (Hermonthis, Aphrodite, Eileithuia and Apollonospolis).

[97]  Strabo 17.1.48–50.

[98]  Strabo 17.1.33–4 (experiences of the Pyramids); 37 (the Labyrinth); 38 (feeding time at Arsinoe); 50 (wagon trip to Philae).

[99]  Strabo 17.1.49. tr. Roller (2014), 757.

[100]  See esp. Philae I. no 43, II nos 130, 142, 143, 144, 151, 158, 168. See Foertmeyer (1989), 33–8 and 72–3 on this graffiti. On the noise of the cataract see Cic. *Rep.* 6.19; Sen. *QNat* 4a 1.3; Plin. *HN* 5.54. On later accounts of the same region, see Cooper (2014), 150–2.

Strabo's description of the Nile course through Egypt is admirably detailed, but his systematic itinerary survey also had the effect of ironing out the various curves in the river between the Delta and the First Cataract. His account repeatedly asserts that the Nile followed a straight course through Egypt, without substantial deviations or bends – a commonplace that he shared with many earlier classical geographers.[101] Yet a glance at a modern map reveals immediately that this is a considerable simplification, and completely occludes the Dendara Bend at Qena. In part, this 'straightening' is a natural tendency of hodological modes of description: by focusing upon specific nodal points and movement between them, rather than their cartographic relations to one another, meandering routes are almost invariably simplified considerably when represented in this form.[102] We experience this phenomenon repeatedly in first-hand accounts of travel along roads and rivers, and can also see it in schematized transport maps like the London Tube Map (or indeed the Peutinger Table), in which cartographic precision is sacrificed for clarity and simplicity. Strabo's dogmatism on this point is all the more striking when we consider his sensitivity to the great curves of the river further south.[103] In the regions that he knew personally, in other words, Strabo insisted (wrongly) that the Nile followed a straight course, while elsewhere he provided a more precise geometrical image. First-hand observation, it would seem, was not always completely beneficial.

## Tacitus on the Ill-Fated Egyptian Journey of Germanicus

A rather different sense of the linearity of the Nile is provided by Tacitus' account of the Egyptian voyage of Germanicus Caesar.[104] In 19 CE, the young prince arrived in Egypt, and travelled up the river as far as the Ethiopian frontier. The episode was politically charged: Augustan law prohibited individuals of senatorial rank from travelling to Egypt without formal permission, and the emperor Tiberius viewed Germanicus'

---

[101] Strabo 17.1.3: 'it alone passes through Aegypt, through the whole of it and in a straight line'; 17.1.4 'The Nile flows from the Aethiopian boundaries towards the north in a straight line to the district called "Delta".'
[102] Janni (1984), 136–40, although at 136 he claims (surprisingly) that Strabo did not know of the great Nile bend between Dongola and Meroe. This is clearly described at 17.1.2. Strabo only 'straightened' the river where he had travelled it himself. Cf. also Brodersen (1995), 59–64.
[103] Strabo, 17.1.2.
[104] Tac. *Ann* 2.59–61. The voyage is also discussed by Suet. *Tib.* 52.2 and alluded to (very briefly) by Vell. Pat. 2.129.3. The fullest scholarly treatment is Weingärtner (1969), but see now Kelly (2010) and Leemreize (2014), 59–63.

presence in Alexandria with suspicion, not least because he was assumed to have his own designs on imperial power.[105] Contemporary commentators still remembered the visit of Germanicus' grandfather Antony to Egypt, and may have been wary of the grandson following this dangerous precedent.[106] The journey also proved to be inauspicious for other reasons. Although Germanicus was welcomed by the human inhabitants of Egypt, the gods (and animals) proved less accommodating: according to several later sources, the refusal of Apis' sacred ox to feed from the visitor's hand at the temple in Memphis was interpreted as a harbinger of the young prince's death shortly afterwards.[107]

Tacitus' account of Germanicus' Nile voyage initially seems like a simple tourist itinerary. While the diplomatic difficulties at Alexandria are briefly noted, there is no reference to the episode at Memphis. He states that Germanicus visited the Canopic and Heraclean mouths of the Nile before travelling south and visiting the major sights on the Nile, from the Pyramids of Giza to the First Cataract.[108] The passage is loosely structured in itinerary form – or at least as a punctuated linear narrative, which recalls the conventions of earlier travel writing. Thebes itself is described briefly, and dominated by the translation of written hieroglyphs in the voice of an aged Egyptian priest: his account of past Egyptian greatness simultaneously recalls Herodotus' digressive asides and explicitly relates the fading of Egyptian grandeur with the rise of Roman power.[109] Similar themes are consolidated in the brief discussion of the tribute lists (*indicta... tributa*) that were also said to have been visible on the temple walls. Thereafter, the key sites of Egypt appear one after another, in rapid succession. Each is graced with a short descriptive or hyperbolic account, whether on the singing statues of Memnon, the size of the pyramids or the peculiar form of the First Cataract rocks:

> But other marvels, too, arrested the attention of Germanicus: especially the stone colossus of Memnon, which emits a vocal sound when touched by the rays of the sun; the pyramids reared mountain-high by the wealth of emulous kings amid wind-swept and all but impassable sands; the excavated lake which receives the overflow of the Nile; and elsewhere narrow gorges

---

[105]  Tac. *Ann.* 2.59; cf. *Hist* 1.11; Weingärtner (1969), 5–9.

[106]  Foertmeyer (1989), 113–4 suggests Tacitus' implicit evocation of Scipio Africanus at *Ann* 2.59 may have been intended to prompt this association.

[107]  Tac. *Ann.* 2.59; Dio Cass. 66.8.6 describes the hostile reception of Vespasian in Alexandria, in implied contrast to Germanicus; cf. Joseph. *Ap.* 2.63 hints at a hostile reception for the prince among the Jewish community of Alexandria. Plin. *HN* 8.185 on Apis's inauspicious behaviour followed by Solin. 32.19 and Amm, Marc. 22.14.8.

[108]  Tac. *Ann.* 2.60     [109]  Tac. *Ann.* 2.60; cf. Luc. 10.268–79 (discussed in Chapter 6).

and deeps impervious to the plummet of the explorer. Then he proceeded to Elephantine and Syene, once the limits of the Roman Empire, which now stretches to the Red Sea.[110]

Brief reflection reveals that the order in which Tacitus presented these sites was determined by literary considerations, rather than either geographical location or the narrative of Germanicus' visit. Thebes and the colossi of Memnon are located far to the south of both the Giza plateau and Lake Moeris, which must be the 'excavated lake' to which Tacitus alludes.[111] The 'narrows and extreme depth' (*angustiae et profunda altitudo*) can only be the First Cataract, which itself lay to the south of Elephantine and Syene. While there is no reason to assume that Germanicus did not visit each of these sites – after all, they were well-established parts of the typical Egyptian 'tour' as Tacitus and his audience must have known – he could hardly have travelled to them in the order in which they are presented here without adding enormous deviations to his route.

Instead, Tacitus was concerned to underscore the hubris of Pharaonic Egypt, already established in the narrative of the priests of Thebes. The statues of Memnon, the 'mountainous' Pyramids and the allusion to Lake Moeris all manifest human claims to authority over nature, which is swiftly undermined. Tacitus' allusions to the almost sublime qualities of the cataract emphasize the scale of human ignorance about the world, a theme which had previously motivated Lucretius and Seneca, as discussed in the previous chapter.[112] In any other writer, references to the decrepitude of the Pharaonic world and the expanding frontiers of the Roman Empire might hint at imperial triumphalism, but this can scarcely be the case here. Tacitus was notoriously sceptical of the imperial pretensions of Rome, and these misgivings are evident throughout his writing.[113] If anything, Germanicus' tour of Egypt must be read as an anticipation of his coming fate. Tacitus may have eschewed the narrative of the inauspicious visit to Apis, but that is because the remainder of his Egyptian geography does the same job for him.[114]

Tacitus' jumbled Nile itinerary should not be read as carelessness or simple ignorance: if the historian's famously exact language were not reassurance enough, his recitation of precise itineraries elsewhere in his works

---

[110] Tac. *Ann.* 2.61 after Jackson (1979), 491–3.    [111] Weingärtner (1969), 136–7.

[112] Discussed more fully in Chapter 4.

[113] Tacitus' hostility to imperialism is a familiar aspect of his writing. See Rutledge (2009b).

[114] Kelly (2010), 231–7 follows similar reasoning, but ultimately detects an optimistic resonance in the passage – a conviction that Roman tyranny will also pass. Cf. also Leemreize (2014), 59–63 for a more positive reading.

reveals the care with which he deployed geographical information.[115] The deft sketches of Northern Europe and Britain in *Germania* and *Agricola* were complemented by a precision within his narrative historical works.[116] Instead, the passage hints at an unexpected result of these linear modes of geographical representation, and of extensive travel within the Nile Valley. Here it is worth stepping back briefly and considering the world of Egypt as it was understood by travellers in the ancient world.

Roman tourists within Egypt did not travel independently, nor were they expected to find their own way. Their movement was aided or hindered by the wind, and was conventionally stopped entirely during the season of the floods. Their stopping points, too, would have been determined by the practical exigencies of river navigation in a way that would not have been true for land travel. In some senses, this dependence on long-standing local practice for Egyptian travel was inescapable in the ancient world, and was only transcended with the introduction of Nile steamers and the opening of the railway line to Aswan in the late-nineteenth century. The negotiation of these difficulties, of course, was the responsibility of local ships' captains, and not the travellers themselves. Consequently, navigation along the Nile was left in the hands of others – a factor which fundamentally affected the way in which the river valley would have been conceptualized by those travelling along it, and by those who read their accounts.

In a recent study, which develops many of the ideas of Michel De Certeau, Tim Ingold has distinguished the punctuated travel of 'transport' with the continuous movement of the 'wayfarer':

> Transport, then, is distinguished not by the employment of mechanical means but by the dissolution of the intimate bond that, in wayfaring, couples locomotion and perception. The transported traveller becomes a passenger, who does not himself move, but is rather *moved* from place to place. The sights, sounds and feelings that accost him during the passage have absolutely no bearing on the motion that carries him forth. For the soldier on parade, eyes turned to the right as his legs beat out an oscillation of metronomic regularity, marching is transport.[117]

This is a form of movement which redefines the landscape as a series of discrete points, which exist only in conceptual relation to one another. As such, it relates directly to the 'hodological' mode of spatial understanding

---

[115] Contra Weingärtner (1969), 137
[116] See, for example, Tac. *Ann.* 6.10. *Agr.* 10–12; *Germ.* 1, 5. And discussion in Clarke (2001) and Thomas (2010).
[117] Ingold (2007), 78. Cf. Deleuze and Guttari (1986), 49–50 for a similar formulation, opposing the 'nomad' and the 'migrant'.

identified by Pietro Janni for the classical world, and apparently exemplified in its itineraries. The most common illustration of this within the modern world is travel by underground train – a mode of transport which not only collapses the spaces between nodal stations, but proudly celebrates this recalibration of the world in texts like Henry Beck's celebrated London Tube map. But the same conceptual principles apply for travel up and down rivers, particularly as a passenger on a tourist vessel.

For the present purposes, an equally vivid point of comparison can be found in the copious modern literature on the Nile. Rudyard Kipling describes precisely this form of transported experience in his wry observations in a letter of 1913:

> For three weeks we sat on copiously chaired and carpeted decks, carefully isolated from everything that had anything to do with Egypt, under chaperonage of a properly orientalised dragoman. Twice or thrice daily, our steamer drew up at a mud-bank covered with donkeys. Saddles were hauled out of a hatch in our bows; the donkeys were dressed, dealt round like cards: we rode off through crops or desert as the case might be, were introduced in ringing tones to a temple and were then duly returned to our bridge and our Baedekers.[118]

Substituting Herodotus for Baedeker, this is probably how Strabo and Aelius Gallus experienced the Nile – as a series of more or less similar stopping points, which were presented to the travellers in turn without a comprehensible context.[119] But Tacitus' account of Germanicus hints at a further level of removal from the landscape – one in which the specific stopping points become jumbled, and in which the linear route, rather than the named points it connects, becomes the defining feature of the journey. We are effectively witnessing the simplification of the populated landscape into an abstracted line of travel.

Here again, there are striking parallels to the presentation of the same country in the spate of modern Nile travel narratives. From the late-eighteenth or early-nineteenth century, European travel along the Nile was common, whether as a trip in its own right, as a feature of a wider Grand Tour of the Eastern Mediterranean, or as a stopping point on the way to India.[120] This fashion generated its own copious literature, and long before the Cook's Tours popularized and regularized these voyages upriver, independent travellers had created a deeply conventionalized form of writing the Nile, as well as of moving along it. While the memoirs of

---

[118] Kipling (1920), 241–2.    [119] Cf. Ingold (2007), 79.
[120] On modern Egyptian tourism, see esp. the papers collected in Starkey and Starkey (2001).

writers like George William Curtis and Amelia Edwards adhered closely to the sequence of their own journeys, and hence contrasted with Tacitus' account of Germanicus' trip, the experience and presentation of specific locations was rarely determined by geography alone.[121] Standard practice on the Nile in the nineteenth century was to sail south when the wind made it possible, and to drift back at a more leisurely pace with the northbound current, stopping off at sites which had been missed on the first frantic rush past.[122] Consequently, the major sights of Egypt were frequently seen, and hence narrated, in a somewhat confused geographical order – a phenomenon which Amelia Edwards in particular lamented.[123] While the parallel with Germanicus is not exact – no eccentricities of the wind could explain a trip which visited the Pyramids between Thebes and Elephantine – there are clear conceptual similarities between these various accounts. In each period, the relative position of the different Egyptian regions was immaterial. What mattered to outside observers was that the country was recognizably linear – a succession of sites that might be visited in a single journey, and which were connected by the Nile.

In itself, this complicates the 'hodological' model of spatial cognition proposed by Janni, and developed by Brodersen. For both of those scholars, linear conceptions of space necessarily depended on the preservation of the order in which places would be visited, if not their positions relative to one another. Yet Tacitus' Egyptian pseudo-itinerary implies that even this order might be lost or confused in the articulation of linear geographies. Doubtless when it came to the practicalities of travel, the precise sequence of stopping points remained important, but the evidence provided by accounts of the Nile suggests that this was not the case once movement through the landscape had stopped and collective responses to the wider world were articulated. Roman commentators far from Egypt could be familiar with the conventional representation of the river as a line, even without travelling there themselves, and even without worrying too much about the precise order in which the places on the river banks appeared. It

---

[121] Curtis (1852); Edwards (1888).

[122] This view of leisurely travel rather occludes the expertise and physical labour of the boats' crews, of course. On the 'orientalist' assumptions underpinning this commonplace, see esp. Cooper (2014), 104–5 and *passim*.

[123] Edwards (1888), 69: 'For the history of ancient Egypt goes against the stream. The earliest monuments lie between Cairo and Siout, while the latest temples to the old gods are chiefly found in Nubia. Those travellers, therefore, who hurry blindly forward with or without a wind, now sailing, now tracking, now punting, passing this place by night, and that by day, and never resting till they have gained the farthest point of their journey, begin at the wrong end and see all the sights in precisely the wrong order.' Edwards was rather proud of the fact that she bucked this trend.

was the line – and not the nodal points that it connected – that came to predominate in such views of the river.

In some senses, the closest visual analogue to this mode of understanding may be found in the famous frontispiece to the Napoleonic *Description de l'Égypte*. Although this image was intended to encapsulate a work of extraordinary encyclopaedic breadth – a work, incidentally, which also included copious examples of more orthodox cartography – it collapses the antique land of Egypt into a single, foreshortened view.[124] [FIG 5.1] Through the centre of the image, and disappearing into the distance, runs the Nile, while along its banks are scattered, more or less haphazardly, the monuments of Egypt, specific and generic alike. Little thought is given to actual geographical location, and the Pyramids of Giza loom over the familiar seated figures of Ramses II from the Temple at Abu Simbel. For the artists of the *Description*, Egypt was a long warehouse, in which the superabundance of wonders was more important than the precise topographical position in which they appeared. The *Description* has rightly been regarded as a foundational text in the development of western 'Orientalism', and there are dangers in pushing an anachronistic correspondence to classical travel writings too far, but this emphatic reminder of political and military authority is salutary.[125] In many ways, the collapsed and jumbled geographies of Nile travellers – and particularly those who engaged with the empire through the writings of Strabo or Tacitus – were closely related to the 'triumphal' assemblages discussed in Chapter 2. The Nile provided one means by which Egypt could be comprehended and ordered in the minds of outside observers, but the precise spatial context in which these component parts were presented was less important than the overarching imperial ontology.

For Egyptian shipmasters, of course, or the boatmen who delighted Strabo on the First Cataract, the Nile was the central reality of their world, to be navigated as seasons and local conditions demanded, and not simply an abstracted line between arbitrary points.[126] The same was very probably true for the vast majority of inhabitants who lived on the banks of the river. For these travellers – 'wayfarers' in Ingold's terminology – the relative locations of settlements, temples, mooring points and sandbanks would

---

[124]   Briefly discussed in Godlewska (1995), 22–4.

[125]   Godlewska (1995) provides a brilliant survey with bibliography. On the importance of the *Description* to Said's formulation of 'Orientalism', see esp. Said (1978), 42–3, 84–7.

[126]   Ancient navigation on the Nile has not been examined in great detail. For a brilliant study of medieval practice, see Cooper (2014), 103–66.

5.1. Frontispiece from the Napoleonic *Description of Egypt*
[Gianni Dagli Orti/The Art Archive at Art Resource, NY]

have been a fundamental part of their knowledge of the river.[127] We get some suggestion of the more or less constant movement up and down the Nile from the copious papyrus evidence, and a number of itineraries survive that can only be the written traces of specific voyages.[128] Texts like the Oxyrhynchus itinerary and the journey attributed to the fourth-century merchant Theophanes occupy an uneasy middle ground between the quotidian 'wayfaring' navigation of the river pilots' learned practice, which had to be aware of currents, shallows and dangers at every stage in the journey, and the 'transported' itineraries typified by Strabo and Germanicus.[129] While these journeys were again defined by the various stopping points on either bank, the timings of both journeys are generous and the pace seems to have been leisurely. Stops for meals or rest are as likely to have been dictated by the whims of the travellers themselves, as by the established norms of the tourist itinerary or the arcane knowledge of the navigator. And for the innumerable journeys of a day or less, which happened throughout Roman Egypt, and which are as likely to have been made over land as on the river, the same was also true: the Nile valley channelled movement through Egypt, but the patterns and rhythms of this movement could vary enormously.[130]

## Satire and Parody

A great deal of writing of the first and second centuries confirms this external caricature of Egypt as a succession of nodal points, each of which was more important for being located on the river than for its precise position along it. Juvenal's famous fifteenth *Satire* opens with a pseudo-geographical section:

> One district reveres the crocodile, another quakes at the ibis glutted with snakes. The sacred long-tailed monkey's (*cercopithecus*) image gleams where the magic chords reverberate from crumbling Memnon and ancient Thebes lies in ruins with its hundred gates. Entire towns venerate cats in one place, in another river fish, in another a dog – but none worships Diana.[131]

---

[127] See Twain (1883), 95: 'Now when I had mastered the language of this water and had come to know every trifling feature that bordered on the great river as familiarly as I knew the letters of the alphabet, I had made a valuable acquisition. But I had lost something too. I had lost something which could never be restored to me while I lived. All the grace, the beauty, the poetry had gone out of the majestic river!' cf. Belyea (1998), 147–8 on similar aspects of 'maps' of the Missouri among the Blackfoot.

[128] Kolb (2001), 100; Mitchell (1976), 111–12.

[129] Adams (2001), 158–62; Matthews (2006) provides a detailed assessment of the Theophanes itinerary.

[130] Adams (2001). Adams (2007) provides a thorough survey of land travel in the province.

[131] Juv. 15.2–8. tr. Braund (2004), 489.

Juvenal's apparent allusions to painted scenes in this *Satire* were discussed briefly in Chapter 3, but the spatial ordering of the text as a whole is also illuminating.[132] The bulk of the *Satire* is devoted to reports of cannibalistic violence between the inhabitants of Ombos (perhaps Naqada) and Tentyra (Dendera) in Upper Egypt, and this opening section was merely intended to set the scene.[133] Many familiar tropes are ticked off – Memnon and Homer's hundred-gated Thebes, as well as the deranged piety of Aegyptus *demens*.[134] What is significant, though, is that these tourist sites and districts are reeled off in quick succession; one location follows another in a parody of the descriptions of Egypt from Herodotus to Strabo.[135] Juvenal's list does not follow a formal geographical order – indeed, several of the allusions cannot be placed at all – but his point is still made: the types of narrative that are satirized here were remembered for their relentless succession of peculiar places, not for the precise order in which they appeared.

Much the same is true of Lucian's *Philopseudes*. In this short dialogue, the prolific satirist of the second century CE discusses lies and truth telling, and takes practised aim at the popular fabrications of Herodotus and Ctesias.[136] Lucian may well have spent time in Egypt towards the end of his life, and cheerfully parodied familiar travelogues of the region.[137] One of the interlocutors in the *Philopseudes* describes how the colossus of Memnon did not just sing to him but recited oracular verses in Greek hexameters, and how a mysterious local priest went from imparting mystic knowledge to riding crocodiles bareback in the river.[138] The precise geography of Egypt was obviously irrelevant to Lucian's main point here, but the various mistakes in the account – apparently confusing Coptus and Thebes, and obscuring the location of Memphis for the purpose of the story – reinforce his principal theme. Juvenal, Lucian and their audiences were tediously familiar with the view of Egypt as a succession of increasingly improbable locations strung out along the Nile: indifference to their relative locations

---

[132] Cf. also the treatment in Swetnam-Burland (2015), 167–81.

[133] The passage is briefly introduced in Tait (2003), 23–4.

[134] Hom. *Il.* 9.383. Cf. Strabo 17.1.46; Plin. *HN* 5.60. On Juvenal's 'imperialist' treatment of Egypt, see esp. Alston (1996).

[135] Foertmeyer (1989), 176–7. Compare Strabo 17.1.40 and 17.1.44, 47, 49

[136] Lucian, *Philops.* 2; compare (most obviously), his *Ver. Hist.* prol. (and *passim*). Geographical themes in Lucian are discussed in Nasrallah (2005).

[137] Baldwin (1973), 17–20; Tait (2003), 24. Cf. also Lucian, *Toxaris*, 27 (alluding to an individual who spent six months travelling on the Nile, saw the pyramids and Colossus at Memnon and was kidnapped).

[138] Lucian, *Philops.* 33. The episode in the following chapter, in which Lucian's boastful narrator attempted to copy the magic powers of the Egyptian priest, was the inspiration behind *The Sorcerer's Apprentice*.

was simply one more feature of these breathless tourist accounts that might be mocked.

This cartographic caricature of Egypt is still more apparent in a some of the prose romances of the second and third centuries AD – the so-called 'Ancient Greek Novels' – and here it is perhaps worth briefly stepping beyond our main chronological parameters to explore this point further. These works were vehicles for the elaboration of some fairly formulaic narratives, with a greater or lesser degree of artistic success, but they did include some geographical detail to lend some verisimilitude to the fabulous stories.[139] In some cases, this is impressive – the account of Nubia in Heliodorus' *Aethiopika* displays a familiarity with the political and cultural confusion in the region beyond the First Cataract, and Achilles Tatius' account of Egypt was clearly influenced by Herodotus.[140] Elsewhere, however, it is the errors that are most illuminating. Typical of this is the second-century *Ephesian Tale* of Xenophon of Ephesus – a 'specimen of penny dreadful literature' according to a recent translator.[141] Relating the marriage, unfortunate separation and eventual reunion of the protagonists Habrocomes and Anthia, the *Ephesian Tale* subscribes to many of the conventions of this literary form, including long episodes set amongst the bandits of the Nile Delta.[142] Towards the end of the work, one of the principal characters, Hippothous, sets out on a voyage up the Nile towards Ethiopia in search of his friend Habrocomes. As we might expect, Xenophon lists the places through which Hippothous is said to have passed, from the Pelusian mouth of the Nile as far as Coptus, just to the North of Elephantine and Syene:

> They gathered a large band of robbers and made for Pelusium; sailing along the Nile to the Egyptian Hermopolis and Schedia, they put into Menelaus' canal and missed Alexandria. They arrived at Memphis, the shrine of Isis and from there travelled to Mendes. And they recruited natives to serve in their band and act as guides. Going through Tawa they reached Leontopolis, and passing a number of towns, most of them of little note they came to Coptus, which is close to Ethiopia.[143]

---

[139] Said (1994), 218; on the fluidity of 'history' and 'fiction' in these works, and hence on the presumed authority of the geographical material within them, see esp. Bowersock (1994).

[140] Heliod. *Aeth.* 8.1, 8.14, 9.1, 9.22 and cf. Strabo 17.1.48; Achilles Tatius 4.11–12. The metanarrative function of the Nile within the *Aethiopika*, in particular, falls some way beyond the scope of this study, but cf. esp. Whitmarsh (1999) and Elmer (2008). The value of Heliodorus as a source on Nubia in the late Roman period is assessed in Eide et al. (1988), 1043–8.

[141] Reardon (1989), 175.

[142] On the trope of the Nile Bandits or *boukoloi* in the Ancient Greek Novels and Egyptian literature, see esp. Rutherford (2000) and the references therein.

[143] Xenophon of Ephesus 4.1.

Hiring local guides must have seemed like a good idea, but it doesn't seem to have done the robbers much good. On the face of it, this reads very much like a standard riparian itinerary, and this must have been what Xenophon intended. There are a handful of familiar places – Pelusium, Alexandria (if only by omission), Memphis and Coptos – and the additional details, like the reference to the shrine of Isis, also sound fitting. Even the reference to 'towns of little note' adds an authentic-sounding feature of a long journey, foreshortened for the purposes of the narrative. As an itinerary, however, this is a nonsense – 'une aimable fantaisie' as one commentator has put it.[144] Other than Memphis and Coptus, all of the places mentioned were scattered around Nile Delta, and can hardly have been connected by a sequential journey. The places are likely to have sounded authentically 'Egyptian' to Xenophon's audience – and with good reason, as they are all attested toponyms – but they are not Nilotic. Not that this mattered for the purposes of the novel: writer and audience both thought of Egypt as a succession of places, strung out along the Nile. The order in which they appeared – indeed, the truth about whether or not they were actually on the Nile – was immaterial within this presentation, and its reception. One commentator has argued that Xenophon's intention here was to create a certain historiographical veracity for his account through an adoption of Herodotean language.[145] If this was the case, the fact that it was the linear form of the Nile geography which provided the ring of authenticity, rather than its content, is significant.

Other works in the same tradition reveal comparable assumptions about Egyptian geography. Philostratus' third-century *Life of Apollonius of Tyana*, is laden with riverine imagery. The protagonist, a semi-mythical first-century philosopher, who wanders the world from India to Ethiopia, is accompanied by a disciple 'Nilus' and an antagonist 'Euphrates', and travels along both rivers in the course of its journey.[146] Although his Egyptian journey is not presented in an explicitly itinerary form, the narrative does purport to progress upriver from Alexandria to the borders of Ethiopia. And yet the geography itself is again confused: Apollonius meets Vespasian in Alexandria, and then travels to Hiera Sycaminos 'on the border of Egypt and Ethiopia'; he visits the colossi of Memnon (where he picks up a guide from Memphis), and only then experiences the sublime grandeur of the cataracts, which are described in considerable detail.[147]

---

[144] Dalmeyda (1926), 49, n.2.   [145] De Temmerman (2012), 506–7.
[146] For a thoughtful interpretation of the Nilotic themes in the *Life*, see esp. Manolaraki (2013), 258–308 and cf. also Elsner (1997). On the generic ambiguity of the text, see Francis (1998).
[147] Philostr. *VA* 5.24–43 (Alexandria); 6.2 (Hiera Sycaminos); 6.4 (Memnon); 6.23, 26–7 (Cataracts).

Several recent interpretations of the text have noted Philostratus' tendency to 'strain geography to its breaking point', and have suggested that this knowing confusion of familiar Nilotic landmarks was intended to indicate the allegorical function of the *Life* as a whole.[148] While the deft interweaving of travel and allegory is certainly crucial to the didactic function of the text, the confident assumption that Philostratus' audience would immediately have identified the topographic confusion of his text is misplaced.[149] A recent translator rightly notes that frequent imperial trips to Egypt would have brought the region to the attention of the wider world, but this need not mean that the precise geography of Egypt would be equally familiar to readers.[150] As we have seen, narratives of travel could frequently confuse and conflate places whether they were intended to be read as history, as satire or as allegory. Philostratus certainly manipulated these topographical conventions to his own narrative ends, but his liberties with topography can only have been apparent to a tiny fraction of his audience.

## Conclusions: Thinking in Lines

This discussion has taken us some way beyond the principal chronological boundaries of this study, and into the imaginative literature of late Antiquity. But there is good reason to think that the processes of cognitive simplification evident in these texts were familiar to the inhabitants of late Republican and early imperial Rome. Over the last generation, scholars have argued about the importance of 'hodological' assumptions in classical and medieval spatial understanding – that the ancient world was most commonly conceptualized in terms of journeys and lines, rather than mapped spaces. For individuals who travelled within the empire, this mode of spatial comprehension seems to have been widespread. Itineraries and *peripli* provided straightforward tools for navigation that were both more easily replicated than two-dimensional maps, and were functional, as more

---

[148] C. Jones (2005), 16. Manolaraki (2013), 275: 'we may infer that Philostratus' geographical implausibility is not driven by cavalier indifference to realism, but by his educative agenda. His absurd Nilotic itinerary from Alexandria to Ethiopia provides an early clue that Apollonius' passage is imaginative rather than geographic, to be followed by a conceptual rather than spatial journey. By rearranging his geography, Philostratus dismantles his audience's expectation of an incremental journey through familiar Nilotic landmarks. His contorted layout draws attention to the river as a signpost to the narrative, rather than as a backdrop to the story.'

[149] Elsner (1997), 29–30 stresses the allegorical (rather than 'empirical') ambitions of the text after Romm (1994), 116–19. Manolaraki (2013), 279–96 argues that a nonsensical geography is fundamental to his method. The issue is substantially complicated, of course, by the complex generic positioning of the text. On which see esp. Kemezis (2014), 63–8.

[150] C. Jones (2005), 16.

recent manifestations of similar technologies may illustrate. Rivers occupy a somewhat anomalous position within this discourse. On the one hand, of course, the physical form of the river, and the experience of travelling along it, lent itself readily to representation (and comprehension) in this form. On the other, the vicissitudes of river travel rather eluded the rigid conceptual framework of the itinerary tradition. A river like the Nile could not easily be defined in terms of roads and well-ordered stopping points, as the somewhat peculiar presentation of Egypt in both the *Antonine Itinerary* and the Peutinger Map may demonstrate.

Nevertheless, the Nile was frequently conceptualized in linear terms by the inhabitants of the early Roman empire, and with good reason. Egypt was frequently experienced as a territory to be travelled through, its wonders presented to spectators as an ordered succession of delights – whether in person, or through the pages of a text. Yet these 'hodological' elements were more fluid than has frequently been thought, and the conception of the river as a line often transcended the need to present its constituent parts in a coherent order. Even among the most careful geographers we see occasional mistakes in descriptions of the Nile – as islands slip up or down stream, or become confused with one another.[151] In part, of course, this may be ascribed to simple carelessness, but the fact that such mistakes could be made without any detrimental effect to the overall shape of these Nilotic geographies is itself telling. In such contexts, the precise order in which Egyptian landmarks might appear in a journey up the Nile was evidently less important than the widespread recognition that they would appear eventually. The Nile was a cabinet of wonders, arranged in linear form.

[151] See esp. the discussion of Seneca and Lucan at 264 below.

CHAPTER 6

# *Triumph and Disaster*
## *Rendering the River in Verse*

It is impossible to appreciate the complexity of Roman geographical understanding in the late Republic and early empire without reference to the
extraordinary corpus of poetry which was composed in that period. For
many writers, in both Greek and Latin, verse was a natural medium through
which to react to the changing world, and many audiences found their own
responses to the developing empire mediated through epic, elegy, lyric or
didactic poetry. A considerable body of modern scholarship has focused
on spatial aspects within Latin verse, but its deeper function in shaping
contemporary comprehension of the world has been neglected. Following the so-called 'spatial turn' in criticism, particular attention has been
focused on the literary function of geographical catalogues, didactic digressions and *topoi*, as well as on the role played by spatial description in the
development of narrative.[1] Several important studies have also highlighted
the political undertones that might be identified in the local landscapes
of poets, or their representations of distant provinces of empire.[2] Consequently, Roman poems have persuasively been read both as proponents of
contemporary ideology, and as forms of resistance to these dominant political discourses. Important as much of this work is – and it has influenced
this chapter profoundly – the precise interdependence between poetry and
other forms of representation deserves closer inspection. Changing representations of the Nile provide one means to approach this.

It is worth stressing from the outset that poetry had always had a central
role to play in the articulation of responses to the wider world. When
Strabo composed his (prose) *Geography* during the reign of Tiberius, he
referred extensively to the *Iliad* and *Odyssey*, and declared Homer to be the

---

[1] The spatial turn in the social sciences is especially associated with the work of Lefebvre (1991), and
Soja (1989). Purves (2010), esp. 1–23 is an important recent application with further discussion of
the scholarship.
[2] Dominik (2009) represents an exemplary reading of the Geopolitics of Virgil, for example. Cf. also
the invaluable study of Spencer (2005).

true ancestor of geographical writing.[3] While Strabo was doubtless concerned to lend his own field a suitably impressive ancestry, the catalogues and descriptive vignettes that were so common in classical and Hellenistic epic did represent an important vehicle for the transmission of knowledge about the wider world.[4] Didactic poetry on a variety of themes also addressed geographical subjects, as the discussion of Lucretius in Chapter 4 may illustrate.[5] Poetry dedicated to geographical description also proliferated. During the last centuries BCE, a number of Hellenistic writers composed verse geographies which drew upon the mathematical and cartographic work of Alexandria, and which influenced prose writers in turn. An Athenian created a verse *periplus* of the coastlines and principal cities of Greece in the first quarter of the first century BCE; he identifies himself as 'Dionysius, son of Calliphon' in an acrostic.[6] Another writer, Alexander of Ephesus, composed a poetic geography which both Cicero and Strabo consulted when contemplating works of their own.[7] At around the same time, writers in Latin followed this lead. Cornelius Nepos and Varro of Reate are cited extensively by Pomponius Mela and Pliny and may well have written in verse, although no secure fragments of these texts survive.[8] Varro of Atax (or Varro Atacinus) certainly did work in this medium: extant sections of his *Chorographia* reveal a rich and wide-ranging survey of the world in Latin hexameters.[9] To judge from these fragments, his poem probably opened with a discussion of the basic mathematical principles behind the structure of the globe, and then added details on specific regions.[10] Perhaps the most famous writer in this tradition, however, wrote towards the end of our period. Dionysius of Alexandria – or Dionysius Periegetes as he is often known – crafted a long description of the whole of the known world in over a thousand Greek hexameter verses

---

[3] Emphatically stated at Strabo 1.1.1–11, and this is an important theme throughout Book 1. Strabo's particularly indignant defence of Homer's apparent ignorance of Egypt and the Nile recurs repeatedly. Cf. 1.2.22–3, 29–31; 7.3.6; 17.1.5. Prontera (1993/2011); Biraschi (2005).

[4] See, for example, the collected essays in Skempis (2013) with the introductory observations of Skempis and Ziogas (2013).

[5] On this tradition, see esp. Conte (1994), 2–9; Volk (2002); Taub (2008) and the comments in Lightfoot (2014), 85–98.

[6] *GGM* 1.238–243; Keyser and Irby-Massie (2008), 260; Marcotte (2000).

[7] Strabo 14.1.27; Cic. *Att* 2.20.6; 2.22.7 (although the latter passage suggests that Cicero did not regard Alexander particularly highly).

[8] Cf. (on Nepos) Pomponius Mela 3.45, 90; Plin. *HN* 3.127, 132; 5.4; 6.5, 31, 199. (on Varro) Plin. *HN* 1.(3–6), and also Gell. *NA* 10.7. Sallmann (1971), 6–20 and 119–26 discusses these debts more fully.

[9] Hollis (2007), 166–79 and 181–92.

[10] Varro Atac. Fr 111, 112, 113 (Hollis). Hollis (2007), 181 suggests that Varro Atacinus' work may have been a Latin translation of Alexander.

during the reign of Hadrian.[11] The work survives in full and clearly betrays its origins in the Hellenistic mathematical tradition.

Important as this didactic tradition was, the two connected genres of epic and elegiac poetry also proved to be fundamental in the articulation and definition of Roman views of the world during this period, and were certainly much more widely read. Both forms reached their sudden apogee in Latin during the last decades of the Republic and the early years of the Principate, and both were intimately bound up in the politics of the changing state.[12] Geographical imagery was common throughout this writing and demands close attention. On the most immediate level, geographical references within the poetry of Tibullus, Propertius and Virgil are invaluable simply for illustrating how far empirical knowledge of the wider world filtered through literate society in this period, and where this information came from. It is conspicuous, for example, that Hellenistic verse and triumphal imagery provided common points of reference for poets, while prose geographical writing and visual projects like the Agrippa 'map' did not.[13] Yet poetry also had a constitutive role to play in the development of Roman attitudes towards the world. The preceding chapters have argued that knowledge about the world was not monopolized by a single political authority, even at the height of the Principate, nor was it articulated only through maps or dedicated prose compositions. Instead, military reports, triumphal parades, wall paintings, didactic treatises and itineraries all contributed in different ways to evolving geographical and political understanding. As poems embedded in the politics of their time, epics and elegies reflected some of this polyvalence, but they also made their own contribution to this discussion.

For writers of epic, geographical points of reference provided an invaluable means to engage with contemporary historical and political concerns. Through reference to Carthage, Troy, Alexandria or the battlefields of Italy, writers could explore and express the changing cultural associations of the wider imperial world. For elegists, the 'real' world – whether of veteran settlements and Italian estates, Roman military campaigns in the provinces

---

[11] Lightfoot (2014) provides a thorough text, translation and discussion.

[12] The bibliography is enormous. The papers collected in Powell (1992) discuss the political resonance of Augustan poetry broadly, see esp. Kennedy (1992). Those in Dominik, Garthwaite and Roche (2009), esp. Rutledge (2009a) approach the politics of elegy under Augustus and his successors.

[13] See esp. Mayer (1986) for illuminating case studies. The possible allusion to a map in Prop. 4.3.37–40 is discussed by Brodersen (1995), 101–2. Yet if this was a display map of the type discussed in Chapter 1, it is conspicuous that Propertius was interested in it as an object of contemplation, rather than as an authoritative source of geographical knowledge. The anonymous *Panegyric to Messalla* (conventionally Tib 3.7) refers to latitudinal bands at Tib 3.7.151–60, on which see Schrijvers (2009), 157–8, but 'triumphal' geography is also prominent in lines 135–46.

or the manifestations of these changes in the city of Rome – was a necessary counterpoint to the imagined idyll of the bedroom or the rustic retreat.[14] These spatial allusions did not claim to reflect accurately the precise topography or geography of the world – nor were they expected to – but they are no less important for that.[15] Read carefully, such imagery highlights the changing associations of specific regions within the Roman world and reveals the layers of cultural memory that accumulated around individual places.[16] Viewed against the other forms of Roman geographical representation – the formal prose treatises, triumphs, landscape paintings and so on – they provide a far richer sense of the cultural geography of the emerging empire.

This general principle might be illustrated by looking briefly at the manner in which Egypt and the Nile were represented in the poetry of the Augustan period. On the face of it, this may seem a well-worn topic. The eighth book of Virgil's *Aeneid*, Horace's ninth epode, and his ode *nunc est bibendum*, along with several elegies of Propertius and Ovid, are frequently invoked as illustrations of Roman chauvinism in the face of the newly-occupied territories in the Nile Valley.[17] We see this particularly vividly in the caustic representations of Cleopatra – 'whore-queen' (*meretrix regina*) in Propertius' words – a vivid metonym for the feminized and corrupting east.[18] If many of these poems betray a certain anxiety in their representations of the queen, not least through their remarkable reluctance to name her, and in the unsettling shifts in emotional register, there can be little doubt that she proved a helpful means by which to underscore the moral legitimacy of the Roman occupation of the east, and of Octavian's victory in civil war.[19] Equally prominent, and equally frequently cited in surveys of this territory, are the Egyptian gods. Virgil opposed the familiar Roman pantheon to the animal-headed gods of Egypt in his seminal portrait of the Battle of Actium, and this image became commonplace in the caricatures of later poets – an apparent assertion of Roman rationality over the boundary-transgressions of the east.[20] Similar charges might also be laid at the common condemnations of Isis in Augustan elegies, and in the more

---

[14] Hardie (1998), 5–27; Spencer (2005).

[15] Note Horsfall (1985), 195: 'No expectation existed in Augustan Rome that the geographical information contained in a work of literature should be precise'. Exactly what this 'precision' entailed, however, remains a matter of considerable interest.

[16] Jenkyns (1998); Spencer (2005) and see also Dominik (2009).

[17] Verg. *Aen.* 8.671–713; Hor. *Epod.* 9, *Carm.* 1.37; Prop. 3.11, 4.6. Discussions of this material have been widespread. Cf. for example Reinhold (1980); Maehler (2003); Manolaraki (2013), 29–37.

[18] Prop. 3.11.39. Wyke (1992); Wyke (2002), 195–243 brilliantly explore the poetic framing of Cleopatra.

[19] Gurval (1998), 137–50; Wyke (2002), 209–10.

[20] Smelik and Hemelrijk (1984) is the classic discussion.

sustained attacks of Juvenalian satire.[21] Viewed from this perspective – which is perfectly valid – the poets of the early Principate illustrated the colonizing confidence of the new Mediterranean Empire, in terms that are immediately familiar from a variety of later colonialisms.

Yet such straightforward classifications can be misleading, and attitudes to the newly-conquered territories of Egypt were often considerably more complex than this image would allow.[22] The peculiar concatenation of generic influences and geographical themes in Tibullus I.7 illustrates the point rather well. The poem was composed in honour of Tibullus' patron, M. Valerius Messalla Corvinus, and combines a celebration of Messalla's birthday with a commemoration of his military triumph over Aquitaine in September 27 BCE.[23] As such, it draws upon and develops the traditions of *genethliakon* (birthday poem), *epyllion* (mini-epic) and *epinikion* (victory poem), and deploys much of the imagery of contemporary Roman triumphs.[24] The most striking aspect of the poem, however, is a substantial encomium to Osiris and the Nile that sits at its heart.[25] Here, Tibullus seems to eschew the themes of military victory, and celebrates instead the role of Osiris-Dionysus as a benevolent bringer of cultivation, wine and song to Egypt and the world. As several recent studies have shown, it is certainly possible to read Tibullus' poem as a reflection of contemporary imperialist assumptions, and his juxtaposition of a martial, Roman west with a more decadent orient remains conspicuous.[26] But this is far from the caricature of a monstrous east so frequently associated with the Augustan poets. Tibullus' Osiris recalls the benevolent, creative figure known to Roman audiences from the first book of Diodorus Siculus' *History*, and perhaps from Hecataeus of Abdera, and thereby also evokes the divine paradigm for Ptolemaic kingship.[27] This imagery was certainly derived in part from the Hellenistic poetry of Callimachus, and there may be echoes of his *Aitia* in the passage, but this was not only a literary conceit.[28] The same section of the poem may also have assumed a general familiarity with

---

[21] Alston (1996); Shumate (2006), 129–58.

[22] Vout (2003) and Gruen (2010), 76–114 are nuanced assessments of the complexity of early imperial responses to Egypt.

[23] Tib. 1.7.9–12. On the poem see esp. Ball (1975); Bright (1975); Koenen (1976); Bright (1978); Konstan (1978); Cairns (1979), 41–4; Moore (1989); Lambert (2003); Lee-Stecum (1998), esp. 205–25 and Bowditch (2011).

[24] Generic issues are discussed particularly in Cairns (1979), 171–3.    [25] Tib 1.7.23–48.

[26] See esp. the nuanced study of Bowditch (2011), and compare Smelik and Hemelrijk (1984), 1928, n.481; Manolaraki (2013), 33–5.

[27] Diod Sic 1.17–20. On this context see esp. Hunter (2006), 53–4.

[28] Tib. 1.7.28 and cf. Callim. *Fr.*383.16. Hunter (2006), 58–9 discusses the implications.

contemporary Isiac hymns.[29] This Egypt is not a distant territory, defined solely by its conquest and abjection, then, but an exotic region rendered partially familiar through literary, religious and even cosmogonic points of reference. As such, Tibullus' poem reflects the sheer political and cultural complexity of geography in the 20s, and the important role of (often fluid) genres in shaping these representations.[30]

The Nile does not appear particularly prominently in the work of the other Augustan poets, but the allusions to the river are illuminating nevertheless. We have encountered some of these already: the Nilotic setting for Virgil's *bugonia* in the fourth *Georgic* was discussed briefly in an earlier chapter, as was Ovid's pointed connection between the river's floods and those of Deucalion.[31] Elsewhere, poets contented themselves with brief allusions to the Nile, succinctly evoking the river, and often in formulaic terms. But these commonplaces or *topoi* are also important, particularly when set within their wider textual and cultural context. By looking at poetic entanglement with other modes of representation, we can begin to appreciate their contribution to contemporary cultural and political discourses. The discussion that follows looks briefly at three particular aspects of these short vignettes – first the common representation of the Nile in terms that recalled the Actian triumph, then the evolution of the *topos* of the seven mouths of the Nile, and finally the association of the river with the death of Pompey. The second half of the chapter examines Lucan's far richer treatment of the Nile in the last books of his *Civil War*.

## The Politics of Geography in Epic and Elegy

Virgil's account of Actium shaped the memory of that battle in the minds of many of his contemporaries. As is well known, the description itself appears at the climax of the famous ekphrasis of the shield of Aeneas in the eighth book of the *Aeneid*.[32] This was to become the canonical description of the Battle of Actium in the period that followed, and it influenced contemporary poets substantially, as we shall see. In his account of Actium itself, the poet famously pits the familiar gods of Italy against the divine menagerie of the eastern gods, under the command of their unnamed queen:

---

[29] Hunter (2006), 56–61; cf. Koenen (1976). Tibullus' own familiarity with Isiac rites is indicated in Tib. 1.3.23–34.

[30] For further discussion see Lambert (2003), Lee-Stecum (1998), 220–4 and 301–3 and Wilson (2009).

[31] See above, 150–1.

[32] Syed (2005), 1–8 introduces Virgil's *ekphraseis* and scholarly responses. Hardie (1986), 336–76 for an influential reading of the shield passage. On the Homeric antecedent, see for example Becker (1995).

> In the midst the queen calls upon her hosts with their native sistrum; nor yet does she cast a glance back at the twin snakes behind. Monstrous gods of every form and barking Anubis wield weapons against Neptune and Venus and against Minerva.[33]

Defeated with the help of Apollo, the eastern allies flee, and find refuge in the Nile. Here, the poet makes direct reference to Vulcan's visual rendering of the scene:

> Amid the carnage, the Lord of Fire had fashioned her pale at the coming of death, borne on by waves and the wind of Iapyx; while over against her was the mourning Nile, of massive body, opening wide his folds and with all his raiment welcoming the vanquished into his azure lap and sheltering streams.[34]

Precisely what Virgil is describing here is deliberately ambiguous, and its poetic inheritance is complex. The ekphrasis was, of course, a staple of the epic tradition, and the digression here was a conscious echo of the description of Achilles' shield in the eighteenth book of the *Iliad*.[35] Like its model, Virgil's shield was thoroughly imbued with geographical and cosmographical elements.[36] Within this particular passage, there are also noteworthy allusions to the Hellenistic poetry of Alexandria. Virgil's portrait of the mournful reception of Cleopatra by the Nile has plausibly been read as an inversion of a similar scene in Callimachus' *epinikion* in honour of Sosibios. In that poem, an androgynous Nile figure joyfully welcomes the triumphal young athlete back to his homeland.[37] Even on the most superficial level, it is clear that Virgil appropriated multiple poetic influences in celebrating Roman victory over Egypt, and the triumph of his own Latin epic voice.

Ekphrasis was a means to reflect upon the nature of poetic description itself, and here the other influences behind Virgil's geographical imagery deserve attention. Conventionally, an ekphrasis was a textual description of a visual work of art, whether this existed in reality or was imagined by the poet himself. Ostensibly, the challenge for the writer was to evoke this artwork in the mind of his audience through the use of language alone, but the practice was frequently more playful than this would imply.[38] Virgil's description of Aeneas' shield illustrates this well. Throughout the

---

[33] Verg. *Aen.* 8.696–700. tr. Fairclough (2000), 109.
[34] Verg. *Aen.* 8.709–713. tr. Fairclough (2000), 111.
[35] Hom. *Il.* 18.468–617.     [36] Hardie (1985); Hardie (1986).
[37] Callim. *Fr.* 384. See Hunter (2006), 144. Stephens (2002a), 255–60 sets this work in its cultural context.
[38] Squire (2009), esp 93–190 provides an important discussion.

digression, Virgil reminds his audience that this wondrous object was forged in metal – thus the seas of Virgil's Actium are cast in gold and silver, its ships in bronze and gold.[39] Yet even as he establishes this conceit, Virgil deliberately deviates from it, and refers to the blood-stained 'ruddy sea' (*rubro litore*), and waves 'reddened with slaughter'.[40] In the passage above, he describes the 'azure lap' (*caeruleum . . . gremium*) of the River Nile.[41] The very impossibility of this colouring on an unpainted metal shield – or rather the poet's emulation of the typical imaginative 'leap' that a viewer of such an object might make in translating the conventions of visual art to a mental image of the scene being represented – is crucial to the literary game as it is played.

The allusion to the Nile goes further than this. Although earlier poets had conventionally included reference to Cleopatra's flight to Egypt in their accounts of the aftermath of Actium, Virgil was the first to introduce the Nile as a specific character within this episode.[42] Virgil's Nile is given a corporeal presence, and familiar clothing as well as a human emotional connection to the defeated queen. The play with the 'laying open' (*pandentem*) of the Nile's 'lap' (*gremium*) locates this vignette in the uncertain middle ground between physical personification and a landscape painting, as well as between narrative description (Cleopatra fleeing to Egypt) and poetic metaphor (the Nile 'welcomes' 'his' queen). Such a scene could not have been represented visually and could only exist as a poetic mediation between multiple different forms of geographical representation. Virgil's Nile is both an impossibility and one which would be completely comprehensible to an audience familiar with the rhetorical practices of ekphrasis and the visual conventions of triumphal display.

Although clearly influenced by Callimachus' vignette, Virgil's Nile differed from the earlier poet's river. In the earlier *epinikion*, the Nile has an androgynous quality, which was probably intended to recall contemporary representations of the Egyptian god Hâpi; in *Aeneid*, we witness a distinctly masculine river god.[43] This was a rendering of a Hellenistic motif in familiar, Roman terms. We can be relatively confident that Virgil's allusion to the personified Nile was intended to evoke the representation of the river in the Triple Triumph of 29 BCE. This is signalled clearly enough by the shift to the description of the triumph itself that immediately follows, and

---

[39] Verg. *Aen.* 8.671–7.    [40] Verg. *Aen.* 8.695.    [41] Verg. *Aen.* 8.709; 8.713.

[42] Most obviously Hor. *Carm.* 1.37.13–21; *Epod.* 9 takes up the narrative of Antony's escape, and flight is also a theme of *Carm. Bell Act* II. On which see Benario (1983). Compare also Ov. *Met.* 5.315–31 on the nymphs seeking refuge in the Nile.

[43] Stephens (2002a), 255–6, on Callimachus' androgynous, nurturing Nile.

indeed the final fifteen lines of the ekphrasis are devoted to the triumphal celebrations themselves.[44] As discussed in Chapter 2, there is good reason to assume that an anthropomorphic river appeared within that ceremony, and the specific location of this passage within the ekphrasis supports this assumption: the account of Cleopatra's flight and her welcome by the Egyptian river appears immediately after the Battle of Actium in Virgil's poem, and before the Triple Triumph – at the point in the digression, in other words, when the distinction between the battle and its ceremonial commemoration are at their most blurred. From this perspective, Virgil's description must be read as a representation of a representation of a representation: a poem inspired by an (imagined) relief, inspired by a triumphal personification. This in turn demands that the audience look again at the description of the battle itself, and acknowledge the extent to which it has been refracted through the conventions of triumphal depiction. Viewed in these terms, the salient points of reference in the battle – Cleopatra herself, the snakes, the sistrum and Anubis – may also allude to the victory trophies that would have been paraded in the ceremony in 29 BCE.[45] These symbols are likely to have become conventional by virtue of repetition, but there is good reason to conclude that they were all features of the Actian triumph, and that after Virgil they came to represent the conflict in the minds of the Roman audience.

Virgil's contemporaries readily adopted this vignette, and it is particularly conspicuous in the Actian elegy of Propertius (3.11).[46] This is a complex poem, in which the poet's captivation by his own beloved is framed in terms of the Augustan victory at Actium, and hence Rome's conquest of 'that woman' (femina), the unnamed Cleopatra. The elegy opens with Propertius' indignant defence of his own surrender to love. After stating that bitter experience has resigned him to this weakness, just as a soldier or sailor has learned to respect the wind or the dangers of battle, Propertius goes on to list the famous women of mythology and history who held their lovers in thrall – Medea, Penethesilea, Omphale and Semiramis. Thereafter, Propertius digresses into a long vituperation of Cleopatra, who threatened Rome by her very existence. If Rome could come so close to enslavement by the Egyptian queen, Propertius argues, what chance would a mere elegist have, when confronted with his own beloved?

---

[44] Verg. Aen. 8.714–28.
[45] On the peculiar triumphal resonances of the snakes, see Kostuch (2009).
[46] Ecphrastic themes are also apparent in Propertius' account of the Temple of the Palatine Apollo 4.6.63–4, but the Nile is less prominently presented here.

It is the specific presentation of the queen and her homeland that is particularly important here. Cleopatra appears in the poem as a very real threat to Rome, and in language that recalls the Virgilian vignette:

> [Cleopatra] dared to pit barking Anubis against our Jupiter and to force Tiber to endure the threats of the Nile, to drive out the rattling trumpet with the rattling sistrum and with the poles of her barge pursue the beaks of our galleys, to stretch effeminate mosquito-nets on the Tarpeian rock and give judgement amid the arms and statues of Marius.[47]

Ultimately, of course, it was Octavian [*Caesar*] who proved more than a match for his female foe, and surpassed the accomplishments of heroes who had come before him, not to mention the elegist himself. In expressing this, however, Propertius switches from an apostrophe to Rome to a direct address to Cleopatra:

> Yet you fled to the wandering outlets of the craven Nile – not that your hands received Roman fetters. You endured the sight of your arms bitten by the sacred asps and your limbs channelling the stealthy route of the numbing poison.[48]

Here again is Actium represented through the theatre of the triple triumph, and the Nile appears in the peculiar spatial syntax of that ceremony. We see the Nile, Anubis, the *sistrum* and the snakes, none of which was present in the battle of 31 BCE, which was fought off the Greek coast, but which featured prominently in the celebrations of 29. Propertius' allusions to the beaks of Roman galleys (*rostra liburna*) add a further resonance, not least because of his reference to 'Actian beaks on the sacred way' in his earlier *recusatio*.[49] The image of Cleopatra in flight also recalls the moment of transition in Virgil's treatment of the subject. While there is no explicit reference to the personification of the Nile in this passage, as there is in *Aeneid* VIII, the river and the triumph remain interdependent within the imagery of the poem.

The political significance of Propertius' elegy has been much debated. Although commentators in the early-twentieth century often read the poem as an uncritical celebration of Augustus – a shift in tone from the cynicism of Propertius' earlier elegies which adopted a more sceptical attitude towards the new state – more recent interpretations have taken issue with this

---

[47] Prop. 3.11.41–44. tr. Goold (1990), 259–61.
[48] Propertius 3.11.51–54. tr. Goold (1990), 261.   [49] Propertius 3.11 44. cf. 2.1.34.

view.[50] The apparent optimism of this elegy, and the enthusiasm with which the reluctant patriot seems to harmonize upon the epic themes being laid down by Virgil at around the same time, is somewhat offset by a darker tone, particularly in its allusions to civil war.[51] As we shall see, this particular tension was also emphasized through Propertius' manipulation of Nile geographies, and specifically his presentation of Pompey's death on the banks of that river. For the present purpose, however, Propertius' adoption of what we might call Virgil's triumphal geography of Egypt seems clear.

A third illustration confirms the point. The *Amores* were Ovid's elegies. In them, he celebrates and laments his love for his married mistress Corinna – probably an elegiac invention, although with typical mischief Ovid occasionally hints that she may have been a real individual.[52] Although the precise sequence of composition and circulation of the *Amores* are unclear, II.13 is certainly the first of a pair of poems, both of which relate to an abortion undergone by Corinna.[53] Here, Ovid prays to the goddess Isis for the recovery of his beloved – an adaptation of a familiar elegiac motif. In the next poem he upbraids Corinna for the abortion itself, drawing upon historical and mythical exemplars in his condemnation.[54] The subject matter of both poems obviously implies the consummation of an affair, and may relate to the previous elegy in the collection, a boast of sexual conquest which Ovid frames in the language of military triumph. The same theme was implicit in the elegy under discussion here.

Ovid opens the poem with an expression of his fear and anger at the dangers faced by his mistress during her abortion. In line 7, this transforms into an appeal to Isis to watch over his lover during her distress:

> Isis, you who dwell at Paraetonium and in the genial countryside of Canopus, at Memphis and palm-growing Pharos, and where the swift Nile, after flowing down in the broad bed, runs out through seven mouths into the waters of the sea, by your *sistra*, by the mouth of worshipful Anubis, I beseech you (so may pious Osiris always be devoted to your rites, the serpent slide

---

[50] Cf. Griffin (1977), who argues that Propertius' sympathetic presentation of Antony undercuts the apparently bellicose tone; Gurval (1998), 190–2; Weinlich (2003), 111–12. Compare the cautionary note of Wyke (2002), 196–7.

[51] Gurval (1998), 208: 'Much like Horace, Propertius fails to applaud the victory at Actium in any purely perfunctory or uncomplicated manner. The reality of civil war prohibits any political panegyric.'

[52] Cf. Ov. *Am.* 2.17.27–30.

[53] Ov. *Am.* 2.13.5–6 hints that the poet is not *absolutely* certain that he was the lover responsible for Corinna's pregnancy, but this does not lessen the irony discussed below.

[54] The prayer on behalf of a sick mistress is a common motif: cf. for example Tib. 1.5; Prop. 2.28. On the prayer to Isis specifically, see Tib. 1.3.23–34.

slowly round your altar, and horned Apis participate in your procession), turn your face this way, and by sparing one, spare two: for you will grant life to my mistress, and she to me.[55]

Ovid's systematic invocation of placenames is noteworthy here: Paraetonium, Canopus, Memphis and Pharos recall the nonsensical linear geographies of the river discussed in Chapter 5.[56] But triumphal themes are also implicit. While there is no explicit reference here to Octavian's triple ceremony in the manner of Propertius, Ovid's evocation of Egypt and the Nile does draw upon the specific symbolism established in *Aeneid* VIII. The references to the *sistra* and the serpents are clear allusions to the established caricature of Cleopatra. The emphasis upon Anubis – and specifically on the mouth (*ora*) of the dog-headed god – is also a reminder of the only Egyptian divinity to be mentioned by both of the earlier poets. Ovid's prayers, in other words, are directed towards the very symbols of submissive and conquered Egypt, which were becoming poetic *topoi* in their own right. Far from being a wholly apolitical account of a territory defined by the worship of Isis, then, this description of the Nile was firmly embedded within the post-triumphal descriptions of the Augustan period.[57]

Yet the Isis of *Amores* II.13 is not the submissive goddess of Virgil or Propertius, but a *triumphatrix* in her own right, a figure to whom the poet comes in supplication. This reversal of fortune hinges upon the references in line 14 to *comes* ('comrade' or 'captain') Apis and especially to the *pompa* of Isis – a term which could signify the religious processions associated with her cult, but also the Roman triumphs in which she had previously appeared.[58] That the poet intended this work to have martial undertones is emphasized by the final couplet and the opening lines of the poem that follows.[59]

Military and triumphal imagery of this kind is latent throughout the *Amores*. In the *recusatio* which opens the collection the martial imagery is particularly prominent: Ovid declares his intention to write epic, but is frustrated in this by the whims of the gods.[60] In the poem that follows, the author presents himself among the triumphal captives of Cupid,

---

[55] Ov. *Am.* 2.13.7–14. tr. Booth (1991), 67.    [56] See above 220–32.

[57] Contra Rosati (2009), 286: 'There is no trace here of the Augustan demonization of the East, and the attitude towards Egyptian cult is quite deferential and appeasing...' This is followed by Manolaraki (2013), 35 'Ovid's appeals are conditioned by amatory contexts which reflect the popularity of the Isis cult among women in Augustan Rome.'

[58] Ov. *Am.* 2.13.14.

[59] Ov. *Am.* 2.13.27–8. Cf. 2.14.1–3 and the discussion of Booth (1991), 70–1 on the links between these passages.

[60] Ov. *Am.* 1.1.1–4.

a god whose conquests rival those of Augustus, another descendent of Venus.[61] Moreover, the poem that immediately precedes II.13 in the collection depicts the poet's fateful 'conquest' of Corinna in precisely this language:

> Encircle my temples, triumphal laurel! I have won victory: look now, Corinna is in my arms – Corinna, who was guarded by her husband, by a chaperon and by a stout door (so many enemies!) to make sure that she could not be captured by any ruse. Worthy of a special triumph is this victory, in which, no matter what else, the beauty is unsullied by blood. My generalship has resulted not in the capture of paltry walls, not of fortifications surrounded by little ditches, but of a girl![62]

The irony of Ovid's boast that his victory was bloodless – a claim reprised in the final couplet – is only revealed in the unhappy poems that follow.[63] Yet this irony runs still deeper. The presentation of the successful lover as triumphator in II.12 is inverted in II.13, in which the poet is shown as a supplicant to Isis. The magnitude of this reversal is underscored by Ovid's concern to describe the Egyptian goddess in terms that Virgil had associated inescapably with the triple triumph of 29 BCE. This was not an 'apolitical' description of a domesticated goddess, then, but a conscious reinvention of the former captive, through the very symbols of her captivity – the Nile, the *sistra* and Anubis above all. In this sequence, the lover-triumphator had become supplicant; the subject Isis had risen to a position of absolute power.

### Nile of the Seven Mouths

A rather different tradition of poetic geography is apparent through commonplaces associated with the number of branches of the Nile as it ran through the Delta and debouched into the Mediterranean. According to the Latin poets, the Nile had seven mouths. Indeed, with the possible exception of the hidden source of the river, this was its most familiar feature in the verse of the period. Catullus seems to have been the first Latin poet to make this connection: he refers to *septemgeminus . . . Nilus*, a description which may have derived from Hellenistic precedent. The image became more firmly established when Virgil employed it as part of the *bugonia* episode in his fourth *Georgic*.[64] Here, debts to earlier Greek

---

[61] Ov. *Am.* 1.2.19–52.    [62] Ov. *Am.* 2.12.1–8. tr. Booth (1991), 63.
[63] Ov. *Am.* 2.12.27–8. On the triumphal theme in this poem, see Booth (1991), 64–5.
[64] Verg. *Georg.* 4.291–2. Cf. 153 above.

poetry can be established with more confidence. The aetiological subject matter of this passage suggests a debt to Callimachus, who may have been the first poet to establish the seven mouths as a commonplace, whether in his lost treatise *On Rivers*, or in another work.[65] Whatever the origins of this tradition were, it rapidly became a *topos* in Latin accounts of the river. It appears twice in the *Aeneid*, and multiple times over the course of Ovid's *Metamorphoses*, as well as in that poet's shorter works.[66] Indeed, almost all of that writer's references to the Nile include an allusion of some kind to its seven branches. Thereafter, multiple Latin poets took up the tag down to late Antiquity.[67] The seven mouths of the Nile became a defining feature of the river in Latin verse.

Prose geographers were rather less confident than the poets that the seven mouths were a definitive feature of the Nile. Most writers agreed that there were seven principal streams, but more detailed discussion of the Delta often complicated things.[68] The complex tangle of waterways could be divided in different ways, and not all of the mouths were regarded as equal. Herodotus initially states that there were five mouths in his survey of Egypt, but later identifies two further channels which he regarded as artificial: whether the Nile had five mouths or seven does not seem to have been a question that particularly moved him.[69] Strabo identifies two principal branches of the river after Memphis, and names five smaller courses, making for the canonical seven, but also notes that there were innumerable smaller mouths of the river – a justifiable observation that doubtless came from his own familiarity with the region.[70] Among Latin prose writers, the pattern is similar. Seneca is entirely silent on the issue. While he certainly knew Ovid's work very well, and drew upon it in his description of the Nile, as we have seen, he states merely that the Nile debouched through 'several channels' (*plura . . . flumina*), and repeats this assertion in his discussion of the theories relating to the flood.[71] Pomponius Mela states firmly that the Nile had seven mouths in his *Chorographia*, but may himself have been

[65] Harrison (2007), 161–2 briefly discusses the Callimachaean themes. Callimachus addresses the Nile (without numbering the mouths) in Fr. 384.

[66] Verg. *Aen.* 6.800, 9.30; Ov. *Met.* 1.422–3, 2.254–6, 5.187–8, 5.324, 9.774, 15.753; *Her.* 14.274; *Am* 2.13.9–10; 3.6.39–40.

[67] Cf. for example Luc. 8.465–6; Juv. 13.27; Stat. *Silv.* 3.5.18–22; Manilius 3.273–4; Claud. *1 Ruf* 185; *Hon et Mar.* 51.

[68] Cooper (2014), 30–33 unpicks the 'overwhelmingly vague and relativistic' classical accounts of the Delta, and see also the illuminating diagrams at 35 and 265.

[69] Hdt. 2.10, and compare 2.17 (where the 5+2 are named).

[70] Strabo 17.1.4. Cf. *Pseudo-Scylax* 106.1–2, which names seven mouths, but stresses that there were only two main channels. And the comments in Shipley (2011), 183–4.

[71] Sen. *QNat* 4A.2.8. 4A.2.22–4.

influenced by the poetic commonplace.[72] Pliny variously states that the Nile flowed through 'many mouths' (*multis... faucibus*), had twelve mouths, including four false channels (*falsa ora*), and that the most important were the Canopic and Pelusian branches. He also noted that seven channels were particularly well-known, and he did regard this number as significant, as we shall see in the Afterword.[73] Nevertheless, it is clear that the seven-fold Nile was more familiar in poetic writing than in other forms of geography.

Latin poets rapidly conventionalized a feature of Nilotic geography which other writers understandably regarded as relatively insignificant.[74] They may have adopted the trope for different reasons – Manilius, for example, felt that the seven mouths provided a helpful analogue to the seven planets, and demonstrated the cosmic significance of the river – but the practice itself is clear. A passage from Propertius illustrates how these poetic commonplaces might interact with other forms of geographical representation. In Chapter 2 we briefly considered the poet's response to the military triumphs of the 20s BCE. In an important *recusatio*, Propertius explicitly referred to the Actian celebrations that he might celebrate if he gave himself over to epic:

> . . . or I should sing of Egypt and the Nile, when, dragged into Rome, it flowed flagging with its seven streams captive . . . [75]

As discussed in Chapter 2, we cannot be entirely confident in Propertius' description of the triple triumph. For the reasons discussed above, it seems likely that the trophy in the procession was an anthropomorphic figure and was probably similar in form to the Nile statues that later became so common throughout the city. It is possible that this figure also included some visual allusion to the multiple channels of the river at the Delta, but it is hard to imagine how this allusion would have been effected: certainly none of the later anthropomorphic rivers include any such feature.[76] Much more probable is that Propertius consciously translated the abstracted grammar of the military display into the language of contemporary poetry, as an illustration both of his capacity to act as Augustus' epic champion and of his refusal to do so. Different forms of geographical representation could certainly interact within this period, but we should not assume that they all spoke the same language.

---

[72] Pomponius Mela, 1.51.
[73] Plin. *HN* 5.54 (many mouths); 64 (12 and 8); 48 (Canopic and Pelusian branches). He lists the best-known seven at 5.64. Cf. below 294–6.
[74] Cf. Cooper (2014), 18.     [75] Prop. 2.1.31–2. after Goold (1990), 105.
[76] See above 95–8 and 185–7. Nevertheless, Bonneau (1964), 329 and Gurval (1998), 29 both assume that Propertius was referring to a physical aspect of the trophy.

### Where Did Pompey Die?

A further ambiguity in poetic geography is apparent in Propertius 3.11. As we have seen, this complex elegy situates Octavian's victory at Actium against the poet's own erotic sufferings. Equally significant, however, are Propertius' subtle evocations of earlier civil wars in his ostensible celebration of the more recent triumph. Within the poem, Egypt did not merely witness the success of the new princeps, but also looked back to the tragic death of Pompey eighteen years earlier, a bleak moment for the troubled Republic. This comes to a head in a peculiar passage:

> Guilty Alexandria, land ever-ready for treason, and Memphis, so often blood-stained at our cost, where the sand robbed Pompey of his three triumphs, no day shall ever wash you clean of this infamy, Rome. Better had your funeral processed over the Phlegrean fields, or had you been doomed to bow your neck to your father-in-law.[77]

What are particularly important here are the geographical resonances of this passage. Propertius' allusion to the *Memphi cruenta . . . harena* clearly situates Pompey's murder within Egypt, and more specifically on the banks of the Nile.[78] This contradicts every reference to the episode in our prose sources. Livy, Velleius Paterculus and Cassius Dio all state that the assassination took place in a small boat off the Egyptian coast: Florus adds the detail that this was near the Pelusian mouth of the Nile, a location which seems to have been widely accepted at the time.[79] The geographical slippage here is not quite as egregious as it might at first seem: Memphis could serve as a synecdoche for the whole of Egypt outside Alexandria, as it was later to do in the poetry of Lucan. Consequently, Propertius was not implying that Pompey was killed well inland, at the apex of the Delta, but this only gets us so far. The allusion to the *cruenta . . . harena* does imply that the murder took place on the banks of the Nile, rather than offshore as actually seems to have been the case.

The location of Pompey's death on the Egyptian sands may have been intended to evoke the spectacular deaths of the arena or to draw a direct parallel between Octavian's final conquest and the most ignominious chapter in the earlier civil war.[80] Outside its immediate literary context, however,

---

[77] Prop 3.11.33–8. tr. Goold (1990), 259.     [78] Butrica (1993) explores this contradiction.

[79] Liv. *Per* 122; Vell. Pat. 2.53.2; Dio Cass 42.5.3; Flor. 2.13.51–2. The association with Pelusium is widely explored by Lucan as at Luc. 8.465–7; 8.826; 9.83. And is itself deployed at 8.543: *Pelusiaci tam mollis turba Canopi*.

[80] Richardson (1977), 362–3.

the image had an interesting afterlife.[81] As we have seen, prose historians continued to narrate Pompey's death as they always had, and Propertius' conceit had little effect. But the same was not always true of poets. In his didactic *Astronomica*, Marcus Manilius specifically refers to Pompey's death on the 'Nilotic coast' (*Niliaco... litore*).[82] Clearly, this was not a direct borrowing from Propertius, but the specific association between the Egyptian river and the triumvir's ignominious end probably had its origins in the earlier poet's work. A rather more significant proponent of the same tradition was Lucan. As we shall see, Lucan devotes considerable space to the murder of Pompey, which provides something of an emotional climax to his epic *Civil War*. His long account of the execution itself reveals clearly that he well was aware of its precise topographical setting.[83] Yet throughout his poem, Lucan places considerable emphasis on the importance of the Nile as the riverine setting for Pompey's death and burial. The latter section of this chapter explores Lucan's multiple Nilotic geographies and the many influences behind them, but Propertius' peculiar elegy may perhaps be discerned behind his treatment of his particular theme.

The passing references to the Nile in Augustan poetry may not seem to have contributed much to the detailed knowledge of the river in the imperial city, but they do reveal a great deal about the developing appreciation of the wider world in this period, and ways in which different media interacted. The elaborate visual affectation in the ekphrasis of *Aeneid* VIII evidently drew upon the familiar geographical language of the Actian triumph, and gives some sense of the resonance of this symbolism, even several years after the ceremony itself. Yet it is likely that it was the very popularity of this poem – and the reprise of the same image in the elegies of Propertius and Ovid that followed in its wake – that helped to underscore this conception of the Nile as a personified but abject river. The poets adopted the visual vocabulary established in the imperial triumphs, then, but they also developed and subverted it, and this repurposing highlights the other ways in which the Nile could be conceived. For Virgil, the Nile was a point of interaction with the Hellenistic tradition of Callimachus; for Propertius a means to undercut Augustan triumphalism with the bleak

---

[81]  Butrica (1993), 344–5 concludes that the reading *harena* ('sands') should be replaced with *uerna* ('native'), based on the historical testimony of Sen. *Brev Vit.* 13.7; *Cons ad Marc* 20.4 and Cic. *Tusc.* 1.86. Even if this interpretation is accepted, the close associations between Nile and Pompey in both Manilius and Lucan still deserve an explanation. This seems to have become a commonplace, even if Propertius didn't mean it.

[82]  Manilius, *Astronomica* 4.50.     [83]  Luc. 8.663–91.

image of Pompey; for Ovid a symbol of the victory of Isis over the elegiac lover, and perhaps over Rome. None of these conceits could have worked without the well-established visual vocabulary of the triumph, but all also depended on a raft of other cultural, historical and even metaphysical associations.

Even poetic commonplaces could shape contemporary geographical understanding profoundly. Epic and elegiac geography frequently rested on heuristics of precisely this kind: by alluding to apparently definitive aspects of a particular feature, a poet could economically evoke it in the mind of his audience. In doing so, the poet associated his own work with the compositions of his predecessors. In purely literary terms, this is not a particularly startling observation, of course: *topoi* had been central to poetry since Homer. But it is important to remember that established clichés of this kind also contributed to the received geographical knowledge of the world in which they circulated. For the educated, Thebes was defined by its Homeric hundred gates as much as by its position on the Nile; indeed, writers of prose geographies could scarcely discuss the city without reference to the familiar formulation in the *Iliad*.[84] In much the same way, the audiences of the early empire came to know the Nile for its seven mouths (and hidden head) as much as for its many other features, which may have been more important to politicians or more interesting to natural philosophers. In due course, indeed, later scholiasts produced geographical cribs to aid readers who were familiar with the placenames of the poets, but were unable to locate these toponyms in the world.[85] Writers of epic and elegy may not have devoted much attention to detailed geographical descriptions, but they could still have a remarkable influence on the understanding of those around them.

## Lucan

Two generations after Augustus, Marcus Annaeus Lucanus composed what would be the fullest poetic treatment of the River Nile as part of his *Civil War* (*Bellum Civile* or *Pharsalia*). Lucan was the nephew of the Younger Seneca and, like his uncle, was a prominent figure at the court of the

---

[84] Hom. *Il.* 9.383–4; Strabo of course pays particular attention to the interface of poetry and geography in this case. Cf. Strabo 1.1.15; 1.2.16; 1.2.29; 17.1.46, the point is briefly addressed in Dueck (2000), 31–2 and cf. Pomponius Mela 1.60; Plin. *HN* 5.60.

[85] The obvious example is Vibius Sequester, an alphabetized gazetteer of the works of Virgil, Ovid and Lucan (and perhaps others) composed in the fourth or fifth century. Riese (1878), 145–59 and Parroni (1965).

emperor Nero.[86] Yet for all of his political connections, Lucan's poem was far from a straightforward celebration of the Julio-Claudians. As its title suggests, the *Civil War* takes as its theme the conflict between Julius Caesar and Pompey, and the collapse of the first triumvirate.[87] It traces the tragic history of the dying republic across the Mediterranean from Gaul and Spain to Thessaly and Egypt, and represents something of a dark cousin to the *Aeneid*.[88] Where Virgil sang of 'arms and the man' (*Arma virumque*) – of the rise of the Augustan Principate against the newly-crafted myths of Roman origins – Lucan's was a poem of *bella . . . plus quam civilia* ('wars . . . more than civil'), of conflicts that spill beyond the restraints even of fratricidal conflict to almost suicidal excess.[89] At the end of his ten extant books, Lucan's epic judders to an unexpected halt; the poem seems to end *in medias res*, with Pompey dead and defeated, but Caesar embroiled in new conflicts in Alexandria, and the Republican champion Cato stranded in the Libyan desert. There is good reason to think that Lucan planned to end his great work here, but the narrative seems unfinished, even if the poem was complete.[90] At various points, Lucan hints that the bloody conflicts that he describes continue to his own day, and even into the distant future. It is this unsettling quality of the epic which makes the perverse Nile a telling emblem for his narrative – a river of limitless floods and unknown source, whose origins may be traced to the very beginning of the world. Significantly, it is on the banks of the Nile that his work comes to its untimely end.

Lucan composed his epic under the massive shadow cast by Nero.[91] Once a favourite of the emperor, by 65 CE the poet's position had deteriorated to the extent that he was implicated in the Pisonian conspiracy to overthrow Nero and met his death shortly afterwards. Quite how the realities of the 60s shaped the *Civil War*, and how far the philosophies espoused in the

---

[86]   On Lucan's life see Fantham (2011). The intellectual culture at Nero's court is helpfully introduced in Dinter (2013b).

[87]   On Civil War as an implicit subject of earlier epics (not least the *Aeneid* itself), see Marincola (2010). For similar themes in Augustan elegy, cf. Hor. *Carm.* 2.1; *Epod.* 7 and 9.

[88]   Hardie (2013), 227–9 outlines the influence of Virgil on Lucan; cf. also Reed (2011) and Casali (2011), who notes the importance of the BC in drawing out the latent political themes in *Georgics* and *Aeneid*.

[89]   This formulation is brilliantly explored by Henderson (1998).

[90]   Masters (1992) makes the case that the poem was unfinished at Lucan's death. Compare Tracy (2011) and (2014) who argues that the ending of the epic represented the point at which Lucan's opposition to Nero shifted from literary to physical opposition. On the 'ending' see further 273–7 below.

[91]   Nero's corpulence is hinted at in Luc. 1.56–8. And cf. Ahl (1976), 30–31. On the political implications of this passage, see n.165 below.

epic affected the poet's response to contemporary imperial power, have been the matter of intense scholarly debate, not least because the political irony of the epic resists straightforward exegesis.[92] This discussion has also encompassed detailed analyses of the poet's treatment of landscape, and particularly rivers, which allow the audience to explore the abhorrent operations of Caesarian political ambition against the ordered structures of the natural world.[93] In recent years, moreover, the representations of Egypt and the Nile in the closing books of the *Civil War* have also been the object of extensive enquiry, both as the setting for Caesar's transformation from triumvir to despot and as a medium for Lucan's engagement with Stoic cosmology and natural philosophy.[94] While a full interrogation of the *Civil War* would be out of place in the present study, a close reading of the poet's Nilotic geography – or more precisely his overlapping Nilotic *geographies* – within the wider discourses of his time help to illuminate these debates. Clearly, understanding of Lucan's poetry necessitates an appreciation of the models against which he worked, and against which the *Civil War* would be read by its intended audience. As we shall see, Lucan was at pains to build upon the poetic precedent established by Virgil and Propertius in their short descriptions of the Nile, but also to manipulate the traditions of prose geography, natural philosophy and doxography, not least in the *Natural Questions* of his uncle Seneca. All of this could be expected to have dramatic resonances in an imperial court that was particularly enchanted with the mysteries of Egypt.

[92] The literature on Lucan's political standpoint is substantial, and a comprehensive bibliography would be out of place here. Of the recent scholarship Johnson (1987) and most strikingly Henderson (1987), 122–164, repr. with modifications as Henderson (1998), 165–210, have stressed the political nihilism of Lucan's position and emphasized the resistance of the text to any straightforward reading as a conscious expression of the poet's belief in nothing. Note the acute challenges of Sklenář (1999) and (2003) and Rudich (1993), 295–6, n.2. Ahl (1976) closely associates the poem with the Pisonian conspiracy (and hence identifies it as a monument of sorts to this resistance). Of the works which seek in Lucan's political philosophy a 'third way' between nihilism and republicanism, see esp. Bartsch (1997), who argues that Lucan's position was dictated by the need to believe in *something* (however absurd), Rudich (1993), 107–85 who regards him as an anti-Caesarean 'dissident' who consciously presented his poem in several different registers, and Leigh (1997), who places particular emphasis on the 'anti-democratic' nature of epic and the spectacles therein, and on Lucan's struggles with the parameters of the genre. Walde (2011) reads the BC as an example of cathartic 'literature of trauma', and thereby places it on a wholly different political trajectory.

[93] See esp. Walde (2007); Wick (2010); Leigh (2000).

[94] Compare for example Tracy (2014), who argues that Lucan represents Memphitic Egypt as a philosophic utopia, which provides a model of intellectual resistance to Caesarism; Manolaraki (2011) and (2013), who regards the digression as a vehicle for anti-Caesarean invective, cosmographic reflection which transcends the narrative structure of the remainder of the epic and a site for Lucan's assertion of poetic virtuosity over Nero; and Barrenechea (2010), who suggests the Nile was intended to demonstrate the limits of Caesar's vainglory and to explore the limits of unreliable narration. My own interpretation of the passage falls somewhere between these three recent positions.

The Nile resurfaces repeatedly throughout the *Civil War*. It makes its first appearance in the twentieth line of the opening book and rises multiple times over the course of the narrative that follows, often in rather incongruous contexts.[95] Yet the most significant descriptions of the Nile appear towards the end of the epic. The last three books of the text are concerned with the fate of the antagonists of the poem after the climactic battle of Pharsalus. Book VIII traces Pompey's flight from the battlefield across the eastern Mediterranean to Egypt. Here, the Nile offers the false hope of refuge for the defeated general and provides a setting for his murder and his eventual commemoration. The book effects a melancholy reflection which draws the narrative out from its historical context into the depths of Egyptian prehistory, and into the distant future. In Book IX, the Republican Cato reflects on Pompey's loss and goes on to face his own struggles in the deserts of Libya. The Nile reappears in Book X, but this time as the object of Julius Caesar's scholarly curiosity. The victorious Caesar engages the Egyptian priest Acoreus in conversation about the river and is presented with a meandering survey of the history of the river, a doxography of explanations for its floods and a short description of its course. While this long digression initially seems a rather strange presence in a poem elsewhere typified by the reckless pace of its narrative, the Nile provides an important political undercurrent to Lucan's work. As we shall see, it is through the twin representations of the Nile at the close of the *Civil War* – as Pompey's tomb and the object of Caesar's scrutiny – that the poet effects the elision between the brutalities of civil war and the Neronian world of his own experience.

### The Nile as Pompey's Tomb

If Virgil's *Aeneid* leads its hero and its audience inexorably towards Rome, Lucan's entropic epic flings its protagonists away from the imperial city with far greater force.[96] The action twists outwards from Italy and reaches a climax of sorts with the conflict at Pharsalus in Book VII. But the attentions of the audience are constantly directed even beyond that battlefield to Egypt, and hence to the post-apocalyptic world that awaits the triumvirs. Throughout the *Civil War*, Pompey's death is repeatedly anticipated and it is repeatedly associated with Egypt and the Nile. Long before the epic staggers into Alexandria, the audience knows what the final destination will be. The headless corpse of Pompey and the blood-stained sands of the Nile

---

[95] Luc. 1.20.      [96] Bexley (2009) explores this instability.

mark the close of the two opening books of the epic – a vivid anticipation of the horror to come.[97] The bloodied Nile is invoked as the site of Pompey's murder in Book V, twice in Book VI, and again in Book VII, before the narrative finally catches up to this foreshadowing.[98] This denouement is also anticipated in visceral rather than geographical imagery: Books III and IV end with the image of other decapitated corpses, at once the creation of civil war and the anticipation of the greatest death of all.[99]

When it comes, Book VIII is almost entirely concerned with this ignominious end: it describes the decapitation of 'head of the world', and the chaos that results.[100] At the opening of the book, Pompey is depicted in flight across the eastern Mediterranean. Reunited with his wife Cornelia, he contemplates the vicissitudes of fate and the possibilities of forging new alliances in order to take the fight back to Caesar. But Cornelia shares with the audience a knowledge that these plans will come to nothing, and that Pompey will eventually meet his death in Egypt. Pompey's fate is determined at the court of the young Ptolemy XIII: he is murdered and decapitated, his head carried triumphantly away, and his body burned, commemorated only by a single, unremarkable headstone.[101] In due course, the different characters of the epic respond to the news of this death and the sight of Pompey's head. Cornelia laments her own role in the spiralling catastrophe of the civil war; Sextus Pompeius, the son of the triumvir, swears revenge on all of Egypt; Cato, the coldly Stoic Republican, commits himself to a futile campaign in the sands of Libya; and Caesar himself responds with crocodile tears and a revived megalomania at the encouragement of Cleopatra.[102]

The anticlimactic denouement of the Civil War (and *The Civil War*) in Egypt is telegraphed throughout the work, not least through the prophetic voices of the epic. The point is vividly illustrated in the prophecy of the witch Erictho in Book VI. To deliver her prophecy, Erictho first reanimates the corpse of a Roman legionary, who then dutifully foretells the respective fates of the triumvirs.[103] This abject oracle first describes the lamentations

---

[97] Luc. 1.683–6; 2.732–6.

[98] Luc. 5.471–5; 6.305–8, 810–12; 7.691–2. And cf. 8.542–4; 9.82, 161–4 and the long description and eulogy at 8.595–72.

[99] Luc. 3.757–61 (an unnamed Roman corpse at Massilia), 4.809–810 (Curio's unburied corpse in Libya); all, of course, recall and retrospectively politicize the similar decapitated body of Pyrrhus in *Aen* 2.567–8. On this echo, see Ahl (1976), 222 and on the implications Casali (2011).

[100] Bartsch (1997), 16–17; On the corporeal imagery of the epic, see further Dinter (2013a), 9–49. Tracy (2014), 31–59 discusses Pompey's precarious position in Alexandria.

[101] Luc. 8.663–711, 736–95.

[102] Luc. 9. 51–116 (Cornelia); 9. 126–66 (Sextus Pompeius); 9. 19–35 (Cato); 9.1035–1108 (Caesar).

[103] Luc. 8.507–830.

of the heroes of the Republic who contemplate the upheaval of the civil war from the underworld, and then the transience of earthly life. His prophecy ends with a chilling assessment of both the profound importance and the essential meaninglessness of its climax:

> The question is, whose grave Nile and whose Tiber will lap
> with waves: for the leaders, the battle confirms their burial alone.[104]

Erictho's zombie reiterates the bleak political message which lurks behind the epic as a whole: the implications of the civil war extended far beyond the identity of the ultimate victor. Were Pompey to prove triumphant, the prophecy implies, little would be changed. Regardless of the victor of the conflict, the fate of the world had already been determined.

In many ways, Lucan's repeated references to the opposed tombs on the Tiber and the Nile refer to the graves of four belligerents, and not just two.[105] In important ways, it looks forward to the events of the 30s BCE, and Octavian's victory, as well as Caesar's. The distinction between Mark Antony's burial in Alexandria and the mausoleum erected for Augustus in the Campus Martius was repeatedly emphasized in the propaganda that presaged the collapse of the second triumvirate and was to remain a central feature of the dynastic ideology of the Julio-Claudians down to the time of Lucan's composition.[106] Lucan underscores these pairings through his repeated insistence that Pompey was indeed killed on the shores of the Nile, rather than off the coast of Egypt as the historical sources would suggest.[107] In this, he effectively performs the reverse operation to that accomplished in Propertius 3.11.33–38, in which the setting of Octavian's victory is indelibly stained by Pompey's blood, as we have seen. Comparable ambiguity underpins Lucan's geographical language in his allusions to, and accounts of, the murder itself. On the one hand, Lucan repeatedly specifies that Pompey met his end on the Pelusian branch of the Nile, at the opposite corner of the Delta from Alexandria. In Book VIII, then, when he refers to the *Hesperius miles*, fated to be buried on the Nile's Pelusian shores, he can only mean Pompey.[108] But this distinction is blurred by the repeated identity of the triumvir's murderers as Pharian, and by the clear implication that it is Alexandria that bears the guilt for Pompey's death.[109] A Roman corpse who met an ignominious death on the shores of the Nile, Lucan's Pompey has a wide historical resonance.

---

[104] Luc. 6.809–11. tr. Braund (1992), 128.
[105] Cf. Berti (2000), 20; Manolaraki (2011), 159–60 and (2013), 77.    [106] Kraft (1967), 199–201.
[107] On the antecedents to this shift in Prop. 3.11, see above 249–51.    [108] Luc. 8.824–5.
[109] Luc. 8.663–91. Note the particular Pharian emphasis in lines 675 and 681.

For good reason, Pompey's death is the point at which the inexorable, careering progress of the *Civil War* briefly pauses while the lasting implications of his tragedy are contemplated. More even than in the description of the dripping battlefield of Pharsalus, it is here where the conflict temporarily runs out of its bloody fuel. Two direct addresses to the Nile provide the breathing space at the heart of this chaos. The first is in the voice of the narrator, and the second ascribed to Sextus Pompeius, the triumvir's son. In each, the river itself is the object of angry vituperation for its role in the collapse of the Republic. Through these lamentations, the audience is moved away from the historical focus of the narrative and into a wider temporal and spatial setting.

In the first, the authorial voice adopts the traditional pieties of hymns to Isis, Osiris and the Nile and twists them into a curse of the river. The familiar pleas for a fertile flood are inverted, as the hostility of the appeal scorches upriver to damn the river at its very point of origin:

> Brutal land, for a crime so terrible, what should I ask you in prayer?
> May Nile be detained in the region where he rises and turn back
> his waters, and may barren fields be in need of winter rains,
> and may you disintegrate entirely into crumbling sands in Ethiopia.[110]

The religious overtones of this bitter apostrophe are made explicit in the lines that follow. Here, the speaker contrasts the welcome granted to Egyptian cults within Rome to the ignominious reception of Pompey in Ptolemaic Egypt. This short passage deploys hostile commonplaces about the region's gods, familiar from the epics and elegies of the Augustan period. But these are not simply the demented animal-gods of Virgil's Actium, but something more destabilizing than that – the 'half-divine dogs' (*semideos . . . canes*) and mortal gods of an unsettling and perverse region.[111]

The lament then shifts its focus to the authorial present. Rome is first upbraided for its failure to receive Pompey's remains, even at the time of writing, despite having erected a temple to the savage tyrant (*saevo . . . templum tyranno*).[112] The narrator goes on to express a resigned satisfaction that the humble grave marker might prompt a reflective tourist or merchant to pay his respects, and that the incongruity of Pompey's grave is the true marker of his greatness.[113] In the final section of the lament, which closes Lucan's eighth book, the temporal focus shifts again, this

---

[110] Luc. 8.826–9. tr. Braund (1992),175.    [111] Luc. 8.832–4.    [112] Luc. 8.835–40 at 835.

[113] Luc. 8.851–58. tr. Braund (1992), 176. There is some thematic recollection here of Prop. 3.7: an elegy on the death of a merchant in Egypt. Tracy (2014), 53 notes the incongruity of this figure in the light of the Golden Age imagery deployed elsewhere in the passage.

time to the distant future. The narrator invokes a time when even the grandest marble mausolea would have crumbled, and Pompey's name have simply passed into legend. One day, Lucan states, the stories surrounding Pompey's grave will seem just as mythical as those attached to Jupiter's tomb on Crete. At that point, the poet implies, Egypt will be glad not to have a permanent marker of this horror:

> One day this will be to your advantage, that no lofty pile
> with marble mass arose, to last into the future.
> No lengthy time will scatter the heap of tiny
> dust, the tomb will fall, and of your death
> the evidence will vanish. A happier age will come,
> when the people pointing out that rock will not be believed;
> and Egypt in the eyes of the crowds of our descendants will be perhaps
> as false about the grave of Magnus as Crete about the Thunderer's.[114]

The power of this image comes from the inversion of two familiar *topoi*. First is the specific association of Egypt with Pompey's death – a connection that Lucan does much to establish over the course of his epic, but which had significant antecedents in Augustan writing, as we have seen. Equally important, however, was the metapoetic conceit that verse would provide a timeless form of memorial, both to the writer and to his subject. In one of his best known *Odes*, for example, Horace proudly claimed that his own poetic fame would outlast even the pyramids.[115] In the concluding lines of his *Metamorphoses*, Ovid made a similar boast that his own epic would survive the Roman Empire and states in the *Amores* that Lucretius will be forgotten with the destruction of the earth.[116] Lucan's hope for a happier age (*felicior aetas*) in which the Civil War is forgotten is also implicitly a desire for a world in which his own *Civil War* is no longer read, but the epic as a whole is motivated by a striking pessimism. In poet's apostrophe to Caesar in Book IX, for example, he is resigned to a world in which the *Pharsalia* – Lucan's as well as Caesar's – will ultimately go on for ever.[117] While the address to the Nile offers the poet the means to navigate in time between Pompey's death, the authorial present and the distant future, then, the inevitable implication of this is simply that the Civil War will continue as long as the *Civil War* is read. The author developed this theme substantially in the last books of his epic, as we shall see.

Similar themes are apparent in the lament of Pompey's son, Sextus Pompeius, at the start of Book IX.[118] Describing his horror at the sight of

---

[114] Luc. 8.865–72. tr. Braund (1992), 176.    [115] Hor. *Carm*. 3.30.1–5.
[116] Ov. *Met*. 15.871–9; *Am* 1.15.23–4.    [117] Luc. 9.983–6.
[118] Nisbet (1982–4/1995) on this speech.

the head of his father carried through the streets of Alexandria, and his grief at the loss even of his father's decapitated corpse, Sextus angrily turns to Egypt. Here, Sextus recalls the themes of the authorial lament, but in more active terms:

> Shall not Amasis, torn out from the pyramid tombs,
> and the other kings go floating down the rushing Nile for me?
> Let all their tombs pay penalty for you unburied, Magnus.
> Isis, power in the eyes of the world, from her tomb shall I evict
> and Osiris clothed in linen I shall scatter through the crowd
> and I shall burn the head by placing gods beneath it. The land will pay
> this penalty to me: I shall leave the fields devoid of cultivators,
> nor will there be anyone to benefit from rising Nile; you will be sole lord
> of Egypt, father, when I have driven out the gods and peoples.[119]

The similarities between these two appeals to the river are important. In one, the narrator calls for time to halt in the form of the Nile itself, and meditates on the passage of human history through the medium of the inexorable flow of the river. In the other, Sextus seeks actively to dissolve the monuments of Alexander, the Pharaohs and the Egyptian gods in the waters of the Nile and leave Egypt outside history in a permanent depopulation.[120]

Both passages draw upon a rich tradition of riparian symbolism in epic poetry, in which rivers were frequently deployed as markers of time.[121] But the bleak morbidity of Lucan's Nile is without obvious parallel. The role of the Tiber in the *Aeneid* provides an illuminating point of contrast. The Italian river provides a reassuring presence within the second half of that poem: it is at the mouth of the Tiber that Aeneas first lands, and on its banks that Augustan Rome will rise;[122] it is Tiber that protects Aeneas and personifies his descendants;[123] and it is the vision of the river as the new Xanthus that helps establish Rome as the new Troy.[124] The river locates Virgil's historical narrative in time and space, and it takes the story of Rome from the fall of Troy to Augustan Rome and back again, both charting Aeneas' journey to the west and framing it as a return home.

[119] Luc. 9.155–164. tr. Braund (1992), 181.
[120] On the precise identity of the royal corpses castigated by Sextus Pompeius, see esp. Nisbet (1982–4/1995), 183–4.
[121] P. Jones (2005), esp. 93–105.
[122] Verg. *Aen.* 2.781–782, 5.83, 796–798 (Tiber as predestined homeland of Aeneas); 7.29–36 (On the landfall at the Tiber mouth); 6.789–800 (on Augustus' Imperial City in Latium). On the various roles of the Tiber in *Aeneid*, see P. Jones (2005), 63–6 and 93–100; Spencer (2005), 50–4; Herendeen (1986), 54–7.
[123] Verg. *Aen.* 7.303–304; 8.31–65, 86–93.     [124] Verg. *Aen.* 3.497–9. Herendeen (1986), 51.

Virgil's can be a violent river, but in the final reckoning it is ordered, and it is always comprehensible. Lucan not only disrupted this order in his own epic river, he delighted in the chaos that resulted – a theme that is developed most fully in the long Nile digression in his final book.

### Caesar's Frustrated Gaze

The Nile digression in the last book of the *Civil War* is undoubtedly the most complex treatment of the river in this period.[125] The only comparable text is the prose discussion in Book IVA of Seneca's *Natural Questions*, and in many ways Lucan's account was written in dialogue with his uncle's work.[126] The passage itself takes the form of a rather one-sided sympotic discussion. Caesar, replete from his feasting on Cleopatra's pleasure barge, seeks to sate his intellectual curiosity in a similar way. To this end, he turns to the Egyptian priest Acoreus, an elderly figure who appeared previously as an ineffectual advisor to the young Ptolemy in the discussions over Pompey's fate.[127] Caesar declares himself to be a scholar who has come to Egypt for enlightenment, and demands the secrets of the Nile floods and its mysterious origins to be explained to him. There then follows one of the longest direct speeches in the whole poem, in which Acoreus first sets the Nile within its cosmic context, linking the floods of the river to the movement of the stars. He then provides a systematic doxography of the Nile floods, boldly compares Caesar's enquiry to the ambitions of a succession of tyrannical rulers, and closes with a substantial discussion of the course of the river from its mysterious origins to Memphis, at the apex of the Delta.

The status of Acoreus within this long passage is complex and has been much disputed. In part, the Egyptian priest fulfils the function of the epic *vates*, or 'bard', a prophetic or didactic figure whose most immediate inspiration is likely to have been Iopas in the opening book of the *Aeneid*.[128] The specific setting of the digression, in the post-prandial splendour of

---

[125] On the digression, cf. Berti (2000); Walde (2007); Barrenechea (2010). Hillard (2002) discusses the historical background to this passage.

[126] On the relative chronology of the *Bellum Civile* and the *QNat*, see Diels (1969), 403–6 and Tracy (2014), 104, n.9.

[127] Tracy (2014), 62–96 provides a thorough reading of Acoreus and argues he was intended as an idealized representation of Egyptian learning, notwithstanding the ambivalent statement at Luc. 8.475. For a contrary reading see Barrenechea (2010), 273–5.

[128] Verg. *Aen.* 1.740–47, on which see Hardie (1986), 51–9. Lucan's debts to Virgil here, and the conscious evocation of the court at Carthage, are discussed by Rossi (2005). Cf. also Manolaraki (2011), 156–7, 174–6; Manolaraki (2013), 103–7.

Cleopatra's barge, also allow the priest to be viewed as a participant in a sympotic exchange, or as an after-dinner speaker, both of which also have some epic precedent.[129] The details of Acoreus' account, however, and particularly its obvious debts to the *Natural Questions*, have also led readers to identify the figure with Seneca and to see in his interaction with Caesar an analogue to the elderly Stoic's instruction of the young Nero. In other aspects, Acoreus might be identified with Lucan himself, or with the priest Chaeremon – another court Stoic, and another Egyptian.[130] What is certainly clear throughout the digression, however, is that the sympotic dialogue on Cleopatra's barge was intended to pass comment on the comparable intellectual aspirations of Nero's circle. This is a connection that Lucan draws more or less explicitly through linguistic echoes of the *Natural Questions*, and which he supports through a deft use of doxographic and geographical discussion. Ultimately, however, it is the focus on the river itself which allows Lucan to blur the chronology between the narrated time of the late Republic and the authorial present of the Julio-Claudian empire. We have already seen how Lucan deployed the Nile as an effective symbol of the passage of time in Book VIII. This technique was to have a still more significant function in his final book. The digression is thus simultaneously important as a reflection of geographical knowledge at the time of his composition; a caustic commentary on imperial hubris, particularly in the field of natural philosophy; and the reformulation of this knowledge as a constitutive part of an ambitious epic with dark political overtones.

The roles of the two participants in the Nile discussion are established immediately and in direct speech. Caesar first demands of Acoreus a summary of the lands, gods and customs of Egypt and declares himself to be the heir of Plato and Eudoxus as a learned pilgrim to the region:

> But though there lives within my breast such enormous energy
> and love of truth, there is nothing I would rather know
> than the causes of the river which lie hidden through so many ages
> and its unknown source: let me have a hope assured of seeing
> the springs of the Nile, and I will abandon civil war.[131]

The way in which Caesar formulates his case is enormously important, both in the precise language that he employs, and in the sentiment behind

---

[129] Cameron (1995), 71–103; Berti (2000), 18, 161; Barrenechea (2010), 269–70 note the sympotic context, and the possibilities therein for metapoetic allusion. Schrijvers (2005), 33–4 argues Acoreus was intended to evoke the after-dinner speech of Cepheus responding to Perseus in Ov. *Met* 4.765–803.

[130] On Chaeremon, see above 179–80.  [131] Luc. 10.188–92.

his closing plea. As we shall see, this is perhaps the most important section of the whole digression in establishing its wider function within the poem.[132] But for Acoreus, this declaration is to be met with a statement of his own. Here, he establishes the occult nature of his cosmological and geographical knowledge and hence his privileged claim to authority:

> To me it is permitted to disclose the secrets of my mighty ancestors,
> Caesar, up to now unknown to the profane multitudes.
> To keep silent about such mighty miracles – let that be piety for others . . . [133]

The Egyptian priest as the guardian of arcane learning was a *topos* in Greek and Roman writing.[134] As several recent studies have demonstrated, this caricature was embraced in the temples of the Nile valley, particularly as the imperial period progressed.[135] It was this reputation that motivated Caesar's enquiry into the mysteries of Egypt, and indeed Lucan's framing of the scene as a whole. Acoreus' response promises a privileged glimpse of secret knowledge, but ultimately proves to be false. The exposition that follows is a mixture of confused (and perhaps deliberately confusing) cosmological lore and summary of Stoic natural philosophy.[136] The latter is a rather elegant versification of Seneca's *Natural Questions* and also recalls the methodology of Lucretius, but it is difficult to escape the observation that there is little that is particularly original in Acoreus' account.[137]

   The first part of the Nile digression proper is focused on the likely causes of the Nile floods.[138] Acoreus outlines and then refutes the 'false belief of the ancients' (*vana fides veterum*) that extensive snowfall in Ethiopia was the cause of the floods. He also dismisses the theories relating to the Etesian winds (here identified erroneously as the 'Zephyrs'), either for driving rain clouds south, or retarding the outflow of the Nile at its mouth. Acoreus goes on to reject the argument that the Nile was joined to other rivers by underground passages, or that it had an Oceanic source. This is a systematic survey of the scholarly territory, and is probably to be read as a conscious recrafting of *Natural Questions* for a new audience. Where there are deviations from established doxography – in Acoreus' failure to associate theories with named authorities, for example, or his silence on the established refutations of all but the first of these arguments – these may be

---

[132]  See below 271.       [133]  Luc. 10.194–6. tr. Braund (1992), 212.
[134]  Tait (2003) provides an excellent overview.       [135]  See esp. Assmann (2003), 409–20.
[136]  Housman (1926), 325–37 produced an emphatic traducing of Lucan's cosmological passage and cf. Diels (1969), who notes the similarly imprecise astrology at Luc. 1.650–5, 8.167–70 and 9.531–2.
[137]  On Sen. *QNat* 4a, see Chapter 4, above. On Lucan's debts to Seneca, see Diels (1969); Berti (2000), 174–85; Tracy (2014), 153. On Lucretian themes (briefly) see Hardie (2008), 315.
[138]  Berti (2000), 187–212 and Diels (1969) 383–94 provide a detailed discussion.

explained by the demands of the verse form and are by no means unique to Lucan.[139] We see the exactly the same features in the brief doxography of Lucretius.

Acoreus punctuates his discussion with statements of others' ignorance,[140] but by the midpoint of the digression, this fiction of privileged knowledge has been entirely abandoned:

> But I – if it is right for me to solve such a great dispute –
> Caesar, I believe that certain waters, long ages after the completion
> of the universe, burst out from shaken veins of the earth
> not by God's intention; that certain waters at the actual construction
> of the universe originated with the whole – and these the Creator
> and crafter of the world himself controls beneath a fixed authority.[141]

That the Nile was one of the primordial waters of the universe, and was moved by forces that were effectively unique to it, corresponds to Seneca's presentation of the river. As we have seen, the loss of a crucial section of Book IVA of the *Natural Questions* creates considerable problems of interpretation, but there is good reason to conclude that Seneca refrained from ruling definitively on the origins of the Nile floods, and that the solution offered by Acoreus more or less corresponded to the opinion of the elderly philosopher.[142] What is equally significant is that Acoreus' long discussion of the mysteries of the inundation, opened as it was by a statement of his own privileged knowledge, ends with a recital of well-established commonplaces which must have been very familiar to an audience at Nero's court (if not at Caesar's).[143]

There is a pause in the digression at this point, in which Acoreus addresses Caesar directly and compares his enquiry to the earlier ambitions of other occupiers of Egypt. This is obviously a crucial passage within the digression, and we will return to it shortly. But Acoreus begins the second part with a reiteration of the impossibility of his task, and his own privileged view. Once more he promises to surpass the rumours of 'lying legend' (*fabula mendax*) and to reveal the course of the river as it was known to him.[144] Once again, the description that follows adheres to many of the conventions of prosaic geographical writing, and at first blush reads like a familiar survey of the river from its source to the Delta. Acoreus addresses many of the

---

[139] *pace* Tracy (2014), 150 and 218–20. On the metrical limitations, see Diels (1969), 387.
[140] See for example Luc. 10.219–20, 237, 239–40.
[141] Luc. 10.262–7. tr. Braund (1992), 214.    [142] See Chapter 5.
[143] Tracy (2014), 149: 'Eager to grasp the inundation's *causas* … *latentis* ('hidden causes'), Caesar has so far only been granted a flowery repackaging of stale clichés.'
[144] Luc. 10. 282–87 at 282.

geographical *topoi* associated with the river – its mysterious origins, the division of the watercourse at Meroe, Philae and the Cataracts and the prominence of Memphis within Egypt – and addresses these in more or less the right order. This last point is more significant than it might seem, and not least because of the tendency of Roman writers to jumble their Nilotic geographies, as discussed in Chapter 5, and in a well-known mistake in Seneca's *Natural Questions*. In that work, Seneca conflates Philae and Meroe in his description of the Nile – a blunder which Lucan corrects.[145] At the very least, then, Lucan's digression provides a competent and attractive survey of the river.

Significantly, Acoreus' description of the Nile is framed as a direct address to the river itself.[146] This apostrophe immediately situates the digression somewhere between disinterested geographical description and religious celebration – an ambiguity that is accentuated by the inevitable recollection of Lucan's own address to the Nile in Book VIII. Thereafter, uncertainties abound. Despite the apparent confidence of his introduction, the most striking feature of Acoreus' digression is the sheer space given to declarations of ignorance. Around half of his description concerns the course of the river in Ethiopia, long before it reaches the familiar territories of Egypt. Here, Acoreus repeatedly emphasizes the elusiveness of the river's course and stresses its hidden origins and unknown course.[147] In its upper reaches, Acoreus' Nile continually frustrates attempts to delineate and contain it. This is a quality that permeates the digression as a whole, even when attention turns to the relatively familiar regions north of the Cataract. Conspicuously, Acoreus' emphasis upon the unknowable source means that his description has no clear beginning; the gradual petering out of the account after Memphis, rather than tracing the course of the river through the Delta and on to Alexandria and the Mediterranean, equally means that the digression has no clear end.

Acoreus' digression is also marked by a surprising imprecision of geographical language. As we have seen, Greco-Roman descriptions of the Nile were most commonly defined by an armature of stopping points along the river. These may not always have been reproduced with absolute precision, and eventually gave way to caricature, but these linear itineraries meant that the Nile was frequently comprehended through the settlements on

---

[145]  See above 169; on Lucan's language here (and the possibility of a fudge on these specifics), see Berti (2000), 234.

[146]  On the significance of the apostrophe, see Manolaraki (2011), 164–6.

[147]  See, for example, Luc. 10.295–8 and 10.300–2.

its banks. Acoreus' Nile fits no such model. His river is charted according to the stars, rather than to terrestrial settlements: significantly, four constellations are named in the description of the river's course and only four human settlements.[148] Of those settlements, three – Meroe, Philae and Abaton (the holy island of Bigeh, located a short distance from Philae) – are islands rather than towns, and thereby emphasize his contention that the Nile was not to be contained or defined by its banks. The well-known fact that Abaton/Bigeh was accessible only to priests further underscores this point.[149] Conspicuously, the fourth of Acoreus' placenames – Memphis – appears only within the context of the limitless Nile floods. The one fixed point in Lucan's Nile geography, in other words, exemplifies the futility defining the river in human terms:

> Memphis first allows you plains and open country
> and forbids your banks to set a limit to your growth.[150]

Unless this couplet is taken to be an allusion to the Delta, Acoreus is silent on the course of the river north of Memphis and includes nothing at all on Alexandria.[151]

Even those parts of the river which are described, moreover, are frequently stretched into almost unrecognizable form. Acoreus' account of the region between Philae (line 313) and Abaton (323) describes a slow-running river, alludes to the trade routes with the Red Sea, and introduces the drama of the cataracts, itself a well-known commonplace in classical writing. These ten lines cover an extraordinary geographical range, despite the fact that Seneca – certainly Lucan's source here – correctly notes that the two islands are located very close to one another.[152] Indeed, the two islands were only a few hundred feet apart. Acoreus and Lucan delight in stretching and distorting Nile geography to emphasize the entropic nature of the river.

---

[148] Berti (2000), 178–81 on the peculiarity of these reference points.

[149] On Abaton/Bigeh, see Diod Sic 1.22.3–6; Sen. *QNat* 4A 2.7; Plut. *De Is et Os* 20; Meyboom (1995), 61–2 and 306–7, n.113.

[150] Luc. 10.330–1. tr. Braund (1992), 215.

[151] This silence has been variously interpreted. Manolaraki (2011) 164 and (2013), 91–2 suggests that the Delta signified the belligerents through its two principal branches, and the omission allowed Acoreus/Lucan to frame the Nile digression as essentially distinct from the historical timeframe of the civil war and cf. Tracy (2011), 39–42. Tracy (2014), 114 further argues that Acoreus refused to impart strategic information to a Caesar more concerned with conquest than with philosophical enquiry.

[152] Sen. *QNat* 4a.2.7. *exiguo ab hac spatio*. The proximity is also stressed by Diod Sic 1.22.3; Plut. *De Is et Os*, 20.

## *Dynamics at Court*

The power dynamics at play within this passage are crucial to the under-standing of its significance, both within the *Civil War* as a whole, and for its immediate audience at Nero's court. As we have seen, the digression is prompted by Julius Caesar's curiosity about the mysteries of the river and his apparent deference to the wisdom of Acoreus. The priest represents the hieratic wisdom of Egypt, which had proven a perennial source of fas-cination for Greek and Roman commentators, and the dialogue between the two characters is a case study in this epistemological tension. Caesar presents his own enquiry as that of an interested tourist or travelling scholar, but appropriates this *topos* of curiosity to his own megalomaniac ends.[153] By contrast, much of Acoreus' response is essentially passive – it promises much, but delivers little. At its midpoint, however, his speech takes a sur-prising turn. Here, he locates Caesar's interest not against the intellectual genealogy that the Roman claims for himself, but in comparison to the political and military rulers who had previously come to Egypt. No heir to Plato, Caesar is instead shown to be the successor to Alexander, Sesostris and the 'mad' Cambyses:

> Your desire to know Nile, Roman, was shared
> by tyrants Pharian and Persian and of Macedon,
> and no age is there which has not wished to grant the knowledge
> to the future – but up to now its natural power of hiding is victorious.[154]

As Jonathan Tracy's recent study has clearly shown, Acoreus' tyrannical genealogy has a rather complex position in Lucan's account of the politics of late first-century Alexandria.[155] Although Alexander is unambiguously presented as a tyrant in this passage, he would hardly have been viewed in such terms in the Ptolemaic court and was held up as a hero by Lucan's (and history's) Caesar. The tradition that Alexander sponsored an unsuccessful expedition upriver may also have originated with Lucan and may simply reflect a common view of the general's all-encompassing ambition. Other sources imply that Alexander did propose an exploration of the kind, but

---

[153] Luc. 10.181–3. It is now conventional to read Caesar's request for knowledge ironically – as an implicit declaration of the superiority of military over intellectual power. Cf. Ahl (1976), 228; Ozanam (1990), 284; Barrenechea (2010). But compare Spencer (2002), 160–1, Rossi (2005), 242–3 and the discussion of these interpretations in Tracy (2014), 100–1. Tracy (2014), 114 perhaps overstates the case by reading this enquiry as a veiled attempt to gather military intelligence (and Acoreus' silence on the Delta as a form of passive resistance).

[154] Luc. 10.268–271. tr. Braund (1992), 214.

[155] Tracy (2014), 182–96. See also Schmidt (1982), who regards the passage as an implicit criticism of Nero's appropriation of the Ptolemaic ruler cult.

there is little other evidence that he followed through on these aspirations.[156] That this was Lucan's conceit rather than Acoreus' is shown by the poet's concern to connect the two generals. In the opening of Book X, Caesar pays homage at the tomb of Alexander. Again, there is no corroborating evidence for this episode – it was Octavian rather than Julius Caesar who visited the tomb – but the passage fulfils an important function in the poem.[157] Through it, Lucan establishes a fascination with the Nile shared by the two tyrants:

> Following the world's slope, he would have gone into the west
> and past the poles, and drunk from the Nile at its source:
> his final day blocked his path and only nature
> could impose this limit on the crazy king.[158]

The subsequent references to Sesostris make a similar point and again fit the demands of Lucan's political message better than the historical context of Acoreus' speech: the mythical king was a heroic figure within Egyptian tradition, and scarcely a tyrant. Cambyses was remembered with hostility in Egypt and may have been loosely linked to the question of the Nile source.[159] Ultimately, there are three messages here: that interest in the Nile is the mark of a tyrant, that nature will always protect its secrets, and that Egypt is the stage on which this futile megalomania is enacted.[160]

Each of these themes builds upon the essential opposition between tyranny and natural order that runs throughout Lucan's epic.[161] Caesar repeatedly scorns sacred boundaries, whether through the crossing of the Rubicon, in the violation of the sacred grove outside Massilia, or in his direct challenge to the gods in the grand storm of Book V.[162] It is only the frustration of his enquiry into the sources of the Nile that halts this continuous transgression – Acoreus' didactic digression both delays Caesar's

---

[156] Arr. *Anab.* 6.1.2; Strabo 15.1.25; Curt. 4.7.2, 8.3; Berti (2000), 215–7. Diels (1969), 395–6 and Tracy (2014), 184–6 are both sceptical about the expedition; Burstein (1976) is more positive, and is followed by Vasunia (2001), 280. Pellacani (2012), 91 suggests that Seneca may also have referred to the expedition in a lost portion of *QNat* 4a.

[157] Cf. Suet. *Aug.* 18.1. Rossi (2005), 251–2 observes that there is no other evidence for Caesar's visit to Alexander's tomb.

[158] Luc. 10.39–42. tr. Braund (1992), 208.

[159] Berti (2000), 219–21. Strabo 17.1.5 alludes to Ethiopian expeditions of both rulers.

[160] Compare Ahl (1976), 229 and Berti (2000) *X* 21–4. On Greek representations of Egypt as a land of tyrants, see esp. Vasunia (2001), 77–87, 183–215.

[161] Berti (2000), 213–14.

[162] Myers (2011) summarizes the theme of boundary violations in the *Civil War*. On the crossing of the Rubicon: Luc. 1.183–227 and the commentary in Herendeen (1986), 60–1; Masters (1992), 1–5; Bartsch (1997), 14; the Storm: Luc. 5.560–702 and the discussion in Ahl (1976), 206–8; Johnson (1987), 105–7; Masters (1992), 143; Quint (1993), 138–39 and cf. also Rudich (1993), 132–3.

relentless progress throughout the world and establishes a physical limit to his destructive avarice.[163] One crucial feature of Acoreus' Nile is that it stands beyond the grasp of Caesar's military power: this is one territory that the new tyrant will never despoil. But it is also significant that Caesar's reckless boundary crossing is halted only by a geographical feature that itself eschews both temporal and spatial limits, whose sublime uncertainty sits beyond the scope of epic poetry itself. For Lucan, this was a means to meditate upon imperial ambition, but also on the limitations of his chosen form to encompass this. This theme is at its most important in the poet's treatment of the ruling emperor Nero.

## Nero and Caesar

The political impulses behind Lucan's *Civil War* have been explored in considerable depth by scholars.[164] The poet's own involvement in the Pisonian conspiracy against Nero and his subsequent execution cast a long shadow over the epic. Whether or not the histrionic celebration of the emperor in the opening book was intended to be read ironically – and scholars remain divided on the issue – the later books have generally been interpreted as a systematic attack on Caesar and hence on the Julio-Claudian Principate.[165] As the *Civil War* progresses, there can be little doubt that Lucan intended his poem to be read in the light of contemporary events, and for his charges against Caesar to apply equally to his successor. At times the poet explicitly includes recent emperors in his attacks on the excesses of 'Caesarism', and the use of the unadorned honorific *Caesar* for both Julius and Nero further blurs the distinction between past and present.[166] Nero is a constant presence throughout the *Civil War*, but it is in the Nile digression where the distinction between the two Caesars is at its most blurred.[167]

---

[163]  Berti (2000), 17–18.        [164]  Cf. 253, n.92 above.

[165]  The celebration of Nero at Luc. 1.33–66 is a crucial and much disputed passage. Ahl (1976), 47–9 and Johnson (1987), 121 regard the celebration of Nero as ironic or parodic: an interpretation disputed by Rudich (1993), 114–15. Masters (1992) and Dewar (1994) regard it as conventional praise. For further discussion of the scholarship on the passage, see Holmes (1999) (who argues for a consciously ambiguous political meaning), an ambivalence picked up by Henderson (2011b), 551: 'When *Bellum Civile* starts thus . . . is it *either* blessing *or* albatross?'

[166]  See esp. Luc. 4.821–4; 7.432–8; 7.368–46; cf. Ahl (1976), 42–4; Johnson (1987), 132; Roller (2001), 37.

[167]  On the inclusion of Nero (and other 'Caesars') in Lucan's attack on Julius Caesar, see Ahl (1976), 49, 55; Holmes (1999), 75–81 at 78; Roller (2001), 37; Rossi (2005), 252–3 and note the emphasis of Luc. 7.639–41.

Within the Nile digression, Lucan attributed to Julius Caesar an interest in Egypt which contemporary audiences would readily have associated with Nero.[168] The last of the Julio-Claudians was an enthusiastic Egyptophile who oversaw the accelerated promotion of the imperial cult within the province,[169] a willing patron of Egyptians within Italy,[170] and an aficionado who maintained his devotion to the region even up to his last moments.[171] These exotic tastes were not unique to Nero – as we have seen, similar motifs were readily adopted by Augustan taste-makers, and there is evidence that Gaius Caligula was also fascinated with the region – but contemporary audiences would certainly have picked up on the immediate resonance of these allusions.[172] Among Nero's courtiers were Seneca and Chaeremon, whose Egyptian interests have already been discussed.[173] Also influential was Tiberius Claudius Balbillus, who was an influential astrologer, and had served as *Praefectus Aegypti* in the late 50s.[174] Lucan makes no reference to the reconnaissance expedition that Nero sent into Ethiopia in the early 60s, but he must have known of it, and the reports that the centurions brought back had a political significance of their own, as we have seen.[175] This fascination for Egypt provides an essential context for the understanding of Lucan's long digression.[176] When the poet sketched his sympotic tableau of an ambitious Caesar eagerly enquiring of an Egyptian priest the origins of the Nile, his primary point of reference was evidently not historical. The immediate audience of the *Civil War* would surely have recognized in the

---

[168] The fullest discussion of Nero's response to Egypt is provided by Cesaretti (1989), which places particular emphasis upon the promotion of a pharaonic Nero within the Nile valley itself and demonstrates at 49–62 that this 'official' Egyptophilia complicated the somewhat stereotyped image of the province within Rome. See also Voisin (1987).

[169] Cesaretti (1989), 19–48.

[170] See for example, Suet. *Nero*, 20.3 and the discussion in Cesaretti (1989), 56.

[171] The tradition that Nero intended to flee to Egypt upon hearing of Galba's usurpation is reproduced by Dio Cass. 63.27.2 and Plut. *Vit. Galb.* 2.1, and cf. Tac. *Ann.* 15.36.1. Suet. *Nero* 47.2 further suggests that the emperor sought the prefecture there as a consolation for the loss of his imperial power. On this tradition, see Cesaretti (1989), 59–60 who notes that it may represent a contemporary smear campaign by Nimfidius Sabinus to encourage the soldiers to elect Galba as emperor. Cf. also Vout (2003), 200 and Tac. *Ann* 16.6 on the embalming of Poppaea.

[172] Caligula's interest in Egypt is extensively discussed in Köberlein (1962). Cf. Suet. *Calig.* 49.2; Philo, *Leg* 172; 250–3; *In Flacc* 23; Joseph. *AJ* 19.80–1. Apion Plistonices was also a prominent figure in Rome after 40 CE and seems to have written works on the natural history of Egypt. Cf. Plin. *HN* 1. Ind.30–2, 35–7; Gell. *NA.* 5.14; 8.2, 10.10 and Aelian *NA* 11.40. Cf. Keyser and Irby-Massie (2008), 104.

[173] On Chaeremon see above 179–80.

[174] Suet. *Nero.* 36; Sen. *QNat* 4a.2.13; Plin. *HN* 19.3. On other courtiers with Egyptian connections, see Voisin (1987), 520–1.

[175] See 206–15 above.     [176] Cf. McCloskey and Phinney (1968).

vainglorious *Julius* Caesar of Lucan's tenth book the contemporary *Nero* Caesar so obsequiously praised in his first.[177]

Lucan underscores the colligation of the two Caesars through the specific language of the opening section of the Nile passage. As we have seen, the digression as a whole is presented as a dialogue, and Acoreus dominates the exchange. But it is Caesar who first introduces the topic of the Nile mysteries, and here we turn back to the peculiar way in which he explains his interest:

> But, though there lives within my breast such enormous energy (*virtus*)
> and love of truth (*tantus amor veri*), there is nothing I would rather know
> than the causes of the river which lie hidden through so many ages
> and its unknown source.[178]

This is, in fact, the only point in the *Civil War* in which Caesar is explicitly ascribed *virtus* – an immensely loaded term that was evidently not employed thoughtlessly by the poet.[179] In fact, the direct inspiration behind Caesar's language here can be found in the *Natural Questions*, as has long been recognized.[180] In one of only three direct references to the ruling emperor in that work, Seneca explains Nero's patronage of the Nile expedition in similar terms:

> I heard two centurions whom Nero, great lover of other virtues and especially
> of truth, (*ut aliarum virtutem ita veritatis in primis amantissimus*) had sent
> to search for the source of the Nile.[181]

Just as Lucan's Caesar is motivated by *virtus* and *amor veri*, so Seneca's Caesar is marked by 'other' *virtutes* and *veritatis in primis amantissimus*. It is uncertain whether Lucan deliberately echoed Seneca in this passage, or whether both writers drew upon official 'Neroese' in framing their accounts

---

[177] Vividly summarized by McCloskey and Phinney (1968), 87: 'In summary, then, what emerges from the last three books of the Pharsalia is the picture of a degenerate court in a luxurious Hellenized country, presided over by base flunkies who dominate a weak, cruel, petty and perverted king... Even more intolerable was a Caesar worse than Caesar, a tyrant whose vices were compounded by the petulant inhumanity of a childlike man who acted thirteen even when he was as old as thirty-two.'

[178] Luc. 10.188–191. tr. Braund (1992), 212.

[179] The transformation of *virtus* within Lucan's poem is typified by the forceful description of its worthlessness in a post-war world at Luc. 1.666–9. On *virtus* in the poem more broadly, compare Rudich (1993), 6–7; Roller (2001), 21–63; Sklenář (2003), 16–31.

[180] Eichberger (1935), 25–8 first noted the echo. For discussion of its significance compare Schmidt (1986), 37; Berti (2000), 170–1 (noting further echoes of *Aen* 2.10 and *Georg* 2.301); Tracy (2011), 38; Tracy (2014), 107–8.

[181] Sen. *QNat* 6.8.3: *Ego quidem centuriones duos quos Nero Caesar (ut aliarum virtutem ita veritatis in primis amantissimus) ad investigandum caput miserat*... tr. Hine (2010), 95.

of inquisitive Caesars, but the verbal similarities are clear.[182] In framing his own interest in this way, Lucan's Caesar unmistakably identified himself as a surrogate for the later emperor.

On the simplest level, the identification of Nero with his ambitious forebear in a Nilotic context might be read as a dig at the hubris of the ruling emperor in sponsoring yet another fruitless expedition upriver. As we saw in the discussion of the *Natural Questions*, the discoveries of the centurions may have been impressive, but they did not provide a definitive solution to the origins of the river, nor did they force Seneca to abandon his deductive approach to the mystery of the Nile floods.[183] Indeed, Nero's attempt to solve by force of arms what was better suited to philosophical enquiry ran exactly contrary to the principles of his former tutor. As Jonathan Tracy has recently argued, the parallels between these didactic pairs – Seneca and Nero on one hand, Acoreus and Caesar on the other – may also have been intended as a comment on the value of appropriate instruction to temper the excesses of a tyrant.[184] Even without this reading, the textual echo clearly situates Nero into the list of curious tyrants that Acoreus develops later in his speech. Alexander, Sesostris, 'mad' Cambyses, Julius Caesar and now Nero had all sought to extend their power to the source of the Nile, and all had come up short. By including Nero within this company, the poet roundly damned his own emperor by association.

The broader significance of this parallel is underscored by the rhetoric of imperialism employed by Lucan. As noted above, Caesar concludes his short declaration to Acoreus with a peculiar claim that he would abandon civil war, if only he could set eyes on the source of the Nile:[185]

> let me have a hope assured of seeing
> the springs of the Nile, and I will abandon civil war.[186]

This is an extraordinary promise, to say the least, but becomes particularly resonant when considered alongside a statement that comes at the very beginning of the *Civil War*. Bewailing the terrors and suffering of civil war (as he is to do throughout the poem), Lucan imagines the triumphs

---

[182] Barrenechea (2010), 265–8; Berti (2000), 170–1 further notes an echo of Virgil, *Georgics* 2.301 *tantus amor terrae*; and *Aeneid* 2.10: *sed si tantus amor casus cognoscere nostros*.

[183] See above 167–8.

[184] Tracy (2014), 259–72. It should be noted, however, that Tracy's reading of Seneca's *QNat* (and particularly his response to the Nile expedition of Nero) is much more positive than that proposed in Chapter 4 above. Compare Manolaraki (2011), 170–1 who regards Acoreus as a more positive reflection of Seneca.

[185] There is a comparable counterfactual at Luc. 3.73–82 (with the Rhine and Ocean as the captives in Caesar's external triumphs, rather than the Nile).

[186] Luc. 10.191–192. tr. Braund (1992), 212.

that might have awaited the Roman people had they avoided the pitfalls of internecine warfare:

> Beneath our yoke already the Seres and barbarian Araxes could
> have come and the race, if it exists, which knows Nile's birth.
> If your love of abominable war is so great, Rome,
> only when you have brought the entire world beneath the laws of Latium,
> turn your hand against yourself; not yet are you without an enemy.[187]

The Seres are normally identified as the inhabitants of China, yet their surprising connection to the African interior recurs in the description of the Nile in Book X. There, Lucan states that the Seres were the first people to witness the Nile after its journey from the equatorial deserts.[188] This might be explained in part as an example of the common conflation of the far south and the far east in much classical writing – or indeed as a 'grotesque poetic conceit' in the reading of Hermann Diels – but the link is not without precedent.[189] It is also conspicuous that Lucan repeats this conceit. The fact that the Seres appear in both passages (and nowhere else in the *Civil War*) suggests a deliberate connection.[190] What is particularly important here is Lucan's implication that the discovery of the Nile source might be a worthy prize for a peaceful empire, and the Seres an exotic group who would thereby be brought under the aegis. The Nile, Lucan intimates, is to be uncovered only in a world without civil war. Yet civil war will end, Caesar counters, only if he might discover the source of the Nile. There is a neat paradox here, but it goes yet further. At the time of Lucan's composition, 'Caesar' was still looking for the source of the Nile. Nero's 'great love' for knowledge thus not only placed him alongside Alexander, Sesostris and Cambyses as one of the great tyrants of history, but revealed him to be the true inheritor of the Caesarean mantle.[191]

  This context also illuminates the important symmetry between the abrupt ending of Acoreus' Nile geography, and the peculiarly truncated nature of Lucan's *Civil War*.[192] That the description of the Nile comes to a surprising end has long been realized: Acoreus traces the river as far as Memphis, but no further, allowing its waters to seep out beyond

---

[187] Luc. 1.19–23. tr. Braund (1992), 3.
[188] Luc. 10.292. On the Seres, see: Ov. *Am.* 1.14.6; Strabo 15.1.34; Pomponius Mela 1.11, 3.60; Plin. *HN* 6.54.
[189] Diels (1969), 397: 'eine groteske Übertreibung des Dichters'; Berti (2000), 228 and cf. esp. Mayerson (1993) 169–174 on the persistence of this confusion. Lucan's immediate source here is likely to have been Verg. *Georg.* 2.121–2, in which the Seres and Aethiopes are juxtaposed; the Seres also appear among Antony's allies in the anonymous work preserved on P.Herc 817. On which see Maehler (2003), 209.
[190] Luc. 10.292.     [191] cf. Johnson (1987), 132.     [192] Brilliantly expounded by Tracy (2011).

their banks before his description reaches the settlements of the Delta or Alexandria. The ending of the epic as a whole has been the subject of rather more speculation, with some scholars arguing that the narrative as it stands is incomplete, and that a more satisfactory conclusion would have been reached with Cato's suicide at Utica, or even Caesar's assassination on the Ides of March.[193] Yet Lucan's Nile geography betrays the poet's conviction that the narrative of the civil war extended far beyond these cathartic deaths and continued even as he laid down his pen. Indeed, the role of the Nile in tying together the worlds of Julius and Nero Caesar, the conquerors of the past and the nameless travellers of the future, provides a possible solution to the puzzle of the poem's end. Like the Nile, the poem refused boundaries; like the description of the river, it ended very deliberately *in medias res*.

## Lucanian Nile-ism

By depicting a river that so vigorously resisted easy definition, Lucan made the Nile recognizably his own. Throughout the *Civil War*, the poet rejects the well-behaved rivers of the Callimachean tradition or the *Aeneid*. Indeed, the transgressive qualities of Lucan's Nile are such that it seeps beyond the confines of its own description and re-surfaces throughout the *Civil War*, not least through the constant references to Pompey's bloody death on its banks. Rivers were a favourite theme of the *Civil War*.[194] Commentators have noted that the violated Rubicon provides a powerful symbol of Caesar's insensitivity towards Roman law, and the invisible Xanthus his indifference to history.[195] The poet also dwells at length on accounts of flooded rivers, culminating, of course, in the long excursus of Book X. Rivers flow throughout Lucan's epic and all of them, ultimately, flow into the Nile. This metaphor is represented literally in Acoreus' discussion of the theory of a vast complex of underground rivers, which concludes:

> then Nile, spewing all rivers
> from a single source, delivers them not through a single stream.[196]

[193] The difficulties associated with the ending of the *Bellum Civile* are variously discussed by Masters (1992), 216–58; Henderson (1998), 183; Rossi (2005), 255–8. Dinter (2013a), 119–54 surveys the manifold endings proposed for the epic.

[194] Cf. Walde (2007).

[195] Luc. 9.974–979. On Lucan's riparian geography in general, see Herendeen (1986), 58–62. Masters (1992), 169 notes Lucan's 'recurrent obsession' with rivers.

[196] Luc. 10.253–254: *tunc omnia flumina Nilus | uno fonte uomens non uno gurgite perfert.* tr. Braund (1992), 213. The precise meaning of the passage, however, is far from clear. Berti (2000), 204

But the same theme is developed just as forcefully in the specific descriptions of the different rivers over the course of Lucan's narrative. Lucan accomplishes this primarily through direct comparison between the Nile and the rivers of Europe and Asia. It is the Tiber that provides the clearest reflection of the Nile.[197] We have already seen how the two rivers are paired together in the prophecy regarding the deaths of Caesar and Pompey.[198] The same comparison between Tiber and Nile is implicit in the account of the restricted flow of the Roman river, choked with the corpses of Sulla's proscriptions: '...At last with difficulty struggling into the Tyrrhenian waves, it streaked the blue sea with its torrent of blood.'[199] Compare the image evoked in the earlier account of the Nile, stained by just one corpse in the aftermath of the next chapter of the civil war:

> Where else now are you taking me? You lead me eastwards,
> Where sea is dyed by Egyptian Nile's flood
> him [Pompey] I recognize, lying on the river's sands,
> an unsightly, headless corpse.[200]

The Euphrates, too, is directly compared to the Nile, in a passage in which the poetic term *Phariae... undae* stands as the Egyptian river: 'But fertile Euphrates floods over fields like the Egyptian waters.'[201] The Po is the subject of explicit comparison as an aside in the celebration of Italian rivers: '[the Po] would be no less than Nile, did Nile not flood | the Libyan sands across the levels of low-lying Egypt'[202] (the Po is subsequently compared with the Danube, as its other great rival). Elsewhere, the Tanais is presented

---

argues that the couplet was an expressive contrast between the single source of the Nile and its multiple mouths, and hence that the *omnia flumina* of 253 was intended to emphasize the volume of the Nilotic stream, rather than its connection to all of the watercourses in the world. While the contrast between single source and multiple mouths certainly seems intended, the emphasis upon the subterranean waterway at 10.249–53 and the inclusion of the Ganges and Po (*inter alia*) as rivers stemming from it surely demonstrate the connection of the Nile to this complex was intended.

[197] The opposition is anticipated in Verg. *Aen.* 6.800: *...septemgimini turbant trepida ostia Nili*. Even without the punning juxtaposition *ostia – Nili* the Nile as a representation of Antony's defeat recalls the repeated use of the Tiber as the symbol of Rome throughout the *Aeneid*. Note also the parallel in Prop. 3.11.42 *...et Tiberim Nili cogere ferre minas*.

[198] Luc. 3.810–811.

[199] Luc. 2.219–220. tr. Braund (1992), 27. The image also recall the corpse-clogged Xanthus at Verg. *Aen.* 5.806–808 and the Tiber as river of blood at *Aen.* 6.86–87.

[200] Luc. 1.683–686. tr. Braund (1992), 21.

[201] Luc. 3.259–260: *sed sparsus in agros | fertilis Euphrates Phariae uice fungitur undae...* tr. Braund (1992), 48. On this poetic terminology, compare Luc. 8.443. On the rhetorical pairing of Nile and Euphrates cf. also Luc. 2.632–635.

[202] Luc. 2.416–417. tr. Braund (1992), 32.

as the geophysical reflection of the Nile: 'For the banks of the Nile are not further than the northern Tanais from Gades in the far west.'[203]

The Nile surfaces again during the account of the Ilerda campaign in the fourth book of the *Civil War*. Lucan's description of the Spanish battlefield circumscribed (and dissected) by the rivers Sicoris, Cinga and Hiberus is among the best known of his topographical passages.[204] The opening image of Caesar and Pompey encamped upon facing hills offers a microcosm of the bifurcated world at war – a neat pattern that is swept away as the flooding waters of the Sicoris cast the landscape into anarchy.[205] The deluge itself has been variously interpreted as an allusion to Ovid's account of Deucalion's flood, as a superlative re-writing of the *Aeneid* storm, and as a wholly Stoic apocalyptic vision in the manner of Seneca's *Natural Questions*, but is perhaps best read as a knowing hybrid of these contrary impulses.[206] Simultaneously an image of primal chaos and of apocalypse, the flood of the Sicorus reads as one of the most affecting images of civil war within Lucan's text. As we have seen, moreover, the Nile also lurked behind Seneca's cataclysm, or perhaps more properly the watery apocalypse framed by both Seneca and Ovid.[207]

Lucan's description of the Ilerda flood was certainly influenced by the account in Caesar's own *Civil War*, and he takes from his source a dramatic comparison of the crossing of the flooded river to British coracles in the Ocean.[208] Yet once more the Nile is cited explicitly as the final point of comparison:

> In this way the Venetan sails upon Po's lagoons and Briton
> on the wide Ocean; in this way, when the Nile covers everything,
> Memphis' boat is constructed from thirsty papyrus.[209]

As Frederick Ahl and Jamie Masters have noted, the juxtaposition of *omnia* and *Nil* within the lines *tenet omnia Nilus | conseritur bibula Memphitis cumba papyro* underscores the meaning of the whole episode with the play on *Nil – Nihil*: Nile – nothingness (or "nil" to preserve the pun).[210] Here, as elsewhere, the flooded Nile provides a dramatic shorthand for

---

[203] Luc. 9.413–414. tr. Braund (1992), 188.
[204] Luc. 4.11–23; see Masters (1992), 46–70 and the bibliography therein.
[205] Luc. 4.48–120; and compare Caes. *BCiv* 1.48.
[206] cf. Ov. *Met.* 1.262. For commentary and references, see Masters (1992), 59–70.
[207] See Chapter 4.
[208] Caes. *BCiv* 1.54. Masters (1992), 67, n.60 notes that Lucan's additional reference to the coracles of Egypt is best read as an allusion to the *caesis... iuvencis* of *Georg.* 4.132, but regards this 'gratuitous allusion' as a nod to Virgil, rather than as a significant invocation of the Nile itself.
[209] Luc. 4.134–6. tr. Braund (1992), 66.     [210] Masters (1992), 66, n.59; Ahl (1976), 121–2.

chaos and nothingness, for the transgression of boundaries that typifies the civil war and forms much of the subject for *The Civil War*.

The rivers of the natural world are not the only streams to be drawn by the current of the Nile. Lucan's repeated reference to the Pompey-stained Nile associates Egypt with the bloody rivers that scar the landscape of his *Civil War*. Still more dramatic is the description of the wholly artificial rivers of the battlefield at Pharsalus – torrents of blood that cascade from mountains of corpses: 'He sees rivers driven on by gore and mounds of corpses high as lofty hills . . .'[211] Once more, Lucan sees the outline of the Nile within this bloody landscape:

> You birds, accustomed to exchange
> Thracian winters for Nile, went later
> to the mild south. Never was the heaven clothed with
> such a cloud of vultures, never did more wings crush the air.
> Every forest sent its birds and every tree
> dripped with bloody dew from gore-stained wing.[212]

Here, it is the migration of the cranes that bind the gruesome landscape of Europe to the great river of the south. The cranes themselves are a familiar enough motif, both from Lucan's own writing and from that of Seneca.[213] More importantly, what we see here – yet again – is the Nile colouring an image of the civil war. And here, at the emotional climax of the epic, the Egyptian watercourse is not just linked to a river, but to a dew of blood, suspended in the air. From the quietly-flowing streams of northern Italy, through the flooding rivers of Spain to the bloodied mists of Pharsalia, it is the Nile that forms the prism through which Lucan views and presents his abject world.

The crucial point here is not just that the familiar rivers of the Roman *oikoumene* recall the Egyptian river, but instead it is that the Nile is consistently invoked as a point of comparison throughout the poet's riparian geography. The river, which had served as a marker of unsettling alterity in much classical writing, which flowed in the wrong direction, at the wrong time, and watered a country vastly different from any other within the world, suddenly appears as the norm within Lucan's blood-drenched universe. The standard by which the rivers of the collapsing world are to be viewed is no longer the idyllic stream or well-charted waterway beloved of the pastoral poets and imperial geographers, but rather the unstable and

---

[211]  Luc. 7.789–191. tr. Braund (1992), 150. And cf. BC 7.700.
[212]  Luc. 7.832–835. tr. Braund (1992), 151.
[213]  Luc. 5.711–713 and Sen. *Oed.* 598ff. and cf. *Octav.* 514 on the beasts feeding at Philippi.

perverse river of Egypt. The Nile offered an evocative symbol of the unreality of civil war: of a world in which what should be land is water, and what should be water is blood.[214] In this unreal – perhaps surreal – landscape, an Egyptian river that flows from south to north, with no obvious source and yet seven mouths, which floods in the summer, and which makes the driest region of the world the most fertile, provides a perfect image for the topsy-turvy, uneasy vision of a world at war with itself.

## Conclusions: Poetic Geographies

The Latin poetry of the late Republic and early empire is enormously valuable as a means of reflecting on the circulation of geographical knowledge and for examining the relative influence of different forms of representation in this period. But these works also had an important constitutive function in shaping contemporary views of the world. In Augustan poetry, this is particularly apparent through geographical *topoi* – commonplaces which collapsed often quite complex features and concepts into definitive metonymic characteristics. For poets of the period, the Nile could be evoked simply enough through reference to the personification of the Actian triumph, and hence to Cleopatra, Isis, Anubis and the *sistra*. Alternatively, the geographical complexities of the Delta, the historic depth of the region beyond, and the mysteries of the flood and the river's origins, could all be conveniently recalled through simply alluding to the seven mouths of the river. This heuristic may have had little practical relevance when it came to understanding the physical geography of the Delta region itself – and was passed over quite quickly by many writers of prose geography – but rapidly entered the popular consciousness as a result of this poetic *topos*. Like the triumphs by which they were so frequently inspired, the poets of the Augustan period were catalysts for the translation of the confusing geography of the world into a convenient imperial grammar.

Lucan's treatment of the Nile suggests something rather different. In his *Civil War*, the Nile was not important simply as a point of reference within the new imperial world, nor was this a point of disinterested metaphysical speculation in the manner of Seneca or the worshippers of the Egyptian cults. Instead, Lucan's was an intensely politicized poetic river that consciously deviated from these precedents. His account built upon the long-standing (and frequently implicit) conventions of orderly

---

[214] Cf. Henderson (1998), 205 and see also O'Gorman (1995), 125–7 on Tacitus' development of this Lucanian trope.

landscapes and dramatic rivers as the stuff of epic, but manipulated this to his own ends. By taking the Nile as his inspiration and metapoetic model, and by embracing the endless, unsettling river in all of its perversity, Lucan emphasized the instability and impossibility of his poetic task. Just as the Nile was endless and knew no bounds, so too did Lucan's war-poem stretch out to infinity. Doubtless the fascination for the Nile at the court of Nero did much to determine Lucan's choice here, and he certainly exploited a range of source material with some sensitivity, but the Nilotic geography that he created was wholly his own.

# Afterword
## The Many Niles of the Elder Pliny

The Elder Pliny's *Natural History* has been a more or less constant presence throughout this study. His work provides the fullest extant description of Agrippa's 'map' and allows us to speculate on its contents; his account of Cornelius Balbus' triumph tells us a great deal about how geographical information was presented in these grand military parades; and our knowledge of Nero's expedition to Meroe and Ethiopia would be much impoverished without his testimony. Pliny is such a rich repository of fragmentary information of this kind that it is sometimes easy to forget about the text in which all of this material was preserved. Yet as several recent studies have demonstrated, Pliny's was an exemplary product of Flavian imperialism – a celebration of the empire of Vespasian and Titus in all of its glorious complexity. Tempting as it may be to plunder the *Natural History* for scraps of information on the lost works of the early Principate, the extant text remains equally illuminating as evidence for imperial geographical understanding in its own right.[1] As a coda and conclusion to the present book, then, it is worth briefly considering how Pliny's manifold representations of the Nile reflected the confused and contradictory geographical assumptions of the world in which he wrote.

The *Natural History* was certainly a vast project.[2] As Pliny declared in the preface, it sought to bring together all of nature into one vast study, to compile the discoveries of more than a hundred authors into a single scholarly archive, and to present in books what would be better preserved

---

[1] Deftly put by Bispham (2007), 45: 'Much Plinian scholarship has driven its seams and galleries through the text in pursuit of these facts, with an absolute disregard of the "geological" context of their acquisition, with little or no interest in Pliny himself or his agendas in writing the HN.' Sallmann (1971) provides a thorough discussion of the *Quellenforschung* of historians of geography in the nineteenth and early-twentieth centuries.

[2] Of the recent scholarship on the text, see esp. Beagon (1992); Naas (2002); Carey (2003); Murphy (2004); Doody (2010) and the essays in Gibson and Morello (2011).

in *thesauri* or treasure-houses.[3] The scale and ambition of the work that resulted are indeed staggering. In thirty-six books, by his count – or thirty-seven if we include his long bibliographic introduction as a separate volume, as most modern editions do – the *Natural History* covers the scope and scale of the cosmos, the geography and ethnography of the world, and its zoology, botany and mineralogy; it includes for good measure detailed summaries of the history of painting, architecture, sculpture and medicine. It draws upon an impressive catalogue of authorities and sets this lifetime of reading within a comprehensible, if sometimes confusing, order. Yet even this vast project has its limitations, created by the shortcomings of earlier authors, the limits of effective autopsy or in some cases the sheer proliferation of information with which its author was confronted.[4] Pliny presents himself as a tireless compiler – an image which the subsequent sketches of his nephew confirmed – yet even he could not hope to include everything within his colossal work.[5]

Geography enjoys a prominent position within the *Natural History* and provides a primary ontology within which Pliny's enormous compendium of learning could be comprehended. After the general introduction to the volume as a whole, and a second book concerned with meteorology and the study of the cosmos, Pliny devotes four books (III–VI) to the physical geography of Europe, Africa and Asia. These volumes represent the fullest Latin geography to survive from the classical period, and for more than a millennium later writers depended upon the material that Pliny assembled in composing their own accounts.[6] These books are systematically ordered. Specific continents or regions are introduced with a survey of their relative dimensions, often through reference to multiple sources, as we have seen.[7] Pliny typically traces coastlines in a form of periplus and adopts similar strategies in recounting major rivers. Administrative lists of cities or regions dominate Pliny's descriptions of interior regions, but these are variously

---

[3] Plin. *HN* Pref. 17; Doody (2009) demolishes the long-held assumption that Pliny was working in a well-established 'encyclopaedic' tradition. And cf. also Doody (2010), 11–39. König and Woolf (2013) set the work in its intellectual context.

[4] The inevitable omissions from the *Natural History* are acknowledged in Plin. *HN* Pref. 12, 15, 18, 28.

[5] Plin. *Ep.* 3.5. On which see Locher (1986); Henderson (2002) and Henderson (2011a). On the self-fashioning in the Preface to the *Natural History*, compare Howe (1985); Isager (1991), 18–31; Sinclair (2003); Morello (2011); Beagon (2013). On its epistemological function, see Doody (2001). Pliny also explicitly laments the impossibility of encompassing everything within his work at *HN* 3.42 (on Greece) and 36.55 (on statues); cf. Carey (2003), 21–2 and Fögen (2013), 87–93.

[6] See esp. Lozovsky (2000) and Friedman (1981) on the impact of Pliny on later geography. The third-century author Solinus proved an important conduit for Pliny's geographical work. On this author see esp. Brodersen (2011) and the essays assembled in Brodersen (2014).

[7] See above 34–6.

arranged and probably date to different periods of the Roman occupation: some are arranged alphabetically, others spatially.[8] In the long account of Italy, for example, the Augustan provinces of the peninsula are presented according to their position on the coast, but the towns within each of them are listed in alphabetical order, in clear deference to the administrative sources at the author's disposal.[9] Elsewhere, multiple sources are either reconciled into a single description or simply presented alongside one another.[10]

Pliny's use of multiple sources was central to his methodology. His stated intention was to create, not an original portrait of the world, but rather a compilation of existing knowledge, and this itself is significant. This approach is telegraphed from the very start of his project. In the opening volume of the *Natural History*, Pliny famously anatomized his work, defining each of the thirty-six constituent books by the facts contained within them, and the authorities that had been drawn upon. Thus, he lists 37 authors for Book III, 54 for Book IV, 60 for Book V and 54 in Book VI. Not all of these sources are cited directly within the account that follows; Pomponius Mela, for example, is listed as a source in the opening bibliography, but is not cited in the main text of the *Natural History*; other sources would appear to have been known at second or third hand, and many sources are cited for more than one book. At the start of Book III, Pliny justifies this explicit appeal to authority, stating that a complete knowledge of the whole of the inhabited world lay beyond the capacities of any one individual, and that he intended to draw upon local accounts wherever they were available to him, an intriguing reversal of Strabo's stated methodology two generations earlier.[11] Viewed as a whole, his great text can sometimes seem like a vast clearing house of imperial knowledge and a compilation of all of Pliny's compendious reading, assembled for the scrutiny of the curious reader.[12]

Pliny's project – and the paradoxes inherent within it – are inseparable from the political context in which it was composed. In this sense, his text is indelibly imbued with imperial assumptions, as was true of all geographical writing in this period. The work is proudly dedicated to Vespasian's

---

[8] Sallmann (1971), 220–36 (with bibliography); Murphy (2004), 134–47. Cf. Brodersen (2010), 834.

[9] Bispham (2007) discusses Pliny's peculiar description of Italy at *HN* 3.38–138. Sallmann (1971), 151–61 provides a helpful survey of Pliny's Spanish sources.

[10] Sallmann (1971), 170–220.

[11] Plin. *HN* 3.1. See also *HN* Praef 21 (on the importance of acknowledging sources where appropriate).

[12] Or – in the words of Syme (1988), 229 'a very sorry and messy compilation'. This in turn has shaped interpretation of Pliny as a geographer. Witness for example Cruz Andreotti (2016), 295.

son, Titus, an old comrade-in-arms of the author and, like his father, celebrated for his scholarly interests.[13] In composing his work in honour of the imperial house, of course, Pliny was making his own contribution to the consolidation of power in contemporary Rome. At the start of the decade, the Flavian triumph marked the successful conclusion of the Jewish War and affirmed Rome's authority at the centre of the world.[14] Grand building projects within the city also reflected this cosmopolitan self-confidence and drew upon themes earlier established in the Augustan period. Pliny added his voice to this chorus of celebration. As we have seen, Vespasian's Temple of Peace articulated triumphal ideology in architectural terms – the spoils taken in Jerusalem were deposited there, but so too were other curiosities from the wider imperial world, including botanical specimens, as well as works of art.[15] At the end of the decade, the Flavian amphitheatre would also provide a spectacular setting for the natural wonders of the world to be brought before the gaze of the city, and for the polyglot inhabitants of Rome to gather together in all of their variety.[16] While Pliny never lived to see the opening of the Colosseum, this imperial self-confidence remains an important theme throughout the *Natural History*. Rome was, for him, the 'the nursling and mother of all other lands', Italy, the 'mother', 'father' and 'parent' of the world.[17] The imperial city provided a 'second sun' to illuminate the world, and the peace brought about by its soldiers promised to bring the whole world into fruitful contact.

Viewed in these terms, the *Natural History* seems an earnest, if rather cacophonous, celebration of the Flavian empire. Indeed, in many ways, the very process of assembling a vast written survey of the world was an inherently imperialistic action, and Pliny evidently recognized this.[18] His was a work that could claim to act as an archive of natural knowledge, and as an authenticator of all of the wonders and marvels (and bits of mundane information) that had washed up in museums, theatres and libraries of the imperial city. This colossal textual catalogue identified, labelled and classified the diverse fragments of the world into something approaching a comprehensible order, and often explicitly drew upon the practices

---

[13] Plin. *HN* Praef 1. Howe (1985), 572–3; Isager (1991), 18–21; Naas (2002), 69–76 and Beagon (2013), 86–9 discuss the political context of the dedication. On the imperial scholars cf. Suet. *Vesp.* 18–19; Plin. *Ep.* 3.5.7; Suet. *Tit* 3; Tac. *Hist.* 2.2–4.

[14] On the triumph, see above 72.

[15] Naas (2002), 467–9; Pollard (2009). Cf. Joseph. *BJ* 7.159–62.

[16] Mart. *Spect.* 1, 3; *Ep.* 12.8.1; Naas (2002), 450–4.     [17] Plin. *HN* 27.3; 37.201.

[18] This is widely acknowledged in the scholarship. Compare Conte (1994); Naas (2002), 416–36; Carey (2003), 33–5; Murphy (2004), 13–16; Evans (2005); Bispham (2007), 43. An important cautionary note is sounded by Doody (2010), 74–5.

of imperial rule to assemble this material. Time and again, Pliny notes first appearances of animals, plants or minerals in Rome, or laments the shortcomings of knowledge at the edges of the empire.[19] Yet this apparent chauvinism is repeatedly tempered. As Pliny celebrated the military and political expansion which had opened up the world to the curious scrutiny of the centre, he also lamented the moral corruption that came with this growth, both through the spread of undesirable practices to new communities, and the introduction of enervating new luxuries to Rome, which resulted ultimately in the decadence of Roman culture and learning.[20]

Pliny's work is profoundly imperial in its perspective and is imbued throughout with the assumptions and ideologies of Roman political and cultural authority, but close investigation of the constituent parts of the *Natural History* immediately reveal the contradictions within this seemingly straightforward orientation. In this, the text reflects clearly the complexities within all political geographical writing in this period, and indeed within contemporary imperial epistemologies more broadly. This is perhaps clearest in the countless contradictions that litter the text. Pliny's multiple, overlapping, palimpsest geographies present a world that proves remarkably unstable in matters of detail, even as it purports to be exhaustive in scope. The gaze affected by the *Natural History* is hardly the even panoptic scrutiny of an omniscient modern state, but rather a cat's cradle of different views that reflect the contested geographies that circulated in the ancient world. In this it reflects quite faithfully the uncertain relationship between political power and authoritative geographical knowledge in the early Roman empire, and the complexities created by multiple modes of representation.

Pliny's treatment of the River Nile illustrates this point rather well. As we have seen, the Nile is discussed at some length in the geographical chapters of the *Natural History*, but Pliny's descriptions are disjointed, repetitive and occasionally contradictory. An account of the course of the River from the Atlas mountains to the Delta in Book V seems to run counter to the description in Book VI, which traces the Nile south from Syene into Ethiopia, and which itself contradicts passing allusions elsewhere in the text.[21] The Nile

---

[19] Murphy (2004), 160–4; Naas (2011), 62. This is illustrated most clearly at Plin. *HN* 8.39 when Pliny notes that the Scandinavian *achlis* had not been seen in Rome (and was all the more unusual for it). Cf. Carey (2003), 85.

[20] Wallace-Hadrill (1990); Citroni Marchetti (1991); Carey (2003), 75–101. Lao (2011) discusses the moral imperative behind the compilation of knowledge against this background, and cf. Beagon (2013), 93–8.

[21] Brodersen (2016), 300–1 notes similar redundancies at *HN* 3.7–30 and 4.110–18 (On Spain); 3.31–7 and 4.105–9 (on Gaul); 5.83–90 and 6.25–8 (on Mesopotamia); 4.49 and 5.141–5 (on the Hellespont).

also appears in a variety of other guises throughout the *Natural History*. There are two different anthropomorphic rivers, for example – one the Basinite statue of the Nile that Vespasian placed in the Temple of Peace, which appears in Book XXXVI, the other a personification of the river as an elderly farmer, which appears in Pliny's account of the cereal wealth of the world in Book XVIII.[22] All of these 'Niles' are unambiguously 'imperial' in their fabrication, but their variety remains illuminating. Vespasian's statue is a reminder that the river had an immediate political resonance at the time of Pliny's composition, which was every bit as important as the post-Actian associations during Augustus' Principate, or the Egyptomania that gripped the courts of some of his successors. Vespasian had, after all, first been proclaimed emperor in Alexandria, Titus had also been welcomed there, and later traditions associated both royal visits with particular prodigies, including an unprecedented inundation.[23] But while Vespasian's anthropomorphic statue 'Romanized' the Nile anew and reasserted the connection between the Egyptian river and a ruling imperial dynasty, it did not occlude the Ptolemaic, Augustan or Julio-Claudian rivers that had come before it or provide a definitive image of the great Egyptian watercourse. Many Niles continued to circulate throughout the imperial city, and Pliny's text reflects many of them.

Pliny has been such a constant presence in the preceding study that a long discussion of the *Natural History* would be out of place here. Nevertheless, two brief case studies will perhaps reiterate some of the central contentions of this book as it draws to its close. First, we look briefly at the somewhat repetitive nature of Pliny's physical descriptions of the river, addressing both his apparent ambivalence on the origins of the Nile, and then the peculiar redundancies within his Egyptian geography. Then we examine the importance of Egypt and the Nile in Book XXXVI of the *Natural History* – Pliny's discussion of marble and the wonders of the world. Vespasian's statue is the clearest manifestation of the river in this section of the text, but it is by no means the only one. It will be suggested here that Pliny's systematic comparison of Egyptian and Roman wonders, his particular emphasis upon the transport of obelisks, and his remarkable description of Rome's sewer system are examples of the kind of metonymic geography discussed in Chapter 2.

---

[22] Plin. *HN* 36.58; 18.167–8.

[23] Henrichs (1968) surveys the territory; Pfeiffer (2010) persuasively argues that the Flavians' devotion to Egypt may have been overstated. Cf. Tac. *Hist* 2.79, 4.81–2; Suet. *Vesp.* 2–3, 6; Dio Cass. 66.8.2 and 66.17.4. On Titus, see Suet. *Tit.* 3–5; Joseph. *Ap.* 1.48; *BJ* 7.116. The sacred aspects of Vespasian's accession in Alexandria are also recalled in Philostr. *VA* 5.27–41 (where the holy man meets the emperor-elect in the city).

## Nile Sources

Pliny opens his description of the Nile in Book V with an acknowledgement of the long-standing mystery of its origins:

> The Nile comes from uncertain sources, wandering as it does for vast distances through harsh and desert lands, and having been explored by unarmed men, without the wars that have uncovered all other countries.[24]

Deprived of the 'wars which have uncovered all other lands' (*sine bellis quae ceteras omnis terras invenere*), Pliny turns immediately to the work of Juba II, the scholar-king of Mauretania, whose geographical and natural historical writings provided invaluable material for the later writer throughout his work.[25] As we saw in Chapter 1, Juba II proposed that the Nile rose in the Atlas Mountains in north-west Africa, a theory that had some considerable heritage in Greek and Hellenistic thought, and which continued to circulate into late Antiquity.[26] Pliny is our principal source for Juba's writing, and he followed the African author in tracing the Nile through various lakes and subterranean passages, before emerging after several days at *fons Nigrum*, turning north and heading to Meroe and then into Egypt.[27] Pliny provides some evidence to support this contention, including a brief reference to the fish and fauna of this African river. While the *Natural History* does not provide a definitive assertion on the origin of the Nile, then, Pliny was sympathetic to Juba's theory, and the geography of Book V was followed by a number of later geographers.[28]

A rather different image of the Nile headwaters is proposed in Book VI, in a passage that was drawn in part from the exploring party sent into the interior by the Emperor Nero.[29] Unlike Seneca, Pliny makes no direct reference to the explorers' journey to the origins of the river. Seneca states that the explorers had claimed to discover a source somewhere in the *immensas paludes* to the south of Meroe, in between a pair of rocks – a topographic commonplace in many accounts of the river's origins.[30] Pliny includes no such reference in his own account, preferring instead to concentrate on the explorers' records of their travels between Syene and Meroe, and noting measurements of distance, along with further ethnographic, zoological and botanical details that may or may not

---

[24] Plin. *HN* 5.51.
[25] Juba is cited by name in 15 of Pliny's 37 books. His African geography is discussed by Roller (2003), 183–210; Sirago (1994), and above 198–9. Sallmann (1971), 85–8 discusses Pliny's debts to Juba.
[26] See above 45–7.   [27] Plin. *HN* 5.51–3.
[28] Solin. 32.1–8; Oros. 1.2.28–33. On which see Merrills (2005), 79–87 (with references).
[29] Plin. *HN* 6.181–7.   [30] Sen. *QNat* 6.8.3–5 and the discussion above 208–9.

have been taken from the *forma Aethiopiae*.[31] Later in the same section, however, he does allude to a possible source in the Ethiopian *paludes*:

> Some have situated a race of Pygmies among the swamps from which the Nile rises.[32]

This reference to 'certain writers' – *quidam* – is a common device of Pliny's and was a means by which he could distance himself from some of the more outlandish material included within his work. In this case, it allowed him to draw upon popular images of Nilotic pygmies, including perhaps those discussed from domestic contexts in Chapter 3, and to provide broad geographical context for them, without making a clear statement about his confidence in this tradition.[33] Nevertheless, these Ethiopian swamps represent a second Nilotic origin within his text.

A third possible source is proposed in Book VIII of the *Natural History*, during Pliny's discussion of African animals. In his account of the *catoblepas*, a mythical quadruped thought to kill humans with its basilisk-like stare, Pliny adds a suitably exotic bit of scene-setting:

> In Western Ethiopia is the *fons Nigris*, which many have reckoned to be the source of the Nile, as they prove by the arguments we have discussed.[34]

Again, Pliny is somewhat elusive in identifying his source here, but it seems likely that his reference to 'many' (*plerique*) writers is actually an allusion to just one: Pomponius Mela was probably the inspiration behind this passage. Mela includes a description of the *catoblepas* in his own account of interior Africa, immediately after his discussion of the *fons Nunc*, which he cautiously links to the western course of the Nile.[35] Although Mela does not draw an explicit connection between the spring and the *catoblepas*, and states only that the *fons Nunc* is 'credible' as the Nile source, this juxtaposition seems to have influenced Pliny.[36] Particularly significant here is that Pliny ostensibly refers his reader back to an earlier part of his work to explain these proofs – *argumenta quae diximus* – but no such discussion exists. In Book V, Pliny does note that the Nile travelled underground for many days from the west before surfacing at the *fons*

---

[31] See above 209.        [32] Plin. *HN* 6.188.

[33] On Pliny's allusions to domestic paintings here, see above, 144–5.        [34] Plin. *HN* 8.77.

[35] Pomponius Mela 3.96–8; Ael. *NA* 7.6 describes the same animal. Cf. Silberman (1988), 318–9; on the 'western Nile' theory more broadly, see 45–8 above.

[36] Pomponius Mela 3.96 *aliqua credibile est*. Desanges (1996) discusses Pliny's further use of Mela on Africa.

*Nigris* – a geography that broadly follows Mela's account.[37] Yet there is no suggestion that this was the source of the river, or was ever thought to have been, and consequently no reference is made to the proofs for this contention.

Pliny, then, presented three possible Nile sources – one in the Atlas mountains, one in the swamps to the south of Meroe, and a third somewhere in between at *fons Nigris* – and never bothered to reconcile them. It is tempting to dismiss these contradictions as a reflection of the magpie-like methodology of Pliny, or of his own carelessness in putting together his descriptions of the world, and these conclusions have some merit. But the contradictions reveal as much about geographical assumptions of Pliny's expected audience as they do about the writer himself. Perhaps most obviously, this demonstrates that no single definitive solution to the mystery of the Nile source was in circulation at the time of Pliny's composition. Had this been the case, his readers would certainly have expected him to defer to it. If author and audience were willing to adopt a certain agnosticism on the origin of the river, moreover, this also implies that their expectations were shaped by the ambivalences inherent in textual accounts (which might express their uncertainty explicitly), rather than in the false certainties of a visual source or map.[38] It was argued in Chapter 1 that the upper course of the Nile is unlikely to have been represented clearly in the public surveys of the Augustan city; Pliny's account would seem to confirm this.

Instead, Pliny's multiple, shifting accounts of the Nile reflect the diversity of media to which the author and his audience might turn in order to make sense of the world. Some Roman subjects looked to monumental visual displays to understand their empire, others to the dry descriptions of prose writers, the trophies borne in military triumphs or the familiar landscape vignettes of distant lands known from domestic contexts, replete with Nilotic monsters and diminutive human figures. Most would have been familiar with many contrasting forms of representation from a variety of different contexts. Pliny's extraordinary portmanteau geography drew upon many of these different types of source and yet reveals that the apparent contradictions between them need not have been especially troubling to contemporary observers. 'The Nile' could at once have emerged in the Atlas mountains, have been discovered by Nero's explorers in Ethiopia and be the setting of the semi-legendary gambolling of pygmies and crocodiles without fear of contradiction. The 'imperial' geography of the late Republic and early empire, then, was created from multiple, dissonant images of the

---

[37] Plin. *HN* 5.52.    [38] Jacob (2006), 263–8.

world, all of which bore the imprimatur of Roman political authority in some ways, but none of which excluded other modes of representation. Pliny's text vividly reflects these contradictions.

## Multiple Egypts

Pliny's descriptions of the human geography of Egypt give a rather different impression of his source use, but here again we witness a concern to use all of the information available to him, even at some cost of clarity. In 5.49–50, he enumerates the nomes of Egypt – the administrative districts which were the principal focus for local government from the Pharaonic period through to the Roman occupation.[39] What follows is a systematic and thorough survey of the territory. Pliny identifies approximately 47 nomes (the precise figure is somewhat blurred by his ambiguity on some names).[40] This is more or less the established figure in for the early imperial period; as Pliny himself notes, different authorities give different figures and occasionally adduce other names for specific nomes.[41] A few lines later, in 5.60–1 and 5.64, he adds a further list of the towns of Egypt, stating that these settlements are the most important of the twenty thousand towns once thought to have been in the region. Conspicuously, in both of these lists, places between Syene and the apex of the Delta are presented systematically in geographical order from south to north (settlements in Lower Egypt are rather more jumbled). There are one or two minor deviations from this geographical ordering in each of these surveys, but in itself this should not perhaps be surprising – as we saw in Chapter 5, places did have a surprising tendency to slip their moorings on riverine itineraries.[42] As a result, the reader is presented with two linear geographies, which more or less overlap despite being separated by only a few chapters. Again, this seems very much a geography by accretion, rather than through systematic selection.

Two features of these passages are particularly worthy of comment. The first, and perhaps most obvious is that Pliny evidently drew upon two distinct sources here, one which listed the Egyptian nomes, the other towns of the region. Given the content, it seems likely that these were administrative sources, analogous to those used in the description of some of the western

---

[39] Yoyotte (1998) provides a succinct overview.     [40] Plin. *HN* 5.49–50.     [41] Plin. *HN* 5.50.

[42] In Plin. *HN* 5.49 the Thinite and Phaturite nomes are both somewhat misplaced. More strikingly, the Panopolite nome, which was situated in Upper Egypt to the north of Ptolemais, appears in Pliny's list alongside districts in the Delta; in 5.60 Phaturis is placed too far south (as it is in the list of nomes in 5.49), and Diospolis Parva is listed before Tentyra, despite being situated upriver of it. On fluidity in riverine itineraries, see above, 228–32.

provinces, although they do not seem to have been listed as such in his opening geography.[43] Inevitably, there are some similarities between the two lists; after all, nomes were generally identified by their largest towns. These had remained broadly unchanged during the period of the Roman occupation and were relatively well established. Consequently, Apollinopolis, Phaturis, Coptos, Tentyra and Lycopolis appear on both lists. But Coptos is located somewhat differently in each, and the precise toponyms employed are frequently different. We can associate the Aphroditopolite and Diaspolite nomes listed in 5.49 with the *oppida Veneris* and *Iovis* of 5.60, respectively, and doubtless many of Pliny's readers could, too, but it seems clear that these were taken from different sources.[44] More striking still are the places which appear in one list but not the other: five towns do not appear in the list of nomes, and four nomes do not have corresponding towns in the later passage. Given this, it is equally significant that Pliny did make some effort to reconcile the two lists that he presented to his audience. He notes that several towns have previously been mentioned (*supra dictum, iam dicta*), and the settlements of Syene, Thebes and Memphis are repeatedly referenced throughout his Egyptian geography as points of orientation for his readers.[45]

Pliny evidently drew upon many different sources in making sense of the Nile. Given his stated methodology, and the peculiar epistemology of the *Natural History*, we would scarcely expect anything else. Yet the implications of this are worth briefly addressing, particularly in light of assumptions about 'official' geographical knowledge in this period. The simple fact that Pliny did not borrow an existing account of the river, in order to embed it within his *Natural History*, strongly suggests that at the time when he was writing, no single source enjoyed such authority. 'Geographical', 'chorographical' and perhaps even cartographic representations of the Nile were certainly known in the early imperial capital: Strabo's detailed descriptions of the river are extant, as are Pomponius Mela's succinct Latin sketches. Seneca and Lucan clearly drew upon established knowledge in their own discussions of the river's course, and the discussion of Vitruvius' sources shows that representations in various media were evidently familiar enough in the city. Yet none of these works seems to have been authoritative enough to represent a single, definitive depiction, or even provided a basic template

---

[43] Sallmann (1971), 204–7 briefly discusses these sources, noting that there is little scholarly consensus on the extent of Pliny's debts. Evans (2005), 50–1 discusses the political implications of similar borrowings.

[44] Winkler and König (1993), 172–3.

[45] Plin. *HN* 5.49, 50 and esp. 5.59. cf. *HN* 6.102–4, 162 for a similar structuring elsewhere in the text.

upon which Pliny could build.[46] Instead, Pliny's was palimpsest Nile, built up of fragments that were trustworthy in themselves, but which frequently sat together uncomfortably. This represented an appeal to a different sort of authority, an attempt to create an image of the Nile that might stand scrutiny in the Flavian city and contribute to his vast project of (almost) universal knowledge, but which did not preclude or invalidate competing geographies in doing so. Instead, Pliny derived his authority from the sheer scale of his project, and the diligence with which he brought it all together. His did not purport to be a definitive account of the world as it actually was, but rather a nearly-complete compilation of others' writings and accumulated facts of the world. Although this methodology was certainly rooted in assumptions of imperial power, and the resulting image helped propagate a vision of a subordinated world, it contrasts sharply with the image of imperial knowledge that has often been assumed of first-century Rome.

## The World in Rome

The great majority of the *Natural History* – the remaining thirty books of the sequence – is not concerned with geographical description in the strictest sense, but still reveals a great deal about contemporary attitudes to the wider world. This is an impression of the *oikoumene* built up of fragments, and endlessly reassembled into different taxonomies. At the start of his account of plants in Book XXVII, Pliny marvels at 'the immense majesty of the Roman peace' which allowed all of these wonders to be brought beneath the gaze of Rome, from the plants of Scythia to the *euphorba* of the Atlas Mountains.[47] Elsewhere, he refers back to his opening account of the world, as if to situate the material he is discussing within an essentially spatial frame.[48] Given this, there can be little doubt that the geography of Books III–VI did have an important ordering function within the work as a whole. But the *Natural History* also reveals the countless new cartographies and modes of understanding that the vast new empire enabled. Like the spectators of Roman triumphs, or the readers of Roman poetry, Pliny and his audience created new maps of the world from the abundant fragments brought within the city itself.

---

[46] Contra (for example) Carey (2003), who argues from Pliny's famous reference to his text as *spectandum* at *HN* 6.211 that it sought to emulate and surpass Agrippa's project. As at 71: 'But the reader is no longer referred to a monument external to the narrative to verify Pliny's account. Instead, we are asked to look at Pliny's geography as we would Agrippa's map.' See also Murphy (2004), 160 who regards triumphs as the 'organizing metaphor' of the geography of the *HN*.
[47] Plin. *HN* 27.1–3, at 3.       [48] See Plin. *HN* 36.54.

The point is illustrated quite clearly in the penultimate book of the *Natural History*.

In Book XXXVI Pliny turns his attention to minerals, and here the Nile has a number of roles to play. The book is ostensibly concerned with marble and the different uses to which it and other quarried stone had been put.[49] Pliny identifies specific sculptors, their prominent works and the stone that had been employed in their creations. This expands into descriptions of important public buildings and private collections, including a prolonged comparison of the great architecture of the wider Mediterranean world with that of the imperial capital. Although Rome is the focus of this discussion, Egypt plays a prominent role throughout, both as the point of origin for different types of marble, and as the location of many important monuments against which the buildings of its capital could be judged.

Underlying Book XXXVI are two of the crucial themes that run throughout the *Natural History* as a whole. On the one hand, the chapter praises imperial power and includes some of the most striking celebrations of Rome within the whole of the text. In Pliny's view, it was the empire that enabled an extraordinary variety of different types of stone to be brought together in fine works of architecture: Roman power simultaneously allowed Ethiopian, Egyptian and Indian sand to be used by Italian craftsmen in cutting marble, it enabled the discovery of new types of stone throughout the world and facilitated the transport of vast monoliths across the Mediterranean.[50] The discovery and quarrying of stone, its manipulation into art, its bringing together into fine collections and the act of writing about all of these processes were predicated on the existence of the Empire, as Pliny well realized.[51] Yet Pliny's celebration of this power was tempered throughout by his own misgivings about the decadent and corrupting nature of extravagant building, and of marble in particular. Book XXXVI opens with a striking assertion that mountains provide the structure of the world, its essential defences against the eroding effects of water and time, and yet had been systematically eaten away by the curiosity and avarice of man.[52] In addressing the wonders of Rome and its empire, Pliny denigrates as many structures as he praises, and he even goes so far as to suggest that the transport of marble should be forbidden.[53]

Equally important, however, is the essential relationship between Rome and the constituent parts of the empire that plays out over the course

---

[49] Rouveret (2003) provides a commentary; cf. Isager (1991), 144–211.  [50] Cf. Plin. *HN* 36.52–3.
[51] Note the comparable treatment of herbs at Plin. *HN* 27.3; Isager (1991), 157–8.
[52] Plin. *HN* 36.1–3.  [53] Plin. *HN* 36.4–6.

of the book: here the distinct spatial ordering of the opening books is supplemented and ultimately superseded. In Book III, Pliny had declared that no other city could be compared to Rome in scale, but it was only in his penultimate volume that the truth of this sentiment was revealed.[54] Pliny's view of Rome as a sort of museum or *Wunderkammer* – a grand inventory of the world, in which his own massive text had an important role to play – underpins the discussion throughout Book XXXVI, and the *Natural History* as a whole. Here, everything was gathered together, creating a chaotic new jumble of associations. This is manifested through Pliny's descriptions of art collections, both public and private, but also through the accounts of architectural *mirabilia* both inside and outside the city.[55] After enumerating the familiar wonders of the eastern Mediterranean, Pliny makes his famously bombastic claim for Rome, a great treasury of marvels, but also a wonder in itself:

> But this is indeed the moment for us to pass on to the wonders of our own city, to review the resources derived from the experiences of 800 years, and to show that here too in our buildings we have vanquished the world; and the frequency of this occurrence will be proved to match within a little the wonders which we shall describe. If we imagine the whole agglomeration of our buildings massed together and placed on one great heap, we shall see such grandeur towering above us as to make us think that some other world was being described, all concentrated into one place.[56]

The essential conceit here – that all of the world is to be found in Rome – is played out through a systematic comparison of the wonders of *orbs* and *urbs*, and the demonstration that nothing found in the wider world was without parallel in the capital.[57] Pliny's description of the marvels of Egypt is particularly important in this and is developed throughout the book. His discussion opens with a long and detailed account of the obelisks of the Nile valley and notes particularly the extraordinary examples from Heliopolis. But equal space is devoted to the transport of several such stones to Rome under Augustus, Caligula and Claudius and to the magnificent ships that carried them across the Mediterranean and which were now worthy wonders in their own right.[58] Pliny argues that the transport of the obelisks along the Tiber also confirms that the Roman river was worthy of comparison with the Nile.[59] The text goes on to discuss the uses to

[54]  Plin. *HN* 3.66.      [55]  Isager (1991), 157–68.      [56]  Plin. *HN* 36.101. tr. Eichholz (1962), 79–81.
[57]  On wonders as a means of negotiating the relationship between centre and periphery, compare Isager (1991), 195–6; Edwards (1996), 101–2; Beagon (2007); Williams (2012), 37–40.
[58]  Plin. *HN* 36.70; Isager (1991), 190–2; Murphy (2004), 51–2; Naas (2011), 62; Leemreize (2014), 75–8.
[59]  Plin. *HN* 36.70. cf. Carey (2003), 86–8.

which these obelisks were put in Rome, and his account of the Augustan *horologium* in the Campus Martius is the fullest account from antiquity.[60]

Throughout his discussion, Pliny systematically compares famous Egyptian monuments to the wonders of Rome and consistently judges the latter to be superior. After describing the Pharos Lighthouse, for example, Pliny sniffily observes that comparable beacons could also be found at Ostia and Ravenna.[61] We see the same in the description of the Labyrinth, a familiar Egyptian wonder near Heracleopolis Magna.[62] Pliny goes into some detail in his description of the labyrinths of Egypt, Crete and Lemnos, but stresses that the lost Italian labyrinth was just as spectacular.[63] On the face of it, Pliny includes no such parallel for the Pyramids, which were certainly widely discussed by Greek and Roman writers and had no conceivable analogue in Rome, but he still managed to find points of comparison.[64] Pliny's assessment of the pyramids is essentially dismissive: he regards them as the creation of a vainglorious kingdom, anxious to keep their populace (*plebs*) occupied. Yet even here, they are trumped by the Roman *mundus alius*: the hundred million sesterces spent by Julius Caesar on his forum was much more than the Pharaohs spent on their expensive boondoggle, and pyramids just as foolish as those at Giza had also ornamented the Italian labyrinth.[65]

This motif of Egyptian stones brought to Rome reaches its climax, of course, in the discussion of Vespasian's Nile statue – a prodigious block of Ethiopian basinites, which not only was transported to the capital, but was transformed into a statue celebrating the very power of the empire. We have already discussed the conceptual significance of this personified figure, in Chapter 2, but it is worth addressing very briefly Pliny's particular emphasis upon the representation of the floods in the sculpture:

> No larger specimen of this stone has ever been found than that dedicated by the Emperor Vespasian in the temple of Peace, the subject of which is the Nile, with sixteen of the river god's children playing around him, these denoting the number of cubits reached by the river in flood at the highest desirable level.[66]

---

[60] Plin. *HN* 36.71–3. On the *horologium* see the discussion at 100–1 above; Parker (2007) provides a clear overview of the obelisks more broadly.

[61] Plin. *HN* 36.73.     [62] Plin. *HN* 36.84; cf. Hdt. 2.148; Strabo 17.1.37.     [63] Plin. *HN* 36.87–93.

[64] If we exclude the smaller pyramid tombs known from the city. On which see Vout (2003), and above 101. Leemreize (2014), 71–5 discusses the attraction of the pyramids as a symbol for Roman writers.

[65] Plin. *HN* 36.103 (Caesar's forum is more expensive than pyramids); 36.93 the *vesana dementia* of the spending on the pyramid-strewn labyrinth. Frontin. *Aq* 116 frames Roman superiority over Egypt more positively.

[66] Plin. *HN* 36.58. tr. Eichholz (1962), 45–7.

Pliny explicitly compares the Nile statue with the famous singing statues of Memnon at Thebes – a parallel which anticipates his discussion of other Egyptian monuments, as we have seen.[67] Moreover, the statue itself draws several major themes of the *Natural History* together. As Pliny presents it, the discovery, transport and use of this massive block of stone are all evidence of the extraordinary power of Rome to reveal and exploit the treasures of the world. The fact that the statue is of the Nile, and that direct reference was made in its fabrication to the fertilizing power of the river, further connects Roman authority with agricultural as well as mineral abundance.[68] It is also significant that the statue is located within Vespasian's Temple of Peace: along with Augustus' forum, this is one of the few buildings that is celebrated without reserve in the text. As it appears in the writing of Pliny and Josephus, the *templum* was a monument to Roman taste and to the benefits of empire and stands as a sort of museological analogue to the *Natural History* itself.[69]

A more surprising link between Egypt and Imperial Rome is established in the peculiar description of the city of Thebes, just across the river from the statues of Memnon. Pliny states that some authorities regarded Thebes as a 'hanging' or 'suspended' town (*pensilis... oppidum*), far grander even than the famed Gardens of Babylon, and beneath which a whole army could be led without any of the inhabitants' knowledge.[70] Pliny is appropriately sceptical about this tradition, noting that Homer offers no corroboration for this story. But equally important is his assertion that even a wonder such as this could be bettered:

> Even so, this is less remarkable than would have been the case had a river flowed through the middle of the town.[71]

The allusion here is to Rome, of course, but this is only made explicit with the subsequent reference to that city as an *urbs pensilis* in its own right.[72] In Rome, it was the sewer complex that transformed the capital above ground into a 'hanging city', and it was Agrippa's famous voyage into these tunnels

---

[67] Plin. *HN* 36.58. On the famous statues at Thebes, well established on the tourist itinerary by this time, see Bernard and Bernard (1960), Bowersock (1984) and Brennan (1998).

[68] Compare the similar discussion of Nilotic fertility in Plin. *HN* 5.58 and 18.167–8.

[69] Naas (2002), 437–45; Pollard (2009). Note Plin. *HN* Praef 19 where the contents of the *HN* are compared to *templis dicata*.

[70] Plin. *HN* 36.94. cf. Diod Sic 2.10; Hom. *Il.* 9.381–4 and the brief discussion in Rouveret (2003), 194–5.

[71] Plin. *HN* 36.94.

[72] Plin. *HN* 36.104. Note also the (more negative) allusion to *pensilis tribus*, wooed by Curio's rhetoric (and revolving theatre), at 36.120.

that confirmed the truth of what had only been myth in Thebes.[73] This is developed further in the discussion that follows:

> Through the city [Rome] there flow seven rivers meeting in one channel. These, rushing downwards like mountain torrents, are constrained to sweep away and remove everything in their path, and when they are thrust forward by an additional volume of rainwater, they batter the bottom and sides of the sewers. Sometimes the backwash of the Tiber floods the sewers and makes its way along them upstream. Then the raging flood waters meet head on within the sewers and even so the unyielding strength of the fabric resists the strain.[74]

The Nilotic resonances of this account are clear, if not explicit. Several commentators have pointed out the close correspondence between the Roman sewers, flowing from the seven hills of the city, and the seven mouths of the Nile.[75] But the parallel runs still deeper. Pliny's discussion of the waters of the sewers reads as an inversion of the doxographies of the Nile inundation that he briefly explored in Book V, and which would have been familiar to his audience from contemporary natural philosophy.[76] The reference to the periodic inundations caused by excessive rainfall recall a popular explanation for the Nile floods. Still more striking is the allusion to the retarding current (*retro infusus*) which reads like a parody of the famous theory of Thales of Miletus, that the Etesian winds prevented the Nile waters from flowing freely into the Mediterranean.[77]

The passage can fruitfully be read as a firm assertion of Pliny's preference for the solid, utilitarian architecture of early Rome over the despotic grandeur of eastern monuments or the fripperies of some more recent imperial projects.[78] He is at pains to stress that the origins of the sewer system were in the pre-Republican period and that it represented an important foundation upon which the later city was built, in moral as well as physical terms. This was also an opinion that was shared by Livy and Strabo and was contrasted with the architecture of other cities.[79] While there is some reason for questioning the absolute sincerity of this praise – sewers remain a peculiar object for wholehearted celebration, and the image of the suspended city sits somewhat precariously over the vituperation with which Book XXXVI opens – Pliny's essential contention here seems clear

---

[73] Plin. *HN* 36.104.    [74] Plin. *HN* 36.105. tr. Eichholtz (1962), 83.

[75] Gowers (1995), 25; Murphy (2004), 189.

[76] Plin. *HN* 5.55–6. On the doxographical tradition, see 157–61 above.

[77] On which see Bonneau (1964), 153–4.    [78] Evans (2008), 124–5.

[79] Liv. 1.56, 5.55.5; Dion Hal. 3.67.5; Strabo 5.3.8.

enough.[80] In the reciprocity between Rome and its world, the city would always be viewed in the more favourable terms.

Yet the implications of this celebration of the *cloaca maxima* require further investigation, particularly in the light of the fragmented geographies discussed in Chapter 2. The precise significance of the Nilotic subtext within this moralizing message is far from clear. Moreover, the relationship between the elusive Nile in this passage and the multiple direct descriptions of the same river earlier in the *Natural History* also remain uncertain. It might be argued that Pliny's intention was to demonstrate that the *mundus alius* had its own Nile, to collapse *urbs* and *orbs*, and to underscore the position of the city as a true microcosm of the world. This was a river that was controlled by the sober building projects of the ancestors and could not subject the Roman world to its whims, in the way that the Egyptian river so notoriously could. It is also possible that these subterranean waters had sublime or cataclysmic resonances, that they were intended as an allusion to the creative (or destructive) waters of the cosmic cycle, and so lent a sublime temporal depth to Pliny's Roman topography.[81] Yet this subterranean Nile evidently did not preclude an appreciation of the river in Egypt, whether as a geographical puzzle, a triumphal trophy or a suitably exotic setting for the discussion of the animals and peoples of interior Africa. Indeed, the Nile of the sewers was dependent upon all of these associations for its own meaning. What this reveals is the essential plurality that underpins the *Natural History*, and indeed, the wider geographical understanding of the early imperial world as a whole.

## Conclusions: Kaleidoscopic Geographies

The present study has argued that knowledge of the wider world was refracted through many different lenses during the late Republican and early imperial period. It has suggested that the dissemination of information through the apparatus of the imperial administration was important, as was argued by Claude Nicolet, and inhabitants of the city did turn to works like the Agrippa survey (whatever that was) to make sense of their place in the world. But study of different representations of the Nile complicates this image substantially. This suggests that alternative views of the new empire could also be assembled in more fragmentary form through triumphs, monumental display or contemporary poetry, which had resonances for different audiences and in different contexts. These modes of

---

[80] Ambiguities: Gowers (1995); Edwards (1996), 106–8.    [81] Suggested by Murphy (2004), 189–90.

representation did not depend upon an established body of authenticated geographical knowledge for their meaning, or produce a coherent image of the world, but rather created their own cognitive contexts in which they could be understood. Simultaneously, the representations in domestic interiors, extraordinary modes of Nilotic reproduction in temples or jumbled reminiscences of travel accounts reveal a plurality of geographical understandings that might have resonance in this period. All of these different modes of representation or comprehension were shaped to a greater or lesser extent by the realities of empire, and all fed into a shared view of Rome as the dominant power over Egypt and the territories of interior Africa. But this shared political context did not resolve the cognitive dissonances between these different media, nor should we assume that it did. There was no single 'imperial geography' in the early empire; there were many.

Pliny's *Natural History* does not reflect all of these overlapping geographies – no text could. He has little to say, for example, on the metaphysical associations of the river, beyond his short doxography of the Nile floods. Similarly, he seems to have engaged relatively rarely with visual representations: as we have seen, his use of the Agrippa 'map' was probably limited to associated textual materials, and he seems to have been somewhat suspicious of the popular misconceptions about Egyptian life that domestic wall-paintings helped to propagate. Yet his fragmented river remains exemplary for the discussion here. Pliny's view of the world has been identified as the panoptic gaze from the imperial centre, and with some justification: his was undoubtedly a text written in the light of the Flavian renaissance. But it also reflects the twitching, restless glances of the viewer, overpowered by endless contradictory distractions. And this is exemplified well in the Nile. Pliny's Nile is a wandering African river, a reinscribed Arabian routeway, a benevolent farmer in a world of plenty, a fictionalized setting for cavorting pygmies, a basinite statue in the Temple of Peace, a highway for the transport of obelisks, and may be detected subliminally in the sewers of Rome. It is this multiplicity that Pliny's *Natural History* is designed to capture and cannot help but express. And it is this multiplicity which best reflects the polyvalent nature of Roman geographical thought in the early imperial period.

# Bibliography

Adams, C. E. P. 2001. 'There and Back Again': Getting Around in Roman Egypt', in C. E. P. Adams and R. M. Laurence (eds), *Travel and Geography in the Roman World* (London), 138–66.

2007. *Land Transport in Roman Egypt: A Study of Economics and Administration in a Roman Province* (Oxford).

Adams, S. and A. G. Robins, 2000. 'Introduction', in S. Adams and A. G. Robins (eds), *Gendering Landscape Art. Issues in Art History* (Manchester), 1–12.

Ahl, F. 1976. *Lucan: An Introduction* (Ithaca, NY, and London).

1985. *Metaformations. Soundplay and Wordplay in Ovid and other Classical Poets* (Ithaca, NY).

Akerman, J. J. (ed.), 2006a. *Cartographies of Travel and Navigation.* (Chicago).

2006b. 'Introduction', in J. J. Akerman (ed.), *Cartographies of Travel and Navigation.* (Chicago), 1–15.

2006c. 'Twentieth-Century American Road Maps and the Making of a National Motorized Space', in J. J. Akerman (ed.), *Cartographies of Travel and Navigation.* (Chicago), 151–206.

(ed.), 2009. *The Imperial Map. Cartography and the Mastery of Empire* (Chicago).

Albu, E. 2005. 'Imperial Geography and the Medieval Peutinger Map', *Imago Mundi* 57.2: 136–48.

2014. *The Medieval Peutinger Map. Imperial Roman Revival in a German Empire* (Cambridge).

Alföldi-Rosenbaum, E. 1975. 'A Nilotic Scene on Justinianic Floor Mosaics in Cyrenaican Churches', in *La mosaïque Gréco-romaine II*. IIe Colloque International pour l'étude de la mosaïque antique (Paris), 149–53.

Allison, P. and F. B. Sear, 2002. *Casa Della Caccia Antica (VII.4.48)*, Häuser in Pompeji, Bd. 11 (Munich).

Alpers, S. 1983. *The Art of Describing. Dutch Art in the Seventeenth Century* (Chicago).

Alston, R. 1996. 'Conquest By Text: Juvenal and Plutarch on Egypt', in J. Webster and N Cooper (eds), *Roman Imperialism: Post-Colonial Perspectives*, Leicester Archaeology Monographs, 3 (Leicester), 99–110.

Alston, R. and E. Spentzou, 2011. *Reflections on Romanity. Discourses of Subjectivity in Imperial Rome* (Columbus, OH).

Andersson, E. B. 1991. 'Metamorphoses in Water', *Latomus*, 50, 544–62.

André, J.-M. 2003. 'Sénèque et l'Égypte: Esquisse d'un bilan', *Revue des Études Latines*, 81, 172–89.

Andrews, J. H. 2001. 'Introduction. Meaning, Knowledge and Power in the Map Philosophy of J. B. Harley', in P. Laxton (ed.), *J. B. Harley. The New Nature of Maps. Essays in the History of Cartography* (Baltimore), 2–32.

Amenta, A., M. M. Luiselli and M. N. Sordi (eds), 2005. *L'acqua nell'antico Egitto. Vita, rigenerazione, incantesimo, medicamento* (Rome).

Arnaud, P. 1983. 'L'affaire Metius Pompusianus ou le crime de cartographie', *Mélanges d'archéologie et d'histoire de l'École française de Rome*, 95.2: 677–99.

1989. 'Pouvoir des mots et limites de la cartographie dans la géographie grecque et romaine', in *Dialogues d'histoire ancienne*. Annales Litteraires de l'université de Besançon, 395 (Paris), 9–31.

1993. 'L'Itinéraire d'Antonin: un témoin de la littérature itinéraire du Bas-Empire', *Geographia Antiqua*, 2: 33–47.

2004. 'Entre Antiquité et Moyen-Âge: l'Itinéraire Maritime d'Antonin', in L. De Maria and R. Turchetti (eds), *Rotte e Porti del Mediterraneo dopo la caduta dell' impero romano d'occidente*. (Rubettino), 3–20.

2007. 'La géographie romaine impériale, entre tradition et innovation', in G. C. Andreotti, P. Le Roux and P. Moret (eds), *La invención de una geografía de la Península Ibérica. II. La época imperial*. (Malaga), 13–46.

2007–2008. 'Texte et carte de Marcus Agrippa: historiographie et données textuelles', *Geographia Antiqua* 16–17: 45–97.

2014. 'Mapping the Edges of the Earth: Approaches and Cartographical Problems', in A. V. Podossinov (ed.), *The Periphery of the Classical World in Ancient Geography* Colloquia Antiqua, 12 (Leuven), 31–58.

2016. 'Marcus Vipsanius Agrippa and his Geographical Work', in Serena Bianchetti, M. R. Cataudella and H.-J. Gehrke (eds), *Brill's Companion to Ancient Geography. The Inhabited World in the Greek and Roman Tradition* (Leiden), 205–22.

Assmann, J. 2003. *The Mind of Egypt. History and Meaning in the Time of the Pharaohs*, tr. A. Jenkins (Cambridge, MA).

Aujac, G. 2001. *Eratosthène de Cyrène, le pionnier de la géographie. Sa mesure de la circonférence terrestre* (Paris).

Austin, N. J. E. and N. B. Rankov. 1995. *Exploratio. Military and Political Intelligence in the Roman World from the Second Punic War to the Battle of Adrianople* (London and New York).

Badoni, F. P. and M. De Vos. 1990. '1.7.1. Casa di Paquius Proculus o di Cuspius Pansa', in I. Bragantini et al. (eds), *Pitture e pavimenti di Pompei*, 1 (Rome), 483–552.

Bakhoum, S. 1999. *Dieux égyptiens à Alexandrie sous les Antonins. Recherches numismatiques et historiques* (Paris).

Bagnall, R. S. 1985. 'Publius Petronius, Augustan Prefect of Egypt', *Yale Classical Studies*, 28: 85–93.

Bailey, C. (ed.), 1947. *Titi Lucreti Cari De Rerum Natura Libri Sex* 3 vols (Oxford).

Baines, J. 2001. *Fecundity Figures. Egyptian Personification and the Iconology of a Genre* (Oxford).

Bal, M. and N. Bryson, 1991. 'Semiotics and Art History', *Art Bulletin* 73: 174–208.

Baldwin, B. 1973. *Studies in Lucian* (Toronto)

1990. 'The Date, Identity and Career of Vitruvius', *Latomus*, 49: 425–34.

Ball, R. J. 1975. 'The Structure of Tibullus 1.7', *Latomus*, 34: 729–44.

Balty, J. 1984/1995. 'Thèmes nilotiques dans la mosaïque tardive du proche-orient', in *Alessandria e il mondo ellenistico-romano. Studi in onore di Achille Adriani,* III; repr. in J. Balty, *Mosaïques antiques du proche-orient. Chronologie, iconographie, interprétation* (Paris), 245–54.

Barchiesi, A. 1997. *The Poet and the Prince: Ovid and Augustan Discourse* (Berkeley).

Barrenechea, F. 2010. 'Didactic Aggressions in the Nile Excursus of Lucan's Bellum Civile', *American Journal of Philology*, 131: 259–84.

Bartsch, S. 1997. *Ideology in Cold Blood. A Reading of Lucan's Civil War* (Cambridge, MA).

2006. *The Mirror of the Self. Sexuality, Self-Knowledge and the Gaze in the Early Roman Empire* (Chicago).

Beagon, M. 1992. *Roman Nature. The Thought of Pliny the Elder* (Oxford).

1996. 'Nature and Views of Her Landscapes in Pliny the Elder', In G. Shipley and J. Salmon (eds), *Human Landscapes in Classical Antiquity. Environment and Culture.* Leicester-Nottingham Studies in Ancient Society, 6 (London and New York), 284–309.

2007. 'Situating Nature's Wonders in Pliny's Natural History', in E. Bispham and G. Rowe with E. Matthews (eds), *Vita Vigilia Est. Essays in Honour of Barbara Levick* (London), 19–40.

2011. 'The Curious Eye of the Elder Pliny', in R. K. Gibson and R. Morello (eds), *Pliny the Elder: Themes and Contexts* (Leiden), 71–88.

2013. 'Labores pro bono public: The Burdensome Mission of Pliny's Natural History', in J. König and G. Woolf (eds), *Encyclopaedism. From Antiquity to the Renaissance* (Cambridge), 84–107.

Beard, M. 2003. 'The Triumph of Flavius Josephus', in A. J. Boyle and W. J. Dominik (eds), *Flavian Rome: Culture, Image, Text* (Leiden), 543–58.

2007. *The Roman Triumph* (Cambridge, MA).

Becker, A. S. 1995. *The Shield of Achilles and the Poetics of Ekphrasis* (Lanham, MD).

Behr, C. A. 1981. *Aelius Aristides. Works.* 2 vols (Leiden).

Bek, L. 1983. 'Questiones Convivales: The Idea of the Triclinium and the Staging of Convivial Ceremony from Rome to Byzantium', *Analecta Romana. Instituti Danici*, 12: 81–107.

Bellen, H. 1991. 'Aegypto capta. Die Bedeutung der Eroberung Ägyptens für die Prinzipatsideologie', in R. Albert (ed.), *Politische Ideen auf Münzen. Festschrift zum 16. Deutschen Numismatikertag* (Mainz), 33–59.

Belyea, B. 1998. 'Inland Journeys, Native Maps', in G. M. Lewis (ed.), *Cartographic Encounters: Perspectives on Native American Mapmaking* (Chicago), 135–56.

Benario, H. W. 1983. 'The "Carmen de bello Actiaco" and Early Imperial Epic', *Aufstieg und Niedergang der römischen Welt*, II.30.3: 1656–62.

Bendinelli, G. 1941. *Le Pitture del Colombario di villa Pamphili*, Monumenti della Pittura Antica Scoperti in Italia, Sezione Terza. La Pittura Ellenistico-Romana, Roma Fasc V (Rome).

Bergmann, B. 1991. 'Painted Perspectives of a Villa Visit: Landscape as Status and Metaphor', in E. K. Gazda (ed.), *Roman Art in the Private Sphere. New Perspectives on the Architecture and Décor of the Domus, Villa and Insula* (Ann Arbor, MI), 49–70.

   1999. 'Introduction: The Art of Ancient Spectacle', in B. Bergmann and C. Kondoleon (eds), *The Art of Ancient Spectacle*. Studies in the History of Art 56, Center for Advanced Study in the Visual Arts, Symposium Papers, 34 (New Haven, CT), 9–36.

Bergmann, B. and C. Kondoleon (eds), 1999. *The Art of Ancient Spectacle*. Studies in the History of Art 56, Center for Advanced Study in the Visual Arts, Symposium Papers, 34 (New Haven, CT).

Bernard, A. and E. Bernard. 1960. *Les inscriptions grecques et latines du Colosse de Memnon* (Cairo).

Berno, F. R. 2003. *Lo specchio, il vizio e la virtù. Studio sulle Naturales Quaestiones di Seneca*. Testi e manuali per l'insegnamento universitario del Latino 79 (Bologna).

Berti, E. M. 2000. *Annaei Lucani Bellum Civile Liber X* (Florence).

Bexley, E. M. 2009. 'Replacing Rome: Geographic and Political Centrality in Lucan's Pharsalia', *Classical Philology*, 104: 459–75.

Bickel, S. 2005. 'Creative and Destructive Waters', in A. Amenta, M. M. Luiselli and M. N. Sordi (eds), *L'acqua nell'antico Egitto. Vita, rigenerazione, incantesimo, medicamento* (Rome), 191–200.

Biraschi, A. M. 2005. 'Strabo and Homer: A Chapter in Cultural History', in D Dueck, H. Lindsay and S Pothecary (eds), *Strabo's Cultural Geography: The Making of a Kolossourgia* (Cambridge), 73–85.

Bishop, P. 1989. *The Myth of Shangri-La. Tibet, Travel Writing and the Western Creation of Sacred Landscape* (London).

Bispham, E. 2007. 'Pliny the Elder's Italy', in E. Bispham and G. Rowe with E. Matthews (eds), *Vita Vigilia Est. Essays in Honour of Barbara Levick* (London), 41–67.

Blouin, K. 2014. *Triangular Landscapes. Environment, Society, and the State in the Nile Delta under Roman Rule* (Oxford).

Blunt, A. and G. Rose (eds), 1994. *Writing Women and Space: Colonial and Post-Colonial Geographies* (New York).

Bömer, F. P. 1969. *Ovidius Naso. Metamorphosen. Kommentar. Buch I-III* (Heidelberg).

Bommas, M. 2012. 'Isis, Osiris and Serapis', in C. Riggs (ed.), *The Oxford Handbook of Roman Egypt* (Oxford), 419–35.

Bonneau, D. 1964. *La Crue du Nil. Divinité Egyptienne. À travers mille ans d'histoire (332 av. – 641 ap. J.C.)* (Paris).

1971. *Le fisc et le Nil* (Paris).

(ed. and tr.), 1971. 'Liber Aristotelis de inundatione Nili', *Etudes de Papyrologie*, 9: 1–33.

1994. 'Le dieu Nil hors d'Égypte (aux époques grecque, romaine et byzantine', in C. Berger et al. (eds), *Hommages à Jean Leclant, 3, Études Isiaques*, Bibliotheque d'Études 106 (Cairo), 51–62.

1995. 'La divinité du Nil sous le principat en Egypte', *Aufstieg und Niedergang der römischen Welt*, II.18.5 (Berlin), 3195, 3215.

Booth, J. (ed. and tr.), 1991. *Ovid. Amores II* (Warminster).

Borca, F. 1998. 'Il paesaggio nilotico nelle letturature greca e latina', *Materiali e Discussioni per l'Analisi dei Testi Classici*, 41: 185–205.

Borjes, J. L. 1989. *Obra Poetica* (Buenos Aires).

Bowden, H. 2010. *Mystery Cults in the Ancient World* (London).

Bowditch, P. L. 2011. 'Tibullus and Egypt: A Postcolonial Reading of Elegy I.7', *Arethusa*, 44.1: 89–122.

Bowersock, G. W. 1984. 'The Miracle of Memnon', *The Bulletin of the American Society of Papyrologists*, 21.1: 21–33.

1994. *Fiction as History. Nero to Julian* (Berkeley).

Bowman, Al. K. 1986. *Egypt after the Pharaohs. 332 BC – AD 642* (London).

1996. 'Egypt', in A. K. Bowman, E. Champlin and A. Lintott (eds), *The Cambridge Ancient History, 10. The Augustan Empire, 43 BC–AD 69.* 2nd edn (Cambridge), 676–702.

Bowman, A. K., E. Champlin and A. Lintott (eds), 1996. *The Cambridge Ancient History, 10. The Augustan Empire, 43 BC–AD 69.* 2nd Edn (Cambridge).

Bowman, A. K. and G. Woolf (eds). 1994. *Literacy and Power in the Ancient World* (Cambridge).

Bowman, G. 1999. 'Mapping History's Redemption: Eschatology and Topography in the Itinerarium Burdigalense', in L. I. Levine (ed.), *Jerusalem. Its Sanctity and Centrality to Judaism, Christianity and Islam* (London), 163–87.

Bragantini, I. 1998. 'VIII.5.24. Casa del Medico', in I. Bragantini et al., *Pitture e pavimenti di Pompei* 8 (Rome), 604–10.

1999. 'IX.5.9. Casa dei Pigmei', in I. Bragantini et al., *Pitture e pavimenti di Pompei* 8 (Rome), 486–527.

Braund, S. H. (tr.), 1992. *Lucan. Civil War* (Oxford).

Braund, S. M. 2004. *Juvenal and Persius*, LCL (Cambridge, MA).

Brenk, F. E. 1999. 'The Isis Campensis of Katja Lembke', in N. Blanc and A. Buisson (eds), *Imago Antiquitatis. Religions et iconographie du monde romain. Mélanges offerts à Robert Turcan* (Paris), 133–43.

Brennan, T. C. 1998. 'The Poets Julia Balbilla and Damo at the Colossus of Memnon', *The Classical World*, 91.4: 215–34.

Bricault, L., M. J. Versluys and P. G. P. Meyboom (eds), 2007. *Nile into Tiber: Egypt in the Roman World. Proceedings of the IIIrd International Conference of Isis Studies, Leiden May 11–14 2005*, Religions in the Greco-Roman World, 159 (Leiden).

Bricault, L. (ed.), 2000. *De Memphis à Rome. Actes du Ier Colloque international sur les études isiaques, Poitiers – Futuroscope, 8–10 avril 1999*, Religions in the Greco-Roman World, 140 (Leiden).

(ed.), 2004. *Isis en Occident. Actes di IIème Colloque international sur les études isiaques, Lyon III, 16–17 mai 2002*, Religions in the Greco-Roman World, 151 (Leiden).

Bright, D. F. 1975. 'The Art and Structure of Tibullus I.7', *Grazer Beiträge*, 3: 31–46.

1978. *Haec mihi fingebam, Tibullus in his World* (Leiden).

Brilliant, R. 1984. *Visual Narratives. Storytelling in Etruscan and Roman Art* (Ithaca, NY).

1999. 'Let the Trumpets Roar!': The Roman Triumph', in B. Bergmann and C. Kondoleon (eds), *The Art of Ancient Spectacle*. Studies in the History of Art, 56 (New Haven, CT), 221–9.

Brodersen, K. (ed. and tr.), 1994. *Pomponius Mela. Kreuzfahrt durch die alte Welt* (Darmstadt).

1995. *Terra Cognita. Studien zur römischen Raumerfassung*, Spudasmata, 59 (Hildesheim).

(ed. and tr.), 1996. *C. Plinius Secundus. Naturkunde. Buch VI* (Zürich).

2001. 'The Presentation of Geographical Knowledge for Travel and Transport in the Roman World: *itineria non tantum adnotata sed etiam picta*', in C. E. P. Adams and R. M. Laurence (eds), *Travel and Geography in the Roman Empire* (London), 7–21.

2010. 'Space and Geography', in A. Barchiesi and W. Scheidel (eds), *The Oxford Handbook of Roman Studies* (Oxford), 827–37.

2011. 'Mapping Pliny's World: The Achievement of Solinus', *Bulletin of the Institute of Classical Studies*, 54: 63–88.

(ed.), 2014. *Solinus. New Studies* (Heidelberg).

2016. 'The Geographies of Pliny and his "Ape" Solinus', in S. Bianchetti, M. R. Cataudella and H.-J. Gehrke (eds), *Brill's Companion to Ancient Geography. The Inhabited World in the Greek and Roman Tradition* (Leiden), 298–310

Brodersen, K. and J. Elsner (eds), 2009. *Images and Texts on the 'Artemidorus Papyrus'* (Wiesbaden).

Brown, S. 1992. 'Death as Decoration: Scenes from the Arena on Roman Domestic Mosaics', in A. Richlin (ed.), *Pornography and Representation in Greece and Rome* (Oxford), 180–212.

Brunt, P. A. 1963. Review of H. D. Meyer, 1961. *Die Aussenpolitik des Augustus und die augusteische Dichtung* (Cologne), in *Journal of Roman Studies*, 53: 170–6.

Buchner, E. 1976. 'Solarium Augusti und Ara Pacis'. *Römische Mitteilungen*, 83: 319–75.

1996. 'Horologium Augusti', in M. Steinby (ed.), *Lexicon Topographicum Urbis Romae*, III (Rome), 35–7.

Bunbury, E. H. 1883. *A History of Ancient Geography*, 2$^{nd}$ edn (London).

Burkert, W. 1987. *Ancient Mystery Cults* (Cambridge, MA).

Burnett, D. G. 2001. *Masters of All They Surveyed: Exploration, Geography and a British El Dorado* (Chicago).

Burns, M. A. T. 1964. 'Pliny's Ideal Roman', *Classical Journal*, 59: 253–8.

Burstein, S. M. 1976. 'Alexander, Callisthenes and the Source of the Nile', *Greek, Roman and Byzantine Studies*, 17.2: 135–46.

    1988. 'Cornelius Gallus and Aethiopia', *The Ancient History Bulletin*, 2: 16–20.

    1996. 'Images of Egypt in Greek Historiography', in A. Loprieno (ed.), *Ancient Egyptian Literature. History and Forms* (Leiden), 591–604.

Burton, A. 1972. *Diodorus Siculus Book I: A Commentary* (Leiden).

Butrica, J. L. 1993. 'Propertius 3.11 and the Death of Pompey', *Classical Quarterly*, 43.1: 342–6.

Cairns, F. 1979. *Tibullus. A Hellenistic Poet at Rome* (Cambridge).

Callebat, L. 2003. *Vitruve. De l'architecture. Livre VIII* Budé (Paris).

Cameron, A. 1995. *Callimachus and His Critics* (Princeton).

Campbell, B. 2012. *Rivers and the Power of Ancient Rome* (Chapel Hill, NC).

Cappel, A. 1994. *Untersuchungen zu Pygmäendarstellungen in der römischen Dekorationskunst* (Würzburg).

Capponi, L. 2005. *Augustan Egypt. The Creation of a Roman Province* (New York and London).

Capriotti Vittozzi, G. 2000. 'Note sulla comprensione dell'Egitto nel mondo romano', *Rivista Storica dell'Antichita*, 30: 121–39.

Carey, S. 2003. *Pliny's Catalogue of Culture. Art and Empire in the Natural History* (Oxford).

Carter, P. 1987. *The Road to Botany Bay. An Essay in Spatial History* (London).

Cary, M. and E.H. Warmington. 1929. *The Ancient Explorers* (London).

Casali, S. 2011. 'The Bellum Civile as an Anti-Aeneid', in P. Asso (ed.), *Brill's Companion to Lucan* (Leiden), 81–110.

Casey, E. S. 2002. *Representing Place. Landscape Painting and Maps* (Minneapolis).

Cesaretti, M. P. 1989. *Nerone e L'Egitto.* Studi di Storia Antica, 12 (Bologna).

Chiai, G. F. 2014. 'The Mediterranean Islands and the Common Sense Geography', in K. Geus and M. Thiering (eds), *Features of Common Sense Geography. Implicit Knowledge Structures in Ancient Geographical Texts* (Berlin), 89–113.

Citroni Marchetti, S. 1991. *Plinio il Vecchio e la tradizione del moralismo romano* (Pisa).

Clark, K. 1953. *Landscape into Art* (London).

Clarke, J. R. 1996. 'Hypersexual Black Men in Augustan Baths: Ideal Somatotypes and Apotropaic Magic', in N. B. Kampen (ed.), *Sexuality in Ancient Art* (Cambridge), 184–98.

    2003. *Art in the Lives of Ordinary Romans. Visual Representation and Non-Elite Viewers in Italy 100 BC- AD 315* (Berkeley).

    2007a. *Looking at Laughter. Humor, Power, and Transgression in Roman Visual Culture, 100BC – AD 250* (Berkeley).

    2007b 'Three Uses of the Pygmy and the Aethiops at Pompeii: Decorating, "Othering", and Warding off Demons', in L. Bricault, M. J. Versluys and

P. G. P. Meyboom (eds), *Nile into Tiber: Egypt in the Roman World. Proceedings of the IIIrd International Conference of Isis Studies, Leiden May 11–14 2005*, Religions in the Graeco-Roman World, 159 (Leiden), 155–69.

Clarke, K. 1997. 'In Search of the Author of Strabo's Geography', *Journal of Roman Studies*, 87: 92–110.

1999. *Between Geography and History. Hellenistic Constructions of the Roman World* (Oxford).

2001. 'An Island Nation: Re-reading Tacitus' Agricola', *Journal of Roman Studies*, 91: 94–112.

2008. 'Text and Image: Mapping the Roman World', in F.-H. Mutschler and A. Mittag (eds), *Conceiving the Empire. China and Rome Compared* (Oxford), 195–214.

Claus, B. 2005. 'Osiris et Hapi: crue et régéneration en Égypte ancienne', in A. Amenta, M. M. Luiselli and M. N. Sordi (eds), *L'acqua nell'antico Egitto. Vita, rigenerazione, incantesimo, medicamento* (Rome), 201–11.

Clifford, J. 1985. 'Objects and Selves – An Afterword' in G. Stocking (ed.), *Objects and Others: Essays on Museums and Material Culture*, History of Anthropology, 3 (Madison, WI), 236–46.

Coarelli, F. 1990. 'La pompé di Tolomeo Filadelfo e il mosaico nilotico di Palestrina', *Ktèma*, 15 (1990), 225–51.

1996. 'Cesare, Iside, e il «Nilo» del Campo Martio' in M. G. Picozzi and F. Carinci (eds), *Studi in memoria di Lucia Guerrini: vicino oriente, Egeo-grecia, Roma e il mondo romano – tradizione dell'antico e collezionismo di antico e collezionismo di antichità* (Rome), 191–5.

1999. 'Porticus ad Nationes', in E. M. Steinby (ed.), *Lexicon Topographicum Urbis Romae*, IV (Rome), 138–9.

Codoñer, C. 1989. 'La physique de Sénèque: Ordonnance et structure des "Naturales Quaestiones"', *Aufstieg und Niedergang der römischen Welt*, II.36.3: 1779–822.

Cohn, B. S. 2006. *Colonialism and its Forms of Knowledge. The British in India* (Princeton).

Collins, R. O. 2002. *The Nile* (New Haven, CT).

Conte, G. B. 1994. *Genres and Readers*. Tr. G. W. Most (Baltimore).

Cook, A. S. 2006. 'Surveying the Seas. Establishing the Sea Routes to the East Indies', in J. J. Akerman (ed.), *Cartographies of Travel and Navigation* (Chicago), 69–96.

Cooper, J. P. 2014. *The Medieval Nile. Route, Navigation and Landscape in Islamic Egypt* (Cairo).

Cosgrove, D. 2001. *Apollo's Eye. A Cartographic Genealogy of the Earth in the Western Imagination* (Baltimore).

2008. *Geography and Vision. Seeing, Imagining and Representing the World* (London).

Courtney, E. 1980. *A Commentary on the Satires of Juvenal* (London).

Croisille, J.-M. 1988. 'Paysages et natures mortes au temple d'Isis à Pompéi', in *Res Sacrae. Hommages à Henri Le Bonniec* (Paris), 124–34.

Cruz Andreotti, G. 2016. 'Rome and Iberia. The Making of a Cultural Geography', in S. Bianchetti, M. R. Cataudella and H.-J. Gehrke (eds), *Brill's Companion to Ancient Geography. The Inhabited World in the Greek and Roman Tradition* (Leiden), 274–97.

Cuomo, S. 2007. *Technology and Culture in Greek and Roman Antiquity* (Cambridge).

Curl, J. S. 1994. *Egyptomania. The Egyptian Revival: A Recurring Theme in the History of Taste* (Manchester).

Curtis, G. W. 1852. *Nile Notes of a 'Howadji'* (London).

D'Arms, J. H. 1999. 'Performing Culture: Roman Spectacle and the Banquets of the Powerful', in B. Bergmann and C. Kondoleon (eds), *The Art of Ancient Spectacle*. Studies in the History of Art 56, Center for Advanced Study in the Visual Arts, Symposium Papers, 34 (New Haven, CT), 301–19.

Dalmeyda, G. (ed. and tr.), 1926. *Les Éphésiaques: ou, Le roman d'Harbrocomès et d'Anthia*, Budé (Paris).

Dan, A. 2014. 'Xenophon's Anabasis and the Common Greek Mental Modelling of Spaces', in K. Geus and M. Thiering (eds), *Features of Common Sense Geography. Implicit Knowledge Structures in Ancient Geographical Texts*, Antike Kultur und Geschichte, 16 (Berlin), 157–98.

Darwall-Smith, R. H. 1996. *Emperors and Architecture: A Study of Flavian Rome* (Brussels).

Dasen, V. 1993. *Dwarfs in Ancient Egypt and Greece*. Oxford Monographs on Classical Archaeology (Oxford).

Daszewski, W. A. 1985. *Corpus of Mosaics from Egypt I. Hellenistic and Early Roman Period*. Aegyptiaca Treverensia. Trierer Studien zum griechisch-römischen Äegypten (Mainz).

Daviault, A., J. Lancha and L. A. Lopez Palomo, 1987. *Un mosaico con inscripciones / Une mosaïque à inscriptions, Puente Genil (Cordoba)*. Publications de la Casa de Velazquez. Série Etudes et Documents, 3 (Madrid).

Davies, P. J. E. 2011. 'Aegyptiaca in Rome. Adventus and Romanitas', in E. Gruen (ed.), *Cultural Identity in the Ancient Mediterranean* (Los Angeles), 354–70.

Dawson, C. M. 1965. *Romano-Campanian Mythological Landscape Painting*, Yale Classical Studies, 9 (New Haven, CT).

D'Errico, D. 1992. 'Materiali di produzione egiziana', in *Alla ricerca di Iside. Analisi, studi e restauri dell'Iseo pompeiano nel Museo di Napoli* (Naples), 77–8.

de Buck, A. 1948. 'On the Meaning of the Name H'PJ', *Orientalia Neerlandica* (Leiden), 1–22.

De Certeau, M. 1984. *The Practice of Everyday Life*. Tr. S. F. Rendall (Berkeley).

De Nardis, M. 1989. 'Seneca, Plinio e la spedizione neroniana in Etiopia', *Aegyptus*, 69.1: 123–52.

De Temmerman, K. 2012. 'Xenophon of Ephesus', in I. J. F. De Jong (ed.), *Space in Ancient Greek Literature. Studies in Ancient Greek Narrative*, Mnemosyne Suppl. 339 (Leiden), 503–16.

De Vos, A. 1990. '1.7.11. Casa dell'Efebo o di P. Cornelius Tages', in I. Bragantini et al. (eds), *Pitture e pavimenti di Pompei*, 1 (Rome), 619–727.

De Vos, M. 1980. *Egittomania in Pitture e Mosaici Romano-Campani della prima età Imperiale* (Leiden).

1990. '1.6.15. Casa dei Ceii', in I. Bragantini et al. (eds), *Pitture e pavimenti di Pompei*, 1 (Rome), 407–82.

De Vos, P. 2007. 'Natural History and the Pursuit of Empire in Eighteenth-Century Spain', *American Society for Eighteenth-Century Studies* 40.2: 209–39.

Degrassi, A. 1954. *Fasti Capitolini* (Rome).

Delano-Smith, C. 2006. 'Milieus of Mobility. Itineraries, Route Maps and Road Maps', in J. J. Akerman (ed.), *Cartographies of Travel and Navigation* (Chicago), 16–68.

Deleuze, G. and F. Guttari. 1986 *Nomadology: The War Machine*, tr. Brian Massumi (New York).

Desanges, J. 1978. *Recherches sur l'activité des méditerranéens aux confins de l'Afrique*, Collection de l'École Française de Rome, 38 (Rome).

1980. *Pline L'Ancien. Histoire Naturelle Livre V.1–46 1ere Parte (L'Afrique du Nord)*. Budé (Paris).

1996/1999. 'Géographie de l'Afrique et philologie dans deux passages de la Chorographie de Méla', *L'Africa Romana*, 11 (1996), repr. in his *Toujours Afrique apporte fait nouveau: scripta minora* (Paris), 123–9.

2008. *Pline L'Ancien. Histoire Naturelle. Livre VI 4e partie. L'Asie africaine sauf l'Egypte et les climates du monde habité*. Budé (Paris).

Detlefsen, D. 1906. *Ursprung, Einrichtung und Bedeutung der Erdkarte Agrippas* (Berlin).

Dewar, M. 1994. 'Laying It On With a Trowel: The Proem to Lucan and Related Texts', *Classical Quarterly*, n.s. 44: 199–211.

Diels, H. (ed.), 1879. *Doxographi Graeci* (Berlin).

1969. 'Lucan und Seneca', W. Burkert (ed.), *Kleine Schriften zur Geschichte der antiken Philosophie* (Darmstadt), 379–408.

Dillery, J. 1998. 'Hecataeus of Abdera: Hyperboreans, Egypt and the Interpretatio Graeca', *Historia*, 47.3: 255–75.

1999. 'The First Egyptian Narrative History: Manetho and Greek Historiography', *Zeitschrift für Papyrologie und Epigraphik*, 127: 93–116.

Dinter, M. T. 2013a. *Anatomizing Civil War. Studies in Lucan's Epic Technique* (Ann Arbor, MI).

2013b 'Introduction: The Neronian (Literary) "Renaissance"', in E. Buckley and M. T. Dinter (eds), *A Companion to the Neronian Age* (Malden, MA), 1–14.

Dion, R. 1977. *Aspects politiques de la géographie antique* (Paris).

Dominik, W. J., J. Garthwaite and P. A. Roche (eds), 2009. *Writing Politics in Imperial Rome* (Leiden).

Dominik, W. J. 2009. 'Vergil's Geopolitics', in W. J. Dominik, J. Garthwaite and P. A. Roche (eds), *Writing Politics in Imperial Rome* (Leiden), 111–32.

Doody, A. 2001. 'Finding Facts in Pliny's Encyclopaedia: The *Summarium* of the Natural History', *Ramus*, 30: 1–22.

2009. 'Pliny's Natural History: *Enkuklios Paideia* and the Ancient Encyclopedia', *Journal of the History of Ideas*, 70.1: 1–22.

2010. *Pliny's Encyclopedia. The Reception of the Natural History* (Cambridge).

2013. 'Literature of the World: Seneca's *Natural Questions* and Pliny's *Natural History*', in E. Buckley and M. T. Dinter (eds), *A Companion to the Neronian Age* (Malden, MA), 288–301.

Dörner, N. 2014. *Feste und Opfer für den Gott Caesar: Kommunikationsprozesse im Rahmen des Kaiserkultes im römischen Ägypten der julisch-claudischen Zeit (30 v.Chr. – 68 n.Chr.).* Pharos, 30 (Rahden).

Douglass, L. 1996. 'A New Look at the Itinerarium Burdigalense'. *Journal of Early Christian Studies*, 4: 313–33.

Downs, R. M. and D. Stea (eds), 1973. *Image and Environment. Cognitive Mapping and Spatial Behavior* (Chicago).

Driver, F. 2001. *Geography Militant. Cultures of Exploration and Empire* (Oxford).

Dueck, D. 1999. 'The Date and Method of Composition of Strabo's "Geography"', *Hermes*, 124.4: 467–78.

2000. *Strabo of Amasia. A Greek Man of Letters in Augustan Rome* (London and New York).

Dueck, D. with a chapter by K. Brodersen. 2012. *Geography in Classical Antiquity* (Cambridge).

Dueck, D., H. Lindsay and S. Pothecary (eds), 2005. *Strabo's Cultural Geography: The Making of a Kolossourgia* (Cambridge).

Dunbabin, K. M. D 2001. *Mosaics of the Greek and Roman World* (Cambridge).

Duncan, C. 1991. 'Art Museums and the Ritual of Citizenship', in I. Karp and S. D. Lavine (eds), *Exhibiting Cultures: The Poetics and Politics of Museum Display* (Washington, DC), 88–103.

Dwyer, E. J. 1992. 'The Temporal Allegory of the Tazza Farnese', *American Journal of Archaeology*, 96.2: 283–300.

Eck, W. 2007. *The Age of Augustus*, 2nd edn (Oxford).

Edney, M. H. 1990. *Mapping An Empire. The Geographical Construction of British India. 1765–1843* (Chicago).

2009. 'The Irony of Imperial Mapping', in J. R. Akerman (ed.), *The Imperial Map: Cartography and the Mastery of Empire* (Chicago), 11–46.

Edwards, A. 1888. *A Thousand Miles up the Nile* (London).

Edwards, C. 1996. *Writing Rome. Textual Approaches to the City* (Cambridge).

Eichberger, K. A. 1935. 'Untersuchungen zu Lucan. Der Nilabschnitt im zehnten Buch des Bellum Civile'. Diss. (Tübingen).

Eichholz, D. E. (ed. and tr.), 1962. *Pliny. Natural History X*, LCL (Cambridge, MA).

Eide, T., T. Hägg, R. H. Pierce and L. Török (eds), 1998. *Fontes Historiae Nubiorum. Volume III. From the First to the Sixth Century AD* (Bergen).

Eide, T., T. Hägg, R. H. Pierce and L. Török (eds), 1996. *Fontes Historiae Nubiorum. Volume II. From the Mid-Fifth to the First Century BC* (Bergen).

El-Sheikh, H. A. 1992. 'Roman Expeditions to the Upper Nile', in G. P. Carratelli, D. Del Re, N. Bonacasa and A Etman (eds), *Roma e l'Egitto nell'antichità classica. Cairo 6–9 febbraio 1989* (Rome), 157–60.

Elmer, D. F. 2008. 'Heliodoros's "Sources": Intertextuality, Paternity, and the Nile River in the Aithiopika', *Transactions of the American Philological Association*, 138: 411–50.

Elsner, J. 1995. *Art and the Roman Viewer. The Transformation of Art from the Pagan World to Christianity*. Cambridge Studies in New Art History and Criticism (Cambridge).

(ed.), 1996. *Art and Text in Roman Culture* (Cambridge).

1997. 'Hagiographic Geography: Travel and Allegory in the Life of Apollonius of Tyana', *Journal of Hellenic Studies*, 117: 22–37.

2000. 'The Itinerarium Burdigalense: Politics and Salvation in the Geography of Constantine's Empire', *Journal of Roman Studies*, 90: 181–95.

2007. *Roman Eyes. Visuality and Subjectivity in Art and Text* (Princeton).

Esolen, A. M. (tr.), 1995. *Lucretius. On the Nature of Things. De rerum natura* (Baltimore).

Evans, R. 2003. 'Containment and Corruption: The Discourse of Flavian Empire', in A. J. Boyle and W. J. Dominik (eds), *Flavian Rome: Culture, Image, Text* (Leiden), 255–76.

2005. 'Geography Without People: Mapping in Pliny *Historia Naturalis* Books 3–6', *Ramus*, 34: 47–74.

2008. *Utopia Antiqua. Readings of the Golden Age and Decline of Rome* (London).

Faider, P. 1930. 'Sénèque en Égypte', *Bulletin de l'institut français d'archéologie orientale*, 30: 83–7.

Fairclough, H. R. 2000. *Virgil*. 2 vols LCL (Cambridge, MA).

Fantham, E. 2004. *Ovid's Metamorphoses* (Oxford).

2011. 'A Controversial Life', in P. Asso (ed.), *Brill's Companion to Lucan* (Leiden), 3–20.

Fasolo, F. and G. Gullini. 1953. *Il santuario della Fortuna Primigenia a Palestrina*, 2 vols (Rome).

Favro, D. 1993. 'Reading the Augustan City', in P. J. Holliday (ed.), *Narrative and Event in Ancient Art* (Cambridge), 230–57.

1994. 'Rome. The Street Triumphant: The Urban Impact of Roman Triumphal Parades', in Z. Çelik, D. Favro and R. Ingersoll (eds), *Streets. Critical Perspectives on Public Space* (Berkeley), 151–64.

1996. *The Urban Image of Augustan Rome* (Cambridge).

Feeney, D. C. 2007. *Caesar's Calendar. Ancient Time and the Beginnings of History* (Berkeley).

Feraco, F. 2008. 'Lucrezio 6, 712–737: la piena del Nilo', *Bollettino di Studi Latini* 38: 583–608.

2011. *Ammiano geografo. Nuovi Studi*, Studi Latini, 76 (Naples).

Ferrari, G. 1999. 'The Geography of Time: The Nile Mosaic and the Library at Praeneste', *Ostraka*, 8: 359–86.

Fitter, C. 1995. *Poetry, Space, Landscape. Toward a New Theory*. Literature, Culture, Theory, 13 (Cambridge).

Foertmeyer, V. A. 1989. 'Tourism in Graeco-Roman Egypt'. Unpubl. PhD Thesis. Princeton University.

Fögen, T. 2012. 'Scholarship and Competitiveness: Pliny the Elder's Attitude Towards His Predecessors in the *Naturalis Historia*', in M. Asper (ed.), *Writing Science. Mathematical and Medical Authorship in Ancient Greece* (Berlin), 83–108.

Forster, E. S. 1966. *Lucius Annaeus Florus. Epitome of Roman History* LCL (Cambridge, MA).

Foucher, L. 1965. 'Les mosaïques nilotiques africains', in *La mosaïque Gréco-romaine II* (Paris), 137–45.

Francis, J. A. 1998. 'Truthful Fictions. New Questions to Old Answers on Philostratus' Life of Apollonius', *American Journal of Philology*, 119.3: 419–41.

Frankfurter, D. 1994. 'The Magic of Writing and the Writing of Magic: The Power of the Word in Egyptian and Greek Traditions', *Helios*, 21: 189–221.

    1998. *Religion in Roman Egypt. Assimilation and Resistance* (Princeton).

Fraser, P. M. 1972. *Ptolemaic Alexandria* (Oxford).

Frede, M. 1989. 'Chaeremon der Stoiker', *Aufstieg und Niedergang der römischen Welt*, II.36.3: 2067–103.

Fredrick, D. (ed.), 2002a. *The Roman Gaze. Vision, Power, and the Body* (Baltimore).

    2002b. 'Introduction. Invisible Rome', in D. Fredrick (ed.), *The Roman Gaze. Vision, Power, and the Body* (Baltimore), 1–30.

French, R. L. 2006. 'Maps on Wheels. The Evolution of Automobile Navigation', in J. J. Akerman (ed.), *Cartographies of Travel and Navigation* (Chicago), 260–290.

French, R. 1996. *Ancient Natural History. Histories of Nature* (London).

Friedman, J. B. 1981. *The Monstrous Races in Medieval Life and Thought* (Syracuse, NY).

Fröhlich, T. 1993. 'Die Wanddekorationen des Peristyls der Casa della Fontana Piccola in Pompeji', in E. M. Moormann (ed.), *Functional and Spatial Analysis of Wall Painting*. Proceedings of the Fifth International Congress on Ancient Wall Painting, Amsterdam 8–12 September 1992 (Leiden), 72–81.

Gais, R. M. 1978. 'Some Problems of River-God Iconography', *American Journal of Archaeology*, 82.3: 355–70.

Galinsky, K. 1969. 'The Triumph in the Augustan Elegy', *Wiener Studien*, 82: 75–107.

    1996. *Augustan Culture: An Interpretive Introduction* (Princeton).

    (ed.), 2005. *The Cambridge Companion to the Age of Augustus* (Cambridge).

Gallazzi, C. B. Kramer and S. Settis. (eds), 2008. *Il papiro di Artemidoro* 2 vols (Milan).

Gallia, A. B. 2002. 'Porticus Vipsania', in Lothar Haselberger (in collaboration with D. G. Romano and E. A. Dumser) (ed.), *Mapping Augustan Rome*, Journal of Roman Archaeology. Supp Series 50 (Portsmouth, RI), 208.

García Moreno, L. A. 1994. 'La República romana tardía y el conocimiento geográfico y etnográfico de Africa', *Africa Romana*, 11: 319–26.

Gautier Dalché, P. 2008. 'L'Héritage Antique de la Cartographie Médiévale: les Problèmes et les Acquis', in R. J. A. Talbert and R. W. Unger (eds), *Cartography in Antiquity and the Middle Ages* (Leiden), 29–66.

Geus, K. and M. Thiering (eds), 2014. *Features of Common Sense Geography. Implicit Knowledge Structures in Ancient Geographical Texts* (Berlin).

Gibson, R. K. and R. Morello (eds), 2011. *Pliny the Elder: Themes and Contexts* (Leiden).

Gill, C. 2003 'The School in the Roman Imperial Period', in B. Inwood (ed.), *The Cambridge Companion to the Stoics* (Cambridge), 33–58.

Gillespie, S. and P. Hardie (eds). 2007. *The Cambridge Companion to Lucretius* (Cambridge).

Godlewska, A. 1995. 'Map, Text and Image. The Mentality of Enlightened Conquerors: A New Look at the Description de l'Egypte', *Transactions of the Institute of British Geographers*, 20.1: 5–28.

Godlewska, A. and N. Smith (eds), 1994. *Geography and Empire* (Oxford).

Godwin, J. 1991. *Lucretius: 'De Rerum Natura' VI* (Warminster).

Goldsworthy, V. 2013. *Inventing Ruritania. The Imperialism of the Imagination* rev. edn (London).

Golledge, R. G. 1999. 'Human Wayfinding and Cognitive Maps', in Reginald G. Golledge (ed.), *Wayfinding Behavior. Cognitive Mapping and Other Spatial Processes* (Baltimore), 5–45.

Goold, G. P. (ed. and tr.), 1990. *Propertius Elegies*. LCL (Cambridge, MA).

Gowers, E. 1993. *The Loaded Table: Representations of Food in Roman Literature* (Oxford).

1995. 'The Anatomy of Rome from Capitol to Cloaca', *Journal of Roman Studies*, 85: 23–32.

Gregory, A. 2007. *Ancient Greek Cosmogony* (London).

Griffin, J. 1977. 'Propertius and Antony', *Journal of Roman Studies*, 67: 17–26.

Griffin, M. T. 1976. *Seneca. A Philosopher in Politics* (Oxford).

2008. 'Imago Vitae Suae', in J. G. Fitch, *Seneca*. Oxford Readings in Classical Studies (Oxford), 23–58.

Griffiths, J. G. 1970. *Plutarch. De Iside et Osiride* (Cambridge).

1975. *The Isis-Book, Metamorphoses Book XI* (Leiden).

1980. *The Origins of Osiris and his Cult* (Leiden).

Grimal, P. 1979. *Sénèque ou la conscience de l'Empire* (Paris).

Gross, N. 1989. *Senecas Naturales Quaestiones. Komposition, Naturphilosophische Aussagen und ihre Quellen*. Palingenesia, 27 (Stuttgart).

Gruen, E. S. 1992. Review of Nicolet 1991. In *Classical Philology*, 87: 183–5.

2010. *Rethinking the Other in Antiquity* (Princeton).

Gullini, G. 1956. *I mosaici di Palestrina* (Rome).

Gummere, R. M. 1962. *Seneca. Ad Lucilium. Epistulae Morales*, LCL, 3 vols (Cambridge, MA).

Gurval, R. A. 1998. *Actium and Augustus. The Politics and Emotions of Civil War* (Ann Arbor, MI).

Hachlili, R. 1998. 'Iconographic Elements of Nilotic Scenes on Byzantine Mosaic Pavements in Israel', *Palestine Exploration Quarterly*, 130: 106–20.

Hales, S. 2003. *The Roman House and Social Identity* (Cambridge).

Hamarneh, B. 1999. 'The River Nile and Egypt in the Mosaics of the Middle East', in M. Piccirillo and E. Alliata (eds), *The Madaba Map Centenary 1897–1997. Travelling Through the Byzantine Umayyad Period.* Studium Biblicum Franciscanium, Collectio Maior, 40 (Jerusalem), 185-9.

Hänger, C. 2007. 'Die Karte des Agrippa', in M. Rathmann (ed.), *Wahrnehmung und Erfassung geographischer Räume in der Antike* (Mainz am Rhein), 135–42.

Hardie, P. 1985. 'Imago Mundi: Cosmological and Ideological Aspects of the Shield of Achilles', *Journal of Hellenic Studies*, 105: 11–31.

    1986. *Virgil's Aeneid. Cosmos and Imperium* (Oxford).

    1998. *Virgil* (Oxford).

    2008. 'Lucretian Multiple Explanations and their Reception in Latin Didactic and Epic', in M. Beretta and F. Citti (eds), *Lucrezio, la natura e la scienza* (Florence), 69–96.

    2013. 'Lucan's Bellum Civile', in E. Buckley and M. T. Dinter (eds), *A Companion to the Neronian Age* (Malden, MA), 225–39.

Harley, J. B. 1988. 'Maps, Knowledge and Power', in D. Cosgrove and S. Daniels (eds), *The Iconography of Landscape: Essays on the Symbolic Representation, Design and Use of Past Environments* (Cambridge), 277–312.

    1989. 'Deconstructing the Map', *Cartographica*, 26.2: 1–20.

Harley, J. B. and D. Woodward (eds), 1987–. *The History of Cartography* (Chicago).

Harrison, S. J. 2007. *Generic Enrichment in Vergil and Horace* (Oxford).

Hartog, F. 1988. *The Mirror of Herodotus. The Representation of the Other in the Writing of History*, tr. J. Lloyd (Berkeley).

Haselberger, L. 2011. 'A Debate on the Horologium of Augustus: Controversy and Clarification with Responses by P. J. Heslin and M. Schütz and additional remarks by R. Hannah and G. Alföldy', *Journal of Roman Archaeology*, 24.1: 47–98.

Haselberger, L., D. G. Romano, E. Ann Dumser (eds), 2002. *Mapping Augustan Rome*. Journal of Roman Archaeology. Supp Series, 50 (Portsmouth, RI).

Henderson, J. 1987. 'Lucan/The Word at War', *Ramus*, 16: 122–64.

    1998. 'Lucan: The Word at War', in *Fighting for Rome. Poets, Caesars, History and Civil War* (Cambridge), 165–211.

    2002. 'Knowing Someone Through their Books: Pliny on Uncle Pliny (Epistles 3.5)', *Classical Philology*, 97: 256–84.

    2011a. 'The Nature of Man: Pliny, Historia Naturalis as Cosmogram', *Materiali e Discussioni*, 66: 139–71.

    2011b. 'In at the Death', in P. Asso (ed.), *Brill's Companion to Lucan* (Leiden), 547–56.

Henrichs, A. 1968. 'Vespasian's Visit to Alexandria', *Zeitschrift für Papyrologie und Epigraphik*, 3 (1968), 51–80.

Herendeen, W. H. 1986. *From Landscape to Literature: The River and the Myth of Geography* (Pittsburgh).

Heslin, P. 2007. 'Augustus, Domitian and the So-Called Horologium Augusti', *Journal of Roman Studies*, 97: 1–20.

  2011. 'The Augustus Code: A Response to L. Hasenberger', *Journal of Roman Archaeology*, 24: 74–7.

Hickson, F. V. 1991. 'Augustus Triumphator: Manipulation of the Triumphal Theme in the Political Programme of Augustus', *Latomus*, 50:124–38.

Hillard, T. W. 2002. 'The Nile Cruise of Cleopatra and Caesar', *Classical Quarterly*, 52: 549–54.

Hine, H. M. (ed.), 1996. *L. Annaei Senecae naturalium quaestionum libros* (Stuttgart).

  2006. 'Rome, the Cosmos and the Emperor in Seneca's Natural Questions', *Journal of Roman Studies*, 96: 42–72.

  2010. (tr.), *Lucius Annaeus Seneca: Natural Questions* (Chicago and London).

Hinterhöller, M. 2009. 'Das Nilmosaik von Palestrina und die Bildstruktur eines geographischen Großraums. Versuche zur möglichen Rekonstruktion, geographischen Interpretation und den Formen der perspektivischen Raumerschließung', *Römische Historische Mitteilungen* 51: 15–130.

Hinze, F. 1959. *Studien zur meroitischen Chronologie und zu den Opfertafeln aus den Pyramiden von Meroe* (Berlin).

Hoffmann, P. 1993. *Der Isis-Tempel in Pompeji* (Münster and Hamburg).

Holliday, P. J. 1997. 'Roman Triumphal Painting: Its Function, Development and Reception', *Art Bulletin*, 79.1: 130–47.

  2002. *The Origins of Roman Historical Commemoration in the Visual Arts* (Cambridge).

Hollis, A. S. 2007. *Fragments of Roman Poetry C.60 BC-AD 20* (Oxford).

Holmes, N. 1999. 'Nero and Caesar: Lucan 1.33–66', *Classical Philology*, 94.1: 75–81.

Hölscher, T. 2006. 'The Transformation of Victory into Power: From Event to Structure', in S. Dillon and K. E. Welch (eds), *Representations of War in Ancient Rome* (Cambridge), 27–48.

Honour, H. 1961. *Chinoiserie. The Vision of Cathay* (London).

Hornung, E. 1971. *Conceptions of God in Ancient Egypt. The One and the Many*, tr. J. Baines (London).

  1992. *Idea into Image. Essays on Ancient Egyptian Thought*, tr. E. Bredeck (Princeton).

  2001. *The Secret Lore of Egypt. Its Impact on the West*. Tr. D. Lorton (Ithaca, NY).

Horsfall, N. 1985. 'Illusion and Reality in Latin Topographical Writing', *Greece and Rome*, 32.2: 197–208.

Houghtalin, L. 1993. 'The Personifications of the Roman Provinces'. Unpubl. PhD Thesis. Bryn Mawr.

Housman, A. E. (ed.), 1926. *M. Annaei Lucani Belli Civilis Libri Decem* (Oxford).

Howe, N. P. 1985. 'In Defence of the Encyclopedic Mode: On Pliny's Preface to the Natural History', *Latomus*, 44: 561–76.

Hudson, B. 1977. 'The New Geography and the New Imperialism', *Antipode* 19.2: 12–19.

Huet, V. 1996. 'Stories One Might Tell of Roman Art: Reading Trajan's Column and the Tiberius Cup', in J. Elsner (ed.), *Art and Text in Roman Culture* (Cambridge), 9–31.

Humbert, J.-M. 1994. 'Egyptomania: A Current Concept from the Renaissance to Postmodernism', in J.-M. Humbert, M. Pantazzi and C. Ziegler (eds), *Egyptomania. Egypt in Western Art 1730–1930* (Ottowa), 21–6.

Hunter, R. 2006. *The Shadow of Callimachus. Studies in the Reception of Hellenistic Poetry at Rome* (Cambridge).

Iacopi, I. 1997. *La Decorazione Pittorica Dell'Aula Isiaca* (Milan).

Impey, O. 1977. *Chinoiserie. The Impact of Oriental Styles on Western Art and Decoration* (Oxford).

Ingold, T. 2007. *Lines. A Brief History* (London).

Inwood, B. 2002/2005. 'God and Human Knowledge in Seneca's Natural Questions', in D. Frede and A. Laks (eds), *Traditions of Theology: Studies in Hellenistic Theology, Its Background and Aftermath* (Leiden), 119–57; repr. in his *Reading Seneca: Stoic Philosophy at Rome* (Oxford), 157–200.

Isaac, M.-T. 1991. Review of Janni 1984. *L'Antiquité Classique*, 60: 511–12.

Isager, J. 1991. *Pliny on Art and Society. The Elder Pliny's Chapters on the History of Art*, Odense University Classical Studies, 17 (Odense).

Irwin, J. T. 1980. *American Hieroglyphics. The Symbol of the Egyptian Hieroglyphics in the American Renaissance* (Baltimore).

Itgenhorst, T. 2005. *Tota illa pompa: der Triumph in der römischen Republik* (Göttingen).

Iversen, E. 1968–1972. *Obelisks in Exile. The Obelisks of Rome* (Copenhagen).

1993. *The Myth of Egypt and its Hieroglyphs in European Tradition* (Copenhagen).

Jackson, J. 1979. *Tacitus. The Annals.* LCL, 3 vols (Cambridge, MA).

Jacob, C. 1992. *L'empire des cartes: Approche théorique de la cartographie à travers l'histoire* (Paris).

1999. 'Mapping in the Mind: The Earth from Ancient Alexandria', in D. Cosgrove (ed.), *Mappings* (London), 24–49.

2006. *The Sovereign Map. Theoretical Approaches in Cartography Throughout History*, tr. T. Conley (Chicago).

Jacobson, D. 1993. *Chinoiserie* (London).

Jameson, S. 1968. 'Chronology of the Campaigns of Aelius Gallus and C. Petronius', *Journal of Roman Studies*, 58: 71–84.

Janni, P. 1984. *La Mappa e il Periplo. Cartografia antica e spazio odologico*. Università di Macerata. Pubblicazioni della facoltà di lettere e filosofia, 19 (Macerata).

Janvier, Y. 1994. 'Vitruve et la géographie', *Geographia Antiqua*, 3: 49–78.

Jashemski, W. F. 1993. *The Gardens of Pompeii, Herculaneum and the Villas Destroyed by Vesuvius. Vol II. The Appendices* (New Rochelle, NY).

Jeal, T. 2011. *Explorers of the Nile: The Triumph and Tragedy of a Great Victorian Adventure* (London).

Jenkyns, R. 1998. *Virgil's Experience. Nature and History: Times, Names and Places* (Oxford).

2013. *God, Space, and City in the Roman Imagination* (Oxford).

Johnson, W. R. 1987. *Momentary Monsters. Lucan and his Heroes* (Ithaca and London).

Jones, A. 2012. 'Ptolemy's Geography: Mapmaking and the Scientific Enterprise', in R. J. A. Talbert (ed.), *Ancient Perspectives: Maps and their Place in Egypt, Mesopotamia, Greece and Rome* (Chicago), 109–28.

Jones, C. P. (ed. and tr.), 2005. *Philostratus. Life of Apollonius of Tyana* LCL (Cambridge, MA).

Jones, P. J. 2005. *Reading Rivers in Roman Literature and Culture* (Oxford).

Kelly, B. 2010. 'Tacitus, Germanicus and the Kings of Egypt (Tac. Ann. 2.59–61)', *Classical Quarterly*, 60.1: 221–37.

Kemezis, A. 2014. 'Roman Politics and the Fictional Narrator in Philostratus' Apollonius', *Classical Antiquity*, 33.1: 61–101.

Kennedy, D. F. 1992. '"Augustan" and "Anti-Augustan". Reflections on Terms of Reference', in A. Powell (ed.), *Roman Poetry and Propaganda in the Age of Augustus* (London), 26–58.

Kern, J. H. C. 1958. 'A Roman "Campana" Relief with Nile Landscape (Pygmy Village)', *Oudheidkundige Mededelingen*, 39: 11–17.

Keyser, P. T. and G. L. Irby-Massie. 2008. *The Encyclopedia of Ancient Natural Scientists* (London).

Kipling, R. 1920. *Letters of Travel (1892–1913)* (London).

Kirwan, L. P. 1957. 'Rome Beyond the Southern Frontier', *Geographical Journal*, 123: 1–19.

1982/2002. 'Greek and Roman Expeditions to the Southern Sudan', in J. Mack and P. Robertshaw (eds), *Culture and History in the Southern Sudan* (Khartoum), 71–4; repr. In his *Studies in the History of Late Antique and Christian Nubia*, Variorum Collected Studies Series, CS 748 (Aldershot), V.

Kleiner, D. E. E. 2005. *Cleopatra and Rome* (Cambridge, MA).

Klementa, S. 1993. *Gelagerte Flussgötter des Späthellenismus und der römischen Kaiserzeit* (Cologne).

Klotz, A. 1931. 'Die geographischen Commentarii des Agrippa und ihre Überreste', *Klio*, 24: 38–58, 386–466.

Klotz, D. 2012. 'Egyptian Hieroglyphs', in C. Riggs (ed.), *The Oxford Handbook of Roman Egypt* (Oxford), 563–80.

Knigge, C. 2005. '"He Keeps the River Nile Flowing, the Field is Full of his Richness". Some Remarks on the Hymn to the Nile and Inundation and Fertility Motifs in Post-New Kingdom Hymns and Related Texts', in A. Amenta, M. M. Luiselli and M. N. Sordi (eds), *L'acqua nell'antico Egitto. Vita, rigenerazione, incantesimo, medicamento* (Rome), 59–67.

Köberlein, E. 1962. *Caligula und die ägyptischen Kulte* (Meisenheim).

Koelsch, W. A. 2004. 'Squinting Back at Strabo', *Geographical Review*, 94.4: 502–18.

Koenen, L. 1976. 'Egyptian Influence in Tibullus', *Illinois Classical Studies*, 1: 127–59.

Kolb, A. 2001. 'Transport and Communication in the Roman State. The cursus publicus', in C. E. P. Adams and R. M. Laurence (eds), *Travel and Geography in the Roman Empire* (London), 95–105.

2007. 'Raumwahrnehmung und Raumerschliessung durch römische Strassen', in M. Rathmann (ed.), *Wahrnehmung und Erfassung geographischer Räume in der Antike* (Mainz am Rhein), 169–80.

2016. 'The Romans and the World's Measure', in S. Bianchetti, M. R. Cataudella and H.-J. Gehrke (eds), *Brill's Companion to Ancient Geography. The Inhabited World in the Greek and Roman Tradition* (Leiden), 223–38.

König, A. 2009. 'From Architect to Imperator: Vitruvius and his Addressee in the *De Architectura*' in L. Taub and A. Doody (eds), *Authorial voices in Greco-Roman technical writing* (Trier), 31–52.

König, J. and G. Woolf. 2013. 'Encyclopaedism in the Roman Empire', in J. König and G. Woolf (eds), *Encyclopaedism from Antiquity to the Renaissance* (Cambridge), 23–63.

Konstan, D. 1978. 'The Politics of Tibullus 1.7', *Rivista di Studi Classici*, 26: 173–85.

Kostuch, L. 2009. 'Cleopatra's Snake or Octavian's? The Role of the Cobra in the Triumph over the Egyptian Queen', *Klio*, 91: 115–24.

Kraft, K. 1967. 'Der Sinn des Mausoleums des Augustus', *Historia*, 16: 189–206.

Kramer, N. 2000. 'Augustus, Cestius und die Pyramide', in M. Dreher (ed.), *Bürgersinn und Staatliche Macht in Antike und Gegenwart. Festschrift für Wolfgang Schuller zum 65. Geburtstag* (Constance), 181–90.

Kuttner, A. 1999. 'Hellenistic Images of Spectacle, from Alexander to Augustus', in B. Bergmann and C. Kondoleon (eds), *The Art of Ancient Spectacle*. Studies in the History of Art 56, Center for Advanced Study in the Visual Arts, Symposium Papers, 34 (New Haven, CT), 97–124.

Laborinho, E. M. 2005. 'Nun, the Primeval Water According to the Coffin Texts', in A. Amenta, M. M. Luiselli and M. N. Sordi (eds), *L'acqua nell'antico Egitto. Vita, rigenerazione, incantesimo, medicamento* (Rome), 221–7.

Laehn, T. R. 2013. *Pliny's Defense of Empire* (London).

Lambert, M. 2003. 'Tibullus 1.7: A Question of Tact?', in A. F. Basson and W. J. Dominik (eds), *Literature, Art, History: Studies on Classical Antiquity and Tradition in Honour of W. J. Henderson* (Bern), 47–60.

Lao, E. 2011. 'Luxury and the Creation of a Good Consumer', in R. K. Gibson and R. Morello (eds), *Pliny the Elder: Themes and Contexts* (Leiden), 35–56.

Lapidge, M. 1989. 'Stoic Cosmology and Roman Literature, First to Third Centuries AD', *Aufstieg und Niedergang der römischen Welt*, II.36.3: 1379–1429.

Leach, E. W. 1988. *The Rhetoric of Space. Literary and Artistic Representations of Landscape in Republican and Augustan Rome* (Princeton).

2004. *The Social Life of Painting in Ancient Rome and on the Bay of Naples* (Cambridge).

Leclant, J. 1976. 'Egypt, Land of Africa, in the Greco-Roman World', in J. Vercoutter, J. Leclant, F. M. Snowden Jr, and J. Desanges (eds), *The Image of the*

*Black in Western Art. I. From the Pharaohs to the Fall of the Roman Empire* (Cambridge, MA), 269–85.

1984. 'Un aspect des influences alexandrines en Gaule: les scènes nilotiques exhumées en France', in *Alessandria e il mondo ellenistico-romano. Studi in onore di Achille Adriani*, III (Rome), 440–4.

Lee-Stecum, P. 1998. *Powerplay in Tibullus: Reading Elegies Book One* (Cambridge).

Leemreize, M. 2014. 'The Egyptian Past in the Roman Present', in C. Pieper and J. Ker (eds), *Valuing the Past in the Greco-Roman World. Proceedings from the Penn-Leiden Colloquia on Ancient Values, VII* (Leiden), 56–82.

Lefebvre, H. 1991. *The Production of Space*, tr. Donald Nicholson Smith (Oxford).

Lehmann-Hartleben, K. 1926. *Die Trajanssäule: Ein römisches Kunstwerk zu Beginn der Spätantike*. Vol I (Berlin).

Lehoux, D. 2012. *What Did the Romans Know? An Inquiry into Science and World-making* (Chicago).

Leigh, M. 1997. *Lucan: Spectacle and Engagement* (Oxford).

2000. 'Lucan and the Libyan Tale', *Journal of Roman Studies*, 90: 95–109.

Lembke, K. 1994. *Das Iseum Campense in Rom. Studie über den Isiskult unter Domitian* (Heidelberg).

Lewin, K. 1936. *Principles of Topological Psychology* (New York).

Lewis, N. 1983. *Life in Egypt under Roman Rule* (Oxford).

Lightfoot, J. L. 2014. *Dionysius Periegetes. Description of the Known World. With Introduction, Text, Translation and Commentary* (Oxford).

Lindsay, J. 1968. *Men and Gods on the Roman Nile* (London).

Ling, R. 1977. 'Studius and the Beginning of Roman Landscape Painting', *Journal of Roman Studies*, 67: 1–16.

1990. 'I.10.4. Casa del Menandro', in I. Bragantini et al. (eds), *Pitture e pavimenti di Pompei*, 1 (Rome), 240–397.

1991. *Roman Painting* (Cambridge).

1993. 'The Paintings of the Columbarium of Villa Doria Pamphili in Rome', in E. M. Moormann (ed.), *Functional and Spatial Analysis of Wall Painting. Proceedings of the Fifth International Congress on Ancient Wall Painting*, Annual Papers on Classical Archaeology, Suppl. 3 (Leiden), 127–35.

Littlewood, A. R. 1987. 'Ancient Literary Evidence for the Pleasure Gardens of Roman Country Villas', in E. B. MacDougall (ed.), *Ancient Roman Villa Gardens*. Dumbarton Oaks Colloquium on the History of Landscape Architecture, 10 (Washington, DC), 9–30.

Livingstone, D. N. 1992. *The Geographical Tradition. Episodes in the History of a Contested Enterprise* (Oxford).

Locher, A. 1986. 'The Structure of Pliny the Elder's Natural History', in R. French and F. Greenaway (eds), *Science in the Early Roman Empire: Pliny the Elder, his Sources and Influence* (Totowa, NJ), 20–9.

Long, A. A. 1985. 'The Stoics on World-Conflagration and Everlasting Recurrence', *Southern Journal of Philosophy*, 23: 13–37.

Long, A. A. and D. N. Sedley (eds), 1987. *The Hellenistic Philosophers* (Cambridge).

Lozovsky, N. 2000. *The Earth is Our Book. Geographical Knowledge in the Latin West ca 400–1000* (Ann Arbor, MI).

Ludwig, E. 1937. *The Nile. The Life-Story of a River* (New York).

MacEachren, A. M. 1986. 'A Linear View of the World: Strip Maps as a Unique Form of Cartographic Representation', *American Cartographer*, 13.1: 7–25.

Mader, G. 1983. 'Some Observations on the Senecan Götterdämmerung', *Acta Classica*, 26: 61–71.

Maehler, H. 2003. 'Roman Poets on Egypt', in R. Matthews and C. Roemer (eds), *Ancient Perspectives on Egypt* (London), 203–16.

Maguire, H. 1999. 'The Nile and the Rivers of Paradise', in M. Piccirillo and E. Alliata (eds), *The Madaba Map Centenary 1897–1997. Travelling Through the Byzantine Umayyad Period*. Studium Biblicum Franciscanium, Collectio Maior, 40 (Jerusalem), 179–84.

Maiuri, A. 1927. 'Reg I Ins VII, Casa nn 10–12', *Notizie degli scavi di Antichità*, 3: 32–83.

——— 1938. *Le Pitture delle case di 'M. Fabius Amandio' del 'Sacerdos Amandus' e di 'P. Cornelius Teges' (Reg. I. Ins 7)*. Monumenti della Pittura Antica Scoperti in Italia. Sezione Terza, La Pittura Ellenistico-Romana. Pompei Fasc. II (Rome).

——— 1956. 'Une nuova pittura nilotica a Pompeii', *Memorie: Atti della Academia Nazionale dei Lincei*, 8 ser. 7: 65–80.

Malaise, M. 1972a. *Les conditions de pénétration et de diffusion des cultes égyptiens en Italie* (Leiden).

——— 1972b. *Inventaire préliminaire des documents égyptiens découverts en Italie* (Leiden).

——— 1985. 'Ciste et hydrie, symboles isiaques de la puissance et de la présence d'Osiris', in J. Ries (ed.), *Le symbolisme dans le culte des grandes religions. Actes du colloque de Louvain-la-Neuve 1983* (Louvain-la-Neuve), 125–53.

——— 2007. 'La diffusion des cultes isiaques: un problème de terminologie et de critique', in L. Bricault, M. J. Versluys and P. G. P. Meyboom (eds), *Nile into Tiber: Egypt in the Roman World. Proceedings of the IIIrd International Conference of Isis Studies, Leiden May 11–14 2005*, Religions in the Graeco-Roman World, 159 (Leiden), 19–39.

Manolaraki, E. 2011. 'Noscendi Nilum Cupido: The Nile Digression in Book 10', in P. Asso (ed.), *Brill's Companion to Lucan* (Leiden), 153–82.

——— 2013. *Noscendi Nilum Cupido. Imagining Egypt from Lucan to Philostratus* (Berlin).

Marcotte, D. (ed. and tr.), 2000. *Géographes Grecs. Tome 1. Introduction Générale. Ps.-Scymnos: Circuit de la Terre*, Collection des Universités de France, no.403 (Paris).

Marincola, J. 1997. *Authority and Tradition in Ancient Historiography* (Cambridge).

——— 2010. 'Eros and Empire: Virgil and the Historians on Civil War', in C. S. Kraus, J. Marincola, and C. Pelling (eds), *Ancient Historiography and its Contexts: Studies in Honour of A. J. Woodman* (Oxford), 183–204.

Martin, G. T. 2005. 'The Egyptian Temple in the Mosaic of Palestrina', in P. Jánosi (ed.), *Structure and Significance. Thoughts on Ancient Egyptian Architecture* (Vienna), 415–25.

Maspero, G. 1879. 'Les peintures des tombeaux Égyptiens et la mosaïque de Palestrine', *Gazette archéologique*, 5: 77–85.

Masters, J. 1992. *Poetry and Civil War in Lucan's Bellum Civile* (Cambridge).

Matthews, J. 2006. *The Journey of Theophanes: Travel, Business and Daily Life in Roman Egypt* (New Haven, CT).

Mattingly, D. J. 1995. *Tripolitania* (London).

  2000. 'Map 36 Garama', in R. J. A. Talbert, *The Barrington Atlas of the Greek and Roman World. Map-by-Map Directory* (Princeton), vol I: 545–51.

Mayer, R. 1986. 'Geography and the Roman Poets', *Greece and Rome*, 33: 47–54.

Mayerson, P. 1993. 'A Confusion of Indias: Asian India and African India in the Byzantine Sources', *Journal of the American Oriental Society*, 113: 169–74.

Mazzoli, G. 1970. *Seneca e la poesia* (Milan).

McCartney, E. S. 1920 'Spontaneous Generation and Kindred Notions in Antiquity', *Transactions of the American Philological Association*, 51: 101–15.

McClintock, A. 1995. *Imperial Leather. Race, Gender and Sexuality in the Colonial Contest* (London).

McCloskey, P. and E. Phinney, 1968. 'Ptolemaeus Tyrannus. The Typification of Nero in the Pharsalia', *Hermes*, 96: 80–7.

McDaniel, W. B. 1932. 'A Fresco Featuring Pygmies', *American Journal of Archaeology*, 36.3: 260–71.

McEwen, I. K. 2003. *Vitruvius. Writing the Body of Architecture* (Cambridge, MA)

McKay, M. 1985. Pygmy Landscapes in Roman Art. Ph.D. University of Toronto.

Melville, A. D. (tr.), 1986. *Ovid. Metamorphoses* (Oxford).

Mendels, D. 1990. 'The Polemical Character of Manetho's Aegyptiaca', in H. Verdin, G. Schepens and E. De Keyser (eds), *Purposes of History. Studies in Greek Historiography from the 4th to the 2nd centuries BC. Proceedings of the International Colloquium Leuven 24–26 May, 1988*, Studia Hellenistica, 30 (Leiden), 91–110.

Merrills, A. H. 2005. *History and Geography in Late Antiquity* (Cambridge).

Meyboom, P. G. P. 1995. *The Nile Mosaic of Palestrina. Early Evidence of Egyptian Religion in Italy* (Leiden).

Meyboom, P. G. P and M. J. Versluys, 2007. 'The Meaning of Dwarfs in Nilotic Scenes', in L. Bricault, M. J. Versluys and P. G. P. Meyboom (eds), *Nile into Tiber: Egypt in the Roman World. Proceedings of the IIIrd International Conference of Isis Studies, Leiden May 11–14 2005*, Religions in the Graeco-Roman World, 159 (Leiden), 170–208.

Michel, D. 1990. *Casa dei Cei*, Häuser in Pompeji, 3 (Munich).

Miller, K. 1895–97 *Mappaemundi. Die ältesten Weltkarten* (Stuttgart).

Mitchell, S. 1976. 'Requisitioned Transport in the Roman Empire: A New Inscription from Pisidia', *Journal of Roman Studies*, 66: 106–31.

Mitchell, T. 1988. *Colonising Egypt* (Berkeley).

Moatti, C. 1993. *Archives et partage de la terre dans le monde romain (IIe siècle avant-Ier siècle après J.-C.)*. Collection de l'Ecole française de Rome (Rome).

　1997. *La Raison de Rome. Naissance de l'esprit critique à la fin de la République (IIe-Ier siècles avant notre ère)* (Paris).

Moffitt, J. R. 1997. 'The Palestrina Mosaic with a "Nile Scene": Philostratus and Ekphrasis: Ptolemy and Chorographia', *Zeitschrift für Kunstgeschichte*, 60.2: 227–47.

Molholt, R. M. 2011. 'Roman Labyrinth Mosaics and the Experience of Motion', *Art Bulletin*, 93.3: 287–303.

Montiglio, S. 2006. 'Should the Aspiring Wise Man Travel? A Conflict in Seneca's Thought', *American Journal of Philology*, 127.4: 553–86.

Moore, T. J. 1989. 'Tibullus 1.7: Reconciliation through Conflict', *The Classical World*, 82: 423–30.

Moorehead, A. 1960. *The White Nile* (London).

　1962. *The Blue Nile* (London).

Moormann, E. M. 2007. 'The Temple of Isis at Pompeii', in L. Bricault, M. J. Versluys and P. G. P. Meyboom (eds), *Nile into Tiber: Egypt in the Roman World. Proceedings of the IIIrd International Conference of Isis Studies, Leiden May 11–14 2005*, Religions in the Greco-Roman World, 159 (Leiden), 137–54.

　2011. *Divine Interiors. Mural Paintings in Greek and Roman Sanctuaries* (Amsterdam).

Morello, R. 2011. 'Pliny and the Encyclopaedic Addressee', in R. K. Gibson and R. Morello (eds), *Pliny the Elder: Themes and Contexts* (Leiden), 147–66.

Morris, J. 2016. 'From Imperator to Agrimensor: Lines of Power'. Unpubl. PhD Thesis. University of Leicester.

Morrison, D. 2010. *The Black Nile: One Man's Amazing Journey Through Peace and War on the World's Longest River* (New York).

Morrissey, J. 2013a. 'Imperialism and Empire', in J. Morrissey, D. Nally, U. Strohmayer and Y. Whelan (eds), *Key Concepts in Historical Geography* (Los Angeles), 17–25.

　2013b. 'The Imperial Present: Geography, Imperialism and its Continued Effects', in N. C. Johnson, R. H. Schein and J. Winders (eds), *The Wiley-Blackwell Companion to Cultural Geography* (Malden), 494–507.

Mouritsen, H. 1988. *Elections, Magistrates and the Municipal Elite: Studies in Pompeian Epigraphy*. Analecta Romana Instituti Danici Supplement 5 (Rome).

Moynihan, R. 1985. 'Geographical Mythology and Roman Imperial Ideology', in Rolf Winkes (ed.), *The Age of Augustus* (Providence, RI), 149–62.

Mozley, J. H. 1929. *Ovid. The Art of Love and Other Poems*, LCL (Cambridge, MA).

Müller, C. 1861. *Geographi Graeci Minores*, 2 vols (Paris).

Mulvey, L. 1975. 'Visual Pleasure and Narrative Cinema', *Screen*, 163: 6–18

Murphy, T. 2003. 'Pliny's *Naturalis Historia*: the Prodigal Text', in A. J. Boyle and W. J. Dominik (eds), *Flavian Rome: Culture, Image, Text* (Leiden), 301–322.

　2004. *Pliny the Elder's Natural History. The Empire in the Encyclopedia* (Oxford).

Murray, O. 1970. 'Hecataeus of Abdera and Pharaonic Kingship', *Journal of Egyptian Archaeology*, 56: 141–71.

Mutschler, F.-H. and A. Mittag (eds), 2008. *Conceiving the Empire. China and Rome Compared* (Oxford).

Myers, K. S. 1994. *Ovid's Causes. Cosmogony and Aetiology in the Metamorphoses* (Ann Arbor, MI).

Myers, M. Y. 2011. 'Lucan's Poetic Geographies: Center and Periphery in Civil War Epic', in P. Asso (ed.), *Brill's Companion to Lucan* (Leiden), 399–415.

Naas, V. 2002. *Le projet encyclopédique de Pline l'Ancien* (Rome).

2011. 'Imperialism, mirabilia and Knowledge: Some Paradoxes in the *Naturalis Historia*', in R. K. Gibson and R. Morello (eds), *Pliny the Elder: Themes and Contexts* (Leiden), 57–70.

Nappa, C. 2005. *Reading After Actium. Vergil's Georgics, Octavian, and Rome* (Ann Arbor, MI).

Nasrallah, L. 2005. 'Mapping the World: Justin, Tatian, Lucian and the Second Sophistic', *Harvard Theological Review*, 98.3: 283–314.

Nelis, D. 2009. 'Ovid, Metamorphoses 1.416–51: *noua monstra* and the *foedera naturae*', in P. Hardie (ed.), *Paradox and the Marvellous in Augustan Literature and Culture* (Oxford), 248–67.

Neudecker, R. 2005. 'Die Pyramide des Cestius', in L. Giuliani (ed.), *Meisterwerke der Antiken Kunst* (Munich), 94–113.

Nicolet, C. 1988. *L'Inventaire du Monde. Géographie et politique aux origins de l'Empire romain* (Paris).

1991. *Space, Geography and Politics in the Early Roman Empire*. Jerome Lectures, 19 (Ann Arbor, MI).

Nicolet, C. and P. Gautier-Dalché. 1986. 'Les "quatre sages" de Jules César et la "mesure du monde" selon Julius Honorius: Realité antique et tradition médiévale', *Journal des savants*, 157–218.

Nisbet, R. G. M. 1982–4/1995. 'Sacrilege in Egypt (Lucan 9.150–161)', *Acta Antiqua Scientiarum Hungaricae*, 30: 309–17; repr in his *Collected Papers on Latin Literature* (Oxford), 182–91.

O'Gorman, E. 1995. 'Shifting Ground: Lucan, Tacitus and the Landscape of Civil War', *Hermathena*, 158: 117–31.

O'Rourke, K. 2013. *Walking and Mapping. Artists as Cartographers* (Cambridge, MA).

O'Sullivan, T. M. 2011. *Walking in Roman Culture* (Cambridge).

Oldfather, C. H. (ed. and tr.), 1933. *Diodorus Siculus. Library of History*, LCL (Cambridge, MA).

Orlin, E. M. 2008. 'Octavian and the Egyptian Cults: Redrawing the Boundaries of Romanness', *American Journal of Philology*, 129: 231–53.

Östenberg, I. 2009. *Staging the World. Spoils, Captives, and Representations in the Roman Triumphal Procession*. Oxford Studies in Ancient Culture and Representation (Oxford).

Ozanam, A.-M. 1990. 'Le mystère et le sacré dans la stoïcisme romain à l'époque néronienne', *Bulletin de l'Association Guillaume Budé*, 3: 278–88.

Panayides, A. M. 1994. 'Überlegungen zum Nilmosaik von Praeneste', *Hefte des Archäologischen Seminars der Universität Bern*, 15: 31–47.

Parker, G. 2007. 'Obelisks Still in Exile: Monuments Made to Measure?', in L. Bricault, M. J. Versluys and P. G. P. Meyboom (eds), *Nile into Tiber: Egypt in the Roman World. Proceedings of the IIIrd International Conference of Isis Studies, Leiden May 11–14 2005*, Religions in the Greco-Roman World, 159 (Leiden), 209–22.

 2008. *The Making of Roman India* (Cambridge).

Parlasca, K. 1994. 'Zur Problematik des Nilmosaiks von Palestrina', in P. Johnson, R. Ling and D. J. Smith (eds), *Fifth International Colloquium on Ancient Mosaics, Bath 1987* (Ann Arbor, MI), 41–4.

Parroni, P. G. 1965. *Vibius Sequester. De Fluminibus, fontibus, lacubus etc.* (Milan).

 1984. *Pomponii Melae. De Chorographia, Libri Tres*. Storia e Letteratura, Raccolta di Studi e Testi, 160 (Rome).

Partsch, J. 1875. *Die Darstellung Europas in dem geographischen Werke des Agrippa*, Habilitationsschrift (Breslau).

 1907. Review of Detlefsen 1906, *Wochenschrift für Klassische Philologie*, 24: 1053–62.

Pascal, C. 1903. *Studii critici su poema di Lucrezio* (Rome).

Pearce, S. J. 2007. *The Land of the Body. Studies in Philo's Representation of Egypt*. Wissenschaftliche Untersuchungen zum Neuen Testament, 208 (Tübingen).

Pellacani, D. 2012. 'Le piene del Nilo. Nota Bibliografica', in M. Beretta, F. Citti and L. Pasetti (eds), *Seneca e le scienze naturali* (Florence), 81–92.

Peters, W. J. T. 1963. *Landscape in Romano-Campanian Mural Painting* (Assen).

Petrain, D. 2014. *Homer in Stone. The Tabulae Iliacae in their Roman Context* (Cambridge).

Pfeiffer, S. 2010. 'Ägypten in der Selbstdarstellung der Flavier', in N. Kramer and C. Reitz (eds), *Tradition und Erneuerung. Mediale Strategien in der Zeit der Flavier* (Berlin), 273–88.

Phillips, R. 1997. *Mapping Men and Empire. A Geography of Adventure* (London).

Piper, K. 2002. *Cartographic Fictions. Maps, Race and Identity* (New Brunswick).

Pittenger, M. R. P. 2008. *Contested Triumphs. Politics, Pageantry and Performance in Livy's Republican Rome* (Berkeley).

Pollard, E. A. 2009. 'Pliny's Natural History and the Flavian Templum Pacis: Botanical Imperialism in First-Century CE Rome', *Journal of World History*, 20: 309–38.

Pollini, J. 1992. 'The Tazza Farnese: Augusto Imperatore "Redeunt Saturnia Regna!"'. *American Journal of Archaeology*, 96.2: 283–300.

Porter, J. I. 2007. 'Lucretius and the Sublime', in S. Gillespie and P. Hardie (eds), *The Cambridge Companion to Lucretius* (Cambridge), 167–84.

Postl, B. 1970. *Die Bedeutung des Nil in der römischen Literatur* (Vienna).

Pothecary, S. 2002. 'Strabo, the Tiberian Author: Past, Present and Silence in Strabo's Geography', *Mnemosyne*, 55.4: 387–438.

Powell, A. (ed.), 1992. *Roman Poetry and Propaganda in the Age of Augustus* (London).

Pratt, M. L. 2008. *Imperial Eyes. Travel Writing and Transculturation*, 2nd edn (Abingdon).

Prontera, F. 1984. 'Prima di Strabone: materiali per uno studio della geografia antica come genere letterario' in F. Prontera (ed.), *Strabone: contribute allo studio della personalità e dell'opera* (Perugia), 187–256.

1993/2011. 'Sull'esegesi Ellenistica della Geografia Omerica', *Philantropia kai Eusebia, Festschrift für Albrecht Dihle zum 70. Geburtstag* (Göttingen), 387–97, repr in his *Geografia e storia nella Grecia antica* (Florence, 2011), 3–14.

2002. 'Geografia', in C. Santini, I. Mastrorosa and A. Zumbo (eds), *Letteratura Scientifica e tecnica di Grecia e Roma* (Rome), 225–45.

2006/2011. 'Geografia e Corografia: Note sul lessico della cartografia antica', *Pallas*, 72: 75–82, repr in his *Geografia e storia nella Grecia antica* (Florence, 2011), 95–104.

2011. *Geografia e storia nella Grecia antica* (Florence).

2016. 'Strabo's Geography', in S. Bianchetti, M. R. Cataudella and H.-J. Gehrke (eds), *Brill's Companion to Ancient Geography. The Inhabited World in the Greek and Roman Tradition* (Leiden), 239–58.

Purcell, N. 1987. 'Town in Country and Country in Town', in E. B. MacDougall (ed.), *Ancient Roman Villa Gardens*. Dumbarton Oaks Colloquium on the History of Landscape Architecture, 10 (Washington, DC), 187–203.

1990a. 'The Creation of Provincial Landscape: the Roman Impact on Cisalpine Gaul', in T. Blagg and M. Millett (eds), *The Early Roman Empire in the West* (Oxford) 7–29.

1990b. 'Maps, Lists, Money, Order and Power', review of Nicolet 1988. in *Journal of Roman Studies*, 80: 178–82.

Purves, A. C. 2010. *Space and Time in Ancient Greek Narrative* (Cambridge).

Quint, D. 1992. *Epic and Empire. Politics and Generic Form from Virgil to Milton* (Princeton).

Rackham, H. (ed. and tr.), 1940. *Pliny. Natural History*. LCL 10 vols (Cambridge, MA).

Radt, S. (ed.), 2002–2011 *Strabons Geographika*. 10 vols (Göttingen).

Rathmann, M. 2012. 'The Tabula Peutingeriana in the Mirror of Ancient Cartography. Aspects of a Reappraisal', in K. Geus and M. Rathmann (eds), *Vermessung der Oikumene* (Berlin), 203–22.

2013. 'Kartographie in der Antike. Überlieferte Fakten, bekannte Fragen, neue Perspektiven', in D. Boschung, T. Greub and J. Hammerstaedt (eds), *Geographische Kenntnisse und ihre konkreten Ausformungen* (Munich), 11–49.

2016. 'The Tabula Peutingeriana and Antique Cartography', in S. Bianchetti, M. R. Cataudella and H.-J. Gehrke (eds), *Brill's Companion to Ancient Geography. The Inhabited World in the Greek and Roman Tradition* (Leiden), 337–62.

Rauch, M. 1999. *Bacchische Themen und Nilbilder auf Campanareliefs*, Internationale Archäologie, 52 (Leidorf).

Rawson, E. 1985. *Intellectual Life in the Late Roman Republic* (London).

Reardon, B. P. 1989. *Collected Ancient Greek Novels* (Berkeley).

Reed, J. D. 2011. 'The Bellum Civile as Roman Epic', in P. Asso (ed.), *Brill's Companion to Lucan* (Leiden), 21–31.

Reinhold, M. 1980. 'Roman Attitudes Toward Egyptians', *Ancient Society*, 3: 97–103.

Rice, E. E. 1983. *The Grand Procession of Ptolemy Philadelphus* (Oxford).

Richards, T. 1993. *The Imperial Archive. Knowledge and the Fantasy of Empire* (London).

Richardson, L. 1974. *Propertius. Elegies I-IV. Edited, with an Introduction and Commentary* (Norman, OK).

Richlin, A. (ed.), 1992. *Pornography and Representation in Greece and Rome* (Oxford)

Ricotti, E. S. P. 1987. 'The Importance of Water in Roman Garden Triclinia', in E. B. Macdougall (ed.), *Ancient Roman Villa Gardens*, Dumbarton Oaks Colloquium on the History of Landscape Architecture, 10 (Washington, DC), 135–84.

Ridley, R. T. 1992. 'The Praetor and the Pyramid. The Tomb of Gaius Cestius in History, Archaeology and Literature', *Bulletino di archeologia*, 13: 1–29.

Riese, A. 1878. *Geographi Latini Minores* (Heidelberg).

Riggs, C. (ed.), 2012. *The Oxford Handbook of Roman Egypt* (Oxford).

Rodriguez, C. 1992. 'The Porticus Vipsania and Contemporary Poetry', *Latomus*, 51: 79–93.

Rodriguez-Almeida, E. 2002. *Formae Urbis Antiquae. Le mappe marmoree di Roma tra la Repubblica e Settimo Severo* (Rome).

Rolfe, J. C. (ed. and tr.). 1979. *Suetonius*, LCL 2 vols (Cambridge, MA).

Roller, D. W. 2003. *The World of Juba II and Kleopatra Selene* (London).

   (tr.), 2014. *The Geography of Strabo* (Cambridge).

Roller, M. B. 2001. *Constructing Autocracy: Aristocrats and Emperors in Julio-Claudian Rome* (Princeton).

Romer, F. E. 1998. *Pomponius Mela's Description of the World* (Ann Arbor, MI).

Romm, J. 1994. *The Edges of the Earth in Ancient Thought* (Princeton).

Rosati, G. 2009. 'Latrator Anubis: Alien Divinities in Augustan Rome, and How to Tame Monsters through Aetiology', in P. Hardie (ed.), *Paradox and the Marvellous in Augustan Literature and Culture* (Oxford), 268–87.

Rossi, A. 2005. 'Sine fine: Caesar's Journey to Egypt and the End of Lucan's Bellum Civile', in C. Walde (ed.), *Lucan im 21 Jahrhundert. Lucan in the 21st Century. Lucano nei primi del XXI secolo* (Munich), 237–60.

Rossi, P. 2012. 'La piene del Nilo nelle Naturales Quaestiones di Seneca', in M. Beretta, F. Citti and L. Pasetti (eds), *Seneca e le scienze naturali* (Florence), 69–80.

Rostovtzeff, M. 1911. 'Die hellenistisch-römische Architekturlandschaft', *Mitteilungen des Deutschen Archäologischen Instituts, Römische Abteilung*, 26: 1–186.

   1941. *The Social and Economic History of the Hellenistic World* (Oxford).

Rotsch, H. 2005. 'The Primeval Ocean Nun and the Terminology of Water in Ancient Egypt', in A. Amenta, M. M. Luiselli and M. N. Sordi (eds), *L'acqua nell'antico Egitto. Vita, rigenerazione, incantesimo, medicamento* (Rome), 229–40.

Roullet, A. 1972. *The Egyptian and Egyptianizing Monuments of Imperial Rome* (Leiden).

Rouveret, A. 2003. *Pline l'Ancien. Histoire Naturelle. Livre XXXVI*, Budé (Paris).

2004. 'Pictos ediscere mundos. Perception et imaginaire du paysage dans la peinture hellénistique et romaine', *Ktèma*, 29: 325–44.

Rowland, I. D. and T. N. Howe (ed. and tr.), 1999. *Vitruvius. Ten Books on Architecture* (Cambridge).

Rudich, V. 1993. *Political Dissidence under Nero: The Price of Dissimulation* (London).

Runia, D. T. 1999. 'What is Doxography?' in P. J. van der Eijk (ed.), *Ancient Histories of Medicine: Essays in Medical Doxography and Historiography in Classical Antiquity*, Studies in Ancient Medicine, 20 (Leiden), 33–55.

Rusch, P. 1882. *De Posidonio Lucreti Cari auctore in carmine De rerum natura 6* (Jena).

Rutherford, I. C. 2000. 'The Genealogy of the *Boukoloi:* How Greek Literature Appropriated an Egyptian Narrative-Motif', *Journal of Hellenic Studies*, 120: 106–21.

2012. 'Travel and Pilgrimage', in C. Riggs (ed.), *The Oxford Handbook of Roman Egypt* (Oxford), 701–16.

Rutledge, S. H. 2009a. 'Writing Imperial Politics: The Social and Political Background', in W. J. Dominik, J. Garthwaite and P. A. Roche (eds), *Writing Politics in Imperial Rome* (Leiden), 23–61.

2009b. 'Reading the Prince: Textual Politics in Tacitus and Pliny', in W. J. Dominik, J. Garthwaite and P. A. Roche (eds), *Writing Politics in Imperial Rome* (Leiden), 429–46.

2012. *Ancient Rome as a Museum. Power, Identity and the Culture of Collecting* (Oxford).

Ryan, S. 1996. *The Cartographic Eye. How Explorers Saw Australia* (Cambridge).

Said, E. 1978. *Orientalism* (London).

1993. *Culture and Imperialism* (London).

Sallmann, K. G. 1971. *Die Geographie des älteren Plinius in ihrem Verhältnis zu Varro. Versuch einer Quellenanalyse* (Berlin).

Salway, R. W. B. 2001. 'Travel, Itineraria and Tabellaria', in C. E. P. Adams and R. M. Laurence (eds), *Travel and Geography in the Roman World* (London), 22–66.

2004. 'Sea and River Travel in the Roman Itinerary Literature', in R. Talbert and K. Brodersen (eds), *Space in the Roman World. Its Perception and Presentation.* Antike Kultur und Geschichte, 5 (Münster), 43–96.

2007. 'The Perception and Description of Space in Roman Itineraries', in M. Rathmann (ed.), *Wahrnehmung und Erfassung geographischer Räume in der Antike* (Mainz am Rhein), 181–209.

Sampaolo, V. 1991. 'II.4.3. Villa di Giulia Felice', in in *Pompei. Pitture e Mosaici III. Regiones II-III-V* (Rome), 184–310.

1992. 'La decorazione pittorica', in *Alla ricerca di Iside. Analisi, studi e restauri dell'Iseo pompeiano nel Museo di Napoli* (Naples), 23–39.

1998a. 'VIII.2.17: Complesso a sei piani delle Terme del Sarno', in Bragantini et al., *Pitture e pavimenti di Pompei* 8 (Rome), 94–135.

1998b. 'VIII.7.28. Tempio di Iside', in Bragantini et al., *Pitture e pavimenti di Pompei* 8 (Rome, 1998d), 732–849.

Schmidt, M. G. 1982. 'Zur Kritik Neros im zehnten Buch der 'Pharsalia', *Zeitschrift für Papyrologie und Epigraphik*, 49: 45–50.

1986. *Caesar und Cleopatra. Philologischer und historischer Kommentar zu Lucan 10,1-171*, Studien zur klassischen Philologie, 25 (Frankfurt).

Schepens, G. and K. Delacroix. 1996. 'Ancient Paradoxography: Origin, Evolution, Production and Reception, Part I: the Hellenistic Period and Part II: The Roman Period', in O. Pecere and A. Stramaglia (eds), *La letteratura di consumo nel mondo Greco-latino* (Cassino), 373–409.

Schnabel, P. 1935. 'Die Weltkarte des Agrippa als wissenschaftliches Mittelglied zwischen Hipparch und Ptolemaeus', *Philologus*, 90: 405–40.

Schrijvers, P. H. 2005. 'The "Two Cultures" in Lucan. Some Remarks on Lucan's Pharsalia and Ancient Sources of Nature', in C. Walde (ed.), *Lucan im 21. Jahrhundert. Lucan in the 21st Century. Lucano nei primi del XXI secolo* (Munich), 26–39.

2007. 'A Literary View of the Nile Mosaic at Praeneste', in L. Bricault, M. J. Versluys and P. G. P. Meyboom (eds), *Nile into Tiber: Egypt in the Roman World. Proceedings of the IIIrd International Conference of Isis Studies, Leiden May 11–14 2005*, Religions in the Greco-Roman World, 159 (Leiden), 223–39.

2009. 'In Praise of Messalla. Hellenistic Geography in Three Roman Panegyric Poems', in M. A. Harder, R. F. Regtuit and G. C. Wakker (eds), *Nature and Science in Hellenistic Poetry*, Hellenistica Groningana, 15 (Leuven), 149–76.

Shackleton-Bailey, D. R. 2003. *Statius. Silvae*. LCL (Cambridge, MA).

Sharples, R. W. 1998. *Theophrastus of Eresus. Sources for his Life, Writings, Thought and Influence. Commentary Volume 3.1. Sources on Physics (Texts 137–223)* (Leiden).

Shcheglov, D. A. 2014. 'Pomponius Mela's Chorography and Hellenistic Scientific Geography', in A. V. Podossinov (ed.), *The Periphery of the Classical World in Ancient Geography* Colloquia Antiqua, 12 (Leuven), 77–94.

Sherk, R. K. 1974. 'Roman Geographical Exploration and Military Maps', *Aufstieg und Niedergang der römischen Welt*, II.1 (Berlin), 534–62.

Shipley, G. 2011. *Pseudo-Skylax's Periplous: The Circumnavigation of the Inhabited World. Text, Translation and Commentary* (Exeter).

Shumate, N. 2006. *Nation, Empire, Decline. Studies in Rhetorical Continuity from the Romans to the Modern Era* (London).

Siard, H. 2007. 'L'Hydreion du Sarapieion C de Délos: la divinisation de l'eau dans un sanctuaire isiaque', in L. Bricault, M. J. Versluys and P. G. P. Meyboom (eds), *Nile into Tiber: Egypt in the Roman World. Proceedings of the IIIrd International Conference of Isis Studies, Leiden May 11–14 2005*, Religions in the Graeco-Roman World, 159 (Leiden), 417–47.

Sidebotham, S. E. 1986. 'Aelius Gallus and Arabia', *Latomus*, 45.3: 590–602.

Siebert, G. 1999. 'Sur la mosaïque nilotique de Préneste. Problèmes d'iconographie, de chronologie et de style', *Ktèma*, 24: 251–8.

Silberman, A. (ed. and tr.), 1988. *Pomponius Mela. Chorographie* Budé (Paris).

Sinclair, P. 2003. 'Rhetoric of Writing and Reading in the Preface to Pliny's Historia Naturalis', in A. J. Boyle and W. J. Dominik (eds), *Flavian Rome: Culture, Image, Text* (Leiden), 277–300.

Sirago, V. A. 1994. 'Il contributo di Guiba II alla conoscenza dell'Africa', *Africa Romana*, 11: 303–17.

Skempis, M. (ed.), 2013. *Geography, Topography, Landscape. Configurations of Space in Greek and Roman Epic* (Munich).

Skempis, M. and I. Ziogas 2013. 'Introduction: Putting Epic Space in Context', in M. Skempis (ed.), *Geography, Topography, Landscape. Configurations of Space in Greek and Roman Epic* (Munich), 1–18.

Skinner, J. E. 2012. *The Invention of Greek Ethnography* (Oxford).

Sklenář, R. 1999. 'Cosmology and Catonian Ethics in Lucan's "Bellum Civile"', *American Journal of Philology*, 120.2: 281–96.

    2003. *The Taste for Nothingness. A Study of Virtus and Related Themes in Lucan's Bellum Civile* (Ann Arbor, MI).

Smelik, K. A. D. and E. A. Hemelrijk, 1984. 'Who Knows not what Monsters Demented Egypt Worships? Opinions on Egyptian Animal Worship in Antiquity as Part of the Ancient Conception of Egypt', *Aufstieg und Niedergang der römischen Welt*, II.17.4: 1852–2000.

Smith, R. R. R. 1988. 'Simulacra Gentium: The Ethne from the Sebasteion at Aphrodisias', *Journal of Roman Studies*, 78: 50–77.

Soja, E. W. 1989. *Postmodern Geographies: The Reassertion of Space in Critical Social Theory* (London).

Sonnabend, H. 1986. *Fremdenbild und Politik: Vorstellungen der Römer von Ägypten und dem Partherreich in der späten Republik und frühen Kaiserzeit* (Frankfurt).

Spano, G. 1955. 'Paesaggio nilotico con pigmei difendentisi magicamente dai coccodrilli', *Memorie: Atti della Academia Nazionale dei Lincei*, 8.6: 335–68.

Speidel, M. P. 1988. 'Nubia's Roman Garrison', *Aufstieg und Niedergang der römischen Welt*, II.10.1: 77–5.

Spencer, D. 2002. *The Roman Alexander* (Exeter).

    2005. *Roman Landscape: Culture and Identity*. Greece and Rome. New Surveys in the Classics, 39 (Cambridge).

Spoerri, W. 1959. *Späthellenistische Berichte über Welt, Kultur und Götter*, Schweizerische Beiträge zur Altertumswissenschaft, 9 (Basel).

Squire, M. 2009. *Image and Text in Graeco-Roman Antiquity* (Cambridge).

    2011. *The Iliad in a Nutshell: Visualizing Epic on the Tabulae Iliacae* (Oxford).

Stanley, H. M. 1899. *Through the Dark Continent. 1899 edn* 2 vols (London).

Starkey, P. and J. Starkey (eds), 2001. *Travellers in Egypt* (London).

Steinmeyer-Schareika, A. 1978. *Das Nilmosaik von Palestrina und eine ptolemäische Expedition nach Äthiopien* (Bonn).

Stephens, S. A. 2002a. 'Egyptian Callimachus', in L. Lehnus and F. Montanari, *Callimaque*, Entretiens Hardt, XLVIII (Vandoeuvres), 235–70.

2002b. *Seeing Double* (Berkeley).

Stewart, P. 2003. *Statues in Roman Society: Representation and Response* (Oxford).

2008. *Social History of Roman Art* (Cambridge).

Stewart, S. 1993 *On Longing. Narratives of the Miniature, the Gigantic, the Souvenir, the Collection* (Durham).

Stinson, P. 2011. 'Perspective Systems in Roman Second Style Wall Painting', *American Journal of Archaeology*, 115.3: 403–26.

Stückelberger, A. 1994. *Bild und Wort. Das illustrierte Fachbuch in der antiken Naturwissenschaft, Medizin und Technik* (Mainz).

Sullivan, J. P. 1985. *Literature and Politics in the Age of Nero* (Ithaca, NY).

Swetnam-Burland, M. 2007. 'Egyptian Objects, Roman Contexts: A Taste for Aegyptiaca in Italy', in L. Bricault, M. J. Versluys and P. G. P. Meyboom (eds), *Nile into Tiber: Egypt in the Roman World. Proceedings of the IIIrd International Conference of Isis Studies, Leiden May 11–14 2005*, Religions in the Greco-Roman World, 159 (Leiden), 113–36.

2009. 'Egypt Embodied: The Vatican Nile', *American Journal of Archaeology*, 113: 439–57.

2010. 'Aegyptus Redacta': The Egyptian Obelisk in the Augustan Campus Martius', *The Art Bulletin*, 92.3: 135–53.

2011. 'Egyptian Priests in Roman Italy', in E. Gruen (ed.), *Cultural Identity in the Ancient Mediterranean* (Los Angeles), 336–53.

2015. *Egypt in Italy. Visions of Egypt in Roman Imperial Culture* (Cambridge).

Syed, Y. 2005. *Vergil's Aeneid and the Roman Self. Subject and Nation in Literary Discourse* (Ann Arbor, MI).

Syme, R. 1939. *The Roman Revolution* (Oxford).

1974/1984. *The Crisis of 2 BC*. Sitzungsberichte der Bayerischen Akademie der Wissenschaften, 7 (Munich, 1974); repr. in his *Roman Papers*, vol 3 (Oxford).

1988. 'Military Geography at Rome', *Classical Antiquity*, 7: 227–51.

Tait, J. 2003. 'The Wisdom of Egypt: Classical Views', in P. Ucko and T. Champion (eds), *The Wisdom of Egypt: Changing Visions through the Ages*, Encounters with Ancient Egypt (London), 23–38.

Takács, S. A. 1995a 'Alexandria in Rome', *Harvard Studies in Classical Philology*, 97: 263–76.

1995b. *Isis and Sarapis in the Roman World*. EPRO, 124 (Leiden).

Talbert, R. J. A. 1989. Review of Nicolet 1988, in *The American Historical Review*, 94.5: 1351.

2008. 'The World in the Roman Traveler's Hand and Head', in J. Rubio Tovar, M. Vallejo Girvés and F. J. Gómez Espelosín (eds), *Viajes y visions del mundo*, Ediciones Clásicas & Canales, 7: 109–28.

2010a. *Rome's World. The Peutinger Map Reconsidered* (Cambridge).

2010b. 'The Roman Worldview: Beyond Recovery?', in K. A. Raaflaub and R. J. A. Talbert (eds), *Geography and Ethnography. Perceptions of the World in pre-modern Societies* (Malden, MA), 252–72.

2012. 'Urbs Roma to Orbis Romanus: Roman Mapping on the Grand Scale', in R. J. A. Talbert (ed.), *Ancient Perspectives. Maps and their Place in Mesopotamia, Egypt, Greece and Rome* (Chicago), 163–92.

Tammisto, A. 2005. 'The Nile Mosaic of Palestrina Reconsidered: The Problematic Reconstruction, Identification and Dating of the so-called Lower Complex with the Nile Mosaic and Fish Mosaic of Ancient Praeneste', *Collection de l'École française de Rome*, 352: 3–24.

Tan, Z. M. 2014. 'Subversive Geography in Tacitus' Germania', *Journal of Roman Studies*, 104: 181–204.

Taub, L. 2003. *Ancient Meteorology* (London).

2008. *Aetna and the Moon. Explaining Nature in Ancient Greece and Rome* (Corvallis, OR).

Taub, L. and A. Doody (eds), 2009. *Authorial Voices in Greco-Roman Technical Writing* (Trier).

Thiering, M. 2014. 'Implicit Knowledge Structures as Mental Models in Common Sense Geography', in K. Geus and M. Thiering (eds), *Features of Common Sense Geography. Implicit Knowledge Structures in Ancient Geographical Texts*, Antike Kultur und Geschichte, 16 (Berlin), 265–317.

Thissen, H.-J. 2006. 'Zum Hieroglyphen-Buch des Chairemon', in G. Moers et al. (eds), *jn.t-Dr.w: Festschrift für Friedrich Junge* (Göttingen), II: 625–34.

2009. 'Plutarch und die ägyptische Sprache', *Zeitschrift für Papyrologie und Epigraphik*, 168 (2009), 97–106.

Thomas, R. F. 1982. *Lands and Peoples in Roman Poetry: The Ethnographical Tradition* (Cambridge).

2010. 'The Germania as a Literary Text', in A. J. Woodman (ed.), *The Cambridge Companion to Tacitus* (Cambridge), 59–72.

Thomas, R. 1994. 'Literacy and the City-State in Archaic and Classical Greece', in A. K. Bowman and G. Woolf (eds), *Literacy and Power in the Ancient World* (Cambridge), 33–50.

Thompson, L. A. 1969. 'Eastern Africa and the Graeco-Roman World (to AD 641)', in L. A. Thompson and J. Ferguson (eds), *Africa in Classical Antiquity* (Ibadan), 26–61.

Tierney, J. J. 1963. 'The Map of Agrippa', *Proceedings of the Royal Irish Academy*, 63C: 151–63.

Todd, R. B. 1989. 'The Stoics and their Cosmology in the First and Second Centuries AD', *Aufstieg und Niedergang der römischen Welt*, II.36.3: 1365–78.

Tracy, J. 2011. 'Internal Evidence for the Completeness of the Bellum Civile', in P. Asso (ed.), *Brill's Companion to Lucan* (Leiden), 33–53.

2014. *Lucan's Egyptian Civil War* (Cambridge).

Tran Tam Tinh, V. 1964. *Essai sur le culte d'Isis à Pompéi* (Paris).

1971. *Le culte des divinités orientales à Herculanum* (Leiden).

1972. *Le culte des divinités orientales en Campanie: en dehors de Pompéi, de Stabies et d'Herculanum* (Leiden).

1983. *Sérapis debout: corpus des monuments de Sérapis debout et étude iconographique* (Leiden).

Trimble, J. 2008. 'Process and Transformation on the Severan Marble Plan of Rome', in R. J. A. Talbert and R. W. Unger (eds), *Cartography in Antiquity and the Middle Ages. Fresh Perspectives, New Methods* (Leiden), 67–97.

Trousset, P. 1993. 'La "carte d'Agrippa": nouvelle proposition de lecture', *Dialogues d'histoire ancienne*, 19.2: 137–57.

Turcan, R. 1967. *Sénèque et les religions orientales*, Coll. Lat. 91 (Brussels).

Twain, M. 1883. *Life on the Mississippi* (London), repr. London 1984.

Tybout, R. A. 2003. 'Dwarfs in Discourse: The Functions of Nilotic Scenes and Other Roman Aegyptiaca', *Journal of Roman Archaeology*, 16: 505–15

Valladares, H. 2012. 'Fallax Imago: Ovid's Narcissus and the Seduction of Mimesis in Roman Wall Painting', *Word & Image: A Journal of Verbal/Visual Enquiry*, 27: 4.

Van der Eijk, P. 1999. 'Historical Awareness, Historiography and Doxography in Greek and Roman Medicine', P. J. van der Eijk (ed.), *Ancient Histories of Medicine: Essays in Medical Doxography and Historiography in Classical Antiquity*, Studies in Ancient Medicine, 20 (Leiden), 1–31.

van der Horst, P. W. 1984. *Chaeremon. Egyptian Priest and Stoic Philosopher. The Fragments Collected and Translated with Explanatory Notes* (Leiden).

van der Vliet, E. C. L. 2003. 'The Romans and Us: Strabo's Geography and the Construction of Ethnicity', *Mnemosyne*, 56.3: 257–72.

van Paasen, C. 1957. *The Classical Tradition of Geography* (Groningen).

Vantini, G. 1994–95a. 'La conoscenza del Nilo nei classici greci e romani', *Nubica*, 4–5: 337–45.

1994–95b. 'Rileggendo il passo di Plinio sulla spedizione di Nerone nel Sudan', *Nubica*, 4–5: 351–3.

Vasaly, A. 1993. *Representations. Images of the World in Ciceronian Oratory* (Berkeley).

Vasunia, P. 2001. *The Gift of the Nile. Hellenizing Egypt from Aeschylus to Alexander* (Berkeley).

Versluys, M. J. 2002. *Aegyptiaca Romana. Nilotic Scenes and the Roman Views of Egypt*, Religions in the Greco-Roman World, 144 (Leiden).

1997. 'The Sanctuary of Isis on the Campus Martius in Rome. A Review Article', *Bulletin antieke beschaving. Annual Papers on Classical Archaeology*, 72: 159–69.

Veyne, P. 2005. *L'Empire Gréco-Romain* (Paris).

2003. *Seneca. The Life of a Stoic* tr. D. Sullivan (New York).

Vidman, L. 1969. *Sylloge inscriptionum religionis Isiacae et Sarapicae* (Berlin).

1970. *Isis und Sarapis bei den Griechen und Römern. Epigraphische Studien zu den Trägern des ägyptischen Kultes* (Berlin).

Virlouvet, C. 1988. Review of Nicolet 1988, *Revue Historique*, 280.1: 244–8.

Voisin, J.-L. 1987. 'Ex oriente sole (Suétone Ner. 6): D'Alexandrie à la Domus Aurea', in *L'urbs: espace urbain et histoire (Is ap. J.-C.)* (Paris), 509–43.

Volk, K. 2002. *The Poetics of Latin Didactic. Lucretius, Vergil, Ovid, Manilius* (Oxford).

von Blanckenhagen, P. H. 1957. 'Narration in Hellenistic and Roman Art', *American Journal of Archaeology*, 61: 78–83.

von Stackelberg, K. T. 2004. *The Roman Garden. Space, Sense and Society* (London).

Vörös, G. 2001. *Taposiris Magna. Post of Isis. Hungarian Excavations at Alexandria (1998–2001)* (Budapest).

Vout, C. 2003. 'Embracing Egypt', in C. Edwards and G. Woolf (eds), *Rome the Cosmopolis* (Cambridge), 177–202.

Waiblinger, F. P. 1977. *Senecas Naturales Quaestiones. Griechische Wissenschaft und römische Form.* Zetemata, 70 (Munich).

Walde, C. 2007. 'Per un'idrologia poetica: fiumi e acque nella Pharsalia di Lucano', in L. Landolfi and P. Monella (eds), *Doctus Lucanus: Aspetti dell'erudizione nella Pharsalia di Lucano* (Bologna), 13–48.

2011. 'Lucan's Bellum Civile: A Specimen of a Roman "Literature of Trauma"', in P. Asso (ed.), *Brill's Companion to Lucan* (Leiden), 283–302.

Wallace-Hadrill, A. 1990. 'Pliny the Elder and Man's Unnatural History', *Greece and Rome*, n.s.37: 80–96.

1994. *Houses and Society in Pompeii and Herculaneum* (Princeton).

1997. 'Mutatis moru: The Idea of a Cultural Revolution', in T. Habinek and A. Schiesaro (eds), *The Roman Cultural Revolution* (Cambridge), 3–22.

2008. *Rome's Cultural Revolution* (Cambridge).

Weingärtner, D. G. 1969. *Die Ägyptenreise des Germanicus.* Papyrologische Texte und Abhandlungen, 11 (Bonn).

Weinlich, B. P. 2003. 'Re-constructing Relationships: The Significance of Name and Place in Propertius 3.22', *Ramus*, 32.2: 102–21.

Wheeler, A. L. (ed. and tr.), 1924. *Ovid. Trista, Ex Ponto*, LCL (Cambridge, MA).

Wheeler, S. M. 1995. 'Imago Mundi: Another View of Creation in Ovid's Metamorphoses', *American Journal of Philology*, 116.1: 95–121.

Whitehouse, H. 1976. *The Dal Pozzo Copies of the Palestrina Mosaic* (Oxford).

1979. A Catalogue of Nilotic Landscapes in Roman Art, Unpub. PhD Thesis (Oxford).

Whitmarsh, T. 1999. 'The Writes of Passage: Cultural Initiation in Heliodorus' Aethiopica', in R. Miles (ed.), *Constructing Identities in Late Antiquity* (London), 16–40.

Whittaker, C. R. 2004. 'Mental Maps: Seeing Like a Roman', in P. McKechnie (ed.), *Thinking Like a Lawyer. Essays on Legal History and General History for John Crook on his Eightieth Birthday* (Leiden), 93–5, 109–10.

Wick, C. 2010. 'Plus quam visibilia – Lukans suggestive Nichtbeschreibungen', in N. Hömke, C. Reitz (ed.), *Lucan's Bellum civile: Between Epic Tradition and Aesthetic Innovation.* Beiträge zur Altertumskunde Bd. 282 (Berlin/New York), 105–18.

Wild, R. A. 1981. *Water in the Cultic Worship of Isis and Serapis.* EPRO, 87 (Leiden).

1984. 'The Known Isis-Sarapis Sanctuaries from the Roman Period', *Aufstieg und Niedergang der römischen Welt*, II.17.4: 1739–851.

Williams, G. D. 2008. 'Reading the Waters: Seneca on the Nile in Natural Questions, Book 4A', *Classical Quarterly*, 58.1: 218–42.

2012. The Cosmic Viewpoint. A Study of Seneca's *Natural Questions* (Oxford).

Williams, G. 1978. *Change and Decline: Roman Literature in the Early Empire* (Berkeley).

Williamson, G. and E. M. Smallwood. (tr.), 1979. *Josephus. The Jewish War* (Harmondsworth).

Wilson, E. 2014. *The Greatest Empire. A Life of Seneca* (Oxford).

Wilson, M. 2009. 'The Politics of Elegy: Propertius and Tibullus', in W. J. Dominik, J. Garthwaite and P. A. Roche (eds), *Writing Politics in Imperial Rome* (Leiden), 173–202.

Wilton, A. and T. Barringer. 2002. *American Sublime: Landscape Painting in the United States 1820–1880* (London).

Winkler, G. 2000. 'Geographie bei den Römern: Mela, Seneca, Plinius', in W. Hübner (ed.), *Geographie und verwandte Wissenschaften* (Stuttgart), 141–62.

Winkler, G. and R. König (ed. and tr.), 1993. *C. Plinius Secundus. Naturkunde Lateinisch-Deutsch. Bücher V-VI* (Munich).

Wiseman, T. P. 1979. 'Strabo on the Campus Martius', *Liverpool Classical Monthly*, 4.7: 129–34.

  1992. *Talking to Virgil: A Miscellany* (Exeter).

Woltjer, J. 1877. *Lucretii philosophia cum fontibus comparata* (Groningen).

Wyke, M. 1992. 'Augustan Cleopatras: Female Power and Poetic Authority', in A. Powell (ed.), *Roman Poetry and Propaganda in the Age of Augustus* (London), 98–140.

  2002. *Roman Mistress: Ancient and Modern Receptions* (Oxford).

Yoyotte, J. 1998. 'Nomes', in G. Posener, with S. Sauneron and J. Yoyotte (eds), *Dictionnaire de la civilisation égyptienne* (Paris), 190–2.

Yoyotte, J., P. Charvet and S. Gompertz 1997. *Strabo: Le voyage en Égypte: Un regard romain* (Paris).

Zanker, G. 1981. 'Enargeia in the Ancient Criticism of Poetry', *Rheinisches Museum für Philologie*, 124, 297–311.

Zanker, P. 1988. *The Power of Images in the Age of Augustus*. Tr. A. Shapiro (Ann Arbor, MI).

  1998. *Pompeii. Public and Private Life*. Revealing Antiquity, 11. Tr. D. L. Schneider (Cambridge, MA).

# Index